Culture in Economics

History, Methodological Reflections, and Contemporary Applications

Many economists now accept that informal institutions and culture play a crucial role in economic outcomes. Driven by the work of economists such as Nobel laureates Douglass North and Gary Becker, there is an important body of work that invokes cultural and institutional factors to build a more comprehensive and realistic theory of economic behavior. This book provides a comprehensive overview of research in this area, sketching the main promises and challenges faced by the field. The first part introduces and explains the various theoretical approaches to studying culture in economics, going back to Smith and Weber, and addresses the methodological issues that need to be considered when including culture in economics. The second part of the book then provides readers with a series of examples that shows how the cultural approach can be used to explain economic phenomena in four different areas: entrepreneurship, trust, international business, and comparative corporate governance.

SJOERD BEUGELSDIJK is Professor of International Business and Management at the University of Groningen, the Netherlands. His Ph.D. (Tilburg University, 2003) concerned the relationship between culture and economic development in European regions. He has published extensively on the relation between culture and economic behavior of firms and individuals, and the relation between culture and national economic development. In 2007 he obtained a prestigious three-year research grant from the Netherlands Organization for Scientific Research.

ROBBERT MASELAND is Assistant Professor of International Economics and Business at the University of Groningen, the Netherlands. His Ph.D. (Radboud University Nijmegen, 2006) analyzed the emergence and impact of the Asian Values thesis. In addition, he has published on topics such as the measurement of values, development models and fairness in trade. In 2008 he obtained a stipend from the Royal Dutch Academy of Sciences, enabling him to work as a researcher at the Max Planck Institute for the Study of Societies (MPIfG) and the Institute for the Study of Labor (IZA) in Bonn.

Culture in Economics

History, Methodological Reflections, and
Contemporary Applications

SJOERD BEUGELSDIJK
ROBBERT MASELAND

CAMBRIDGE
UNIVERSITY PRESS

CAMBRIDGE UNIVERSITY PRESS
Cambridge, New York, Melbourne, Madrid, Cape Town, Singapore,
São Paulo, Delhi, Tokyo, Mexico City

Cambridge University Press
The Edinburgh Building, Cambridge CB2 8RU, UK

Published in the United States of America by Cambridge University Press, New York

www.cambridge.org
Information on this title: www.cambridge.org/9780521193009

First published 2011
Reprinted 2012

Printed at MPG Books Group, UK

A catalogue record for this publication is available from the British Library

Library of Congress Cataloguing in Publication data
Beugelsdijk, Sjoerd, 1976–
Culture in economics : history, methodological reflections, and contemporary
applications / Sjoerd Beugelsdijk, Robbert Maseland.
      p.   cm.
Includes bibliographical references and index.
ISBN 978-0-521-19300-9
1. Economics – Sociological aspects.   2. Culture – Economic aspects.   I. Maseland,
Robbert Karel Jozef, 1975–   II. Title.
HM548.B488   2010
306.3 – dc22   2010040290

ISBN 978-0-521-19300-9 Hardback

Contents

Figures

Tables

Boxes

Prologue

"Well, culture counts. In the first two chapters, I speak about geography, which I think is terribly important. But once you get past geography and want to know why certain areas have done better than others within the same geographical context, then you have to recognize that culture counts."

(David Landes, interview in *Challenge* 1998)

"We do have a great deal of recent research modeling specific norms and their impact set in a game-theoretical framework, but examining the overall consequences of culture for economic performance is still in its infancy."

(Douglass North 2005: 57)

Why a book on culture in economics?

Culture matters! If there is a one-liner summarizing the rationale for this book, it is this one. Recently many economists have turned their attention to the role of culture and have included culture in their economic theories. This interest is also reflected in books by prominent scholars who have argued that a closer study of the role of culture in economics is required. For example, Nobel Prize winner Douglass North argues that culture is fundamentally related to economic outcomes. As North puts it in his most recent book on economic change: "Our task is to explain the diverse belief systems that have evolved historically and in the present, which have very different implications for structure, organization, and economic success of societies" (North 2005: 69). A similar plea for a closer analysis of culture can be found in Greif's 2006 seminal work on institutions and economic development (Greif 2006). According to Greif, insufficient attention is paid to the fact that unobserved institutional elements, i.e. culture, can vary systematically across societies and directly influence the effectiveness of institutions. Two societies with the same formal rules specifying property rights will experience very different levels of investment if different beliefs about the enforcement of these rights prevail in each (Greif 2006: 20–21). Such statements by Greif and North reflect a broader consensus among many economists that culture matters and deserves scholarly attention. The fact that Tabellini's presidential lecture at the 2007 meeting of the European Economic Association was entitled "Institutions and culture" sends a clear signal to the community of economists: we need to incorporate culture in our economic framework (Tabellini 2008b). This book is an attempt to put this discussion on culture in economics into a broader perspective and sketch the added value of including culture in economics along with questions that arise when doing so.

This said, scholarly work about culture remains highly scattered and diverse. Contributions are spread thinly not only over various areas of economics but also over neighboring disciplines such as sociology, anthropology, political science and management. In this book, we have attempted to bring together these scattered contributions in a single volume. We discuss the ways in which economists have incorporated informal norms, values and culture in their work, contrasting and complementing these with perspectives from other disciplines. Assessing these contributions critically and from an historical perspective allows us to discuss our achievements thus far and also point out some of the main difficulties and challenges lying ahead of us. In doing so, we have written a book that is unique in the sense that we bring together several streams of research that would normally be found in an array of journals, conferences and workshops in economics, sociology, political science, anthropology and management.

Finally, although this book is not intended to be a classical textbook with supporting case material and assignments, we do think it is a valuable resource for economics professors teaching courses on culture and institutions as well as graduate students in economics. As we have previously taught courses on institutional economics, culture and economic behavior and international political economy, we have experienced the need for a book summarizing the culture debate and putting it into broader perspective. As far as we know, only David Weil's most recent textbook (2009) on economic growth contains a separate chapter on culture. Although he provides an informed and succinct overview of the reason why culture is important to economics, our ambitions go beyond arguing that culture matters. We wish to show where this interest in culture comes from and discuss the history of culture in economics to understand contemporary developments. Even more so, we wish to push the methodological and theoretical research frontier in this field. For econ-students, our book is a useful resource for evaluating the recent cultural turn in the economics discipline. By providing such an historically embedded analysis of the way economists have dealt with culture, we also aim to counter recent criticism indicating that many economists are trained as mathematicians and have forgotten the broader societal context in which economic activity takes place (*see* Paul Krugman, *The New York Times*, September 2, 2009). Because we have made great efforts to not turn a blind eye toward developments in other social sciences, social scientists from any discipline will recognize many of the themes discussed. For non-econ-students this book may, therefore, serve as a relatively simple introduction to the way culture has been included in economics.

Overall structure

The book has two main parts and a conclusion. The first part is mainly concerned with historical and methodological issues that need to be considered when including culture in economics. We structure the various approaches to "culture" by sketching the historical and methodological context in which the discussion on culture has evolved. Also, we point out some non-economic contributions to culture and economy, in so far as they seem useful to economists interested in culture. This is the task of the first part of the book, which constructs a framework from which to assess the various contemporary contributions to the field of cultural economics. The second part contains four contemporary applications.

We center the discussion in the first part on three closely related key challenges or tensions. The first relates to the fact that whereas culture deals with structures that are deemed given to the individual, economists start from a model of reality in which behavioral patterns and outcomes are retraceable to individual, purposeful decision-making. As a result, economists studying culture face a challenge of aligning cultural (exogenous) *structures* to economic *agency*. Second, we note that the concept of culture refers to properties at the *collective*, macro-level while most economic theory operates at the level of the *individual* or is derived from the micro-economic behaviour of individual agents. Hence, culture research in economics encounters a problem of realigning the collective and the individual, or more practically has to find a solution for the problems associated with the aggregation from micro to macro and vice versa. The third theme concerns the tension between economists' focus on establishing *universal* insights and principles on the one hand and the presence of a diversity in cultural logics and perceptions of reality on the other. This *context specificity* is hard to align with this basic assumption of universalistic behavior. This tension between universalistic and particularistic is related to the phenomenon of a cultural bias.

These three themes return in the second part of the book when we discuss contemporary applications of cultural economics. We have chosen to discuss entrepreneurial culture, trust, international business and comparative corporate governance for two main reasons. First, they are highly topical in the sense that they can be found on the agenda of many economists interested in culture. This is reflected in the choice of panel sessions at conferences and the popularity of these topics among Ph.D. students. Second, by limiting ourselves to these four different topics that we consider to be representative, we intend to cover the broad scope of culture studies in economics. Despite the shared focus on culture, the four topics show minimal overlapping, thereby maximizing the lessons that can be learned from these specific topics. Each of these chapters deals with different practical issues that arise when incorporating culture in economics and serves to illustrate the abstract themes discussed in the first part.

The final part of the book, Chapter 10, concludes and provides several main methodological concerns, theoretical challenges and empirical opportunities for further work on culture in economics. The book has a common denominator, but we have tried to write it in such a way that the chapters can also be read as stand-alone contributions.

Chapter overview

In the first chapter we seek to define culture. Given the variety of methodological perspectives and scholarly and disciplinary differences, it is impossible to come up with one (new) all-encompassing definition. Kroeber and Kluckhohn (1963) have already counted more than 170 definitions of culture in the literature. In reviewing the literature, we are, however, still able to compile a list of defining and recurring characteristics of many definitions of culture. After having established these key characteristics of a definition of culture, we describe the difference between culture and closely related concepts such as nationality, ideology, institutions and ethnicity.

In Chapter 2 we provide an historical overview of thought about culture in economics, putting the removal of culture from economic thought after the Second World War in its historical context. This history is meant to show that, in spite of the renewed interest in linking culture and economy, the way in which the two concepts have grown apart over time continues to frame the current debate about culture in economics. It is argued that the status of the debate in the 1950s should be seen not so much as a starting point of the debate about culture and economy but as the culmination of a longer development in which conceptions of culture and "the economic" had gradually evolved in opposite directions. Culture, or better, perhaps, morality, which was the more common term in early days, had been an inherent part of economic studies since the early work of Adam Smith but was, however, outsourced to sociology and anthropology in the early twentieth century.

Chapter 3 follows up on this historical overview by putting into context the recent surge in studies on culture. We do this by analyzing the specific reasons for the current inclusion of culture in the economic framework. We describe the role of failing World Bank policies, the break-up of the Soviet Union, increased data availability, the Asian Values debate, and the rise of New Institutional Economics.

Having described both the time-line of culture's inclusion, exclusion and inclusion again, and the underlying rationale for this development, we put the relation between culture and "the economy" in theoretical perspective in Chapter 4. We distinguish between three broad approaches: culture and economy, culture as economy/economy as culture, and a third, more meta, perspective focusing on the culture of economics. The first approach, labeled culture and economy for lack of anything better, conceptualizes culture as an exogenous factor. It can be included in economic models as a source of preferences, as a source of constraints or as deviations from the model. Each of these options is elaborated upon in this chapter.

Parallel to this approach whereby culture is perceived as an exogenous factor, more inclusive approaches exist as well. Some authors have sought to extend the economic framework to cover all social and cultural phenomena, viewing culture as economy. Gary Becker and the Chicago School are examples of this, as is the cultural materialism of anthropologist Marvin Harris. Alternatively, ethnographers and economic historicists have developed analyses in which culture is studied as an encompassing whole covering every sphere of life. In this line of work, economic behavior enters as a cultural phenomenon that is subject to cultural studies. These approaches we classify as *culture as economy/economy as culture*.

The final and more meta-analytical approach addressing the role of culture in economics concerns those who study the ideas of economists from a cultural perspective. It deals with the *culture of economics*. Whereas the first approach (culture and economy) is especially most familiar to and most popular among economists, the second and certainly the third approach are less well known. In order to provide a full sketch of the landscape of studies addressing the link between culture and "the economic," we do, however, consider it necessary to discuss these approaches as well.

Chapter 5 concludes the first part of the book. Given the landscape sketched in Chapter 4, we focus on the methodical side of the "cultural economics." We discuss the variety of (empirical) approaches that can each be associated with the theoretical streams of research as described in Chapter 4. Because of its popularity in economics, we concentrate on those approaches associated with the "culture and economy" strand. This implies that we discuss cross-cultural experimental approaches and contributions from cross-cultural psychologists who have operationalized culture by means of large-scale, cross-societal value surveys. We discuss well-known databases such as the World or European Values Survey and Hofstede's and Schwartz's work on culture dimensions. The availability of these databases yields new possibilities for empirical research.

Part II consists of four chapters dealing with topics which contemporary economists are interested in and are still working on. In the first application in Chapter 6, we discuss the role of entrepreneurial culture. Many economists, ranging from entrepreneurship and innovation economists to growth economists, have referred to such an ideal of entrepreneurial culture. Entrepreneurial culture is often the residual in economic explanations, but, beginning with the work by McClelland (1961), entrepreneurial trait research has provided a renewed impetus to the (empirical) study of entrepreneurial culture. As we discuss in this chapter, the discussion on entrepreneurial culture centers around the tension between structure and agency and the difficulty in translating insights from entrepreneurial trait research at the individual level to the notion of an entrepreneurial culture at the collective level.

The highly topical issue of trust is discussed in Chapter 7. Economists frequently operationalize culture in terms of generalized trust, as, for example, in Tabellini's 2007 presidential lecture at the European Economic Association referred to previously (also in Fehr's 2008 presidential lecture on trust at the same meeting (Fehr 2008) and Dixit's presidential lecture at the 2009 meeting of the *American Economic Association* (Dixit 2009)). We provide an overview of the studies using trust as an indicator of culture and discuss the strengths and weaknesses of such an interpretation of culture. We also discuss the (economic) consequences and the antecedents of societies characterized by high or low trust levels. In doing so, we show how economists struggle to trace the origin of trust and the associated problem of infinite regress. Moreover, we discuss the difficulty in coming up with a universal measure of trust because trust has been argued to be (partly) context specific.

In Chapter 8, we turn toward a more business-oriented approach, i.e. we enter the field of international business. Logically, culture has traditionally played a major role in understanding the patterns of international investment and cooperation across borders. The field of international business deals with the challenges arising from these cultural differences. More specifically, we discuss the relation between cultural differences and investment behavior of multinationals and the influence of (differences in) value patterns of managers working across borders. The tension between universal approaches and context-specific rationality is an important part of the discussion in this chapter.

The final application in Chapter 9 deals with the relatively recent literature addressing the reasons for international differences in corporate governance regimes. Contemporary studies of differences in investor protection regimes explicitly mention the role of legal origin in explaining differences in degree of investor protection. Similar to the literature on trust, studies in the field of comparative corporate governance and legal origin have embedded their explanation in the broader cultural or institutional turn in economics. We discuss the different concepts associated with this literature and draw implications for our broader research agenda on the inclusion of culture in economics. More specifically, we focus on the optimality of culture or, in other words, the question of whether there is one unique best culture (from an economic point of view) or whether multiple equilibria exist that perform similarly.

The book concludes with a discussion of what we have learned so far and what roads we need to follow if "cultural economics" is to make a meaningful and lasting contribution to economic thought. Given the enormous amount of work on culture, both in the past and by our contemporaries, this book is by definition a far from exhaustive overview of conceptualizations of culture and the way economists have dealt with culture. On the basis of this limited overview, we do, however, feel that (i) we provide a general insight into the various trends in cultural economic research that exist, (ii) we indicate where they are coming from and where they are heading and (iii) we highlight the important challenges and possibilities confronting research into culture in economics.

The book's message

We intend to provide an overview of the literature addressing the role of culture in economics and, at the same time, take a position in this broader debate. Our critical reflection on how culture made its way back into economics and how contemporary debates in economics are shaped by the interest in culture should not be mistaken for a negative evaluation of this literature. In fact, we are optimistic about the future development of economics. The current attention devoted to culture in economics (and context in general) is a sign of the strength and maturity of the economic discipline. Economists today are incorporating insights from other disciplines, reflecting upon their assumptions, reaching out to critics in a constructive dialog and amending their theoretical premises in order to develop more meaningful and precise insights. All this bodes very well for the future. At the same time, we are not naïve. As economics has moved beyond its traditional limits, many latent discussions buried for decades underneath a blanket of consensus over how to do proper economics have suddenly started to re-emerge. Whereas "as in most other sciences, the majority of the economists do their work with little explicit reflection on the philosophical assumptions that underlie their research" (Hodgson 2007:

211), the inclusion of culture in economics forces us to (re)think some of these pillars. It puts old questions, such as those about structure and agency, collectivism and individualism, and universalism versus particularism, back on the agenda while also triggering a couple of new ones. Up until now, unfortunately, contributions to the debate about culture in economics have, generally speaking, not taken up these challenges very well. The deeper methodological and theoretical implications of incorporating culture in economic thought have not generally been acknowledged, let alone adequately responded to. The immediate danger is that, as a result, the discussion about culture in economics will not be able to move beyond the level of platitudes such as "culture matters" and push economic theory forward in a meaning-ful way. In this case, people are likely to lose their interest in the issue sooner or later and write off the newly re-emerged field as a theoretical dead-end. Such a fate is avoidable and should be avoided. Beyond the conceptual and methodological difficulties lies a potentially blossom-ing field of inquiry. In order to reach that point, this book seeks to dissect the current debate and expose those challenges that have to be addressed in order for the new cultural economics to flourish.

Acknowledgments

Parts of this book have been presented at numerous places and we are grateful for all the comments we have received over the last couple of years. We thank the Netherlands Organization for Scientific Research (NWO) and the Royal Dutch Academy of Sciences (KNAW) for pro-viding funds that have given us both the opportunity to concentrate on writing this book. We also thank our colleagues at Nijmegen Uni-versity and the University of Groningen. Extensive discussions over lunch with André van Hoorn, Floris Heukelom, Eelke de Jong, Jan Peil, Harry Garretsen, Roger Smeets, Remco Zwinkels, Bart Frijns and Albert de Vaal have definitely contributed to the quality of the book. We also thank Arjen Slangen of the University of Amsterdam for shar-ing his useful and critical insights on the role of culture in international business. Of the many people at various conferences with whom we have discussed the contents of this book, we would like to specifically thank the organizers and attendants of the workshop on culture and economy at the EAEPE Conference in Bremen, 2006. Of course, any errors are ours, and interpretations of general developments in the field are even more ours, but the opportunity to use you as sparring partners is greatly appreciated.

Although it has already been some years, the working group on European Values at Tilburg University was probably the first group to exhibit the ambition to write a book like this. We are still grateful for the discussions with the members of that pioneering group, consisting of sociologists, management scholars, political scientists and economists. More specifically, we would like to thank Wil Arts, Paul Dekker, Loek Halman, Sjak Smulders, Jaques Hagenaars, Lans Bovenberg, Niels Noorderhaven and Wim van der Donk. We have all gone our separate ways, but the seed for this initiative was planted in those meetings in 2002 and 2003.

We would also like to thank our colleagues at the departments which were so kind to host us for several days and, sometimes, even several months. More specifically, we thank Nicolai Foss and Torben Pedersen of Copenhagen Business School, Rajneesh Narula at the University of Reading, Lee Hock Guan of the Institute of Southeast Asian Studies, the staff at the Max Planck Institute for the Study of Societies in Cologne, Marco Caliendo and Werner Eichhorst at the Institute for Labor Studies (IZA) in Bonn, and Tina and Bjorn Ambos at the University of Vienna.

Finally, we would like to thank Ton van Schaik, Floris Heukelom, Angela Wigger and three anonymous reviewers for reading parts of the book and the final manuscript. You have come up with useful comments and questions that triggered us to further sharpen our discussion. All remaining errors and misinterpretations are ours.

Final remark

The title of the book reflects our ambition to discuss the role of culture in economics and the way in which scholars have attempted to (re-)align the premise of economic rationality with the foundations of social behavior. The title is deliberately chosen. We do not wish to suggest that we provide *the* framework on culture and economic behavior, nor do we describe the foundations of a new field called cultural economics. However, for reasons of readability, we will occasionally refer to the broader field of studies on culture in economics as "cultural economics."

PART I

History and methodological reflections

1 | *Defining culture*

1.1 Introduction

To most of us, culture means something like a society's traditions, its values, norms and beliefs. Culture also refers to artistic activity, its products and the historical heritage of a society. In addition, most of us would agree that culture is linked to the collective identity of communities and, as such, refers to differences between societies.

What ties all these meanings together? What is culture *exactly*? It is when we start thinking about these questions that things start to get blurry. In spite of the attention that has been paid to culture in social sciences over the centuries, we are still no closer to an unambiguous, widely accepted definition of the term. Conceptualizations of culture vary across disciplines, between schools and simply between authors. In their authoritative review of the culture concept, Kroeber and Kluckhohn (1963) had already counted more than 170 different definitions of culture in the literature. Another half a century of social sciences later that number has increased only further. Although we all seem to have vague ideas of what culture is about, it seems to be very difficult to agree on its exact definition.

This lack of a clear-cut, unambiguous definition is a rich source of misunderstandings in debates. The fact that most of us have a notion of what culture is in the back of our minds only adds to this. If an anthropologist and an economist are discussing the role of culture in economic development, they may think they understand each other, but are they really discussing the same things? The former may believe they are talking about ideas and values that are the contested product of current political–economic processes, while the latter may interpret culture as ancient traditions that are inherent to a society's static identity. Without making clear what we understand by culture beforehand, any discussion of the role of culture in economics is bound to be fruitless.

Before we start our discussion of culture in economics, we therefore first have to make an attempt to define the object of our inquiry and delineate culture more precisely. Needless to say, we do not claim to be able to come up with a definition of culture that trumps all existing ones. What we will do in this chapter is stipulate what we understand by culture throughout this book, so as to familiarize the reader with the scope and limits of our discussion. In order to do that, it serves to shortly review various conceptions of culture that can be found in the literature. In doing so, we rely on the classic overview of Kroeber and Kluckhohn (1963), complemented by more recent literature.

1.2 Culture as artificial

A very basic way to delineate culture is by focussing on its opposition to nature. Culture is generally understood to refer only to those aspects of the environment that have been made or shaped by humankind. This element has been stressed especially in definitions stemming from the first half of the twentieth century. For example, Ostwald (1907: 510) defines culture as "that which distinguishes men from animals." Another such definition runs "the man-made part of the environment" (Herskovits 1948: 17). A more recent contribution in this line is Inglehart (1990: 18), who argues that "while human nature is biologically innate and universal, culture is learned and may vary from one society to another."

An interesting observation about these definitions is that, apart from natural differences, they exclude virtually nothing. Culture covers all aspects of social reality. This view of culture as a "comprehensive totality" (Kroeber and Kluckhohn 1963: 85) is especially prominent in cultural anthropology. Perhaps one of the most famous definitions of culture capturing this view is the classic one formulated by Tylor [1871]. According to Tylor, culture is "that complex whole which includes knowledge, belief, art, morals, law, custom, and any other capabilities and habits acquired by man as a member of society" (1924 [1871]: 1). Others include Boas' (1930: 79) statement that "culture embraces all the manifestations of social habits of a community," or Malinowski's definition of culture as "an integral composed of partly autonomous, partly co-ordinated institutions. It is integrated on a series of principles such as the community of blood through procreation; the specialisation in activities; and last but not least, the use of power in political organisation. Each culture owes its completeness and self-sufficiency to the fact that it satisfies the whole range of basic, instrumental and integrative needs" (1969 [1944]: 40).

Obviously, the distinction from biological and physical aspects of reality alone does not get us very far in delineating culture. Culture still means close to everything. If we want to give the debate about culture in economics any direction, we need to identify other dimensions of the concept.

1.3 Culture as ideas and worldviews influencing behavior

Closely related to the nature–culture dualism is the distinction between mind and matter. Since the second half of the twentieth century, authors discussing culture generally interpret culture as being about the worldview of people rather than the material world out there. The view of culture as everything that humans made gave way to a view of culture focussing on everything that humans thought, felt and believed. Except perhaps in the sphere of arts, culture has come to be not so much about material artefacts themselves as about the perceptions, ideas, norms and values underlying them.

This is most obvious in anthropology, where culture came to be identified with systems of meaning. Clifford Geertz, probably the most famous ethnographer of the second half of the twentieth century, typically defines culture as "an historically transmitted pattern of meanings embodied in symbols, a system of inherited conceptions expressed in symbolic forms by means of which men communicate, perpetuate, and develop their knowledge about and attitudes towards life" (Geertz 1973: 89). Geertz's view is symptomatic of anthropology, which usually understands culture as complexes of distinctive properties, including norms, worldviews and beliefs (Wolf 1999: 21). Outside anthropology, this interpretation of culture is widespread as well. We encounter it in the works of Hall (1995) or Wuthnow, who writes about culture as "overarching symbolic frames of reference, which we shall refer to as meaning systems, by which people come to grips with the broader meaning and purpose of life" (Wuthnow 1976: 2–3). It "is at base an all embracing socially constructed world of subjectively and inter-subjectively experienced meanings" (Wuthnow *et al.* 1984: 25). Cross-cultural psychologist Geert Hofstede (1991: 5), finally, has something similar in mind when he describes culture as "the software

of the mind." Culture, in most contemporary conceptions, refers to
the intangible. It is about values, ideas, routines and beliefs held by
people. But does this mean that all ideas and beliefs are cultural?

1.4 Culture as group distinction

One of the most crucial aspects of culture is that it is about distinction.
It has to do with how groups differ from one another. This element of
distinction is stressed in various definitions that can be found in the literature. Geert Hofstede defines culture as "the collective programming
of the mind that distinguishes the members of one group or category
of people from another" (Hofstede 2001: 9). Other examples include
Kluckhohn and Leighton (1946: xviii), who maintain that "a culture
is any given people's way of life, as distinct from the life-ways of other
peoples"; Hall (1995: 176), claiming culture is "the systems of shared
meanings which people who belong to the same community, group,
or nation use to help them interpret and make sense of the world";
Gellner (1992: 18) arguing culture is "a shared set of ideas, held to
be valid simply because they constituted the joint conceptual banks of
custom of an ongoing community"; or Schweder (2001: 3153), who
defines culture as "community-specific ideas about what is true, good,
beautiful, and efficient."

While distinction from other groups is an important element of a definition of culture, questions remain about how to identify the groups
in which culture is thought to be residing. To derive one's conception
of culture from collective identity requires clearly demarcated groups,
so that collective identities are unambiguous. However, as the definitions by Hofstede (2001) or Gellner (1992) indicate, it is often culture
itself that distinguishes members of one group from another. Culture
is not only an aspect of distinctive groups, it is also a means to distinguish groups. This element can also be found in older writings on
culture, such as in Wallis' (1930: 9) definition of culture as "the artificial objects, institutions, and modes of life or of thought which are
not peculiarly individual but *which characterize a group*" (emphasis
added) or Benedict's argument that "what really binds men together
is their culture" (Benedict 2005 [1934]: 16). This two-way reasoning
is potentially problematic. It means that to identify culture we have to
look at differences between groups, while to identify groups we have
to look at culture. The way out of this is to look for any clusters in

the distribution of ideas, values and beliefs as culture of an apparent group. Indeed, Hofstede takes such an empirical approach in his work, not defining cultural communities *a priori*, but identifying cultural boundaries and differences on the basis of patterns in survey data (*see* Chapter 5). A definition that takes this route explicitly is the one by Brumann (1999: S1), which says that culture refers to "the clusters of common concepts, emotions, and practices that arise when people interact regularly."

There are limits to such an approach. For one thing, empirically derived clusters in habits, ideas and behavior often overlap, so that any individual belongs to various cultures simultaneously. Individuals share ideas, values and symbols with their religious communities, their country, their street, their age group and the supporters of their favorite soccer club. All these units might be taken for cultural communities, and it is next to impossible to come up with exclusive, clearly demarcated groups of people who are the holders of a distinctive culture (Sen 2006). What is more, it has been shown that identities are fluid. Whether national identity, gender, age, class or family serves as dominant basis for identity is dependent upon the context (Eriksen 1993). The fluid character of cultural identity is more fully recognized in the description of culture by Collier (1989) as an "historically transmitted system of symbols, meanings, and norms. The emphasis in this conceptualisation is upon identities, inter-subjectively defined by similarities in symbols and norms, which are posited to potentially change during the course of a conversation . . . In some encounters, nationality may be a key construct, but in others, gender, the relationship, or one's professional position may be key constructs in the understanding and accounting for outcomes. Therefore, I believe that identity adopted, managed, and negotiated during an encounter can be an important focus. Culture can be measured thus as background and heritage, and as emergent patterned conduct around a particular thematic identity" (Collier 1989: 295). The cultural group to which one belongs, and its difference from other groups, is not a fixed given. Individuals constantly switch identities, depending on the context. This multi-layered and fluid character is by itself no problem, but it does make things difficult when we want to move beyond theory development and pinpoint cultural groups and differences in practice. Letting go of the link to collective identity is no option either, however, as the element of distinction between groups is essential to how culture is understood.

Culture refers to ideas that are (supposed to be) shared among a group. Without this element, it is more useful to talk simply of ideas, tastes, norms or values in general.

1.5 Culture as inherited, unquestioned given

Culture refers to what is shared among a group, but most of us would not argue that any set of ideas that a number of people happen to hold at a particular time makes up their culture. For any shared set of ideas to be part of the culture of a group, it has to be perceived as inherent to that group. In other words, to individual members of the group it must be a given, following from their collective identity. This element of culture is stressed in Gellner's definition (1992: 18), which runs: "a shared set of ideas, held to be valid simply because they constituted the joint conceptual banks of custom of an ongoing community." The idea of culture as a system of norms and beliefs that individuals inherit rather than consciously choose can also be found in the definitions of culture used by anthropologists such as Tylor or Geertz, who portray culture as inherited, "comprehensive totality" (Kroeber and Kluckhohn 1963: 85). Inglehart (1990: 18) also describes culture as a system transmitted from generation to generation. What all these definitions imply is that culture is assumed to be a given to the individual member of a group. It is simply held valid, unquestioned by the individual as a member of the cultural community.

This view of culture as unquestioned makes it possible for researchers to demarcate culture from economic or political patterns of thought and behavior, while allowing them at the same time to incorporate culture as a factor influencing such behavior. In sociology, for example, culture has been generally understood as the realm of intimate communitarian ties that bind, as opposed to ideology which denotes scenarios of factional strife among self-seeking interest groups (Wolf 1999: 21). Culture is thus distinguished from purposeful, self-interested (political) action, though communitarian ties may still inform such political strife (e.g. Huntington 1996). In those schools within social sciences that focus on rational choice by individuals rather than collective action, we can see something similar occurring. According to the rational choice framework, people make decisions based on preferences and limited means, seeking to optimize outcomes. In such a framework, culture enters as an external force, influencing the individual rational agent. Political scientist Chai (1997: 45), for example, sees culture "as the basis for individual preferences (goals) and beliefs." Alternatively, culture can be treated in the manner of Coleman (1990), as "norms that mandate action that is not in one's own interest or proscribe behaviour that is" (DiMaggio 1994: 29).

Within economics we observe the same trend. Culture is typically turned into a factor influencing rational behavior, while not being subject to rational design itself (e.g. Williamson 2000). Lal (1998) talks about "unintended consequences" in this respect. Culture is understood as those things that were not rationally chosen but are given to the individual. It serves as an input for (bounded) rational choice. This latter element is obvious in the definition of culture employed by Douglass North: "the transmission from one generation to the next, via teaching and imitation of knowledge, values, and other factors that influence behavior" (North 1990: 37; the definition is taken from Boyd and Richerson 1985: 2). Other economists have interpreted culture more limitedly as informal institutions (Greif 1994; Williamson 2000), shared values and preferences (Fernandez 2008; Guiso *et al.* 2006; Tabellini 2007a, 2007b) or religious beliefs (Barro and McCleary 2003; Guiso *et al.* 2003; McCleary and Barro 2006). What all these interpretations have in common is that culture is explicitly reduced to an exogenous input factor influencing behavior and choices, which makes it compatible with the framework commonly employed by economists. Conceptualizations of culture as an exogenous factor allow it to enter the causal framework of economics without many (apparent) problems.

1.5.1 Challenges to culture as inherited given

This view of culture as inherited, comprehensive totality is not universally shared. In anthropology, it has been challenged in recent decades by a focus on the production and negotiation of culture in individual practices. As noted, the project to define culture in terms of distinctive properties of given groups runs into the problem that in real life groups are not given. Anderson (1991) argues that all collectives transcending the level where people have face-to-face relations with each other are in fact "imagined communities." An Islamic IT specialist from California and a Presbyterian plumber from Detroit may never have met, may not have anything in common and may not have any mutual acquaintances, yet, they might still feel they are bound together by way of both belonging to the community of the United States of America. Because of the fact that an imagined community called America exists, they are each other's "fellow Americans."[1]

This opens the door for a conception of culture in which culture is not so much an inherited, given "thing" but a schema produced, reproduced and negotiated by agents in their practices. As Anderson has shown, national identity is not self-evident; it is the product of an historical process in which the imagined community of the nation has actively been constructed. America, like France or China, has been made by the people, through their imagining. If culture is understood as that which distinguishes the way of life of one imagined community from another, it follows that culture is also a factor in this imagining. Sharing a common system of symbols, meanings and norms binds people together in an identifiable group. It is our shared culture that tells us who we are, making us different from other groups. In contemporary contributions, culture is therefore often seen as "a term of differentiation that separates 'us' from 'them' through the construction of general characteristics that are meant to define, and mark off, a given group or collectivity vis-à-vis another group or collectivity" (Hau 2000: 126).

The conception of culture as being produced and renegotiated by individual agents through their actions and practices is typical for contemporary anthropology and cultural studies. In the words of anthropologist Richard Fox (1985: 197): "there is no weight of tradition, only a current of action." Culture is not a given to be re-enacted but is "always in the making." It is still only occasionally that this interpretation of culture as contested and negotiable enters economics (*see* Heydeman 2008 for an example).

As a consequence of the more dynamic understanding of culture, attention in anthropology has shifted to the social processes of the construction and reproduction of culture, away from the product of this process. The question is no longer what culture is but how culture is produced, by whom and why. Since culture serves as a way of marking off one group vis-à-vis the other, as Hau (2000) maintains, the construction of culture has important political and economic effects.

---

[1] That is not to say that the state of the USA is imagined; it is only to say that the American nation is an imagined community.

For example, consider an employee who is part of a certain company. Companies might push a process in which being part of the company evolves into a distinctive business culture, with its own norms, symbols and meanings. As a result, the employee's sense of belonging to the firm is strengthened – it is now not only a job contract but also a set of collectively shared meanings, norms and symbols that binds her to the company. At the same time, the gap with other companies has become larger, as they have distinctly different cultures. Such a cultural binding of employees to the company gives the company a stronger position in its wage bargaining with employees, since people are less inclined to leave their cultural in-group.

Politically, the construction of distinctive, national cultures has been an important factor in the legitimation of nation-states. In this respect, Appadurai (1996: 15) speaks of culturalism as the mobilization of cultural differences in the service of national or transnational politics. The construction of a distinctive culture has the effect of mobilizing people toward a given end, such as the erection and defence of a unified state on certain territory. Note that although it may be constructed to that end, culture can have this effect only because its members usually do not perceive it as constructed. This idea also is central in the ideas of cultural theorist Peter Berger, who argues that man "forgets that the world he lives in has been produced by himself" (Berger and Pullberg 1965, 2000). Were people to perceive their national cultural identity as a product of the political interests of the state, they would be less willing to make sacrifices for their country. It is because people assume culture to be given and do not question their cultural identity that culture is able to mobilize people and make them endorse culturally specific institutions that are not always in their own interests.

1.6 Competing terms: ideology, institutions, ethnicity, nationality

By now, we are able to identify a few distinctive aspects of culture. As we have seen, culture is most usually interpreted as being:

a. human-made
b. about ideas and worldviews underlying behavior
c. about distinction between collective identities
d. assumed as given to the individual.

These characteristics allow us to distinguish culture from closely related terms such as ideology or institutions. Ideology shares aspects (a) and (b) with culture, but it differs on aspects (c) and (d). As noted by Wolf (1999: 21), ideology commonly refers to purposive, self-interested conflicts between factions within communities. It is perhaps the essence of ideology that it is discursively debated rather than unquestioningly shared by the whole of a community. That makes it essentially different from culture.

Institutions are often defined as "the rules of the game" (North 1990) or, slightly more elaborately, as "a self-sustaining system of shared beliefs about how the game is played" (Aoki 2001). The concept of institutions, like culture, relates to ideational and behavioral structures that are created by humans and influence their decision-making. In contrast to culture, however, institutions need not be related to collective identity. Also, they are to a stronger extent prone to questioning as individuals may contest and at least try to redesign them according to their preferences. An extensive literature in game theory exists, successfully demonstrating that institutions may evolve out of conscious, purposive action of individuals (e.g. Axelrod 1984; Kreps 1990; Lewis 1969; Greif, Milgrom and Weingast 1994). However, the abilities of individuals to design or alter institutions instrumentally are usually seen as limited. North, for example, describes the evolution of institutions as incremental change (North 1990). The most important difference with culture lies therefore in aspect (c) – institutions are not necessarily limited to a specific group.

That is not to say that institutions are never given to any particular society. There are many examples of institutions not meeting these criteria. It is to say that institutions, in contrast to culture, are not *necessarily* specific to a community and treated by its members as given. This leads us to conclude that culture and institutions are not exclusive categories. Structures are neither culture nor institutions: culture refers to a subset of institutions deemed inherent to a community and therefore lying outside the realm of what the individual may question or change (Roland 2004).

Whereas the element of collective identity distinguishes culture from other institutions, concepts such as ethnicity and nationality share this reference to identity. Here, the difference lies in aspect (b): in contrast to culture, both ethnicity and nationality do not refer to ideational factors exogenously influencing beliefs, values or behavior. Neither one's ethnicity nor one's nationality in itself says anything about one's ideas, values or behavior. Nationality is fundamentally a political identity. It follows from citizenship, which in itself tells us nothing about customs, ideas or appearance. Ethnicity refers to sub-societal communities, based on ethnic markers such as alleged racial or physical traits, language, religion or descent. Such markers are usually perceived to be primordial – that is, they are seen as ancient givens, preceding social constructs.[2] As a result, even totally assimilated migrants acting and believing in the same way as their fellow citizens may still be identified as ethnically distinct groups.

Obviously, nationality and ethnicity are often correlated with differences in ideas and behavior and may have a cultural dimension to them. It is important to note, however, that this is by no means automatically the case. To use the terms interchangeably, or to assume ethnic groups or nations to be the units in which culture resides, is thus potentially problematic. Although cultural, ethnic and national communities may often overlap, culture is not nationality, nor is it ethnicity.

1.7 Conclusion: culture in this book

We have identified culture as a subset of institutions related to societal collective identity. At the same time, we have learned from modern anthropology that collective identities are not givens but that they are fluid constructions. Communities, in the words of Anderson (1991), are always imagined. The combination of these insights enables us to identify culture as we understand it. Throughout this book, we loosely define culture *as those behavioral and ideational structures that are deemed essential to the constructed identity of a community.*

This delineation immediately triggers some critical questions. Who is deeming these structures essential? Who constructs the community's identity? Who decides which individuals are making up the community? Indeed, we think that these attributions are by definition contestable. Some people perceive English language as essential to American identity, others do not. What is more, those who do are likely to have different ideas about what American identity is and possibly even

---

[2] Note that this perception by the members of the ethnic community, or by other groups in society, of these traits as primordial does not mean that they actually are.

about the demarcation of the community of Americans. Culture is in the eye of the beholder.

The eyes of which beholders do we take as guidance in our discussion? Throughout this book, we let ourselves be guided by the perspective taken by the authors we discuss. In some cases, authors do not explicitly present their work as part of the culture–economics literature and only loosely or indirectly refer to culture. However, if an author discusses structures of behavior or ideas that he perceives as inherent to a group's identity, we treat this as an instance of research dealing with culture nonetheless. That is not to say that we necessarily agree with this perception. In fact, a common theme throughout the book is our questioning of such attributions. We often criticize the added explanatory value of seeing certain institutions as cultural. Also, we portray some doubts about attributing culture to pre-defined communities such as nations. A discussion of legal heritage (Chapter 9) is included, for example, because the authors involved in this discussion tend to present legal systems as inherited social structures that are specific to a society and influence its economic outcomes. Although they use the term "culture" loosely, and do not always present their work as contributions to culture-based research in economics, we do include these authors in our book. Likewise, when discussing trust (Chapter 7) we take the perspective of authors that see trust as a proxy for culture and have also explicitly presented trust as such. In sum, all topics and associated chapters are a deliberate choice and serve as input in our quest to understand how culture has made its way (back) in contemporary economics and how such a development shapes theories and raises methodological challenges. Having provided a working definition in this chapter, we turn, in the following chapter, to the analysis of how culture disappeared from economics. We subsequently discuss why and how culture re-emerged in economics.

2 | How culture disappeared from economics

2.1 Introduction

We have started our story about culture in economics with the difficult question what culture is and how to define it. We identified a number of essential aspects of what people understand by culture in the previous chapter. In this chapter and the next three, we delve into the question how this idea of culture may possibly enter economic thought.

Looking at the elements of culture that we have discussed, it is immediately obvious that such a task will not be easy. To economics, or at least the version of economics that became dominant in the twentieth century, culture is a very strange animal indeed. Economists tend to analyze behavior and society from the perspective of rational choice. Culture, meanwhile, is deemed inherited and given to individuals, lying outside the realm of instrumental design. Moreover, culture is about identities emerging at the level of collectives, whereas modern economics studies reality through the lens of individual decisions. Finally, the notion of cultures as constituting worldviews implies that there are various ways of perceiving reality, resulting in various logics of behavior. Economics, by contrast, aims to establish universal principles of behavior. These oppositions make it not very surprising that culture has not received much attention from economists until recently. Economics and culture are difficult to reconcile.

It was not always like that, however. The contemporary interest in the relation between culture and economics and how to include culture in economics is not something completely new. Early economists did not yet believe that issues like morality, beliefs and traditions lay outside the normal bounds of economics. Up until the early twentieth century, what we now call culture and economics were naturally studied together. Scholars such as Adam Smith, Karl Marx, Gustav

Schmoller, Max Weber and Thorstein Veblen have all contributed more or less explicitly to the subject in the past.

Why has culture disappeared from economics? How did this process happen? This chapter traces the development of cultural and economic thought up until the mid-twentieth century, by which time culture had disappeared from economics almost completely. It argues that, through shifts in the meanings of both culture and economics, the two concepts came to eventually acquire the conflicting connotations we have described above, resulting in culture's ejection from economics. In the next three chapters, we discuss why economists nevertheless gradually became interested in culture again and how culture has entered their analyses since.

In discussing the relation between culture and economy we distinguish between two broad phases, which we subsequently discuss in this chapter. In the first section, we trace the evolution of culture as a relevant category for understanding the world, including the economic sphere. In the second section, we discuss the events that are associated with the separation of economic and cultural studies. These events ultimately culminated in the idea of culture entering – or rather, being removed from – economics as "tradition," most obviously in modernization theory. The chapter concludes with a discussion, which highlights the impact of the historical background on the contemporary debate about culture in economics.

2.2 A history of culture in economics

To understand how culture has been related to economics over the past centuries, we first need to delve into the history of the "culture" concept. In Chapter 1, we have identified several aspects of contemporary understandings of culture: it is related to collective identity; it is about ideational structures, influencing behavior; it is a human-made system; it is assumed to be inherited and given. These characteristics of the word "culture" have not always been the same. Meanings of culture have shifted over time and differed between languages. Detailed historical accounts of this evolution in Western thinking can be found in Kroeber and Kluckhohn (1963), Markus (1993) or Brons (2005). Here we limit ourselves to key developments relevant to the discussion about culture in economics.

2.2.1 From culture to progress

The term "culture" stems from the Latin *cultura*, a derivative from *colere*: to grow, to cultivate. On top of its literal agricultural meaning, ancient authors such as Cicero also used the word metaphorically as *cultura animi*, the "cultivation of the mind." In medieval times, with their focus on religious worship rather than human development, this meaning of the term more or less disappeared, only to return during the Renaissance. Then, the metaphorical meaning soon replaced the agricultural one as the dominant understanding of culture.

Culture thus entered modern thought with the meaning of the individual process of moral and intellectual development. A "cultured" individual was someone who was well educated, refined and erudite. While this remained the primary meaning, two gradual shifts in the meaning began to take place in the seventeenth and eighteenth centuries. First, the term came to denote not only the process of individual development but also the product of it (Kroeber and Kluckhohn 1963: 37; Markus 1993: 9). Culture became a "thing", which people possessed or did not. Second, the seventeenth and eighteenth centuries saw a shift from culture as individual development toward culture as development of societies as a whole. The idea of "more and less cultured societies" emerged, put forward by authors such as Montaigne and Pufendorf (Brons 2005: 99–100; Kroeber and Kluckhohn 1963: 31; Markus 1993: 10).

At this point in time, culture, as in the original use of the word as *cultura animi*, still represented a normative standard rather than a factor influencing behavior. It was the way individuals and peoples ought to become, not a description of how they were. A first step toward a more descriptive interpretation of culture occurred during the Enlightenment. Especially in Britain – most notably in Scotland – a new view of history had emerged, centering around the idea of *progress*. Scottish authors, who were simultaneously confronted with new images and information about "less cultivated" colonies and with their own peripheral position within Britain, developed the idea that history could be seen as societies evolving progressively, in stages. David Hume (1976 [1757]), for example, developed this idea of progression with regard to the history of religion. The idea of progress had been informed by the so-called *Querelle des Anciens et Modernes*, i.e. the struggle between those who continued to hold classical culture as the normative standard and those who began to challenge the prescriptive relevance of ancient culture for modern times. In the latter view, societies were no longer compared to an ideal defined by an image of the classic age but came to be described in their own terms. The idea of a universal, trans-historical human nature and ideal society began to make way for a more pluralistic view in which different societies were seen in their historical context (Baars 1988). History thus came to be classified in distinctive periods; the idea of progress subsequently added structure and direction to this classification.

The idea of culture as development of societies fitted neatly within these ideas. Culture as a normative standard still set the direction of development, but the idea emerged that different societies were at different levels of this universal development toward "culturedness" (Kroeber and Kluckhohn 1963: 32). It was within this context that the first theories about culture, history and economics came about.

Adam Smith

Adam Smith has often been labeled the founding father of economics. He earned this distinction for his seminal *The Wealth of Nations* (1999 [1776]), in which he argued that division of labor and trade, inspired by self-interest, is the source of wealth and economic prosperity. However, it is clear that Smith, the importance of this work notwithstanding, was certainly not the first one to write about the economy. Also, it might be noted that in his own time, Smith was much more renowned for his other major book, *The Theory of Moral Sentiments*, first published in 1759 (Smith 1976 [1759]).

The paradox of Smith's current stature is better understood if we consider his work in the context in which he wrote. Smith's major works, *The Theory of Moral Sentiments* and *The Wealth of Nations*, are to be seen not as positivist analyses of society – which would be an anachronism – but as normative, political economy. It was not a pure description of a situation that existed everywhere; self-interested behavior and the predominance of free commerce were by no means universally accepted. Smith's work primarily served as a call for allowing the situation he described to come about, with his theories providing the moral justification for it.

Thus, although Smith might not exactly have been the father of economics, in many ways he was the father of an economics that dealt with market society, and as such, the first one to write about the economic system that we know today.

The eighteenth century was a time of great changes in British society. On the eve of the industrial revolution, Britain had been experiencing a change from a pre-market into a market society. This entailed nothing less than a breakdown of the old order. A new society was rapidly emerging, which was not constituted by guilds, feudal lords and serfs any more but by capitalists, landlords and workers. The new economic system was no longer governed by fixed, hierarchical, ascribed roles but by the free employment of production factors. Instead of traditional relations, the market came to be the organizing factor of economic life, if not society as a whole. Commerce acquired a central role in the organization of society, where it previously had been a marginal phenomenon. The breakdown of the old order and its replacement by "capitalism" was by no means a smooth, uncontested process. It first required "freeing" labor from the land to which it was tied, which occurred as a consequence of the enclosures of previously common lands. This process turned the feudal lord into a landlord, and by dispossessing the peasant, it created a new kind of labor force, obliged to work for wages. The enclosures were a brutal and often violent process. In addition to physical repression, it meant the disappearance of the certainties and logic of the old order. A society governed by contractual bargaining on the market instead of by religious and personal considerations implied all kinds of existential uncertainties. As late as the 1810s, anti-capitalist movements such as the Luddites would be resisting this new society. It was in and about this context that Smith wrote.

The new social order emerging in Britain brought the individual to the fore. The emerging market society was a place in which individuals interacted freely with each other and in which everyone sought to improve themselves, without being constrained by ascribed roles and closed positions as existed in feudalism. Such a situation was easily associated with chaos and therefore it required a philosophy of how a society comprised of individuals working on their own accord would still be functioning in an orderly manner. Smith provided such a theory. In *The*

Theory of Moral Sentiments, he described how individualism would not lead to a breakdown of all morality but how moral sentiments could be rooted in an individualist, anthropocentric worldview. He argued that individualism would not result in a war of everyone against everyone, but that inborn inclinations to mutual sympathy ensured an orderly, moral and progressive society. In *The Wealth of Nations*, Smith did the same for economic order and prosperity. The two books, especially when taken together, thus provided a justification for the kind of society that was emerging.

At the same time, the writings of Adam Smith in this respect reflected the ethical teachings and principles with which English society was imbued. As Max Weber would later argue, Puritanism advocated the idea that everyone had/should have a calling. If everyone took up this calling earnestly, working hard and doing one's best in order to honor God, the division of labor and its benefits for society as a whole came about indeed. But rather than as strictly utilitarian, Puritans interpreted such usefulness for the common good as an aspect of the purposeful organization of society meant to glorify God. The moral message portrayed by Smith is indeed much the same as the Puritan ideal: strive hard within one's individual calling, for the benefit of such conduct reaches beyond individual gain, fitting the purposeful system (Weber 1992 [1904–1905]: 161).

In other words, what Smith was writing about was not (simply) an analysis of the economy, even when in *The Wealth of Nations* he specifically addressed production and wealth. Rather than that, Smith was the advocate of a total social and moral order, on the one hand new, and on the other drawing from ethical principles coming from religious sources. To Smith, this order was rooted in individualist liberalism, of which economic principles such as the division of labor were just an aspect. In his work, there was not yet a division between economy and society, or culture. Economics, in Smith's work, was a societal and moral, political subject. The really revolutionary aspect of *The Wealth of Nations*, when compared with the work of mercantilists or physiocrats, was perhaps the ethico–political idea that the wealth of nations was to be understood as the product of commercial and entrepreneurial activity. With Smith, the wealth of a nation is not determined by the riches of its royals, as the mercantilists argued; it is defined as the product and income of equal, free individuals. In this sense, Smith's work is a radical, political statement and a redefinition of society as a whole, rather than simply an economic theory.

If we accept that Smith was describing a whole social system rather than just an economic principle, it follows that in Smith's work we find a theory about the relation between what nowadays (!) would be called culture and the economy. A society of free individuals engaging in commercial relations with each other would be both orderly and prosperous. Commerce created a society which was civilized, because commerce was a necessary condition for arts and moral development (Smith 1983 [1763]: 137). In other words, rather than proclaiming an entirely egoistic society of everyone against everyone, commercial relations bred liberty and virtues. Such a liberal society, with its moral and material prosperity, was perceived to be the most advanced stage of history, in which commerce was the structuring element. Thus, where Smith can be said from a contemporary perspective to speak of relations between economy and cultural aspects, he views the culture he describes and advocates not as differentiated but as the universal endpoint of development through commerce. Culture or civilization equals the market society, which through commercial development will eventually emerge in every society, however savage it is now.

In the thoughts of Smith and his contemporaries, we see how the idea of cultivation of an individual's moral and intellectual qualities has been transplanted to the progress of societies. General visions about the evolution of societies emerged, covering morality, religion, commercial relations and political structures. In these broad theories, culture and economy did not exist yet as separate social categories. To speak of this literature as being about culture *and* economy is an anachronism. Also, Smith's thought differs from current work on culture in the fact that the moral, commercial and political development Smith envisaged was not deemed specific to any community. Societies differed in "the degree to which cultivation has progressed" (Kroeber and Kluckhohn 1963: 32), but the direction of this progress was universal. These two aspects changed with the emergence of a new interpretation of culture, inspired by the Counter-Enlightenment.

2.2.2 The "essentialization" of culture

If we think of culture nowadays, we usually do not consider it to be the universal product of societal development. Rather than that, culture is deemed particular to a society and although rooted in history, this history is typically considered specific to the society as well. This is what we mean by essentialism: the idea that certain attributes – in this case, culture – are specific and inherent to the identity of a certain group or society.

An essentialist interpretation of culture started to emerge from the late eighteenth century, fully blossoming in the nationalist nineteenth century (Wolf 1999). This process took place in a few steps. To start with, in German philosophical discourse, a distinction came to be made between culture and civilization. This distinction had its roots in the rejection by Romantic authors of the Enlightenment worldview of universalism and reason. Romanticists began to stress the peculiar, the traditional and irrational instead. In this line of thought, the term "*Zivilisation*" began to be reserved for the universalist, rational society authors such as Smith had envisaged. It referred to the development of artificial structures of behavior and manners. To the Romanticists, the outward decorum of such *Zivilisation*, being opposed to the natural tendencies and genuine development of human beings, only restricted individuals and societies in their advancement. Contrasted to such artificial constraints was "*Kultur*," which denoted the actualization of the innate qualities and identity of human beings. *Kultur* was deemed something positive and referred to the genuine cultivation of human nature, as opposed to the adoption of alien manners and restrictions of *Zivilisation* (Brons 2005: 100; Markus 1993: 16).

At first, this new view upheld the eighteenth-century idea of culture as the fruit of cultivation. The idea of a universal development path was altered in a more pluralistic understanding of historical development. Authors such as the influential Johann Gottfried Herder thus began to pay attention to what made particular peoples unique (Kroeber and Kluckhohn 1963: 38–39). The study of history began to make place for the study of multiple histories of particular peoples. The idea that each people had a *Volksgeist*, i.e. a specific, inner essence from which its language, folklore and historical development unfolded, began to take hold. The idea of a *Volksgeist* gave rise to the emergence of a new science of *Völkerpsychologie* (ethnic psychology), seeking to identify this shared psychological essence that bound together a people and set it apart from other peoples (Wolf 1999: 28). In this new development, culture acquired two dimensions. On the one hand, it was still something a society could have more or less of; the "cultured" societies were still opposed to the savage, primitive peoples. On the other hand, however, each society now was considered to follow a unique development path, determined by the cultural identity of the people. Culture gradually became something specific. Within economic thought, we can see this development in theories of scholars such as Wilhelm Roscher, gradually evolving into the ideas of the Historical School.

The Historical School

The Historical School in economics generally refers to a rather diverse set of authors of various generations. Hence, any summary of the contribution of the Historical School in a few pages is necessarily as incomplete and simplistic as such a project would be when dealing with neoclassical economics. When discussing the way historicists tended to approach culture and economy, we necessarily limit ourselves to tentative, broad generalizations.

The main idea that bound authors such as Wilhelm Roscher, Bruno Hildebrand, Karl Knies and Gustav Schmoller was a common understanding of economics as an historical, cultural and political science. They were concerned with the economy as a function of individual motivation and morality. Historical Economists rejected the assumed, imposed idealist construct of self-interested rationality proposed by classical economics. Instead of simply stating that human motivation was universally self-interested, they sought to investigate the ethics and motivations of individuals, viewing this as the basis for how economies functioned. In addition to an explanatory interest in ethics as a crucial variable guiding behavior and constituting society, historicists viewed economics as an ethico–political science. Economics was a science explicitly directed at policy applications; the distinction between pure theory and practice was to be dissolved. However, if economic performance was a function of the morality in a society, to say anything about economic policy implied taking stances toward morality.

Ethics in this respect was confronted as an empirical science. Research and theory development would result in statements about moral decay and progress of societies that were not merely idealist speculations but firmly grounded. Thus, theories of societal progress, embedded in moral development, were developed by authors such as Roscher, Hildebrand and Schmoller. To the latter, "economy is part of culture built into the world of nature, a product of man's intellectual efforts... with cultural progress the psychological-ethical causes become relatively more important" (Betz 1997: 97). This clearly refers to an understanding of culture as cultivation of morality, overcoming the natural state. However, the whole project of putting economy in an historical–cultural perspective was informed by an awareness of specific characteristics setting societies apart. Schmoller, for example, calls attention to the point that "Ein Sinken der Zuckerpreise in England bewirkt eine steigende Konsumtion, das gleich Sinken bei uns bewirkt das nicht, weil bei uns die Sitte des Zuckerkonsums eine andere ist" [A drop in the price of sugar causes a rise in consumption in England while the same drop does not have such an effect with us (in Germany, auth.), since our habits with regard to sugar consumption are different] (Schmoller 1874, in Koslowski 1997: 6). One could therefore argue that historicists were confronted with a continuous tension between a concern with specificity and the desire to develop economics into an ethico–political science, requiring moral standards. The position to which they tended was one of cultivation of specific characteristics. Culture thus was differential, but still a product of development.

This position is perhaps most clearly taken by Wilhelm Roscher, although in some ways being predecessor rather than member of the Historical School. Whereas the later historicists would make a more downrightly hermeneutic turn and dissociate themselves avidly from classical and neoclassical economics, Roscher was more accommodating. He did not seek to develop a new theory of economics, but tried to transplant the historical method into economics as it was. Economy, in his view, was not a system but a description of historically variable economic relationships (Priddat 1997: 20). Roscher sought a "factual" rather than an idealist science.

However, Roscher did cling to the idea of objective principles that are a-historical themselves, guiding history. He believed that history was governed by developmental laws, similar to natural laws. Empirical description is only the observational aspect of a preceding fundamental knowledge of such laws (Roscher 1918 [1854]: 82–83, §29). In other words, any specific empirical description should be in terms of the encompassing framework of historical laws. This historical description hence was in need of a comparative approach: the parallels between different economic phenomena are to be treated as objective truth when "there is a standard by which to measure them: this standard takes the form of a law of history" (Priddat 1997: 23). These laws of history referred to general patterns in the development of specific characteristics of different societies, however. In this way, Roscher sought an "historical–physiological method," looking for a "simple description of, firstly, the economic character and needs of a nation (Volk), secondly the laws and institutions created to fulfil the former and finally the degree of success they have had. In other words, a simultaneous description of the anatomy and physiology of economics" (Roscher 1918 [1854]: 77, §26). He believed that history portrayed a cyclical structure: each society goes through a period of growth, maturity and decay. However, each people had its own path and own period of maturity.

Later Historical Economists moved away somewhat more from the idea of universal laws. Knies, for example, maintained that "the claim of universal and unconditional theoretical validity is but a product of its own time" (Betz 1997: 91). In other words, standards and motivations were made the subject of inquiry, historicized as well. They were not just specific to societies; they were specific to historical periods as well. Although the emphasis thus very gradually shifted from the idea of cultivation to a focus on the historical specificity of societies, the main idea of culture as cultivation and development of a societally specific moral character was maintained. Culture was thus understood as essentialist cultivation.

Methodologically, historicists sought to develop economics more clearly as part of the *Geisteswissenschaften*, the moral sciences. The underlying idea here was that sciences studying behavior had an object that was fundamentally different from natural sciences. For one thing, human beings had free will, ruling out the search for universal principles that directed natural science. What bound all humans together was the fact that they were fellow humans and their actions and ideas had purpose and meaning, which could be recognized and understood by each other. Although society could not be reduced to causal principles, its workings could and were understood by people. This understanding was what the *Geisteswissenschaften* were about; instead of an *Erklären* (explanation), historicists sought a *Verstehen* (understanding). The idea of *Geisteswissenschaften* implied a hermeneutic turn, arguing that the object of a discipline such as economics was to be the study of meaning. Meanings of processes and practices could be uncovered by confronting details from various angles and putting them in perspective of the whole. This approach was already advocated by Roscher, arguing that details should be viewed in their relation with the entire field of economics and the whole of national life as well (Roscher 1918 [1854]: 82–83 §29). Through such confrontation of parts and whole, one could ultimately gain a *Verstehen* of a society and the meaning of the actions by individuals that were part of it.

The ideas of the Historical School have had a huge impact on the development of debates about the role of culture in economics, even though the authors associated with this school themselves are mentioned relatively rarely nowadays. The Historical School obviously had an important influence on Max Weber's study of the origins of Western capitalism as an evolution of morality – the topics addressed and approach betray a strong similarity. On a deeper level, some peculiarities of the Historical School would make themselves felt in debates for a long time. For one thing, the essentialist ideas of authors such as Roscher were structured around the idea of society as nation. The history, the moral character and economy were all viewed from this perspective: the nation, or *das Volk* (people), was where culture resided. Cultural differences were differences between nations. As a corollary, the nation itself was homogenized and approached as a closed, given entity not subject to questioning. There existed such a thing as *the* German moral character and *the* British culture. Such essentialist notions of culture and development amounted to an approach to the study of economy that might be called "methodological nationalism": the idea that any analysis of culture should start out from the unit of the nation.

Against the background of an emergent German nation-state seeking a common identity, this is hardly surprising (Kroeber and Kluckhohn 1963: 52). More generally, the idea of national cultures can be clearly linked to the emergence of nation-states in the nineteenth century and was instrumental to this political project. The idea of geographically located groups with unique, collective identities, whose ideas and values were deeply and fundamentally different from other groups, were what justified a nation's claims for control over a certain territory. It is therefore not surprising to find the idea of nations each having their own national development path and culture to have dogged development economics after the Second World War – many newly independent countries were confronted with a similar challenge of building unified nation-states, legitimizing their existence and supporting the role of the state. This essentialist focus on the nation as the unit having a distinguishable moral character and culture would continue to work through in work on culture and economy, however. It left a firm imprint on much of the revival of cultural economics in the final decades of the twentieth century, for example in the empirical cross-country comparative studies.

In addition to "methodological nationalism," the hermeneutic turn made by the Historical School would continue to influence an important strand of thought with regard to studies of culture in other disciplines. The approach of anthropologists like Geertz, for example, is building on the idea that social science should be concerned with the study of meaning, through a *Verstehen* of other people, rather than with looking for universal causal laws. The opposition between approaches favoring some form of hermeneutics and approaches seeking general laws makes itself felt even today.

In a more negative way, it might be argued that the Historical School has had an impact on the development of debates about culture and economy because of the way it hung on to an ethico–political economics. The ethical economics historicists were committed to was not only to be about ethics and politics but was also to have a normative character itself. The mixing up of these two ideas contributed to the neglect of morality by later theorists. In the circles of those seeking a pure, non-normative economic theory, the inclusion of ethics in one's analysis became suspect. The idea took hold that if one was looking for general, non-normative insights, one should refrain from ethics. Hence, even though direct references to the work of people such as

Roscher and the Historical School have become rather sporadic in the literature nowadays, its impact cannot be underestimated. However, the essentialism of the German Historical School was not the only important development in thinking about culture and economy in the nineteenth century.

2.2.3 The politicization of culture

The distinction between *Kultur* and *Zivilisation* not only instigated a shift to the essentialist interpretation of culture which can be found in the works of the German Historical School. The idea of *Zivilisation*, denoting a system of norms and rules of entirely human, artificial origin, capable of oppressing humans rather than following from their nature, also inspired a radical critique of society that can be found in its most virulent form in the works of Karl Marx. In this line of thinking, the idea of an inevitable progression toward a state of civilization, governed by reason and individual self-interest, was taken over from Enlightenment economists such as Smith. This view of progress was combined with two elements of Romanticism: the less optimistic perception of progress and civilization, and the idea that the rational structures and organizations called civilization were something different from the irrational, traditional and moral aspects of society. This combination led to the first theories that could be said to be about culture *and* economy, in the sense of a relation between two different things. In this theory, social norms, beliefs and values were the mental representations of a system of politico–economic relations and conflict. Instead of the essentialist notion of culture developed by Roscher and others, Marx questioned culture, religion and social values critically from the perspective of political economy.

Karl Marx and Marxism

Although Adam Smith went into history as the founding father of economics, when it comes to academic and societal influence he definitely has to succumb to Karl Marx. The founder of "scientific socialism," Marx inspired generations of social activists, social scientists and quite often a blend of these to adopt a critical approach toward economics and society. Although commonly known – and denounced – as the ideologue of communist movements all over the globe, Marx's magnum opus, *Das Kapital* (1867), is actually an analysis of the capitalistic market economy, rather than dealing with communism or socialism.

To Marx, the essence of capitalism[1] is the use of capital to produce more capital. This occurs through the exploitation of labor. Like other classical economists such as Smith and Ricardo, Marx saw labor as the only production factor capable of actually producing value. However, labor employed in the capitalistic production process typically produces more value than what is needed to sustain it. The laborer needs to work to ensure survival, receiving payment that makes this more or less possible. However, the laborer conducts more work than would strictly be needed for survival. In this "overtime," which represents labor inputs that are not paid for by the capitalist, surplus value is produced by the laborer. This surplus value results in a difference between production costs and rewards and makes the production process profitable to the capitalist.

The reason why laborers can be forced to work more than they would strictly need to for their survival lies in the monopolistic control over the means of production by the capitalist. Because the laborer is dependent on capital to produce anything, this puts the capitalist in a position to exploit labor and, in a way, steal part of the value produced by laborers. In other words, capitalism rests on a system of exploitation and oppression.

This is not the place to go into the details of Marx's analysis of the capitalistic mode of production. Suffice to say that capitalism, according to Marx, is a system of inherent conflict between laborers, who have an interest in limiting their labor inputs to the amount needed for their survival, and those who control the means of production, who seek to lengthen the period in which the laborer produces surplus value as much as possible. According to Marx, such conflict arising from privileged control over means of production is universal, but its form is dependent on the specific mode of production. The conflict acquired a different form in feudalism, for example, since the distribution of control over means of production was different. Historical development takes the form of the decline of one mode of production and its replacement by another one.

---

[1] Although the term "capitalism" is hardly used in *Das Kapital*.

This occurs because each mode of production has inherent contradictions, which eventually result in crisis and its downfall (Marx 1859: 7–11).

For the relation between culture and economy, it is important to note that any such mode of production is not just an economic affair but creates an entire system of social structures and ideas supporting it. For example, the exchange of goods typical of capitalism presupposes that goods are comparable, because they represent value. After all, if there was no common dimension to all products, no exchange would be possible. If value is the common aspect of all goods, and value is created by labor, this presupposes that all labor is indirectly seen as equivalent. In other words, the market exchange of goods indirectly implies that the labor of a peasant is comparable to the labor performed by a nobleman. This requires a social outlook that is most likely to come about in the abstract vision of mankind typical of Christian doctrines such as Protestantism or Deism (Marx 1978: 32, 36). In many other societies, the works of a nobleman would be classified as of an entirely different quality than the works of a commoner, ruling out equal exchange between the two. Thus, capitalism entails a certain outlook to match economic structures. More generally, the social relations of production form a complex system that goes beyond mere economic relations and affects social, psychological and religious conditions.

The relation between these elements is given by the principle of historical materialism (not Marx's term). Marx divides society into an economic structure and a judicial and political superstructure. According to historical materialism, the economic structure of a society is the real basis on which this superstructure is built and determines the social outlook and beliefs held by society (Marx and Engels 1848: 480). In other words, the mode of production of material life sets the social, political and religious conditions in a society (Marx 1859: 8–9; Marx 1978, section 1, footnote 33). Economy thus has primacy in the Marxist worldview. Also, Marx's theory is decidedly structuralist. Economic structures govern society and even individual actions, since the actions of a capitalist are only a function of the needs and purposes ascribed to capital. The capitalist will internalize these functions, changing, for example, the economic necessity of savings into the moral requirements of abstinence and frugality (Marx 1978: 457). In this way, the individual actor is governed by the laws of economic structures of its own making.

These structures also govern historical developments. As noted, according to Marx, the historical evolution of a society occurs on the basis of the development of the contradictions within its mode of production. That also means that other "revisionist" attempts to change society, through political and social channels, are futile. As long as a mode of production has not entered a crisis of its own making, resulting in the downfall of a particular division of labor, any solution or moderation of the conflict between laborers and capitalists is impossible (Marx 1978: 373).

The relation between culture and economy in Marx's thinking thus focusses on the economic. Culture, morality and religion are internalized social relations that are economic in essence. In this way, they support the economic substructure and help to oppress labor by sustaining a mode of production and distribution of control over means of production. The connection with the notion of *Zivilisation* is clear: *Zivilisation* also referred to artificial, man-made constraints and restrictions that prevent human beings from their full actualization. In Marx's thinking, the superstructure of society has a similar effect. Morality, religion, social, legal and political structures are not intrinsic to national, historically rooted identities, as Roscher wants it, but are part of hegemonic systems of oppression and class conflict. The main difference with the *Zivilisation* concept is that the superstructure, according to Marx, is not an arbitrary set of rules and relations but a symptom of historical laws as well. To Marx, however, that does not preclude an explicitly critical stance.

Such ideas have been worked out in various ways by followers of Marx. Sometimes, historical materialism has been taken to denote a uni-directional causal relationship from economy to culture. Such views have been denounced by many others, however, branding them as vulgar materialism, economism or economic determinism. For example, Brewer (1990) asserts that Marx's doctrine of historical materialism never was supposed to mean that any real society could be reduced to a single abstract mode of production. Rather than that, modes of production should be seen "as basic forms of organization which can be combined and elaborated in many ways in different historical circumstances" (Brewer 1990: 14). What is more, the relation between economic structure and cultural super-structure is dialectical rather than monocausal. Although the mode of production is the primary driver of socio-cultural change, culture also affects the economic structure. Engels (1888: 93), for example, maintains that the rapid development of the United States has in part been due to the American entrepreneurial spirit. That said, Marx shared with his predecessors the idea that the rational logic of civilization (used more or less as a synonym for capitalism, according to Brons 2005) would ultimately determine the direction of the universal history of mankind. The logic of historical development was thus in the end set by economic structure, not culture.

One of the most important Marxist authors who did stress the cultural side of the reciprocal relationship between superstructure and structure was the Italian communist Antonio Gramsci. Gramsci sought a more nuanced and comprehensive understanding of class conflict, which was less exclusively historically materialist. In Gramsci's view, class domination did not rest only on the formal political system and institutions imposed and defended by the state; it also spread into social and cultural life, creating a system of ideas, habits, beliefs and social relations that actively supported the situation of repression and dominance by one class. Working classes were not only oppressed by the formal relations of the capitalist system of production, the state or its laws and institutions; their oppression also had infiltrated ideas, beliefs, values and norms, which served to put them in a position of exploitation. The total of all this material, intellectual and ideological dominance together formed what Gramsci called hegemony (Gramsci 1980). Similar ideas were later worked out in the context of developing societies in Paolo Freire's *Pedagogy of the Oppressed* (1972), in which he set out a program for liberating poor classes in developing countries from the mental oppression resulting from decades of colonial and capitalist exploitation.

It is debatable which of these views most closely resembles the true position of Marx and even more so whether that question is of any relevance or not. What these approaches share is a critical attitude toward culture and economic structures, questioning the content of moral, ideological and social structures from the perspective of political economy. This can be said to have been Marx's greatest contribution to economic and social science: his call for a reflective, critical stance that was almost lacking in political economy until then. Such a critical attitude, which sees culture as a political–economic, problematic structure, continues to inform thinking about culture and economy today.

In the nineteenth century, we thus have a dual understanding of culture and its role in economic processes. On the one hand, there is the view of culture as *essentialized self-actualization*, informing the German Historical School, among others. This was the way most people saw culture: as a set of characteristics inherent to a society's identity and steering its development. On the other hand, there is the critical view inspired by Marx, which challenges this meaning and function of culture, seeing it as part of *hegemony*. In this critical perspective, culture was seen as a reflection of the political and economic order in society, serving to legitimize and support this order. Rather than taking over the way culture and economy were understood within and by society, Marx and his followers sketched a different, counter-hegemonic understanding of society, from which point of view issues such as culture, law and economy were critically addressed. It should be noted that this view, being a critique, does not dispute that culture *was* commonly understood within society as essential self-actualization. What it challenged was that this was the way society *ought* to be understood, seeking a critique rather than a reproduction of such understandings. It argued that although people generally see culture as an inherited set of characteristics inherent to a society's identity, it is in fact an ingredient of hegemony, to be explained out of underlying political–economic structures.

This dual understanding of culture already bore the seeds of another, more methodological opposition that came into full prominence only after the Second World War. Roscher and the German Historicists were committed to studying economy and society as they were, using the concepts and understandings available within the social system itself. Marx, by contrast, considered that these concepts and understandings were products of the system and reflected its structures and power relations. Therefore, any analysis making use of the concepts and understandings present in the field could not lead to critical insights into social and economic mechanisms. Marx sought to develop an alternative framework, the meta-historical reality of class struggle, which provided the structures on which critique could be grounded. In other words, the German Historicists – like the classical economists, as Marx would have argued – analyzed society from the (subjective) perspective of the insider, while Marx sought to develop an objective point of view by creating an outsider position. This tension between (alleged) insider and outsider positions continued to play a role in debates about culture, and culture and economy. This tension became even more challenging because imperialism affected the interpretation of culture.

2.2.4 The traditionalization of culture

The rapid changes which Europe faced in the latter part of the nineteenth century had an impact across the globe. What some people labeled as the first wave of globalization ultimately challenged the existing notions of culture and society as well. After all, the idea that different societies were on different development paths, set by the cultural characteristics of their nations, was primarily designed for the understanding of Europe. However, the late nineteenth and early twentieth centuries were also the epoch of imperialism and a limited European focus did not suffice any more.

Any country with any aspirations in Europe was active in building itself an empire. This project was often not only political; increasingly, it was felt that imperial power also brought a responsibility toward the natives to educate and civilize them. Imperial powers apparently not taking this responsibility were publicly denounced (for example, Joseph Conrad's *Heart of Darkness* about Belgian Congo or Multatuli's "Max Havelaar" about the Dutch East Indies). Imperialism thus created a partition of the world as civilized and "savage," which also affected the understanding of culture. Within the Western world, people like Roscher had discussed the differences between the developments of various Western nations. In the global imperialistic arena, however, all these nations could be classified together as civilized and as such opposed to the rest of the world. This ultimately caused a change in the understanding of culture.

As noted, the understanding of culture as essentialized self-actualization was two-dimensional. From the Enlightenment stemmed the notion of culture as something of which a society could have more or less. A more "cultured" society had developed more fully and was at the forefront of technological, artistic, political and economic achievements. Culture in the sense of civilization was associated with the triumph of reason and opposed to barbarism and irrational traditionality. Simultaneously, under the influence of Romantic nationalism, the process of cultivation of a society had become something specific to each society, so that each nation had its own development path. Cultural differences were not only differences of degree but differences in kind as well.

Under the influence of imperialism, these two dimensions began to drift apart, starting to denote different concepts. In the paternalistic context of the imperial powers, the idea of "culturedness" as the result of progress and cultivation of inner qualities was applied to the development and achievements of Western, "high" cultures. These achievements were not particular to or typical of a specific development path. Rather, they were the (desirable) fate shared by the whole of humankind, being the endpoint of all development. To denote this development, the term "culture" was gradually dropped in favor of terms such as "civilization" and "modernity." Only in the context of arts and literature do we still find the term "culture" to mean the cultivation of intellectual and aesthetic ideals that are characteristic for the cultured person.

The word culture, when applied to societies, thus came to denote the differential dimension mainly. Since modernization was considered to be a universal, homogenizing process, cultural differences existed only where there had not been development yet. Culture – the particular, the specifically own – became the deviation from the mold of modernization. From cultivation it turned into tradition, becoming the opposite of the idea of modern development. Development indicated progress and rationally designed change; culture, which still existed only where development had not taken place, began to imply stability, irrational tradition and changelessness. It was often opposed to civilization and associated with less developed societies (Kroeber and Kluckhohn 1963: 19–20). Development was a process that was the same everywhere; culture entailed the specific deviations from it. And perhaps most crucially, where civilization was modeled after the own, culture was a term reserved for The Other. The educated West was modern, whereas the unenlightened peoples of the world – including, perhaps, the poor and less educated mob in the core societies – had these irrational habits and remnants of the past called culture (Brons

2005: 106–107).[2] Thus, the use of the term "culture" came to reflect and support the distribution of power in the world. Western powers could legitimize their dominance by the fact that they portrayed the rational, civilized type of behavior and thinking that was universally desirable. They had the task of leading the "others" out of their particular cultural ways.[3] Culture, in the world of imperialism, had become something of the uneducated. It was something to get rid of.

2.3 A history of culture vs. economics

The process described in the previous sections obviously affected the thinking about culture and economy. Until the late nineteenth century, the social sciences were not as differentiated in separated disciplines to the extent that they are now. The political economy of Smith and Marx was indeed political, not only economic, and included analyses and topics that mainstream economists nowadays would not consider to be part of the economic discipline. To Roscher, even more so, economics was "a political science, a science concerned with the evaluation and government of people . . . I don't presume to know anything unless I understand its relationship to the state, to the law, to religion and art, to every aspect of a nation" (letter to Gervinus [1840], cited by Priddat 1997: 19). Max Weber, widely considered to be one of the founding fathers of modern sociology, held a chair in economics.

2.3.1 The emergence of economics as a cultureless science

The current boundaries between the social science disciplines took a long time to establish. The line between sociology and economics

---

[2] This tendency to see culture as something especially relevant in non-Western countries continues today. A search in ISI Web of Knowledge reveals that studies about economy are more than twice as likely to address culture if they are also about the Third World.

[3] See, for example, the "benevolent assimilation proclamation" by President William McKinley upon the colonizing of the Philippines by the US in 1898: "The mission of the United States is one of the benevolent assimilation, substituting the mild sway of justice and right for arbitrary rule. In the fulfilment of this high mission, supporting the temperate administration of affairs for the greatest good of the governed, there must be sedulously maintained the strong arm of authority, to repress disturbance and to overcome all obstacles to the bestowal of the blessings of good and stable government upon the people of the Philippine islands under the flag of the United States."

in particular continued to be fuzzy for a long time, with sociologists such as Weber and Durkheim dealing with many of the same issues as apparent economists like Veblen. The origins of the separation of social sciences lay in part in the so-called *Methodenstreit*, in which the theoretical approach of marginalist economists was opposed to the alleged descriptive empiricism of the historicists. Within economics, the marginalist approach eventually proved to be victorious. It was a slow process, however, with institutionalists such as Veblen and John R. Commons successfully resisting marginalist dominance for a long time, so that it was not until after the Second World War that the victory of economic orthodoxy was more or less complete. The *Methodenstreit* of the 1880s, centering upon the opposition between the Historical Economist Gustav Schmoller and the economist Carl Menger over the methodological course economic science should take, was but a first step in the process. In this heated debate, Menger (1969 [1883]) argued that at least for the purpose of theory we ought to explain all external economic phenomena in terms of internal economic orientation. In other words, economic activities, such as acts of production, saving and consumption, ought to be analyzed as outcomes of rational choice in the procurement and deferral of pleasure (Bond 2006: 3). Other motives or factors that might inform or influence economic actions are of no relevance to the economist, in this reasoning.

Whereas the historicists saw the profit-seeking, purposeful thinking of capitalist society as an historically specific form of behavior, Menger declared that such economic rationality was a universal trait of behavior on which the science of economics should be founded. From the perception of the historicists, this meant that Menger was taking out one historically constituted way of behaving and declaring it the universal norm. In this view, the economist Francis Edgeworth was an interesting transitory figure. Much like Menger, Edgeworth sought to found economics on the assumption that all people are pleasure seekers. However, rather than translating this into a universal model of behavior, Edgeworth argued that some were better pleasure seekers than others; women and people of low birth were deemed less well equipped to make the contemplatory efforts needed to maximize pleasure. On the whole, due to the foolishness of those less capable people, society underperformed when it came to maximizing pleasure (Edgeworth 1879). To Edgeworth, therefore, utility maximization was not a universal trait of human behavior but something specific to educated white men. Still, the model was to be the foundation of the science of economics, for it set the norm to which the world should (and would) eventually adhere. In Edgeworth's thinking, we see a transformation from utility maximization as a desired behavior, as yet portrayed only by educated, enlightened males, toward rational utility maximization as an axiomatic model of behavior. At the end of this process, rationality was not an objective any more but an assumption.

This interpretation of what economics was about was not unanimously shared, however. Indeed, many authors, both historicists and theoretical economists, felt that the abstract approach of neoclassicism, reducing human motives to the margins of purposive rational action, was too restrictive to understand economic phenomena in their totality. In the first instance, the main adversaries of the approach advocated by Menger were authors belonging to the Historical School. They were followed up by a new breed of economic scholars, seeking to develop theories that covered the social, cultural and political aspects of economic phenomena. Max Weber coined the term *Sozialökonomie* for this project; in Anglo-Saxon countries *institutional economics* was more widespread.

Max Weber

Max Weber (1864–1920) has become known as one of the founding fathers of modern sociology. He was an important figure in the intellectual climate of early twentieth-century Germany and has had an enormous influence on the social sciences that is felt even today. Within economics, however, his stature seems to have faded somewhat, even though he spent much of his career studying socio-economic subjects. His career might be divided into two phases.

Weber's early works were more downrightly socio-economic in character. Inspired by the tradition of the German Historical School, Weber studied specific economic historical subjects such as the development of Roman land tenure, viewing such issues within the entire social and historical context. In 1904–1905, Weber published *Die Protestantische Ethik und der Geist des Kapitalismus* in two parts in the *Archiv für Sozialwissenschaft und Sozialpolitik*. The article set the stage for the rest of Weber's work, which increased in scope substantially.

In *Die Protestantische Ethik*, Weber sets out to trace the development of Western capitalism, arguing that it had its roots in the worldly asceticism associated with certain branches of Protestantism (Calvinism, Puritanism, Pietism and Baptism). The argument is elaborate and consists of various steps. First, Weber argues that the tendency of the capitalist to work hard seeking profit and the propensity to save and invest should be seen as a moral phenomenon, or an ethos. Importantly, Weber maintains that capitalism itself is of all times and places. However, a capitalist economic action is simply "one which rests on the expectation of profit by the utilization of opportunities for exchange, that is on (formally) peaceful chances of profit," thus differentiated from profit through plunder or expropriation (Weber 1992 [1930]: 17–18). What sets the Western economy apart from such universal capitalism, which is but a form of organization, is a capitalist spirit. In the Western economy, "man is dominated by the making of money, by acquisition as the ultimate purpose of his life. Economic acquisition is no longer subordinated to man as the means for the satisfaction of his material needs" (Weber 1992 [1930]: 53). It is this ethos or spirit of capitalism which is the object of Weber's inquiry.

In the second step, Weber argues that the origins of this ethos lie in the ethical principles of Protestantism. The inquiry of *Die Protestantische Ethik* is part of a wider project to study the influence of certain religious ideas on the economic spirit, which would also cause him to study other world religions such as Confucianism, Judaism and Hinduism (Weber 1989; Weber 2005). In his study of Protestantism, Weber states that Calvinism promoted a worldly asceticism. The doctrine of predestination maintained that one either was elected or not, which was known to and decided by God only. This implied that there was no "magical" control over one's fate, as was the case in Catholicism, in which good deeds could cancel out wrongs done, or where holy sacraments had such effects. Thus, the doctrine promoted rationalization.

Rationalization, however, is a process requiring an object – there needs to be something which is rationalized. This "something" Protestantism provided in the idea of calling. Although predestination meant that one's ordeal was beyond one's control, it was held to be "an absolute duty to consider oneself chosen, and to combat all doubts as temptations of the devil, since lack of self-confidence is the result of insufficient faith, hence of imperfect grace ... on the other hand, in order to attain that self-confidence intense worldly activity is recommended as the most suitable means" (Weber 1992 [1930]: 111–112). This latter idea follows from a view of the world as a purposeful system meant for the glorification of God. Intense worldly activity in this view amounted to doing what God had required one to do. Thus, asceticism, a tendency which had always been present in Christianity, was translated into a serious and solemn focus on one's works in the world, rather than in the move away from the world promoted by the hermit and monastic traditions of Catholicism (and other religions). In this context, the idea of work as a calling (*Beruf* in German or *beroep* in Dutch) emerged. One had a duty to find one's specific place within the organized, rational system of society and to fulfill the tasks to which one was called to the utmost. This view required constant self-control and a deliberate regulation of one's life; it compelled the "methodical rationalization of life" (Weber 1992 [1930]: 128). Thus, the Protestant ethic promoted purposeful dedication to one's task, stimulating division of labor and capitalist economic action.

The duty to engage in rational, intense, solemn worldly activity naturally led to wealth. Wealth, however, constituted a danger. On the one hand, Calvinists had argued that wealth was good because it enhanced the prestige of the faithful, proving the purposefulness of the creation. On the other hand, Puritans argued that wealth and comforts all too easily could lure one into idleness. Not leisure and enjoyment, but activity served to increase God's glory (Weber 1992 [1930]: 157). As a result, a morality emerged centering around rational conduct based upon the idea of a calling, in which intense, purposeful worldly activity was encouraged, but the enjoyment of its fruits discouraged. In other words, riches were not a problem; consumption was. Wealth had to be applied for practical, purposeful causes. Naturally, such an attitude promoted capital accumulation. To Weber, it is this set of moral ideas that have shaped modern Western capitalism – even though nowadays their religious basis has got lost.

The importance of *Die Protestantische Ethik* lay not only in this message but also in the theoretical and methodological ideas underlying the work. Weber wrote the work in an academic context characterized by the opposition between the Historical School of economics and Marxism. With both he shared an approach to study economy in an historical perspective. However, Weber was decidedly more influenced by the former and *Die Protestantische Ethik* in some ways could be read as a frontal attack against Marxist Historical Materialism. The work firmly denounced the notion that ideas could be reduced to material factors. However, Weber equally challenged simplistic Idealism, which argued that ideal factors determined historical development, including the economy. Rather than that, Weber's work could be read as claiming that there is no unidirectional relation between ideas and material factors and in general that there are no laws of history (Giddens 1974: 33; 1992: xx). Capitalism, as a system of organizing economic action, could and had emerged in any society. The form it acquired in Northwest Europe and New England, however, was an historically specific product of a particular set of circumstances. Neither the unlimited expansion of capitalist economic action nor the form it acquired in the West was the inevitable outcome of historical evolutionary principles.

Just as Weber rejected the idea that certain developments were inevitable because of laws of history, he also objected to claims about the moral quality of social phenomena. Rationalization is the main leitmotif in his historical research and Weber held there was a logical distinction between ratio and morality. Social science should and could refrain from moral statements, in his view. Rationalism is guided and informed by moral ideas, but rationalism itself cannot judge moral ideas and objectives; these have another source. Because of this moral irrationality of the world, there are no more or less rational ethical systems (Giddens 1974: 44). The Protestant ethic, in Weber's story, was thus an irrational moral force, upon which a process of rationalization was based creating modern Western capitalism. There is thus ultimately nothing rational or desirable about Western capitalist society, or at least not in the sense that it is more rational than the rationalization occurring on the basis of Confucian principles in China, for example.

The influence of these ideas on discussions about culture and economy has been profound. On the more superficial level, it set the stage for a focus on practical morality as the differential element between societies, which would make itself felt up until the recent cross-cultural values-studies literature. The concern with religion as a source of such values has continued to influence debates as well, especially with regard to East Asian development. In his focus on the Spirit (*Geist*) of capitalism, Weber took another step in the direction of separating material, behavioral structures on the one hand and ideas and symbolic systems on the other. The *Geist* of capitalism refers to the system of thoughts, convictions and ideas that underlie the capitalist behavior. It is this, rather than capitalist actions themselves, that makes modern capitalism stand out. In this sense, the notion of *Geist* is somewhat similar to current notions of culture in economics: an ideational and symbolic system influencing economic behavior.

Weber's most profound impact on the discussion, however, was perhaps his renunciation of laws of history, claiming the moral irrationality of the world. By this step, Weber's work moved again further away from ideas of culture as related to processes of cultivation. The values that set societies apart were themselves not subject to rational inquiry and universal principles; Weber merely studied the subsequent development on the basis of them. Thus, Weber's work could be interpreted as a framework of general development (rationalization) on the basis of specific characteristics (moral values). In this respect, his work was an important source for the modernization theorists of the 1950s and for the varieties of capitalist literature that have become popular more recently (although in Weber's case, it would probably be more appropriate to speak of the "variety of rationalizations"). Moreover, by making his logical distinction between rationality and morality, Weber played an unintended but important role in the removal of issues of culture from economics and the way the social sciences would become separated – economics studying rationality, sociology focussing on the empirical study of specific values.

With authors such as Max Weber in Germany, Marcel Mauss in France and Thorstein Veblen on the other side of the Atlantic, economics was not yet reduced to analysis in terms of marginal utility. They were part of a large branch of economists seeking to analyze "capitalist behavior" as something historically specific that needed to be explained. In this explanation, they did not limit themselves to one set of human motives in the way neoclassical economics did. Rather, socio-economists and institutional economists argued that the behavioral and economic regularities that an economic science should seek to uncover were emerging from sources other than just behavior motivated by marginal utility. In Weber's *The Protestant Ethic and the Spirit of Capitalism*, for example, the ethical system gave explanations for the rise of capitalism and accumulation, seeing accumulation as an outcome of ethical principles rather than as a hedonistic goal achieved by purposive action. That is not to say that theory on the basis of marginal utility was dismissed. It was only, as Weber put it, "subject to marginal utility" itself (Weber 1908) – one explanation among others.

Without going into the details of the various theories developed by socio-economic and institutional economic authors, what is interesting here is that over time they would be gradually pushed to the fringes or removed completely from the body of economic thought (Morgan and Rutherford 1998; Rutherford 2001). Menger's position would slowly grow to be the dominant view in economics. This process took longer in some places than others. In England, the combination of the hierarchically structured academic and cultural life and the dominance of an important neoclassical economist such as Alfred Marshall caused the English version of the *Methodenstreit* to be cut short. Across the Atlantic, the marginalist approach also gained the upper hand early on, but it would not be before the Second World War that the challenge put forth by historicism was subdued in the United States (Ross 1991). The end result, however, was the same everywhere: the neoclassical interpretation of economics had become the dominant one.

This process, initially evolving around the question of how to conduct economic science, eventually became a division of studies of the economy into economics on the one hand and economic sociology and economic anthropology on the other. The way Menger had defined economic science, in terms of method rather than in terms of a clearly delineated research object, implied that different approaches were perhaps possible but were not economics. Economics was concerned with those regularities in behavior that could be derived from the internal economic orientation, i.e. rational choice. It was not about understanding each and every aspect of economic phenomena from a comprehensive range of perspectives (Bond 2006). This opposed economics to the social or historical description and analysis of economic phenomena. Joseph Schumpeter, in an attempt to resolve the *Methodenstreit*, first made this division of labor explicit. Schumpeter maintained that both sides in the *Methodenstreit* were basically right, but they differed in their perspectives and "their interests in different problems" (Schumpeter 1908: 7). Economics aimed at "pure theory," based on individuals making marginal choices. The inputs for such decisions, such as the origins of preferences and institutional constraints, were important but not for the "pure theory" of economics. For economics, "it is irrelevant why people demand certain goods" (Schumpeter 1909: 216). These questions are there for other social sciences to study.

The evolution of economics as a science defined by a method rather than a research object would eventually culminate in the famous definition of economics that came to define the discipline: "economics is the science which studies human behavior as a relationship between given ends and scarce means which have alternative uses" (Robbins 1932: 16). Robbins' definition takes the focus on the universal structures of rational choice even one step further than Menger's approach by placing differences in preferences outside the domain of economic studies as well. In Robbins' definition, economists focus purely on the structure of rational choice; the explanation of all contextual and individual differences is left to other sciences.

2.3.2 The removal of context

As long as one believes that there is a specific field of phenomena that are economic in nature, the idea that there are meaningful things to be said about these phenomena from perspectives other than marginal theory is unavoidable.[4] Weber's *Sozialökonomie*, advocating a vision of economics in which all acts of value creation and consumption have meanings that can be understood, is an example of such a rival view. The disregard for such other perspectives and factors within economic science implied that the discipline "economics" was not equal any more to "the study of economic phenomena." Scientific studies of economic phenomena were possible that were not economics.

---

[4] As we will describe in the next chapter, Chicago economist Gary Becker would later radicalize Robbins' stance and abandon the idea of economics as a science studying economic phenomena altogether. Instead of viewing economics as the science dealing with economic explanations of economic phenomena (thus maintaining two understandings of what is economic), Becker took an (arguably more consistent) approach of defining economics purely in terms of a mode of explanation, in principle applicable to all phenomena.

A first step in this development was, ironically, the rise of institutional economics in the United States, founded by Thorstein Veblen. This movement rejected neoclassical economic theory, seeking instead a more comprehensive, historically and culturally contextualized approach. Veblen was sharply aware of the de-historicized, de-socialized character of neoclassical economics. In his 1898 seminal paper "Why is economics not an evolutionary science?," he singles out the political economist Cairnes as an advocate of "pure theory," arguing that such a "pure theory" is a "theory of the normal case" (Veblen 1998 [1898]: 409). Although being stripped of all moral connotations that the idea of the normal order of nature might have, neoclassical economic theory, according to Veblen, is still formulated in terms of normality and natural law. It takes a certain conduct – economic rationality – which, instead of being viewed as a particular conduct in a certain time and place, is said to be the normal structure which all behavior universally tends towards. Such theories, in Veblen's eyes, are what set economics apart as relatively backward among the social sciences. Whereas modern sciences are evolutionary, focussing on explanations of dynamic processes in terms of cause and effect, economics clings to a metaphysical vision of the world in which the world is the way it is simply because that is the normal, natural order.

It has been the subject of discussion whether Veblen intended to develop a positive, evolutionary research program for economics to replace neoclassical analysis. Although many of his predecessors have interpreted him thus, there is also quite a lot going against such an interpretation (Peukert 2001: 548). In the latter view, Veblen did not level his criticism against the state of economic theory because he thought that evolutionism was a better or more scientific program; rather, he saw the move toward evolutionary sciences as part of a general historical development under the influence of industrialization and mechanization, which induced people to think of the world in terms of mechanistic, causal processes, without ulterior goals or meanings (Tilman 2004: 157). Evolutionary sciences were thus not superior, they were merely more modern (Peukert 2001: 548). Veblen can also very well be read as proposing a positive, evolutionary research program. In 1896 he wrote in a letter to a former student that "economics is to be brought in line with modern evolutionary science, which it has not been hitherto. The point of departure of this rehabilitation, or rather the basis of it, will be the modern anthropological and psychological sciences . . . (economics) is to shape itself into a science of the evolution of economic institutions" (quoted in Hodgson 2004: 135). The result should be "an evolutionary economics (which) must be a theory of a process of cultural growth as determined by the economic interest, a theory of a cumulative sequence of economic institutions stated in terms of the process itself" (Veblen 1998 [1898]: 413).

This explicit call for a grounding of economic theory in psychological and anthropological insights eventually proved counterproductive in stemming the tide against an interpretation of economics as "pure theory" alongside other social sciences that more directly dealt with the world "out there." Economic theory was to be based on insights from modern psychological theory; these ideas were an input, not part of economic inquiry. Whereas former approaches had taken economics as being about the analysis of human behavior, which automatically included the analysis of human nature and the motives behind behavior, explicitly building on psychology institutionalism reproduced the notion that there was a realm for psychology and a realm for economics. By focussing on the importance of irrationalities, Veblen confirmed rationality as a norm; by insisting on introducing psychology into economics, he confirmed that the two were different things. Similarly, whereas ideas, beliefs, morality and habits had been naturally included in the interpretation of the economic of authors ranging from Smith to Schmoller, Veblen considered it necessary to explicitly drag them in. Claiming that modern capitalism was much more "primitive" and "barbaric" than commonly presented, Veblen challenged the conception of Western behavior as rational, but also reproduced the opposition between rationality and barbarism, primitivity and cultural traditionality. Before, culture had not been a term often mentioned within economics, although many of the contributions by economists in the preceding centuries would from our current perspective entail studies in culture and the economy. Where previous authors, such as Adam Smith, had felt that it went without saying that economic studies dealt with the progress of society as a whole, at this point in time Veblen felt it necessary to point out that "in economics, the subject of inquiry is the conduct of man in his dealings with the material means of life, (so that) the science is necessarily an inquiry into the life-history of material civilization . . . like all human culture this material civilization is a scheme of institutions – institutional fabric and institutional growth" (Veblen 1909: 628). In his opposition to an economic analysis cleansed of culture, institutions and psychology, Veblen reproduced the notion that culture and psychology were no longer by definition part of economic analysis – although they certainly had to be incorporated for economics to be useful. Emphasizing "cultural habit and belief (institutions) in economic behaviour" he views economic interests and activities as "only 'vaguely isolable' from, the larger web of cultural processes that make up individual lives and integrate social relations and events," but isolable nonetheless (Jennings 1998: 528).

Culture had become something distinguishable from, though extremely relevant to, economic behavior. Veblen thereby ironically gave his opponents the ammunition to discharge his institutionalism as being cultural science, sociology or psychology, but not economics. The distinction between cultural factors and economic phenomena was a first step in the removal of context from economics. The second step was the redefinition of non-orthodox authors as not really economists. Already in his obituary, his pupil Mitchell says of Veblen that "many economists held that whatever his work may be, it is not economic theory" (Mitchell 1929: 649). After the Second World War, Veblen would enter economic textbooks only – if at all – as someone who had studied some marginal peculiarities within the overall accepted neoclassical economic theory.[5]

In a similar way, a scholar like Max Weber, analyzing the economy in its totality and applying a range of explanations, of which the historically specific focus on marginal utility was only one, would find himself redefined as a sociologist rather than an economist in a few decades. A prominent economist playing a crucial role in this process was Joseph Schumpeter (Bond 2006). Although Schumpeter, who was committed to the study of the economy from the perspective of utilitarian motives, wrote about Weber in flattering terms, he also made it clear that in his view, Weber was "a sociologist. It was only indirectly and secondly that he was also an economist – although he was a

---

[5] Added to the matter of scientific disciplines, Bartley and Bartley (2000) make the case that Veblen's ideas, often quite unsympathetic to the dominant classes in society, led vested interests to seek to eliminate Veblen's intellectual legacy. Veblen became the subject of a stigmatizing campaign, defaming his reputation. Veblen had already been subject to slander and this went on after his death. According to Bartley and Bartley (2000), a central role was played by his biographer, Joseph Dorfman. This added to the marginalization of his legacy.

sociologist who focused primarily on economic phenomena" (Schumpeter 1954 [1920]: 112–113). Later on, in his *History of Economic Analysis*, Schumpeter (1955: 819) would go even further, arguing that Weber was not an economist at all. In Schumpeter's view, Weber was a scholar who was primarily interested in the understanding of historical meaning of actions and events. Although this was interesting, it was not economic science.[6] Thus, whereas Weber originally had been concerned with the theoretical analysis of economic phenomena from a plurality of perspectives, in their total historical, social and cultural context, the increasingly tight grip of neoclassicism over economics meant that his contributions came to be reinterpreted and reduced to the analysis of contexts. Moreover, the context of neoclassical economic theory was reinterpreted not as constituting economic rationality but as intervening, limiting and distorting the universal patterns of economic rationality.

What had formerly been economics thus came to be divided into a theoretical economics proper, focussed on the universal behavioral principles of the rational individual, and an economic sociology meant to complement this theory by adding the specific social–cultural context of economic processes. The point was perhaps made most explicitly by someone who arguably could be seen as one of the founding fathers of modern neoclassical economics: Vilfredo Pareto. Pareto argued that a distinction ought to be made between strictly economic behavior, being the outcome of "a series of logical reasonings," and behavior determined by what he called "custom" (Pareto 1972 [1906]: 29–30; Bourdieu 2005b: 209). The former belonged to economics, the latter to the other social sciences. In this way, economic sociology emerged as a complementary discipline to economics proper, studying those peculiarities of economic phenomena that deviated from the economic theoretical model.

In the same way that an economic sociology came about as a complement to economics, a sub-discipline called economic anthropology

---

[6] Ironically, Schumpeter himself would go on to experience the same fate. In his short overview of the most important economic thinkers, first published in 1953, Robert Heilbroner devotes a highly approving chapter to Schumpeter. Yet, he asks of Schumpeter's contributions: "Is this economics? Not by any of the conventional conceptions. It is better described as historical sociology" (Heilbroner 1999: 308). Almost needless to say, Weber does not even make it into the book.

emerged. The difference was this: where economic sociology focussed on *those aspects of society* for which economic theory did not apply, economic anthropology was designated *those societies* where economic theory was not relevant. Much like Weber and Veblen, an author like Marcel Mauss, who had gained fame with the cross-cultural study of economic processes (e.g. his famous *The Gift*, published in 1925), was thus interpreted out of economics into anthropology. Unlike economic sociology, which came to be more or less reduced to the study of context of economic behavior, economic anthropology was still concerned with economic phenomena in their social totality, that is, the economic as undivided from the social, normative, religious, etc. However, this total, cultural approach to the study of economic phenomena over time came to be considered of relevance only to non-Western, non-developed societies.

2.3.3 Universal rationality vs. specific culture

The finer details of the broad theoretical developments sketched above are described in other works about the history of economic thought. What is of relevance for the place of culture in economics is that economics became concerned with one universal aspect of human behavior, in principle unlimited in scope, whereas disciplines such as economic sociology focussed on the particular deviations from this aspect; these non-economic approaches had the task of bridging the gap between the economic *Güterwelt* (Durkheim and Fauconnet 1903: 487) and real-life situations.[7] Economics was to be concerned with "pure theory," other social sciences with particular context. This idea created an opposition between an economic logic, based on competition and efficiency, and a social logic, subject to socially constituted norms, meanings and rules of fairness (Bourdieu 1998b). The distinction between universal, rational economic behavior on the one hand and the specific, social–cultural behavior on the other was ultimately

---

[7] This *Güterwelt*, to Durkheim, was a world that existed only in the minds of economists; it was "un monde isolé qui demeure à jamais identique à lui-même et au sein duquel les conflits entre des forces purement individuelles sont régis par des lois économiques immuables" (Durkheim and Fauconnet 1903: 487–88, in Swedberg 1994: 72). The economic world was separated from real life by being subject to universal, immutable laws without deviations. Adding the deviations gave the real world.

retraceable to the distinction that had evolved in the nineteenth century between civilization (culturedness) and culture (tradition). Economics studied the rational aspect of society – civilization – while other disciplines studied culture (Brons 2005: 113).

This division of the sciences, in a sense, reflected the dominance of the way of life of Western educated elites over other social structures; neoclassical economics, emerging as the dominant party, was concerned with the norm, the other social sciences with the deviations from this norm. Culture – in the new interpretation of anti-rational tradition – thus became the subject of the context-oriented social sciences, being removed from the increasingly abstract models of economics. It was in this context that culture ultimately disappeared from the mainstream economic lexicon. Culture, as particular deviations, had no place in a science devoted to understanding these aspects of behavior that were universal. Sure enough, institutional economists such as Veblen and Commons continued to be prominent for a long time. But one should note that even these authors, had they been starting their careers a few decades later, would most likely have been working in a social sciences department rather than been classified as economists. The division of labor, in which neoclassical economists studied a-contextual rational choice under scarcity and (economic) sociologists studied the particular contexts, was thus upheld. The work of old institutional economists was deemed not theoretical enough to be real economics (Coase 1984: 230), even though it might have been of minor interest when applying economic theory to real-life situations. Even an influential contemporary institutionalist such as Hodgson actually advocates a return of the old institutionalist approach on the basis of the impurity principle – the idea that there are always sub-systems within capitalism (or any economic system) not organized on that system's basis (Hodgson 1995). In other words, the advantage of an institutionalist approach above neoclassicism is deemed to be that it adds specific context to the general model, thus reproducing the existing dichotomies.

2.3.4 Development economics: where culture and economics still met

After the Second World War, the abstract, technical approach to economic theory became increasingly dominant. Whereas in the 1930s, economic theory had still been presented largely by way of verbal expositions, in the 1950s this made way for the formal mathematical method. Simultaneously, economics became decidedly less pluralist in this period. The tradition of institutional economics had slowly disappeared or was removed from the economic to the sociologic.

There are many reasons for this development, which have been discussed extensively in other works (e.g. Morgan and Rutherford 1998; Rutherford 2001). For now, the main interesting observation is that the apparent consensus among economists should be seen in the light of a common enemy: Marxism.[8] After all, these were the heydays of the Cold War, in which the communist and capitalist systems vied for global dominance. In this context, deviations from teachings unambiguously supporting capitalism were suppressed. It paid to present a theory underpinning the market model as established truth, so that economic affairs became subject to technocratic debate only. The message of this project was simple: the capitalist system was not only superior in moral terms – because it guaranteed freedom – it could also objectively be shown that it was good economics.

That message was to be propagated especially in the arena where much of the Cold War was actually fought, the Third World. In the search for the dissemination of economic systems and securing larger parts of the globe under one's sphere of influence, a new branch of economics came about, concerned with the development of the newly independent former colonies. Authors such as Rosenstein-Rodan (1943) and Rostow (1960) were (unintentionally) instrumental in providing theoretical support for what was essentially a political project – securing the allegiance of Third World nations by sending them aid. As a result, economics was (re-)discovering the less developed world.

It is interesting in itself to note that the new concern with the economic development of former colonies was thought to merit a special development economics. After all, logically speaking, concern with the Third World does not have to lead to a special theory for the Third World – application of the existing theoretical concepts was

---

[8] And, during the Second World War, fascism. The traumatic experience of the Second World War also created a deep distrust for scientific programs such as those envisaged by Roscher and the Historical School; ideas about intrinsic national cultural character came to be eschewed, portraying all developed (!) societies as basically similar. This probably contributed further to the universalism of neoclassical economics.

also an option.[9] Yet, apparently, the Third World was considered to be a place different enough from the developed world for it to be subject to different economic principles and mechanisms. At the same time, the entire Third World, essentially different as it was from the developed world, was deemed homogenous enough itself to be captured by one development economics, with the same economic laws applying whether in Korea, Senegal, Chile or Bhutan. What bound all these diverse regions was their status of less-developedness. The emergence of development economics as a sub-discipline of economics thus reflected the division of the world in a developed, rational part, and a Third World that was defined largely in terms of opposition to the Western model. The ideas that informed the assignment of culture to anthropology and sociology, while maintaining the supposedly universal rational behavior as the domain of economics, were thus reproduced. The main difference was that economics now began to devote attention to a part of the world that was previously the monopoly of ethnology or anthropology. But in developing a special kind of economics for this purpose, it approached the less developed world from the same point of view that once excluded the colonies from its analysis altogether.

Naturally, therefore, development economics came to be the special arena in which economics continued to be approached in a broader, more contextual manner than in the abstract models of the mainstream core. The Third World was the one place where economics and culture continued to meet. After all, an economics that was to be relevant in a context governed by tradition had to take a more comprehensive view. The Third World was and remained a place in which behavior was subject to structural mechanisms, cultural ideas and customs. An approach focussing on rational individuals capable of independent action and choice was not deemed applicable. Thus, at a time when culture disappeared from the scene in mainstream economics, it survived within development economics. If one is looking for interesting work about culture and economy stemming from this period, therefore, it is to be found mainly in this direction, most notably *modernization theory.*

---

[9] As neoclassicals began to argue in the late 1970s again, initiating the take-over of development economics by neoclassicals.

Modernization theory

Theories about development emerging in this period can by and large be classified under the header modernization theory. Modernization theory was concerned with the problems and possibilities for turning the (former) colonies into prosperous, modern societies. Authors such as Rostow (1960), Hoselitz (1954, 1957), Eisenstadt (1968), Nash (1964) and McClelland (1961) held the assumption – often implicitly, sometimes explicitly – that "developedness" was a single, objective state that was the endpoint for all societies (even though lip service was paid to the possibility of a diversity of paths toward it). Therefore, developed societies could function as examples for less developed countries. They were simply farther ahead on the same line. Roscher's idea of using historical knowledge to derive the universal laws of development was adopted, but the knowledge considered relevant was about the history of Western societies only; after all, these were the ones that had developed. A universal development model was thus based on the historical evolution of Western powers. Outside the Western world, development was taken to have been absent.

These ideas meant that, even though the economic situation formed the initial inspiration for many of them, modernization theorists were not concerned with economic growth only. Instead, they sought to replicate the way in which rich countries had grown rich, because that was the only way they knew it could happen. This entailed economic development as simply an aspect of a much broader process of social and cultural change called modernization. For example, to Manning Nash "modernity is the social, cultural, and psychological framework which facilitates the application of science to the processes of production. And modernization is the process of making societies, cultures, and individuals receptive to growth of tested knowledge and its employment in the ordinary business of daily living" (Nash 1964: 226). Such an application of science to production amounted to the solution to poverty, in his eyes. However, that "involves a value system conducive to the relatively unhampered search for new knowledge, a positive approval of innovation, and a high tolerance for ontological uncertainty. It also requires a social structure where political and class groups are willing to run the risks of innovation as these may affect the distribution of income and power. And it requires mobility of resources and manpower: some assurance that effort and reward are linked in a socially recognized and enforceable manner. It requires the kinds of persons who will make innovations, apply them to the processes of production, move to economic opportunities, and permit a good part of social honor and prestige to be determined by success in the economic sphere" (Nash 1964: 226). This citation is typical of modernization theory in the way that it turns the condition of the US of the 1950s into a universal prerequisite for development. Also, it betrays a strong belief and trust in modern technology and science as solutions to underdevelopment. To Nash and many other modernization theorists, poverty was ultimately a matter of lack of science in production. By adopting superior Western technology, less developed nations would immediately reach Western standards of living. On this basis, many aid projects had gone under way aimed at disseminating modern technology in the Third World. It turned out, however, that in spite of its unambiguous superiority, Western technology was often resisted and not applied. This put theorists on the look-out for all kinds of social, political and cultural obstacles that prevented a smooth application of science to production, which needed to be addressed. The problem of development became the problem of "adapting and communicating modern techniques to less developed areas" (Hoselitz 1954). Modernization, in this sense, had a strongly pedagogic tone. Societies had to change and learn how to behave and to appreciate superior technology, which required a certain social and cultural outlook.

When it came to this wider social and cultural context of development, McClelland's book *The Achieving Society* (1961) was especially influential. In it, McClelland proclaimed that economic development and prosperity were dependent on "modern" entrepreneurial attitudes, which could be transferred through the schooling system (*see* Chapter 6). Again, the message of such work was that the free market with its entrepreneurial attitudes was the right path to development, calling developing nations to cast aside the traditions inhibiting them and modernize. In a way, it was an attempt to create a world in a mirror image of the US. Culture, in this story, was mainly presented as a problem. Developing nations were constrained by cultural rules and customs that prevented them from rational economic behavior, functioning markets and

development. Thus, culture, as trad
don in order to develop. Only by a p
could a society really – in the words (
and fly on to modernity.

Of course, there were dissenting '
strategy to development which viewe
cle. An important early critic of this de
Hirschman, argued that "the method
history of one or several economically
certain situations that were present at
opment was brought actively under wa
countries, and then construing the abser .... as an
obstacle to development" (Hirschman 1965: 385–386). Hirschman
labels approaches such as this "ethnocentric."

In reaction, a slightly more nuanced view on the role of culture
in development emerged that focussed not only on obstacles but
also on the way in which some societies were able to overcome
their problematical traditions, and on traditions that could prove
to be assets to development (Eisenstadt 1968: 447). The possibility
was acknowledged that "traditional societies" had some valuable
cultural traits as well. Such "right" traditions – i.e. traditions that
were already in line with modernity – could be instrumental in modernization. In this way, Marion Levy Jr. argued that the different
development paths of China and Japan could be traced back to the
fact that individualism in China had been absent, whereas in Japan
it was not (Levy Jr. 1962). Japan had the right culture to develop
and therefore it had modernized more successfully.

Modernization theory thus reserved a rather explicit role for culture. On the one hand, cultural change was an important aspect
of any development process. On the other hand, cultural characteristics could facilitate or hinder modernization, so that cultural
differences between countries might be the source of their differential development records. Culture, in this thinking, was something
to abandon or exploit.

We noted already that modernization theories reproduced much of
the thinking of earlier authors such as Roscher. Both Roscher and
modernization theorists shared a belief in the existence of universal

laws; both shared an approach in which these develop-
were to be derived from historical observation; and both
a much broader perspective than an exclusively economic
n addition to these similarities, there is another strong parallel
tween the two, what we have called a "methodological nationalism."
Roscher saw the nation with its culture and own history as the natural unit of analysis for studying development. Modernization theorists
did the same. Under the influence of trends in economic thought in
the developed world, economic development was deemed a project of
macro-economic policy. The newly independent national governments
saw it as their task to develop their countries economically and socially.
Five-year plans were written in many countries. This approach was not
restricted to those countries in the communist sphere of influence, since
recipients of US aid such as South Korea or Taiwan also developed
through such plans and high levels of government interference.

Contemporary versions of modernization theory have eliminated
some of the more problematic areas of earlier theories, such as the
stark opposition between traditional culture and modernity or the
extreme one-size-fits-all approach, while maintaining the general idea
of a universal development trend to be followed by all societies. A
modern sociologist/political scientist such as Ronald Inglehart (1977,
1990, 1997) has suggested that several amendments are necessary if
researchers want to continue working with modernization theory. The
first amendment is that humankind has entered a new historical stage,
that of post-modernity or post-industrialism. This new stage is not
only accompanied by new technological developments (information
and communication technology) and economic changes (globalization
of markets, flexibility of work), it also brings new values, particularly
post-materialistic rather than materialistic ones. The second amendment is that we must not focus all our attention on long-term developments but also need to take into consideration short-term changes,
such as the different phases of the business cycle, and short-term events,
such as wars and revolutions. A third amendment is that we must
incorporate in modernization theory the theoretical notion of path
dependency. This implies that although the direction of change may
be common in various societies, each society develops according to its
own speed and in a distinctive way reflecting a society's social–cultural
experiences and historical heritage. "Economic development tends to
push societies in a common direction, but rather than converging, they

seem to move on parallel trajectories shaped by their cultural heritage" (Inglehart and Baker 2000: 49).

Although Inglehart and Baker (2000) build on both modernization and culturalist theory, they also react against the deterministic character of these theories. Their central thesis is that economic development has systematic, and to some extent predictable, cultural and political consequences. These consequences are, however, not iron laws of history but probabilistic trends. In other words, the probability is high that certain changes will occur as societies develop economically, but the question of whether they occur, and if so, to what degree and in which form, depends on the specific cultural and historical context of the society in question. Economic development brings cultural changes, but a history of Catholic, Protestant, Orthodox, Islamic or any other religious tradition gives rise to cultural zones that persist after controlling for the effects of economic development (Inglehart and Baker 2000; Petterson 2006).

2.4 Conclusion

This chapter has presented an overview of thinking about culture in the context of (studies of) economic development and the economic sphere throughout the ages. It has argued that culture, since its conception as the cultivation of virtues and knowledge during the Renaissance, experienced quite a transformation until it came to acquire the meanings that we usually give it today. The golden threads in this history are summarized in Table 2.1. From individual cultivation, culture first came to denote the progress of the universal cultivation of society. As such, it was understood in the ideas of authors such as Adam Smith or, in a different way, Karl Marx. Under the influence of Romantic nationalism, the idea that culture (*Kultur*) was not universal but specific to societies emerged. This shift inspired authors associated with the German Historical School, including Max Weber. Eventually, culture came to be associated with static differences between societies, while the universal progress element was removed to the concept of civilization. Economics, with its emphasis on the universal structures of individual rational choice, inherited civilization. Culture was left to other social sciences.

It should be noted that this has been *a* – not *the* – history of culture and economy. As any writing of history is laying a structure over

Table 2.1. *A history of culture and economic thought*

Time	Significant historical trends	MEANINGS OF CULTURE	ECONOMIC THOUGHT
1500		Moral education	
	Renaissance	↓	
1700	Enlightenment	Collective moral education	
	Idea of Progress	↓	
1800	Romanticism	Stage of collective moral development	Adam Smith
	Nationalism	↓	
1900	Imperialism	Type of collective moral development	Roscher
			German Historicists
		Civilization: rational conduct, developedness	Weber
		Culture: specific collective identity	Veblen
1960			Modernization theory
			Neoclassical economics

events to connect them in a meaningful way, many other histories could have been written on the topic. Since this chapter is part of a book about current and future research on culture and economy, we have focussed on a history of relevance to contemporary discussions. The chapter is not aiming to present a comprehensive overview of the history of economic thought, historiography or the genealogy of culture; the history presented here is the limited product of our focus on certain themes throughout the development of the debate. We think these themes are highly informative for assessing current theoretical developments because they highlight problems and considerations that are playing important roles now.

The most important insight of this chapter is that the history of the concept of culture and the history of economics are intertwined: culture was part of economic thought (or, more accurately, the other way around). It was only at the beginning of the twentieth century that the interrelated evolution of the concept of culture, split up into a "cultural" and a "cultured" meaning, and the establishment of the boundaries between economics, sociology, history and anthropology, caused culture to disappear from economic thought. Culture came to be constructed as opposed to the research object of economics. Whereas economics had grown to be the study of the universal, normal and rational, culture had developed into a concept denoting particular varieties, the irrational deviations of this economic model. In so far as culture still entered economic thought, it tended to be at the fringes of analysis. Culture was invoked to study the marginal peculiarities of our behavior that could not be explained in terms of (bounded) rational behavior by acting subjects any more, or of behavior as a whole in marginalized, undeveloped societies.

Given this opposition between culture and the economic that has evolved over centuries, the question arises: why did economists nevertheless grow interested in employing culture again in recent decades? More importantly, how do they try to overcome opposition and bring the two together again? These are the questions we turn to in the next three chapters.

3 | Explaining the rise of culture in modern economics

3.1 Introduction

Where the previous chapter told the story of culture's gradual disappearance from economics, this chapter tells the story of its comeback. As argued, by 1950 culture had all but disappeared from economics. This was the result of a long process in which culture and the economic had acquired almost opposite meanings.

The contrast between cultural and economic perspectives that came to characterize the state of thinking by 1950 is summarized in Table 3.1. In this list of oppositions, one can still recognize the distinction between culture and civilization as it emerged in the nineteenth century – economics inheriting the latter. Also, we see once again the various elements of the definition of culture discussed in Chapter 1. Culture, being about patterns of thought and behavior that are deemed inherited and unquestioned, is at odds with the economic model of the social as constituted by rational agents, purposively designing outcomes. Furthermore, culture focusses on collective, emergent properties, whereas economics looks at society from the perspective of individual behavior. Finally, the idea of cultural diversity inspiring different worldviews and patterns of behavior in different societies is alien to the economic quest for universal principles.

Given these rather fundamental oppositions, one would not expect culture to enter economic thought ever again. Yet, from the last decades of the twentieth century onwards, we can observe a steady rise of economic studies into culture, most of them applying quantitative methods to pin down the effects of cultural differences on economic outcomes (Barro and McCleary 2003; Fernandez 2007, 2008; Franke, Hofstede and Harris Bond 1991; Guiso, Sapienza and Zingales 2006, 2009; Granato, Inglehart and Leblang 1996; Harrison 1992; Luttmer and Singhal 2008; Noland 2005; Pryor 2005; Swank 1996;

Table 3.1. *Culture vs. economics*

Culture is:	Cultural perspective:	Economic perspective:
Inherited and unquestioned	Exogenous structures	Rational agents
Related to collective identity	Collectives	Individuals
Worldviews influencing behavior	Context-specific insights	Universal principles

Tabellini 2007a, 2007b, to name a few). Other studies take a more historical approach, focussing on differences in culture, institutions and their effects on long-run development (Clark 1988; Greif 1994, 2006; Kuran 2003, 2009; Landes 1998). Culture has also featured in theoretical work (Heydemann 2008; North 1990, 2005; Williamson 2000).

The question is, what accounts for the sudden return of interest in culture among economists? In this chapter, we argue that the comeback of culture is part of broader trends in and outside economics (cf. Roland 2004). On the one hand, the success of the version of economics that prevailed after the Second World War led it to transgress into areas it had hitherto left to other sciences, thereby encountering issues that were more usually linked to cultural analysis (e.g. Becker 1973; Becker and Murphy 2000; Levitt and Dubner 2005). On the other hand, from the 1970s onwards, important developments in economic research and economic reality brought questions to the fore that standard economic theory was not capable of answering satisfactorily. An explosion of experimental research, taking off in the early 1970s, eroded the trust in models assuming full rationality and efficient markets (Camerer and Fehr 2006; Conlisk 1996; Kahneman and Tversky 1979; Thaler 1992, 2000). The financial crisis of 2008 seems to have finalized this (*The Economist* 2009; Hodgson 2009). Other developments include a growing awareness of long-run differences in economic practices and outcomes between societies, triggered by the spectacular rise of East Asia in recent decades and the relative lack of development in Africa. The lack of satisfactory economic explanations for this inspired an expanding literature on the "deep" determinants of economic development, for which culture could enter as a candidate (Acemoglu *et al.* 2001; Diamond 1997; Glaeser *et al.* 2004; Hall and

Jones 1999; Landes 1998; La Porta *et al.* 2008; Rodrik *et al.* 2004). The rise of East Asia also had the (temporary) effect of introducing the idea that there may be more than one way to look at economics and issues of development, thus challenging the idea of one theory for all. Communism's demise played a role here as well – where the communism–capitalism stand-off had hitherto masked much of the variety among capitalist societies, its disappearance suddenly sensitized researchers to differences between market economies for which they had no explanation.

Developments such as these invited economists to look beyond the traditional boundaries of their discipline. Some turned toward cognitive sciences and psychology for improvements to the rationality postulate, seeking a paradigm that is better grounded in empirical observation and capable of explaining more (Denzau and North 1994; Kahnemann 2003; Thaler 1991, 1993, 2005); others decided to focus on the historical and social contexts in which economic processes take place. The so-called New Institutional Economics, associated with authors such as Douglass North, Oliver Williamson and Avner Greif, is an example of the latter. The varieties-of-capitalism approach provides another (Albert 1991; Hampden-Turner 1994; Hall and Soskice 2001). When economists thus ventured beyond their traditional paradigms, culture – defined as the opposite of what economics used to be about – naturally came into the picture.

Developments in other disciplines have made this step toward culture easier for economists. The emergence of cross-cultural datasets, as developed by Inglehart (1977, 1997a), Hofstede (2001) and Schwartz (1994, 2006), and projects such as the Chinese Culture Connection and GLOBE (Chinese Culture Connection 1987; Harris Bond 1988; House *et al.* 2004) enabled researchers to study culture using quantitative methods. In political science, culture became a topic of interest with the works of Huntington (1993, 1996; Harrison and Huntington 2000), and a literature on the effects of cultural differences emerged (Jackman and Miller 1996; Lane and Ersson 2005). Finally, anthropology, the place where culture was studied traditionally, began to move away from interpretive and postmodernist extremes toward a more dynamic, if not strategic, view on culture that is easier to reconcile with the economic perspective (Fine 2002).

These are the stories this chapter will tell. The account of culture's comeback begins where the story of the separation of culture and economics ends: the mid-twentieth century. Discussing the period from the Second World War onward allows us to trace the slow advance of culture in economics, up to its present relative popularity.

3.2 Modern economics: the cultureless science

After the Second World War, economics had scant attention for culture. To some extent, this neglect of culture set it apart from other social sciences. However, it also reflected a more general trend. Culture – and especially national culture – as a research topic met with hesitation within social sciences at the time. The comparative study of national cultures (within economics exemplified by the German Historical School) had been popular ever since the nineteenth century and even earlier, resulting in diverse works such as Voltaire's *Essai sur les moeurs et l'esprit des nations* (1963), Wilhelm Wundt's ten-volume book series on *Völkerpsychologie* (1911–1920), or Ruth Benedict's *Patterns of Culture* (2005).

By 1950, however, something had changed. On the political side, the developments of the 1930s and 1940s had caused people to be extremely wary about claims about national characters. The devastating impact of political nationalism, culminating in two world wars, had made the attribution of specific characteristics, ideas, values and identities to any nation or people highly suspect. Much – though not all – of what had been published as scientific studies of national character was exposed as having been little more than a pseudo-scientific, thin veil for nationalist myths and racial stereotypes. But not only the increased wariness of all that reeked of nationalism and racism made people hesitant toward studies of national culture – a growing disenchantment with colonialism also had its effect. Arguments about a nation's or people's cultural character had not been made only about the nations of the developed world; ideas about the cultural propensity toward laziness of various peoples, or the incompatibility of peoples' cultures with things such as rational thought or democracy, had been legitimizing the colonial project all along. With de-colonization, more and more people started to see through such mechanisms. Colonial prejudices came under attack, dealing another blow to national character studies (e.g. McGowan and Purkitt 1979). Although studies into the culture of non-developed countries had a brief moment of popularity on the waves of modernization theory (most notably

McClelland 1961), such endeavors were increasingly criticized as well (Hirschman 1965). Studies into national cultures had been corrupted by nationalism, racism and colonialism, it was widely felt. In cultural anthropology – where culture was unavoidable as a topic – authors responded by developing theories stressing the commonalities and rationality of various cultures (e.g. Levi-Strauss 1980, 1966) or by taking an interpretive turn, focussing on the insider's perspective (e.g. Geertz). These approaches generally abandoned the nation as the unit where culture resided. National culture had become a minefield few people still dared to tread on and most authors turned their back to it, at least until research methods would become available that avoided the pitfall of stereotypes and would result in more reliable knowledge (Hofstede 2001: 13).

On top of this general trend, neoclassical economics had a few specific problems of its own with culture. Its firm adherence to the self-interest axiom and its focus on methodological individualism made it especially problematic to take in culture (Blaug 1992; Hermann-Pillath 2006). Culture was often perceived as a coherent and comprehensive whole, to the extent that individuals almost vanish. Popular ideas about "the Japanese culture" or "the African culture" illustrate this. The "atomistic" approach of neoclassical economics obviously has difficulty coping with such a concept (Hermann-Pillath 2006). If the behavior of each and every one of "the Japanese" is reducible to something called "Japanese culture," what role is there still to play for a theory about individual decision-making? What is more, if such cultures are deemed inherited and given to individual agents, how can we reconcile them with the idea of rational agents designing outcomes purposively? Finally, the idea of cultural variety determining behavior conflicts with economics' adherence to self-interest as a universal motivation among people. By focussing on the universal elements of human behavior, economics almost automatically excludes cultural differences.

All this led to culture being neglected within the social sciences, and even more so among economists. It is only a little bit of a caricature to describe post-Second World War economics as a hard, technical science, employing formal analytical models that focussed exclusively on rationality and self-interest. Yet, it was in this economics that culture would go on to slowly gain a place for itself.

3.3 Culture's comeback

The return of economics to "soft issues" took place in two phases. The first was one of expansion of economic thought. In this phase, economic theory began to be applied to an increasing number of research areas traditionally left to other disciplines, and other social sciences started to incorporate elements of the economic rational choice model. The second phase was something of a backlash against this trend. The application of economic principles to many areas made people more aware of the limitations of the economic model. In response, economics began to devote more attention to insights from psychology, sociology and cultural sciences to complement its analysis.

3.3.1 The expansion of economic thought

Whereas economics and other social sciences for a long time co-existed (as we discussed in the previous chapter), from the late 1970s onward they found themselves increasingly competing for the same domain. This had much to do with the interpretation of the subject of economics, formulated by Lionel Robbins in 1932, that became dominant after the Second World War. Robbins (1932) had defined economics as "the science which studies human behavior as a relationship between ends and scarce means that have alternative uses." Economics, according to this definition, focusses on only one aspect or type of actions, which is by no means all there is to social behavior. In this sense, Robbins' definition clearly demarcates the field of interest for economics. However, it may be noted that economics in Robbins' perception does not have a specific domain of the world as its subject, in the way that psychology studies the mind, anthropology studies non-Western societies and business studies focusses on the behavior of companies. Although limiting economic analysis to one class of behavior, Robbins' definition allows economics to turn towards all these things. Usually, economists had refrained from applying their analyses beyond the marketplace or economic planning agencies, but the theory was not principally limited to such domains. Indeed, in the early 1970s, Chicago economists led by Gary Becker began to apply economic analysis to spheres traditionally left aside by economists, such as marriage and the family (Becker 1973; Cochrane 1975; Schultz 1975).

They argued that these spheres were equally subject to the principles of economic rationality and could be analysed from the same point of view as consumption and trade. A clear expression of this line of thinking can be found in Stigler and Becker's 1977 article titled "De Gustibus non est Disputandum," in which they wrote that "tastes neither change capriciously nor differ importantly between people. On this interpretation one does not argue over tastes for the same reason that one does not argue over the Rocky Mountains – both are there, will be there next year, too, and are the same to all men" (p. 76) and "*all* changes in behavior are explained by changes in prices and income, precisely the variables that organize and give power to economic analysis" (p. 89, emphasis in original).

A similar process was under way in development economics, led by, among others, Ian Little, Bela Balassa, Anne Krueger and Deepak Lal. These authors argued for a return to basic market principles in development theory and practice, or rather, for a dissolving of development economics as a separate theory from standard economics (e.g. Lal 1985). Here, too, the message was that no spheres existed that were subject to mechanisms different from the economic and that market principles could and should be applied in the context of developing countries as well. It led to the situation in which "development economics today is mainstream economics applied to poor countries" (Kanbur 2002).

All these developments amounted to the same message: whereas up until then economics had left certain issues to sociologists, psychologists and anthropologists, the approach advocated by the new breed of neoclassical authors questioned the *raison d'être* of other social sciences. If economic rationality applied in all spheres, separate disciplines for the study of developing economies, sexual relationships, religious dogmas or the appreciation of art were unnecessary; the standard economic model sufficed. This message amounted to a reinventing of the whole world as a market and went a long way toward dissolving the divisions between economics and sociology. However, it did so by a process that could be called the *economization of sociology*. Subjects previously assigned to sociology now were claimed by economic theory, until eventually rational choice came to be accepted as the basis for social theory within sociology as well. The rise to prominence of rational choice sociologists such as Coleman (1990) can be seen as the continuation of this trend, partly initiated by Becker.

This expansive tendency of the economic model was linked to the social–political developments at the same time, as the "neoliberalism" that spoke from it had a major impact on policy practices. With regard to development, for example, the neoclassical revival was reinforced by the increasing role and leverage of the International Monetary Fund (IMF), as many developing countries had to apply for assistance in the early 1980s. As a condition for such assistance, the IMF demanded market-style reforms. Eventually, the so-called Washington Consensus emerged, focussing on economic growth, to be brought about by structural adjustment: reforms including "sound" exchange rates, financial openness, trade liberalization, privatization, deregulation and balanced budgets.

More or less the same prescriptions were applied to all developing countries in need of assistance or aid. This "blueprint" approach was informed by a view of economics as a stock of objective knowledge, representing universal, inevitable principles. When many of the structural adjustment programs proved to have serious social costs in the short term, this was seen as an unfortunate but unavoidable price for economically necessary measures (often referred to as dynamic adjustment costs). Specific contexts did not matter; the same market principles applied anywhere.

3.3.2 The limitations of the market model

The second phase of integration of culture and economy came as a reaction to this creeping advancement of economistic ideas into spheres not considered to be subject to economic principles. Cracks in the Washington Consensus view began to emerge from the late 1980s, with critics pointing at the dismal effects of structural adjustment programs in many developing countries. It would take at least another ten years, however, for this critique to reach the inner circles of the World Bank and the IMF. The assumption of the position of Chief Economist and Senior Vice President of the World Bank by Joseph Stiglitz in 1997 signaled a growing awareness of the limits of the neoliberal model in development and poverty reduction. The "mixed successes" of structural adjustment programs were only one source of inspiration for this turnaround; another important development was the collapse of the communist bloc in 1989 and the associated introduction of the free market model in the former Soviet states.

The fall of the "Second World" was of importance not only for political realities – it was an important event for economic thought as well. Initially, many liberal thinkers celebrated it as the victory of the liberal-democratic market model, some even going as far as to announce the end of history (The Economist, December 26: 1992; Fukuyama 1992). It was perhaps the culmination of the neoliberal project that sought the universal dissemination of market principles. However, this claim of ultimate victory triggered reactions. For one thing, the reshaping of formerly communist countries in a capitalist vein soon proved much more difficult than had been previously acknowledged. Radical liberalization wreaked havoc in many post-communist societies, where living standards fell substantially upon the transition to a market economy. Here, the blueprint neoliberal reform recipes often proved to be problematic, causing a collapse of all kinds of social security mechanisms, rising unemployment and a tendency toward corruption and plutocracy. As a result, economists grew more aware that the implicit idea behind many of these reforms – that one could bring about a functioning market economy by simply removing the state – was too simplistic. Increasing attention came to be devoted to the role of institutions in the economy and to the particular problems and challenges arising from the social context in which economic policies were implemented.

At the same time, the disappearance of the common enemy of communism created a sudden awareness of the differences within the camp of market economies, perhaps born out of a craving for some form of counterweight against the strict, neoliberal interpretation of capitalism. Thus, a literature emerged devoted to the analysis of the *varieties of capitalism*, calling attention to contextual differences of institutions and culture (e.g. Albert 1991; Hampden-Turner and Trompenaars 1994; Hodgson 1995; Dore *et al.* 1999; Hall and Soskice 2001). Albert (1991), who played a major role in starting the debate, announced a new opposition between "le modèle néo-américain," focussing on short-term profit and individual endeavor, and "le model rhénan," focussing on collective performance, consensus and the long term. The argument was that differences in values, institutions and cultural context allowed for other forms of capitalism than the Anglo-Saxon type.

This branch of literature, often focussing on the firm level, was complemented by a reinvigorated enthusiasm for empirical, cross-cultural comparative studies. Whereas after the Second World War investigations into national identities had come to be distrusted as unscientific prejudices, by now large cross-cultural datasets had become available, providing a more solid ground for studying cultural differences. Examples include the European and World Values Surveys (Inglehart 1977, 1981, 1997), the datasets developed by Hofstede (2001) and Schwartz (1994, 2006) and other projects such as the Chinese Culture Connection and GLOBE (Chinese Culture Connection 1987; House *et al.* 2004). (*See* Chapter 5 for a detailed discussion.)

In economic statistics, important new data sources became available as well. Since 1968, the United Nations had been sponsoring the International Comparison of Prices Program, which was intended to provide internationally comparable statistics about the economic conditions of countries. This project eventually resulted in the Summers–Heston dataset (otherwise known as the Penn World Tables), published in 1991 (Summers and Heston 1991). The availability of comparable economic data triggered a mushrooming pile of publications dealing with the empirics of economic growth, in which economic performance was explained by an ever expanding set of variables, culminating in Sala-i-Martin's (1997) ominously titled paper "I just ran four million regressions." In combination with the new values surveys datasets, the Summers–Heston data facilitated the emergence of a vast literature about culture and economic performance, all of it using cross-cultural comparative methods. A not nearly exhaustive sample includes Franke *et al.* (1991), Dieckmann (1996) and Granato *et al.* (1996), regressing economic growth on cultural variables. Others have related culture to central bank independence and price stability (De Jong 2002), innovation (Shane 1993), and entrepreneurship, redistribution and national savings (Guiso *et al.* 2006). Barro and McCleary (2003), Guiso *et al.* (2003) and McCleary and Barro (2006) all set out to establish a relationship between religion and economic growth, while still others focus on the influence of trust and per capita growth (Knack and Keefer 1997) (*see* Part II for more details).

Although this reinvigorated interest in different forms of capitalism was stirred by the increasing dominance of capitalist systems after 1989, it was certainly not the only source of inspiration – the awareness of differences between capitalist countries had also received a huge boost from an older trend in international economics: the economic rise of Japan and the East Asian Tigers in its train.

3.3.3 The Asian Values debate

The spectacular rise of a group of East Asian countries was a riddle to many observers. It is quite telling that a 1993 publication by the World Bank, analyzing the economic development of Korea, Taiwan, Hong Kong, Singapore, Malaysia, Thailand and Indonesia, was entitled "The East Asian Miracle" (World Bank 1993). To many economists, accustomed to stories of development failures and stagnation, the economic history of these East Asian countries was nothing short of miraculous. The search for a convincing explanation for East Asian economic growth triggered all sorts of hypotheses. Among these, a prominent theory was the proposition that something called "Asian Values" had been responsible for the success.

Early contributions relating economic growth in Asia to culture were generally dealing with Japan and focussed on the role of the Confucian heritage (Dore 1967; Kahn 1979; Levy Jr. 1962). With development taking off in other parts of East and Southeast Asia as well, the debate intensified in the late 1980s and early 1990s (Dore 1990; Dore and Whittaker 2001; Levy Jr. 1992; Harris Bond 1988; Harrison 1992; Hitchcock 1994; Lodge and Vogel 1987; Nuyen 1999; Patten 1996; Chinese Culture Connection 1987). In general, the stress on the Confucian element decreased, with the more neutral term Asian Values rising in prominence.[1] According to the Asian Values thesis, Asian culture encouraged thrift, work and investment in education. Apart from values directly affecting the economy, Asian Values also included filial piety, collectivism, consensus-seeking, discipline and respect for authority. These values were indirectly assumed to be responsible for

---

[1] The inclusion of predominantly Islamic countries such as Malaysia and Indonesia in the Asian Miracle made the link with Confucianism problematic. However, also in an allegedly Confucianist place like Singapore, Confucianism was less prominent than authors in the Asian Values tradition often presumed. The evolution of Singapore's religious education program in secondary schools in the early 1980s illustrates this. Confucianism did not feature at all in the initial outline of the program (in contrast to Buddhism, Hinduism, Islam, Bible Studies and World Religion studies). When it was eventually added, Singapore had to import teachers from abroad to lecture in Confucian Ethics, as the expertise was lacking at home. Finally, very few students were opting for Confucianism, with the majority of Chinese students picking Buddhism instead (Hill 2000: 19–20). A second reason for downplaying religious heritage in the Asian Values discussion was the fact that governments saw religion as potentially stirring up ethnic divisions (Hill and Lian 1995: 205–210; Maseland and Peil 2008).

the Asian Miracle by nurturing rational, capable and insulated bureaucracies willing to bring about economic development for society as a whole (Dore and Whittaker 2001).[2]

The emergence of this thesis was not surprising. Culture had always been the one thing developing countries were considered to be rich in. Not coincidentally, the only field in economics in which culture and social context had continued to play a significant role after the Second World War was development economics. In fact, the very idea of a separate economics for developing countries had been informed by a tendency to think of the world dichotomously, opposing traditional, irrational developing countries to the modern, developed world. Development, in the modernization theory of the 1950s and 1960s, meant to become more like developed countries. Simultaneously, however, the development debate was informed by an opposition between East and West, in which "the West" stood for the developed, European and North American modern societies and "the East" for traditional, mystic, agricultural societies. These dichotomies overlapped, as the common use of the term the West for rich, developed countries illustrates. East vs. West, traditional vs. modern and undeveloped vs. developed were all binary oppositions that partitioned the world along more or less the same lines.

For a long time one problem with such a division of the world into a developed, rational part and a less advanced, traditional part had persisted: Japan. Here was a country that was at the same time developed and non-Western. As such, it did not fit into the simple dichotomy of modernization, and it attracted much scholarly attention (e.g. Levy Jr. 1962; *see also* Hodgson 1995: 582). Japan was a "them" that somehow had become an "us" at the same time.[3] The problem worsened when "the Asian anomaly" spread to other countries and regions, such as Korea, Taiwan, Hong Kong, Singapore, Malaysia and Thailand. Interest in this Asian Miracle increased accordingly.

---

[2] This part of the thesis invited a critical literature challenging the link between Asian culture and modes of government and governance (e.g. Barr 1999; Khoo 2002). A particularly contentious issue was the compatibility of the alleged Asian respect for authority and collectivist orientation with democratic rights and principles (Bae 2008; Kim 1994; Li 1997).

[3] A telling illustration of this ambiguous status of Japan is the fact that the Dutch Central Bureau for Statistics (CBS) classifies Japanese immigrants officially as "western immigrants" (CBS 2004).

The culturalist turn in the debate about Asian development was therefore perhaps unsurprising. After all, we were still dealing with a part of the world that was supposed to be the opposite of modern rationality, a cultural place steeped in tradition – the fact that the dichotomy developed–undeveloped had to be altered was no reason to let go of the other oppositions. Thus, we find Ronald Dore *et al.* proclaiming that "Japan and Germany remain very different. Japan's economic institutions are deeply socially embedded" (Dore *et al.* 1999: 117), or Donald Katzner arguing that "[T]here is little justification for introducing self-interest or rationality as a major assumption in explanations of Japanese economic behavior" (Katzner 2008: 25). The message is clear: when the East develops, that development must be rooted in its traditions.

Even when talk about Asian Values decreased after the Asian financial crisis of 1997, by then it had already provided a major impetus for the revival of culturalism in economics in general. The simultaneous rise of culturalism in the debate about East Asia and the increasing attention to East Asia in the economic debate in general had worked together to make paying attention to culture acceptable in economics. It was on the waves of the Asian Values debate, therefore, that economic historical works promoting the idea that culture had been responsible for the rise of the West also began to re-emerge. The most prominent of these have been David Landes' *The Wealth and Poverty of Nations* (1998) and the collection by Harrison and Huntington (2000). Culture, still a decidedly oddball topic in the 1980s, became a force to be reckoned with.

3.3.4 Culture hits the mainstream: New Institutional Economics and behavioral economics

As we have argued, the increasing connections between economics and other social sciences over the past decades developed in two ways. First, there was what one might call an *economization of social science*, represented by the upturn of rational choice sociology and the rising dominance of the Chicago School. This movement was carried by influential authors such as Gary Becker and James Coleman. Rather than genuine integration of different views, this process could more accurately be understood as the annexation (sometimes also referred to as colonization) by neoclassical economic analysis of spheres previously ascribed to other disciplines. The neoclassical counterrevolution in development economics, led by authors such as Deepak Lal, Anne Krueger, Ian Little and Bela Balassa, also fitted this movement.

Second, in part as a reaction to this "annexation," attention to the complementary context of economic behavior began to increase from the late 1980s. As a result, what one might dub a *sociologization of economics* took place, in which economics was imputed with more realism and practical relevance by taking into account the impact of other, "softer" factors. The varieties of capitalism approach, the explosion of empirical literature on the basis of datasets provided by Inglehart, Hofstede and the like, as well as the Asian Values literature, are all examples of this trend.

Whereas the second class of approaches certainly had been on the rise from the 1980s, this still did not touch the theoretical core of economics. They were in principle empirical approaches, not so much attacking economic theory as complementing it. Even the economic historical work of someone like Landes (1998) did not specifically address economic theory. All that changed with the advent of New Institutional Economics (NIE), which was essentially a theoretical project. Carried by authors such as Douglass North, Ronald Coase and Oliver Williamson, New Institutional Economics was perhaps the most important new line of thought combining economics with the subjects of other social sciences. It derived this status from managing to combine the two trends discussed above. It was born out of an insight that inclusion of the complementary context was necessary for any meaningful description or analysis of reality, but insisted that these complementary factors should be approached from the perspective and with the tools provided by economic theory. In other words, social context mattered, but it was economic theory that was needed to analyze this context. This integrative approach can be found in the work of Douglass North.

Douglass North

Douglass North (1920–) started his career as an economic historian, working on the subject of US economic growth, studying it from a neoclassical perspective. In the early 1970s, he turned to the economic history of Europe, which involved questions about deep structural transformations in society and economic system. North soon found that to analyze such transformations, neoclassical tools were unsatisfactory. He therefore sought to develop an institutionally focussed analysis, resulting in a series of books, starting with *The Rise of the Western World* (1973), *Structure and Change in Economic History* (1981), *Institutions, Institutional Change and Economic Performance* (1990) and, most recently, *Understanding the Process of Economic Change* (2005). Each of these removed North further from the standard neoclassical framework, although he always maintained its core arguments about market exchange and scarcity as the basis for his work.

Institutions, to North, are the rules of the game. Analyzed from a neoclassical perspective, such social rules and norms develop through reactions to changes in prices and opportunities. In the neoclassical framework, such market processes would in principle lead to an efficient equilibrium. In the real world, though, institutions are not always efficient. Moreover, inefficient institutions not only exist, they also persist. History shows divergent paths of development. This provided a puzzle to North, which he attempted to solve in *Institutions, Institutional Change and Economic Performance* (1990), arguably his most important work.

His basic argument is that neoclassical economics is mistaken in assuming perfectly informed, rational individuals taking decisions in a world without transaction costs. If information is costly and people are henceforth only boundedly rational, they tend to construct institutions – norms, values, rules of behavior – that will make decision-making easier, more predictable and less uncertain. However, these institutions – being inflexibilities in behavior, as it were – result in transaction costs. The level of these transaction costs differs and this is what determines the relative efficiency of a society's institutions and the performance of its economic system.

Institutions can change because of individual behavior in reaction to variations in prices and perceived opportunities. However, the adaptability of institutions is limited because they are rooted in deeper lying institutions, such as socially held convictions and beliefs, religions and culture. Although these levels are subject to evolution, the impact of individual action on them is unknown to the individual actor, which tends to take this culture, religion, etc. as given characteristics of its environment. This embeddedness creates transaction costs that prevent radical changes in the institutional structure, allowing only incremental change in institutions. Thus, differences in development paths between societies are explained: societies do not simply learn and copy successful strategies of others.

What we see here is a concern with extending the neoclassical framework to make it more realistic. Thus, transaction costs are invoked and assumptions of perfect rationality are loosened. At the same time, the emergence and development of these deviations from the neoclassical model are analyzed with more or less neoclassical tools. In later work, such as Denzau and North (1994) and North (2005), North seeks to substantiate the concept of bounded rationality by going more deeply into cognitive science. The aim here is to understand the way in which the mind and brain work and how that relates to the way in which people make choices and the belief systems that they have. Here we see the same concern with developing a more realistic model of human decision-making and action, in order to understand global historical processes. Still, the focus on individual decision-making, market exchange and some form or degree of economic rationality is maintained.

New Institutional Economics, in its attempt to incorporate what previously were considered to be side issues into an adapted economic core model, could be seen as an attempt at genuine integration of the study of economy and "soft issues" such as culture and institutions. This was not to be an "economics-plus." Rather, NIE strived to offer a more comprehensive, realistic economic theory that could cover a wider range of issues and developments. It is debatable whether new institutionalism has been successful in this respect (more about this in Chapter 4), but the ambition is important.

Parallel and partly complementary to the development of NIE, important methodological developments have taken place in microeconomics with the development of behavioral economics, specifically game theory. Using traditional game-theoretical methods, (micro) economists have accumulated a large body of evidence over the past three decades showing that "many people violate the rationality and preference assumptions that are routinely made in economics" (Conlisk 1996: 674; Camerer and Fehr 2006: 47). Although many of these insights into human behavior were already acknowledged and vividly described by Adam Smith (*see* Ashraf *et al.* 2005), this literature spanning micro-economics and psychology has shown that "people do not frequently form rational beliefs, objectively irrelevant details affect their behavior in systematic ways, they prefer to be treated fairly and resist unfair outcomes, and they do not always choose what seems to be in their best interest" (Camerer and Fehr 2006: 47).[4] And as a result of both behavioral heterogeneity and versatility, small differences in institutional starting points have major effects in outcomes (Bowles 2004). The relationship between interacting individuals with heterogeneous preferences and aggregate outcomes is at the top of the agenda of many behavioral economists.

Perhaps starting with Kahneman and Tversky's 1979 seminal *Econometrica* article on prospect theory, the publication of *Advances in Behavioral Economics* by Camerer, Loewenstein and Rabin in 2003 marks and summarizes this development of research on the psychological underpinnings of (micro) economic decisions (*see* DellaVigna (2009), Earl (2005) and Lewin (1996) for classical overviews of research in psychology and economics). The claim of behavioral economists is that the assumptions underlying their models are more realistic than in the neoclassical model. Criticism of the method employed in behavioral economics is scarce given its current popularity, but that does not mean that everyone shares the added value of this new (latest) wave of research in economics. For example, Rubinstein (2006) claims that the psychology and economics literature has replaced the "dead parrot" of full rationality with one that is equally dead, and points to the equally unrealistic assumptions made in this newly emerging field.

Although many researchers in this area use experiments, behavioral economists are methodological eclectics (Camerer and Loewenstein 2003) and have started using a range of methods, including computer simulations and brain scans, leading to a new sub-field called neuro-economics (e.g. Camerer *et al.* 2005). In a way, one defining aspect of current research in behavioral economics is the attention for

---

[4] Note that this does not imply that outcomes in line with the standard economic model cannot occur. Depending on the structure of agent heterogeneity and the structure of social interactions, collective outcomes close to the predictions generated by the model based on Economic Man are realistic (Camerer and Fehr 2006).

context. Instead of treating context as a nuisance variable (e.g. as in experimental economics), behavioral economists (or better, social scientists, because the scholars involved are not solely economists and include psychologists as well, e.g. the 2002 Nobel Prize winner in economics was the psychologist Daniel Kahneman) are specifically interested in these context effects and see them as "treatment effects" (Camerer and Loewenstein 2003). Phenomena such as framing effects, anchoring and preference reversal all imply that preferences are not the pre-defined exogenous sets of indifference curves as found in microeconomics textbooks (DellaVigna 2009; Guiso 2008).

It is clear that both NIE and behavioral economics signaled a broadening of economic theory which made it attentive to social context and created a theoretical environment in which culture could reside. As a result, culture started to attract attention from what might be called "serious" economists working outside the new institutional school (e.g. Lal 1998; Barro and McCleary 2003). In early twenty-first-century economic thought, culture definitely matters.

3.4 Meanwhile, in cultural sciences

3.4.1 An interpretative development

Around the same time that economics began to look more closely at culture as a factor of interest, other disciplines, most notably anthropology, began to raise serious doubts about the concept. These doubts had to do with the origins of anthropology, which descended from colonial studies of indigenous peoples. The study of other cultures had originally been developed as an instrument of colonial administration. After de-colonization, cultural anthropology became increasingly aware of this historical burden. However, despite repeated efforts, it turned out that it was rather difficult to get rid of this legacy completely. Eventually, the concepts of culture and cultural studies themselves were suspected of being affected.

A first step in the project to eliminate the colonial burden was to break with the study of other cultures from the perspective of the outsider, as colonial administration as well as modernization theorists had done. Outsiders were commonly Westerners, and describing other cultures from their point of view usually resulted in little more than distorted comparisons with Western conceptions and experiences.

Cultures had to be described from the perspective of the native rather than that of the Western visitor. A more interpretive, subjective approach to studying cultures and societies was advocated by ethnographers such as Clifford Geertz (*see* Chapter 4).

The move toward an interpretive anthropology, while addressing some of the more profound problems of ethnocentrism, was in the first instance concerned with finding better, more authentic knowledge rather than with the problem of colonial legacies. The awareness that these two issues were intertwined, since colonialism had caused distortions that went deeper than commonly thought, hit the debate in full force with the publication of the groundbreaking *Orientalism* by Edward Said in 1978.

Edward Said's *Orientalism*

In 1978, Edward Said published *Orientalism*, in which he traced the depiction of something called "*the Orient*" in European writing throughout the ages. It became a hugely influential work, inspiring an arguably new literature that could be called post-colonial theory, dealing with issues of power, knowledge and, amongst others, economic dominance (Ghandi 1998: 64). This canonical status of *Orientalism* is perhaps surprising to the economically inclined reader. How could a work that dealt principally with books and literary analysis have such an impact on theories about colonialism, power and social reality? After all, was it not concerned with texts rather than the political–economic reality? The answer to these questions is that, to Said, texts are always worldly, i.e. they are events that are part of the social world which they help to reproduce.[5] They reveal and encode the prevailing structures of attitude, reference and preoccupation of the world around them. In this sense, textual "discourse analysis" is inseparable from the project of social science (Ghandi 1998: 68).

In *Orientalism*, Said argues that in European literature, science and popular myth, the Orient and Orientals as concepts have been created as mirror images of the West. The binary opposition

---

[5] To some extent, there is a parallel with the way in which McClelland (1961) uses texts to uncover core ideas about achievement and entrepreneurship in societies. We discuss this literature in Chapter 6.

between East and West, or Orient and Occident, in which the West always had the upper hand, created a consistent, paradigmatical image of the Orient, a "region" that as a conceptual unity existed mainly in the heads and books of Europeans, but whose geographical boundaries were considered to lie between Morocco and the Eastern shores of Indonesia. "Orientalism was ultimately a political vision of reality whose structure promoted the difference between the familiar (Europe, the West, 'us') and the strange (the Orient, the East, 'them'). This vision in a sense created and then served the two worlds thus conceived... A certain freedom of intercourse was always the Westerner's privilege; because his was the stronger culture, he could penetrate, he could wrestle with, he could give shape and meaning to the great Asiatic mystery, as Disraeli once called it" (Said 1995: 44). This Orientalist discourse reflected the power distribution in the world, or as Said argues, it is "fundamentally a political doctrine willed over the Orient because the Orient was weaker than the West, which elided the Orient's difference with its weakness" (Said 1995: 204). Orientalism, i.e. the project of studying, teaching and writing about the Orient, was informed by and created the notion that traditional and despotically inclined Orientals required domination and being led by rational, purposive action-oriented Westerners, thus constituting an essential cognitive accompaniment of Europe's imperialism (Ghandi 1998: 67). The consequence of the inequality between West and East in the Orientalist discourse is that the Oriental is always represented, without being given the opportunity to present him/herself. The result is not so much that a distorted image of the Orient has come about – since "the methodological failures of Orientalism cannot be accounted for either by saying that the real Orient is different from Orientalist portraits of it, or by saying that since Orientalists are Westerners for the most part, they cannot be expected to have an inner sense of what the Orient is all about – but that 'the Orient' is itself a constituted entity, and that the notion that there are geographical spaces with indigenous, radically 'different' inhabitants who can be defined on the basis of some religion, culture, or racial essence proper to that geographical space is equally a highly debatable idea" (Said 1995: 322). "The Orient" is a constructed "anti" of what European society aspired or considered itself to be, fitted in a geographical framework; those things "we" are not and do not want to be, are Eastern. This role of the Orient as the opposite of the West meant that "Orientalist ideas could enter into alliance with general philosophical theories (such as those about the history of mankind and civilization) and diffuse world-hypotheses" (Said 1995: 204). This way, the Orient not only became the opposite of the West, it also became the model of a "backward," "traditional" society. Where the West was rational, modern, liberal, progressive and strong, the East was mystical, traditional, despotic, static and weak. Being Oriental came to be an immobilized or unproductive quality; hence, even when the Orient is being approved, it is through such phrases as "the wisdom of the East" (Said 1995: 208) pointing at an altogether unpractical metaphysical wisdom rooted in ancient traditional values and beliefs, which has been acquired simply through being around for millennia rather than through conscious efforts.

The importance of Said's work was that it made clear that the way in which we write about "the Orient" is inextricably connected to the political context in which we write. Even more strongly, *Orientalism* showed that the very idea of the Oriental as a research object and a category different from ourselves was already informed by such political relations. The work thereby highlighted the necessity for awareness of these contexts and for a reflexive approach that takes into account the political content of texts. Social science could no longer pretend to be merely concerned with truth or authenticity, since claims to either of them were inevitably tainted with partiality. Rather, the project of social sciences consisted of texts that were social acts in themselves and thereby had social and political consequences, on the basis of which they needed to be assessed.

In *Orientalism*, Said argued that European thought and writings over the centuries had created an opposition between East and West, in which the East came to be a synonym for everything that the West aimed not to be. Moreover, the book showed that such conceptions, reflecting the colonial distribution of power, are still present in contemporary writing. The Asian Values debate, for instance, is an example of how the idea of Asia as an irrational, mystic and traditional place continues to affect contemporary economic analysis. *Orientalism* was a wake-up call for those who believed that colonial prejudices and dispositions in academic writing had ended with de-colonization. It triggered a round of intense introspection in anthropology, culminating in the (in)famous *"writing culture"* debate (Clifford and Marcus 1986). The insight about the East as the dichotomous opposite of the West was applied to "other" societies in general. It was argued that ethnography divided the world in two parts: one part that was writing and one that was being written about.[6] The part that was writing – "us" – was monopolizing the right to produce knowledge, denying the other part – "them" – the right to present itself. This situation reflected and reproduced the distribution of power in the world. Thus, according to the writing culture argument, the very nature of ethnography itself was imbued with political–economic inequalities.

The story of the radicalization of such reflections on postmodern anthropology is interesting, but beyond the scope of this book (*see*, for example, Clifford 1989; Fernandez 1986; Roth 1989). The postmodern shift in anthropology makes the discipline probably too unpalatable to economists to be of direct relevance to the debate about culture in economics. The importance of the anthropological debate for economics lies primarily in its acute awareness of cultural bias and the insight that this problem is rooted deeply in cultural research. Also, the criticism hitting anthropology triggered a move away from its previous focus on other cultures as comprehensive, static systems. To describe people in terms of the strange cultural systems they lived in was to ignore the fact that people in "other" cultures were also thinking, consciously making choices and actively shaping their lives and environments. The focus on the strangeness of the other culture blocked one's view to the kind of choices and actions that all people have to make. In order to avert all this, anthropology began to develop a view of the world in which agents were actively involved in shaping and negotiating their identities. Social structures and beliefs came to be seen as dynamic, fluid and contested. This dynamic view of culture is characteristic of contemporary anthropology; it is not limited

---

[6] The phrase "writing culture" had an intentionally dual meaning. On the one hand, it referred to the actions of students of culture, who were in the business of writing about culture. Writing culture thus meant "the writing of culture." On the other hand, it denoted the fact that the writing of culture itself was a culture shared by ethnographers. Here, writing culture was understood as a "culture of writing (about the other)," which was to be subjected to analysis and reflection.

to its postmodern influenced versions but shared by other schools in the discipline.

3.4.2 A functionalist development

Of course, the interpretive development discussed above has not been the only movement in the field of cultural studies. From the 1970s, a functionalist movement went directly against the postmodern trend in anthropology. Rather than focussing on the particular and the insider perspective, this school placed itself in the tradition of social science that sought to develop cross-cultural objective schemas to categorize and explain different cultural beliefs. The work of Mary Douglas stands out in this respect. Douglas is most famous for her grid/group model, which she uses to classify societies along two dimensions. Grid is about behavior and indicates the degree to which people are constrained by rules; group is about identity and focusses on the strength of group ties (Douglas 1973). The underlying argument is that grid and group refer to fundamental problems which every society faces, so that they form universally valid categories. Douglas uses this classification to show that these two basic, universal features of social relations – the extent to which we are constrained by rules and the importance of group ties – generate cultural biases and are replicated in people's cosmological beliefs, values and preferences. Cultural beliefs mirror social relations and serve to validate them, thus preserving the social order and its power distribution (Douglas 1973). In other words, thought modes can be explained by their functionality for the social order (Douglas 1986).

Its focus on cross-cultural regularities and functional explanations for cultures directly positions this work opposite to the dominant stream in anthropology at the time. Although Douglas attracted a group of devoted scholars, her work may actually be more popular outside anthropology than within the field (*see* Beidelman 1993 for an anthropologist's perspective on Douglas' work). Especially in political sciences, the framework has been extensively used. Examples include theories of political preference formation (Wildavsky 1987), policy analysis (Schwarz and Thompson 1990) and studies of perception of environmental pollution and risk (Douglas and Wildavsky 1982). Douglas' work is also closely related to contemporary innovations in cross-cultural psychology led by Geert Hofstede and Shalom Schwartz, who also came to develop a system of dimensions to classify societies and cultures, partly motivated by functional explanations (*see* Chapter 5 for an extensive discussion of this work). Cultural dimensions of this kind have regularly been employed in economic work studying the impact of culture, though application of the grid/group framework itself to economic issues is relatively rare (exceptions include Caulkins and Peters 2002; Douglas and Isherwood 1979; Linsley and Shrives 2009).

A reason might be that economists are usually primarily interested in the consequences of cultural differences (Tabellini 2008a), whereas Douglas' framework is first and foremost designed to explain them. The logic runs from social relations to "cosmologies," i.e. beliefs, values and ideas justifying the social order, not the other way around. The grid/group system seeks to classify social relations, which lead (though not deterministically) to cultural biases. It is explicitly not a system for classifying cultural biases determining social relations and institutions (Douglas, letter October 1983, cited in Spickard 1989: note 12). What is more, in line with the general developments in anthropology, this school of thought is strongly focussed on the dynamics of culture, especially in its later versions (Douglas 1999; Thompson *et al.* 1990). The argument here is that all types of cultural bias are always potentially present in any group of people and are always vying for dominance. In this conflict, individuals constantly (re)negotiate, move around and change allegiances, thus continuously changing the cultural landscape.

The awareness of cultural bias and the dynamic perspective of culture which can be found throughout current anthropology make it possible to escape the pitfall of cultural determinism that always looms in studies of culture in economics. What is more, it opens up the way for an analysis of the origins and evolution of culture rather than just its impact. Theoretically, the enhanced focus on agency is in principle closer to the methodological premises of economics than conceptualizations of culture in terms of encompassing, inherited systems. All this makes contemporary anthropology potentially relevant to discussions about culture in economics. We discuss this potential more fully in the next chapter.

3.5 Conclusion

In this chapter, we have discussed the various sources of what we argue is a revival of culture in economics. It has been shown that the economization of social science by economists such as Becker and

Krueger, the sociologization of economics by authors such as Inglehart, Barro and Albert, and the people involved in the Asian Values
debate all came together to create a renewed interest in culture in
economics. New Institutional Economics and behavioral economics,
meanwhile, offered the directions for a theoretical foundation of such
a project. However, so far, the literature about culture and economics
stands out as a loose collection of ideas, united mainly by a sense
of serious differences between societies and a perception that there is
more between heaven and earth than rational choice and self-interest.
It is not precisely clear how new institutionalism can be reconciled
with the variety of capitalisms approach, or how the Asian Values thesis relates to cross-country comparisons, especially given the former's
demise after the Asian financial crisis of 1997. The main conclusion
that can be drawn when looking at this diverse literature is that there is
a strong revival of interest in culture in economics. Culture is back and
culture matters. Beyond that, we still have little clue of how culture can
be related to the economy. Culture matters for economics, but how?
This is the question we take up in the next chapter.

4 | Culture in economics: contemporary theoretical perspectives

4.1 Introduction

In Chapter 2 we have seen how culture and economy got separated theoretically, resulting in the disappearance of culture from the economic lexicon by the mid-twentieth century. Chapter 3 provided reasons for the return of interest among economists in the role of culture in recent times. In this chapter we continue this discussion by assessing the various ways in which culture may enter economics.

Attempts at integration of culture and economics broadly fall into four categories, as illustrated in Table 4.1.

First, there is a literature in which the economic model of behavior is basically maintained, with culture being added as an exogenous factor explaining what the economic model by itself cannot. We refer to these approaches as "Economy and Culture." We discuss this literature in Section 4.2. Second, there is a literature which can be said to bring together culture and economics by analyzing both economy and culture from a cultural perspective. Many people have argued, for example, that economic rationality is an historically and culturally specific phenomenon, rather than a universal behavioral structure. In this interpretation, a society's economy is just one of many aspects of the overall culture of that society. If the economy is a manifestation of culture, it follows that it is to be analyzed by cultural sciences rather than that it requires a discipline of its own. This line of thought, which we denote "Economy as Culture," we will discuss in Section 4.3. Third, a literature exists making exactly the opposite claim: rather than subjecting the economy to a cultural analysis, it argues that culture is to be analyzed by economics. Gary Becker did so when he declared all areas of social life subject to economic analysis, thus denying the existence of a separate realm of culture to which economics was not applicable (*see* Chapter 3). We denote this approach "Culture as Economics" and discuss it in Section 4.4. The fourth category of literature

Table 4.1. *Structure of Chapter 4*

Combination	Integration	Reflection
Culture and economy	Economy as culture	Culture as economics	The culture of economics and economists

is of a higher order, focussing on the practice of economics itself. Authors in this category, which we discuss in Section 4.5, have analyzed what might be called the "Culture of Economics." The argument here is that economists as members of the economic community share certain beliefs, orientations, meanings and dispositions, which can be interpreted from a cultural perspective. The chapter ends with a short summary and conclusion.

4.2 Economy and culture

The fact that, within modern economics, culture has largely been defined as opposite to the economic does not mean that it is impossible to add culture to economics. The opposition allows culture to be seen as entirely exogenous to the economic. That means that the several exogenous factors present in the model can serve as inroads for culture.

The economic model of behavior in such a view can be summarized as follows: an individual actor having certain preferences is confronted with a scarcity of means and decides upon an outcome on the basis of the confrontation of these two. In the orthodox neoclassical version, such a decision is purely economically rational. More recent developments often replace pure rationality by what is called bounded rationality, denoting the point that individuals are plagued by a lack of information and uncertainty about outcomes of actions (Conlisk 1996). The importance of such developments notwithstanding, the basic structure of the behavioral model has not been altered. This structure is given in Figure 4.1.

Individual Preferences	+	Constraints	=	Outcomes

Figure 4.1. Structure of economic model of behavior

Given this model, culture can enter as an exogenous factor in three ways. First, it can enter as preferences, or a source of preferences. Second, it can enter as a source of scarcity: constraints. Third, it can enter as deviations from the model, that is, culture explains those outcomes that have come about in ways other than the economic model suggests. For each of these possible inroads, it is possible to find authors having taken them.

4.2.1 *Culture as (source of) preferences*

Neoclassical economics, while studying choice on the basis of individual preferences, has always explicitly left the formation of preferences outside its analysis. Instead, it has preferred to deal with individual choices, *given* certain preferences. Underneath this lies a view in which morality and rationality are separated, which we can also find in Weber's position about the world's "moral irrationality." The basic argument here is that rational social science can analyze and discuss matters of the ratio, but that it is impossible to come to rational assessments of morality. To Weber, there are no rational ethical systems; rationalization, in which he was primarily interested, occurred *on the basis of* morality, which is itself irrational (Giddens 1974: 44). Rationality is a process of confronting means and ends efficiently, and/or deciding upon action on the basis of effectiveness with regard to certain values. In both cases, ends and values are the object of rationalization, while not subject to rational evaluations themselves. Similarly, neoclassical economics focussed on the rationality of individual choices on the basis of "moral" preferences, which it refrained from expressing verdicts about. It was concerned only with the efficiency of these choices, but left the formation of preferences to the individual. This, of course, was also a political stance: rather than making explicitly political claims about which preferences individuals ought to have, neoclassicism held on to the liberal principle of self-determination. It thereby deviated from Marxian economics, for example, which argued that material structures determined people's beliefs and preferences, implying that these could be (mis)guided. Value formation was an entirely exogenous affair and something occurring prior to the economic model.

With preferences and values being exogenous inputs to the economic model of behavior, they form a convenient route for adding culture to

the model. In this case, culture enters "as the basis for individual preferences (goals) and beliefs" (Chai 1997: 45). Thus, having established
culture as (a source of) preferences allows us to fill in the formal models of neoclassicism substantially. This is the line – at least implicitly
and indirectly – taken by the many recent empirical studies of culture
and the economy on the basis of large-scale, cross-country survey data,
such as Barro and McCleary (2003), Granato, Inglehart and Leblang
(1996), Hampden-Turner and Trompenaars (1993), McCleary and
Barro (2006) or Shane (1993). The argument in such studies runs that,
for example, if people are risk averse, they will choose risk-reducing
social arrangements such as bank credit, whereas risk-loving people
will opt for stock markets to finance their investments. If the Dutch
like leisure more than the Americans, the Dutch will work less, even
when controlled for differences in real wages and tax effects. If we
are able to establish such differences in preferences between various
cultures, we should, on the basis of economic theory, be able to predict
outcomes and explain certain differences between countries. Although
such research is conducive to answering many specific questions, such
as why stock markets are more developed in society A, the use of this
approach, in the end, is limited.

Perhaps the main drawback of taking the route of preferences for
adding culture to the economic model is the fact that it does not
develop or alter the economic model, but merely fills it in. Whereas
the neoclassical model of choice and behavior describes only abstract
structures of behavior, the culture-as-preferences approach translates
the model's abstract predictions to concrete, substantial decisions. In a
sense, the approach is similar to market research: we can predict which
"product" people will choose on the basis of their preferences we have
studied (*see*, for example, de Mooij and Hofstede (2002), in which
cultural differences are invoked to explain variations in consumption
patterns across countries). Theoretically, however, the approach is not
likely to push forward any theoretical boundaries; its main use lies in
filling in the existing theoretical model and answering specific empirical
questions.

To incorporate culture through the route of preferences requires a
specification of the kind of preferences that are deemed to be cultural
and a theory about how they relate to other types of preferences.
Not all preferences are cultural; otherwise, it would not be clear what
the added value of talking about culture would be. One intuitively

plausible way to distinguish cultural preferences from others is to argue that culture is produced by collective social processes, whereas other preferences are exogenous givens at the individual level. However, if cultural preferences are the outcome of social processes, it follows that their formation is subject to analysis. Seen from this perspective, only when combined with an elaborate theory about the nature, emergence and development of cultural preferences, adding culture as a source of preferences could fundamentally contribute to our understanding of the economy and economic decision-making.

Unfortunately, little theory has been developed in this direction so far (*see* Chapter 5 for a fuller account). The work of Mary Douglas and her followers, discussed in the previous chapter, and Wildavsky's (1987) analysis of preference formation in particular, forms an important exception. Here, the argument is that preferences are generated by social relations and reflect the way society is organized. Another partial exception is Tabellini (2008a), who develops a model of preference evolution on the basis of parents optimally choosing what values to pass on to their children. Much like Wildavsky (1987), Tabellini (2008a) concludes that differences in institutions and technology in the end determine differences in values. For example, the presence of well-functioning legal institutions makes the transmission of generalized values optimal, since the more distant transactions such values foster are successfully enforced by these institutions. It should be noted that employing functionalist explanations such as these to complement the culture-as-preferences approach results in a two-way causality. If preferences are generated by the way we organize society, and societal organizations are in turn determined by our preferences, the result is that society ends up along a self-reinforcing path.

A different approach is taken by Mark Casson (e.g. 1993; Casson and Godley 2000), who argues that culture (in economics) can be seen as collective subjectivity. More concretely, culture denotes the subjective preferences and subjective beliefs about probabilities shared by a collective. The latter takes us toward a view of culture as defining the (perceived) means in choices; the former is in line with addressing culture as preferences. However, Casson (1993) goes beyond much of the literature in this category by setting out to develop a theory of the emergence of the kind of collective subjectivities he calls culture. He argues that if we take preferences and beliefs to be malleable rather than fixed, collective subjectivity will emerge on the basis of dominance by leaders, imposing their preferences and beliefs on to others through force and manipulation. Although this leaves many loose ends (for example, why culture apparently has a stability and closedness that mere imposed preferences by a leader are not likely to have), the attempt at taking the debate about culture and economics into a more constructive sphere by developing theory about cultural development, as well as the attention for the role of power in such processes, is an important step forward. Analyzing the formation of cultural preferences from a political–economic perspective, Casson (1993) moves away from a "culture and economy" approach toward a "culture as economy" approach, in the tradition of Becker. Economic analysis provides the final answer, as culture becomes something that economic theory can explain.

4.2.2 *Culture as (source of) constraints*

An alternative route to including culture in the economic model of behavior other than through exogenous preferences is by presenting culture as (a source of) constraints in the rational choice model. This is the way culture is approached in NIE, which treats culture as a constraint for institutional development.

The core idea of NIE is that individuals do not possess perfect information but are coping with uncertainty. To deal with uncertainty (North (2005) refers to this as a non-ergodic world), institutions are invented; social rules and norms of behavior that make social reality more predictable. Channeling human actions into fixed patterns and reducing the range of possible courses of behavior which one has to take into account, institutions have a dampening effect on uncertainty and the costs associated with that. However, while on the one hand reducing uncertainty about outcomes and behavior of others, institutions also "define and limit the set of choices of individuals" (North 1990: 4). In other words, institutions – the "rules of the game" as they are defined by North (*ibid.*) – pose constraints for individual choices. As a consequence, by making some things unnegotiable, they cause inefficiencies, rigidities and market imperfections. Although institutions are necessary for facilitating cooperation and interaction, they do so while bringing about transaction costs. The degree of these costs is, however, dependent on the quality of institutions. To North

(1990), herein lies the answer to the question of global economic divergence: economic divergence is a consequence of differences in institutional quality.

Such an argument logically leads to the question of why such divergence would persist. If societies know that their institutions are relatively inefficient compared with the institutions of others, why do they not throw out their own institutions and copy those institutions of more "successful" economies? In the new institutional argument, institutions enter as human-made constraints that are more or less rational (if not consciously designed) answers to problems of information shortages and uncertainty. However, when institutions are human-made, they should in principle be alterable as well, so one would expect institutional (and therefore, indirectly, economic) convergence to take place. More fundamentally, viewing institutions as adaptable puts their function as persistent constraints in a problematic position. Institutions can constrain only if people are bound by them, not when they are contingent agreements that can be adapted at will.

It is at this point that culture comes in. There are two closely related arguments in NIE explaining why institutions are not adapted at will and redesigned after more successful examples. The first argument is that institutional development itself is constrained by history, so that institutional evolution is *path-dependent*. Choices in the past define the range of possible institutional developments in the present, so that institutions cannot be overhauled suddenly. The second argument states that institutions are *embedded*, in this case meaning that there are informal constraints such as norms, values and beliefs, in which institutions are nested and which limit the extent to which institutions can be changed (North 1990: 83). Changes in formal rules that go beyond the informal institutions of a society are unlikely to be effective because, due to enforcement costs, efficacy requires people to believe formal rules to be just (North 1992: 478). Stability, then, "is accomplished by a complex set of constraints that include formal rules nested in a hierarchy, where each level is more costly to change than the previous one" (North 1990: 83). Therefore, even revolutions and discontinuous changes tend to portray a high level of continuity, in spite of possible initial appearances. The reason for this is that "formal rules change, but the informal constraints do not" (North 1990: 91). In other words, culture is added as a constraint for institutional evolution.

Table 4.2. *Economics of institutions according to Williamson (2000)*

Level	Frequency	Purpose
Embeddedness: informal institutions, customs, traditions, norms, religion	10^2 to 10^3	Often noncalculative; spontaneous
Institutional environment: formal rules of the game – esp. property (polity, judiciary, bureaucracy)	10 to 10^2	Get the institutional environment right. First-order economizing
Governance: play of the game – esp. contract (aligning governance structures with transactions)	1 to 10	Get the governance structures right. Second-order economizing
Resource allocation and employment (prices and quantities; incentive alignment)	Continuous	Get the marginal conditions right. Third-order economizing

Other new institutional authors such as Williamson and Lal have expanded the argument of cultural constraints. Both Williamson (2000) and Lal (1998) sketch the economy as a system of several levels, from the level of specific allocation on to the levels of legislation, culture and those such as evolutionary biological constraints and material natural constraint. Each higher level sets the limits for adaptations on the level beneath it, because higher levels typically change more slowly. In Williamson's version, specific timetables for various levels are even set (Table 4.2).

In all these ideas, culture is added as the ultimate source of constraints. It is because institutions can be changed to only a limited extent that they can serve as institutions, channeling human behavior into more predictable patterns. The reason that institutions can be changed to only a limited extent in the end is that they are hierarchically nested with culture on top. Culture, in this line of thinking, changes only slowly and, moreover, not according to consciously intended design (Roland 2004). It is thus that culture can serve as the ultimate source of constraints in the model.

Although the inclusion of culture in the new institutional model of the economy is promising, it begs many of the more interesting questions. As in the culture-as-preferences approach, a substantive theory about what culture is and how it evolves is lacking. To their credit, most of the authors involved acknowledge this. North, for example, argues that "cultural evolutionary theory is in its infancy and is not of much immediate value in analyzing changing specific informal constraints" (North 1990: 87). Williamson (2000) calls for more research on the level of embeddedness; economic sociologists Smelser and Swedberg do the same (1994: 18). If one is to assess the theory, for this reason, the question should perhaps not be whether NIE is currently providing meaningful insights about the role of culture in economy but whether it can reasonably be expected to do so in the future. In this respect, there are two obstacles that the theory needs to confront.

First, it should be noted that the idea of culture as a source of constraints depends on the evolution of culture as an unintended, incremental process. If culture were subject to conscious, rational design, it would not be serving as a source of constraints because it could be changed at will by the actors bound by it. Culture, in other words, develops by following mechanisms and processes unknown to economic actors; they fail to see or predict the effect of their actions on their cultural environment. When cultural evolution is a process that cannot be known completely by economic actors, however, it logically follows that there are limits to the knowledge economists can develop about it as well. The idea of culture as a source of constraints thus depends on the vision of cultural evolution as a black box, insensitive to conscious design. The model makes the development of a substantive theory about culture and cultural evolution problematic.

In fact, the main substantive statement about cultural evolution in this line of thinking is that culture evolves slowly and incrementally. It is in this respect, however, that the culture-as-constraint approach treads on thin ice. Recall from the previous chapter that contemporary anthropology argues that culture ought to be approached as a dynamic and constantly in the making rather than as a static set of traditions. It has been shown that cultural change is possible and in fact is occurring everywhere. Moreover, post-colonial authors have argued that much of what nowadays is viewed as the static cultural heritage of less developed societies can often be traced back to colonial policies. By contrast, new institutional economics (in so far as it turned toward culture) has tended to approach national cultures as static, or at least very slowly adapting givens. Arguments for this proposition are mostly lacking. In Williamson (2000), it is not very clear where the differences in adaptive speed come from or how the specific timetable is derived. Moreover, Lal (1998), although mimicking much of Williamson's argument, comes up with entirely different time frames. In his view, the forces working toward market equilibria adapt constantly, whereas equilibrating forces of material beliefs work within the lifetime of a generation and deeper-rooted cosmological beliefs exhibit equilibria that take at least two generations to change. Again, arguments beyond intuitive appeal for these time frames are lacking.

Second, invoking culture as a source of constraints for institutional development triggers the question as to why we are not dealing with institutions directly. This concern is aggravated by the lack of substantive theory and definitions of culture (*see* Chapter 1). The way North delineates culture is illuminating in this respect. Culture – the intergenerational transmission of factors that influences behavior (North 1990: 37) – comes into play as a source of constraining factors, but is not analyzed, or even defined directly. Culture is addressed as a black box resulting in constraints for institutional change. However, if we are not ready to define and theorize culture beyond its impact on institutions, invoking culture becomes merely a more complex way of assuming that institutions change only incrementally. In short, the role ascribed to culture in new institutional economics is as yet both quite fundamental and marginal. It is a necessary prerequisite for the theory to hold (at least partly), but apart from this purpose, little attention is paid to it. Theoretically, it has not yet evolved into a theory about culture and its evolution. As a consequence, the danger exists that culture serves mainly as a stop-gap needed to maintain the choice-under-constraints model. The inclusion of culture in economics through the route of constraints requires more theoretical work in order to deliver a fundamental contribution.

4.2.3 Culture as deviation from the model

In addition to introducing culture as a source of preferences or constraints, it can be introduced as a deviation from the model. In this case, the inclusion of culture is not meant to enhance the explanatory power of the economic model itself, but is put forward as an explanation of those outcomes that the model fails to explain. One can find this approach in the work of Coleman, among others, treating culture as "norms that mandate action that is not in one's own interest or proscribe behavior that is" (DiMaggio 1994: 29). Clark (1988) finds that differences in work pace between countries cannot be explained by differences in training, experience, education, nutrition, incentives, management and labor organization alone. This breach of economic theory leads him to conclude that cultural differences must be a factor. However, he is unusually critical of his own approach, arguing that incorporating culture as a residual is not going to get economics anywhere – the search is for factors underpinning these observed differences.

Many other authors are not as reflective, unfortunately. The approach to incorporate culture as residual has been especially popular among descriptive studies of economically successful societies. High savings rates, entrepreneurial behavior, economic performance and long-term employment systems in Asian countries that cannot be explained by "normal" economic theory are often "explained" by calling them cultural (e.g. Daly 1998; Dore 1990). Lincoln *et al.* (1978) reveal a cultural effect on organizational structures by showing that firms with a high number of Japanese employees tend to behave differently from American-dominated firms. The cultural savings thesis has been tested more systematically by Carrol *et al.* (1994), focussing on differences in savings rates between countries as evidence of cultural differences.

A more recent example of the culture-as-deviation perspective is the "epidemiological approach," mostly associated with Raquel Fernandez (2007, 2008; Fernandez and Fogli 2005, 2006). Fernandez shows that immigrants tend to portray behavior that is in many ways somewhere in between behavior observable in the country of origin and that portrayed by the population of the host country. After controlling for competing explanations, the author infers from the observation of these behavioral differences that there are cultural differences and that cultural differences matter. Luttmer and Singhal (2008) follow the same approach to study cultural determinants of redistribution, although they do not compare only actual behaviors (voting) but also the preferences for redistribution of various immigrant groups. Algan and Cahuc (2010) study migrants' inherited social structures in the context of their trust levels (*see also* Chapter 7). The logic is the same:

all observed differences that cannot be explained otherwise are dubbed cultural in origin, which is deemed to explain them.

Some cross-cultural experiments, such as Gächter and Hermann (2009), Henrich *et al.* (2006) or Herrmann *et al.* (2008), make a similar argument. Observed differences in behavior between pre-defined groups are provided as evidence for the role of culture in human behavior. For example, Henrich *et al.* (2006) show that the willingness to administer costly punishment in games is correlated with the group to which one belongs. They conclude that "different groups arrive at different 'cultural' equilibria" (Henrich *et al.* 2006: 1770). In all these instances, the observation of inter-group differences in behavior that cannot be explained otherwise is taken to be proof that culture matters.

Historically, it is not terribly surprising to find such an approach in the literature about culture and economics. To a large extent, of course, it fits the ideas and delineations on the basis of which the division between economics and sociology had been finalized in the early twentieth century. The evolution of the concept of culture as the particular, static context put it in natural opposition to economic theory, as has been argued in previous chapters. The growing awareness of the limits to the economic model implied that people increasingly went looking for approaches that could fill the gap. It was almost inevitable that they would stumble upon culture in this quest. After all, the way in which the social sciences had been divided had created a situation in which culture began where economics stopped. Under these circumstances, showing the limits to the economic approach became more or less synonymous with showing that culture was important.

Basically, this sub-field maintains the division of sciences devoted to culture and sciences devoted to economic structures and behavior. From the point of view of theory development, it is therefore not very promising. A characteristic feature of this literature is the relative lack of attention for a well-crafted definition of culture, being more or less understood as "that which lies beyond the limits of the economic approach" or, more generally "those behavioural differences that are not explained by individual factors." Although the insight that the economic model has its limits in itself is important, calling what lies beyond these limits culture has little added value when this culture is not properly theorized subsequently. The effect of such lack of theorization and definition is that culture is often reduced to a residual factor, discouraging further scientific inquiry rather than stimulating it. This is explicitly recognized by Clark (1988), who acknowledges that if culture remains only an unexplained anomaly, it will be able to explain anything. Calling high savings rates cultural might pose as an explanation for a while, but upon closer scrutiny it turns out to conceal rather than answer questions.

4.3 Economy as culture

Thus far, we have discussed approaches to culture and economics that have tried to address culture while maintaining the economic model. Alternatively, there have been approaches seeking to replace the situation of a separate economic theory and theory of culture by one, unifying, comprehensive theory, which covers both economy and culture. Such approaches address the economy and culture from the perspective of a common framework, instead of maintaining a theoretical boundary between cultural and economic analysis.

Given the division of social sciences, such theories come in two basic flavors. First, a wide array of ethnographers, anthropologists and historical sociologists have approached economic behavior as a cultural phenomenon. In this perspective, human behavior can be understood only in its cultural and historical context, which covers every sphere of life, including what we might call the economy. Authors as diverse as Clifford Geertz and Karl Polanyi are examples of this economy-as-culture approach. Second, there are those authors who have sought to extend the economic framework to cover all social and cultural phenomena. This approach, associated most strongly with Gary Becker and the Chicago School, approaches culture as part of, and governed by, the economy. We will discuss this latter approach in the next section.

4.3.1 The cultural context of the market economy

The study of economic behavior as a social activity, to be analyzed from the same theoretical and methodological perspective as other types of behavior, was obviously most widespread in the period before and around the separation of economics and sociology. In the previous chapters, we have encountered the approaches of authors such as Roscher, Schmoller and Mauss, analyzing economic phenomena from a perspective of social and cultural analysis. Adam Smith and

Max Weber highlighted the moral foundations of market economies, implying that a certain system of norms and values was required before the modern market economy could come about.

Although – as has been argued – such work went into decline after the Second World War, with authors increasingly being assigned to either economics or social/cultural sciences rather than both,[1] there have always been some noteworthy exceptions continuing an approach to economics as an historical and cultural science. Probably the most prominent in the post-war period was Karl Polanyi.

Karl Polanyi

Karl Polanyi, born in Vienna in 1886 and raised in Budapest, was an economic journalist turned historian, whose various works consistently defy the trend of specialization in the social sciences. His main work, *The Great Transformation* (1975, first published in 1944), offers an insightful and critical story of the origins and development of capitalism. Other works, such as *Trade and Market in the Early Empires* (1957) and the unfinished *The Livelihood of Man* (published posthumously in 1977), extrapolate the themes addressed in *The Great Transformation*, the latter attempting to translate them into a grand framework for understanding "the" economy.

The quotation marks in "the" economy are there for a purpose. To Polanyi, there is no "the" economy; each society has its own way of organizing production and consumption. Polanyi rejects Robbins' definition of economics as the science devoted to the study of choices under scarcity. Instead, he defines economics substantively, as the science that deals with the various ways in which human beings interact with their physical and social environment in order to survive and reproduce (Polanyi 1977: 19–34). The objective of this science is not to discover universal economic laws and principles but to understand how different societies deal with the challenge of material survival and reproduction.

---

[1] In the case of Adam Smith, this was obviously not the case. However, the idea that commerce was a civilizing force, creating a morality that was necessary to restrain the relentless pursuit of self-interest, seemed to get lost in the popular reading of Smith, only to resume from the 1980s (e.g. Hodgson 1988; Peil 1999; Buchan 2006).

A major focus within this quest is on the relation between the organization of material reproduction and the rest of society. Polanyi argues that the organization of the provision of economic needs usually occurs by the same social structures that govern the rest of society. The norms and roles governing social and political relations in medieval societies, for example, were the same as those which governed its economic life. Being a blacksmith in a medieval city was not just a profession, it also denoted a political status (free citizen) and social identity. Over the past centuries, however, Polanyi sees a great transformation occurring, in which a separate economic sphere has been created, dis-embedded of its social context. Economic relations are separated and governed by different institutions than the rest of society. In Polanyi's words, "a self-regulating market demands nothing less than the institutional separation of society into an economic and political sphere . . . normally, the economic order is merely a function of the social, in which it is contained . . . nineteenth century society, in which economic activity was isolated and imputed to a distinctive economic motive, was, indeed, a singular departure" (Polanyi 1975 [1944]: 71). This transformation is the essence of the ascent of the market system, in which the economy is placed outside society, even replacing society eventually while following only its own logic. This logic, in Polanyi's story, is then not the set of universal principles of neoclassical "formal" economics but an historically situated, ideologically motivated construction of social relations governing production and interaction – the subject of "substantive" economics.

Central in Polanyi's story stands the observation that the market is but one of various ways of economic organization. To Polanyi, economies can be classified according to the form of integration dominant in them. Integration is present in the economic process to the extent that the movements of goods and persons, which overcome the effect of space, time and occupational differentials, are institutionalized so as to create interdependence among the movements (Polanyi 1977: 35). It is, one might say, the corollary to any division of labor. There are three main forms of such integration, namely reciprocity, redistribution and exchange. In modern capitalism, exchange based on markets and focussed on prices is dominant, but at other times in history reciprocity and redistribution have had a much more central place in society. Pre-capitalist societies had no separate economic sphere with a distinct and explicit set of motives and functions (Stanfield 1998: 367). All this is not to say that markets themselves are recent phenomena; "the institution of the market was fairly common since the later Stone Age," as Polanyi argues, but "its role was no more than incidental to economic life" (Polanyi 1975 [1944]: 43).

The advent of modern capitalism, however, brought supremacy of the market. The uncontrolled economic system of the market economy, heedless of all human needs but profit, rapidly replaced the social-economic orders that were in place, in which economic action had been embedded in social life. Thus, labor became a commodity, to be traded and used as input for production. The idea of labor as a social act performed by and inextricably connected with the entire lives of human beings disappeared. Hence, with society being governed increasingly solely by the economic logic of the markets, social relations and valuations came under threat. About the market economy, he writes: "Instead of economy being embedded in social relations, social relations are embedded in the economic system... for once the economic system is organized in separate institutions, based on specific motives and conferring a special status, society must be shaped in such a manner as to allow that system to function according to its own laws. This is the meaning of the familiar assertion that a market economy can only function in a market society" (Polanyi 1975 [1944]: 57).

Polanyi, however, also observes a countermovement, in the form of a "protective response" to this onslaught of markets. Governments have introduced legislation to protect labor; central banks, trade unions and various social movements have emerged, both progressive and conservative – all initiatives to counter the self-regulatory market. This opposition between the expansionary, disembedded market system and the declining mechanisms of reciprocity and redistribution supports the instability of modern capitalist society, in Polanyi's view. The tension between growing "market monopoly," so to speak, and protective responses was what created crises.

In many ways, Polanyi's work is based upon the opposition between the economic and social–cultural context dwelled upon in the second chapter. However, instead of unwittingly reproducing this opposition, he considers it a crucial historical phenomenon, to be analyzed, explained and – the social activist in him – countered. The good society is one in which the roles of reciprocity and redistribution are again recognized and all has not been left to self-regulating markets. The neglect by economic theory of factors such as culture and society, to Polanyi, is part of the ideological construction of the market system. He dismisses formal economic theory not so much on the grounds that it is wrong but on the ground that its formalism is ethnocentric, the theory being a cultural artefact of modern market society. At best, neoclassicism could be seen as analysis of the economic system as it is. By assuming the principles governing this economic system to be universal, neoclassical theory ignores important questions such as how the market society has come about and why it did so. More to the point, however, is the interpretation of economic theory as the ideological motivation and justification of the self-regulating market economy. Polanyi, in other words, saw the elimination of the social and cultural in economics as a phenomenon inextricably intertwined with the emergence of the market economy, being the theoretical equivalent of the disembeddedness of the market system.

In the work of economic historians like Polanyi, the system of economic organization that we have come to call the market is interpreted as a particular, contextual social construction. Other forms of economic organization are possible and actually turn out to be ubiquitous throughout history. A similar approach and argument can be found in the works of Robert Heilbroner. Heilbroner argues that any society needs to find its particular answers to three basic questions: mobilization, allocation and distribution (Heilbroner 1999; Heilbroner and Milberg 2002). Three basic categories of answers are the market, command or tradition. The parallel with Polanyi's trinity of exchange, redistribution and reciprocity is evident. What these works have in common is that they see each form of economic organization – whether it is the market, hierarchy or traditions – as historically and contextually determined. They reject the orthodox economic view that the model of individuals pursuing self-interest within a market economy captures a universal structure of behavior, arguing that the market economy as we know it is a phenomenon that was specific to a time and place instead.

The idea that a market economy is historically and culturally specific has also been put forward by other authors. We have already discussed Weber and Smith in this respect. More recently, anthropologists and historians have also argued that the rational, purposeful individual pursuing self-interest is a modern Western construct rather than a universal structure of behavior (e.g. Sahlins 1976). Landes (1998) argues that the Western conception of time, which after the invention of the mechanical clock was measured in regular intervals rather than as a continuum, allowed the emergence of the notion of progress that was necessary for the modern capitalist economy. Whitrow (1988) adds to this that the Western, and more in particular the Puritan, conception of time as an objective constraint, separated from nature, underpins ideas of causality, purposeful behavior and scarcity that are essential to the type of behavior expected in the market economy.

Some authors move beyond the historical and contextual specificity of "the" market economy to discuss culturally and historically specific forms of market economies. The sociologist Richard Sennett describes how the so-called new economy, with its flexibility, unstable institutions and global orientation, is accompanied by a culture that supports it. In this "culture of the new capitalism," as Sennett calls it, individuals are oriented toward short-term change, focussed on potential ability rather than accomplishment and attuned to "singular events, one-off transactions" rather than continuous structures and sustained relationships that can be directed toward collective progress (Sennett 2006: 178). The economic organization that we see in our (post)modern capitalist societies, in this perception, is not simply a (pure or not) market economy, as neoclassical theory would maintain, it is an entire, historically specific system of economic organization which includes certain institutions, a certain work ethic and certain behavior and beliefs.

The "varieties of capitalism" and new economic sociology approaches have taken the same tack (Hall and Soskice 2001; Nee and Swedberg 2005). The basic proposition in these approaches is that there is no such thing as "the" market economy, but that each and every market economy is different, based on different institutions. This institutional context is socially and historically specific and needs to be analyzed as such. Comparative research is therefore necessary in this view.

What these approaches have in common is a view of market economies as historical phenomena, specific to the time and place in which they have emerged and flourished. Whereas neoclassical economics provides insights into the workings of the market economy (and then only about those parts of any real-life economy that is actually governed by markets), it cannot say anything about the market economy's emergence. Substantive, historical economics is therefore needed in the perspective of the economy as a social–historical phenomenon. In other words, it is not economy plus social–cultural context that is addressed in these approaches, it is a view of the economy, i.e. a sphere of life in which we behave more or less in line with economic theory, as an historical and cultural construction itself.

4.3.2 Economy as system of meaning: anthropological approaches

The economy-as-culture approach can also be found in anthropology as it emerged after the Second World War. Anthropologists like Clifford Geertz shifted from the "scientistic" analysis approach to social studies, which applied analytical categories to societies in order to establish general patterns and relations, toward an interpretive view. The objective of social science, in this view, was to uncover the system of meanings attached to social phenomena by members of a society themselves. Since this approach focussed on the life-worlds, meanings and knowledge societies had developed, it avoided an *a priori* categorization of societies in a cultural, social and economic sector. Culture – the system of meanings attached to society – naturally included the economy.

This trend in anthropology must be seen as a reaction against the approaches to the study of "less developed" societies popular at the time, most notably modernization theory. As we have seen in the previous chapters, modernization theory could be criticized for being ethnocentric. The unidimensional, unidirectional, evolutionary view of development it exhibited was still essentially a colonial project; it made clear which societies were on top of the ladder and which on the bottom. Less developed societies, thereby, were sentenced to a "comparative existence." The very idea of describing Third World societies in terms of what they were not – i.e. modern, or developed – denied these societies an identity in their own terms. They (theoretically) existed only in comparison to the norm of developedness and were reduced to objects governed by structural processes and relations that had been formulated by Western scholars and inspired by Western historical modes of development. Such theories turned "less developed societies" into objects of the actions of the developed West, denying them the capacity for autonomous action.

This critique bit especially hard in anthropology, because of its roots in studies in service of colonial administration. The story of cultural anthropology in the last half-century is one of a discipline trying to come to terms with its historical background as colonial science, leading to a lengthy period of intense self-reflection, eventually radicalizing in the works of Edward Said (1995) and Clifford and Marcus (1986). The way social sciences approached culture came under heavy fire. The interpretive shift advocated by the likes of Geertz can be seen as a first step in this process. In the end, the concept of culture itself even came into question.

Interpretive anthropology hovered around the practice of ethnography, the (qualitative) description of societies and the social phenomena therein. It was more wary of ethnology, the practice of deriving general laws from the study of societies. Rather than constructing an elaborate taxonomy of culture or finding universal laws of cultural development, which always involved applying an external categorization to social reality, interpretive anthropology aimed to present knowledge that was *authentic*. This required comparative research[2] or grand theoretization to be replaced by an in-depth, *thick description* of one society at a time from the inside out.

The difference between this thick-description approach of ethnographers such as Geertz and the approach associated with modernization theory can be elucidated by introducing the difference between the *emic* and *etic* perspectives. In this distinction, originating in linguistics, emic indicates the perspective of the insider, whereas etic refers to that of the outside observer. Geertz, focussing on the intrinsic cultural distinctions that are meaningful to the members of the society itself, is concerned with the emic. Modernization theory, understanding "other" societies in terms of their imperfect fit with the capitalist model, including

---

[2] At least, comparative research in the traditional sense of the word. One could argue that ethnography itself is comparative research, making the ethnographer more aware and reflective of their own culture by experiencing comparison during fieldwork.

entrepreneurship, scientific "attitudes" and other ideas borrowed from the condition of Western modernity, is an example of etics.

Clifford Geertz

Ethnographer Clifford Geertz (1926–) is perhaps the most important anthropologist of his generation, a status only underlined by his being a main target of criticism by later generations of ethnographers (*see* next section). Geertz has been concerned with examining the meaning of cultural behaviors through interpretation. He argued that people shape patterns of behavior and attach meaning to their experience, and these meanings should be the object of inquiry for social sciences. Because each culture is unique in this respect, any attempt at finding universal laws is flawed. To Geertz, the project to describe and understand a society or a culture in terms alien to that culture is fundamentally misguided. Such an approach is not deemed capable of providing an authentic account of a culture; in order to do so, one should describe a culture in its own terms. This invalidates grand, overarching theorization about culture and societies, such as the one developed by modernization theory. As Geertz has noted, "though those with what they take to be one big idea are still among us, calls for a 'general theory' of just about anything social sound increasingly hollow, and claims to have one megalomanic" (Geertz 1983: 4).

To Geertz, culture is essentially a semiotic concept. He argues that "man is suspended in webs of significance he himself spun," so that he takes "culture to be those webs, and the analysis of it to be therefore not an experimental science in search of law but an interpretive one in search of meaning" (Geertz 1973: 5). The analysis of culture, in this perspective, is the study of meanings given by people to the world around them. In this approach, Geertz sought to move the social sciences away from emulation of the natural sciences and toward a connection with humanities. Rather than studying generalized structures and seeking causal laws, social science should focus on locally interpreted experience and meaning.

In Geertz' line of thinking, an etic perspective, introducing all kinds of categories and concepts that have meaning only to the observer, is of limited value and by itself cannot lead to authentic knowledge of culture; it is at best a first step. The approach of thick description, by contrast, is thought to lead to idiosyncratic knowledge – knowledge that is "true" locally, i.e. in the meanings and interpretations that are given within the local culture. General, nomothetic causal laws are deemed impossible in the social sciences, since there are no universal principles and structures that could be known objectively; everything is always interpreted locally. It is the task of the social scientist to study this locally interpreted world. Such an effort is always frustrated by the problem that the scholar's knowledge is itself an interpretation, making it difficult to truly grasp the genuine native's perspective. In this respect, the interpretive approach is heavily informed by relativism. Arguing that "culture is context," Geertz maintains that in so far as there are generalities a social science can study, they are to be found only within a culture because they are created by it and hence do not exist cross-culturally.

Thick description is concerned with observing and writing down in full detail rather than categorizing and structuring in pre-conceived analytical categories, which would cause biases and blind spots in observation. The idea is that any action, however small, is informed by, and therefore refers to, a wider web of meanings, which can be studied through a focus on these specific actions. Actions are symbolic "texts" referring to the system of meaning that is a culture. Through observation and description of actions, one can approximate the native's point of view. Only such an approach of thick description of societies in their own terms and meanings, it is argued, can result in knowledge of culture that is authentic.

For the study of culture and economy, this approach means that the two are inseparable. If culture is the web of meanings and significance spun by humans, then that includes the meanings and interpretations of economic activity. What is more, since culture is the system of meanings created by society according to this approach, no single aspect of it can be understood independent of its position within the entire web of meaning. This leads to a study of economic phenomena focussing on their meaning, provided by their context. In this spirit, Kopytoff (1986) argues for a cultural biography of commodities, in which the meanings attributed to a commodity in the various stages of its life-cycle and various contexts it enters are studied. An excellent example of such a study is Ziegler (2007), who analyzes the international flower trade, assessing the different cultural meanings of flowers and trade relations along the commodity chain. Studies like these cover economic phenomena, but focus exclusively on their cultural content. Rather than adding to it, cultural analysis replaces the economic framework.

4.4 Culture as economics

In the same way that economic behavior can be studied as a cultural phenomenon, it is possible to analyze culture from an economic perspective. After all, as we noted in the previous chapter, Lionel Robbins' formal definition of economics in principle allows economic analysis to be applied to every sphere of life.[3]

4.4.1 The Chicago School

In the previous chapter, we showed how authors of the so-called Chicago School began to unlock this potential in the 1970s. Economic analysis came to be applied to topics that traditionally had been left to other social sciences (*see* Lazear 2000 and Fine 2002 for overviews of this trend). The economist who probably did the most to expand the boundaries of economics into the other social sciences was Gary Becker, who transgressed into fields as diverse as racial discrimination, crime, drug addiction and marriage and divorce, all from the perspective of rational, utility-maximizing individuals. Perhaps even more important for our purpose is his work on modeling tastes. Rather than taking tastes as exogenous input into the rational choice model, Becker sought to make them endogenous. In order to do so, he did not go out to borrow insights into the formation of tastes from psychology or sociology, as one might perhaps expect. Instead, Becker assumed tastes to be identical across individuals, while recasting consumption as production so that changes in prices and in income became the driving forces in understanding behavior (Becker 1965; Stigler and Becker

---

[3] We use "formal" here in the sense in which Polanyi uses the word. Polanyi contrasts the formal definition of economics – referring to a form of behavior, namely economizing – with his own substantive definition, delineating economics as the science that deals with that part of society that we call "the economy" (Polanyi 1977).

1977). Equally bold is Becker's analysis of social interactions. Rejecting the idea that economic rationality automatically implies selfishness, he shows that by defining utility functions appropriately, economic analysis can take into account "concern for the actions of others" (Becker 1976; Becker and Murphy 2000). Thus, one can explain collective processes such as fashions and other dynamic structures. In a similar vein, economists have also transgressed into the domain of religion, analyzing church attendance as an investment under uncertainty (the uncertainty being whether one is rewarded in the afterlife) (Azzi and Ehrenberg 1975; Mangeloja 2005), and specific religious norms and rules as mechanisms to raise the costs of exit (Iannacone 1992b; Iannacone and Berman 2006). Lazear (1999) applies economic analysis to questions of multiculturalism and cultural assimilation, showing that small minorities are more likely to assimilate than larger ones because the incentives are stronger.

Apart from the latter, none of this addresses culture explicitly, though the analysis of social interactions and the emergence of collective tastes, fashions and religious norms comes close. In fact, economic imperialism, as the approach has been called by its critics (e.g. Fine 2002) and, approvingly, by some of its advocates (e.g. Lazear 2000), can be said to negate the existence of a sphere called culture, which refers to collective processes beyond the scope of individual rational choice. When nothing lies beyond the scope of individual rational choice any more, culture becomes an empty concept.[4] Meanwhile, various elements that we usually think of as belonging to the realm of culture – tastes, religion – are subjected to economic analysis. In this sense, the Chicago School can be said to constitute a culture-as-economy approach.[5]

---

[4] The only way in which Lazear (1999) invokes culture is as a "thing" which individuals may choose to acquire or not. This decision is operationalized as the choice to study a language. Culture is effectively stripped of its meaning, turning it into a good of which the consumption is subject to economic principles. Although in name about culture, Lazear's analysis could, without many amendments, be applied to membership of tennis clubs or the decision to buy a car to visit another town.

[5] Economic imperialism has always been controversial. The model of the *homo oeconomicus* that it puts forward has been considered as exposing a bleak, miserable view on humanity. It is not hard to see why. In a review of microeconomic models of fertility, Cochrane (1975) identifies models in which children are seen as a zero-utility byproduct of sexual activity, models in which

4.4.2 *Cultural materialism*

In an entirely different part of the academic world, anthropologists have also been working on economic interpretations of culture, although in ways that are far removed from those of the Chicago School. Seeking to develop a scientific theory about the emergence of cultural practices and beliefs, Marxist-inspired anthropologists have argued that traditions, customs and beliefs could be traced back to practical, material problems which the society in question faced. Cultural materialism, as this approach is called, holds that "human social life is a response to the practical problems of earthly existence" (Harris 1979: ix). The name most readily associated with this movement is Marvin Harris. Borrowing from Marx and Engels, Harris claims that all social arrangements and symbols follow from the "infrastructure" of a society: the way in which society solves the material problems of meeting subsistence requirements and reproduction. For this reason, Harris assigns priority to the study of the material conditions of sociocultural life, as these determine societal practices. He argues that similar technologies, applied to similar environments, will result in similar socio-cultural arrangements. Infrastructure is determined in part by natural circumstances, as it "is the principal interface between culture and nature, the boundary across which the ecological, chemical, and physical restraints to which human action is subject interact with the principal socio-cultural practices aimed at overcoming or modifying those restraints" (Harris 1979: 57).

A famous example of Harris' cultural materialism is his analysis of the sacredness of cows in India. To some, this might seem an irrational religious belief in a country with both more cows and more malnourished people than any other place in the world. Harris, however, argues that religion is not the source of the norm; indeed, "religion has affected India's foodways, but India's foodways have affected India's religion even more" (Harris 1985: 51). Instead, Harris claims that the religious

they enter as investment goods, and models in which children are consumer goods, whose utility has to be weighed against the utility of other consumer goods forgone by having children. Few real-life parents would consider their family choices in these terms and would be prone to dismiss such theories as irrelevant. In its defence, the economic approach to social issues has been able to expose some structures underlying behavior, while – in the more modest versions – not claiming that these structures are all there is to human social activity.

prohibition on killing cows is a response to the need for plow animals. Stray cows are not nobody's property, in this perspective; they are a form of communal property, owned by the poorest of India's farmers whose farms are too small to keep any plow animals (or, nowadays, tractors) of their own.

A problem of cultural materialism is that it has difficulty accounting for strong, enduring differences in economic performance. If cultural evolution is in the end governed by an economic logic, we should expect cultural forces restricting economic life to be adapted or abandoned, at least in societies close to the margin of subsistence (Clark 1988). Social norms that reduce material output per person will literally die out, as those evading them have a higher chance of surviving. This kind of economic logic implies that all societies in the long run should tend toward economically successful cultures.

On a theoretical level, cultural materialism (like economic imperialism) has been charged with reductionism by critics, as it is alleged to bring down the richness of human culture and society to a few material principles. Its focus on etic research aimed at discovering general laws brought cultural materialism into conflict with those seeing in anthropology as a humanistic discipline rather than a scientific one (e.g. Clifford Geertz, Edward Evans-Pritchard). At the same time, the work of Harris and his followers offers a research program and perspective that provides interesting points of contact with economics. In fact, cultural materialism, while resoundingly Marxist in orientation, is in a lot of ways remarkably similar to Douglass North's or Oliver Williamson's new institutional economics. Both approaches claim that institutions and conventions should be seen as (remnants of) answers to economic challenges (whether subsistence, reproduction or uncertainty).

4.4.3 Strategic identity and the economics of identity construction

A further step along the "culture as economics" line is what might be called the strategic identity perspective. In this approach, it is not so much the content of specific cultural customs that is explained economically as the use of the categories "culture" and "ethnicity." Ethnography has not been limited to the approach of authors such as Geertz, viewing ethnic and cultural identity as following from subjective feelings of belonging based on shared primordial attachments.

Another tradition exists which, building on Gramsci, traces ethnic and cultural identity to instrumental manipulation in service of collective political–economic interests (e.g. Wallerstein 1960). Ethnic and cultural identity, in the latter view, is seen as a way of masking divergent interests, thus serving as an instrument of exploitation. Also, culture and ethnicity have been argued to be means for mass mobilization or for legitimization of nationalist ideologies of states.

This "instrumentalist" tradition (Young 1983) has been criticized for its overemphasis of structure at the expense of the role of the individual agent. By ignoring the emotive and psychological aspect of group identity, it begged the question why people would feel attached or committed to any cultural group identity in the first place. In response, attention began to shift away from explanations of the origins of cultural categories toward an analysis of how identities are constructed in practice. The answer to this question was sought in the strategic and tactical employment of cultural and ethnic identities (Bentley 1987; Lyman and Douglass 1973; Yelvington 1991). It was recognized that (cultural) identities are optional as people can usually draw from several sources of identity. Ethnicity and culture are negotiated by individuals in their daily activities and social encounters, on the basis of their interest. The emphasis of choices between multiple potential identities makes the strategic identity perspective especially relevant in the context of multiculturalism and migrant communities (Kahani-Hopkins and Hopkins 2002; Stanczak 2006). Dávila (2001) and Sunderland *et al.* (2004), for example, show how Hispanic identity in the United States has been shaped by marketing processes by companies targetting "the Hispanic market" and consumers responding to such strategies.

Whereas on first sight all this probably smacks too much of social constructivism to be very attractive to mainstream economics, the shift away from a holistic vision of culture toward a focus on the way culture and ethnicity are constructed in individual practices actually offers interesting openings for economic analysis or business studies. In contrast to the interpretive approach advocated by Geertz, the strategic identity perspective shares with economics a view of human action as rationally oriented toward practical goals. The focus on individual practices and choice is much easier to reconcile with the economic framework than the focus on cultures as comprehensive systems of meanings. In the combination of economic analysis and the strategic identity perspective lies a very interesting field of research, which might be called the "economics of identity construction." Crude first attempts in this direction include Akerlow and Kranton (2000) and Lazear (1999), who develop formal models in which they analyze identity and cultural assimilation respectively as choices made by rational agents. These contributions still take cultures and identities as fixed, given things between which agents can choose. A further step would be to analyze the evolution of culture from the point of view of purposeful individuals invoking and giving shape to identities on the basis of their economic objectives. Early examples of such analyses include Maseland (2006) and Maseland and Peil (2008), who show how an Asian identity in which the Asian economic model was rooted has been actively constructed by agents pursuing their political–economic interests.

The strategic identity perspective is perhaps of more relevance for the future of the debate about culture in economics than any of the other perspectives discussed in the last two sections. All these approaches put forward a common framework that is applicable to study virtually all aspects of social reality. In the culture-as-economy approaches, everything is reducible to economic principles. In Geertz' economy-as-culture perspective, every aspect of social reality is seen as an indispensable part of the totality that we call culture. Whereas to Becker or Harris everything is economic, one could say that in Geertz' understanding of culture, everything is culture. Each of these approaches achieves the objective of a unitary framework for studying culture and economy only by negating the other. Usurpation is the keyword here, not integration. In this sense, one could say that advocates from both camps take positions at ends of a continuum. The opposition between economics and cultural sciences is maintained; it is just denied that the other perspective has anything useful to offer. The strategic identity perspective, with its focus on purposive action of subjects constructing and renegotiating structures of meaning and identity, has the potential to escape from this opposition – it offers an area of study where economics and anthropology may meet.

4.5 The culture of economics

So far, we have discussed approaches that maintained the opposition between culture and the economic (Section 4.2), as well as approaches that advocated either an exclusively cultural or an exclusively economic analysis (Sections 4.3 and 4.4 respectively). Another class of approaches operates on a meta-level, subjecting economic and cultural sciences to analysis themselves.

Such reflexive approaches come in two flavors. First, one could see scientific research as an economic phenomenon, subjecting it to economic analysis. Economists have demarcated a research field called the "economics of science" (Heukelom and Maseland 2010; Sent 2005) and arguments based on such reflexivity have been made (Davis and Klaes 2003). Economic thought can be seen as the product of a process of weighing costs and benefits, rather than as "scientific truth."[6] Although this literature is interesting, the study of the economics of economic thought lies beyond the scope of this book. In this section, we will limit ourselves to the second variety: the analysis of the culture of economics.

4.5.1 Economics and hegemony

The idea to include economic thought in an analysis of historical culture can in some form already be found in the work of Karl Polanyi. As we discussed before, Polanyi argued that the way of organizing the economy is socially and historically embedded. Polanyi went further than this, however, arguing that the thinking about economic processes is socially and historically specific as well. Economic theory reflects and shapes the construction of the economy in a society. Within Polanyi's ideas about the emergence of the market economy, the development of economic thought played an important role. The construction of an economic sphere separated from society, in his view, was supported by the emergence of neoclassical theory, with its thoroughly formal interpretation of economics. The removal of social context from economic rationality in theory and the disembedding of the economy from society in practice were two sides of the same coin.

In this sense, the science of economics can be seen as a cultural artefact of modern capitalist society. Such arguments can be taken further,

---

6 In this respect, McCloskey (1983) argues that economists in possession of true knowledge about the economy rendering them able to make accurate predictions would, if they behaved according to economic theory, not publish or disseminate such knowledge. Rather, they would keep it to themselves and act upon it, since that is the more profitable behavior.

so that economic theory is interpreted not only as constituted by the "culture of capitalism" but also as justification and underpinning of the market system, evoking parallels with Gramscian studies about hegemony (*see* Chapter 2). Already in 1899, US economist Edward Seligman had argued that classical economic theory was nothing but the ideology of the dominant classes and that as such it was instrumental in maintaining the status quo (American Economic Association 1899). More recently, these elements have come back in the works of Bourdieu. Like Polanyi and the approaches of economic sociologists, Bourdieu (2005a, 2005b) argues that economic reason should be seen as historically and socially constituted. To simply assume economic rationality as a universal, a-contextual structure of human behavior, as neoclassical theory does, is to be rejected. In Bourdieu's view, economic structures are not universal givens but are created by agents. In turn, economic structures determine these agents, that is, they influence who they are, how they are prone to act and what they believe. Because of this mutual dependence of disposition and structure, ideas about how the economy works can be self-validating. In particular, economic theory has the peculiar propensity for "making itself true" because it orients "the economic choices of those who dominate economic relationships" (Bourdieu 1998a). The economic structures and dispositions that are described by economic theory are actually created by agents in practice because they base their decisions on economic theory. What is more, these choices and the structures they create are imbued with the symbolic force of economic theory. The way economic decisions are made by the economically powerful is not a matter of decisions one can agree or disagree with; they are presented as inevitable. The way our economy is organized mirroring the world of economic theory follows from the universal mechanisms described in the de-historicized and de-socialized truth of economic theory. In this perspective, whether one likes it or not, this is the way the economy works. Only people without sufficient knowledge of economics would make different decisions than the ones in accordance with economic theory. Such "economistic fatalism" can be found in neoliberalism, which Bourdieu describes as "a powerful economic theory whose strictly symbolic strength, combined with the effect of theory, redoubles the force of economic realities it is supposed to express. It ratifies the spontaneous philosophy of the people who run large multi-nationals and of the agents of high finance" (Bourdieu 1998b:

126). Economics, in this view, amounts to a set of beliefs, inspiring a project that seeks to recreate the world in the mirror image of economic thought; a world without collectives in which individual pursuit of self-interest is all that matters.

It might be noted that Bourdieu's point has a strong similarity with that of Richard Sennett, whom we discussed before. Like Sennett, Bourdieu maintains that a new system of capitalism is under way, which has a systemic and cultural component. The new capitalism is about flexibility, short-term pursuit of self-interest and the marginalized role of collectives. It affects work ethic, identities and social ties. Like Sennett, Bourdieu is highly critical of this development. However, Bourdieu goes a step further than Sennett in arguing that economic theory – which in his view is a moral, ideological project – plays a central role in bringing about this new capitalism. Instead of simply casting aside economic theory in favor of a sociological analysis, as the "economy as culture" literature is prone to do, Bourdieu makes economic thought the subject of his analysis. Thus, by questioning it, he is able to surpass the opposition between culture and the economic.

4.5.2 The culture of economists

One does not need to succumb to such a radical perspective in order to analyze economics as a cultural phenomenon. In a well-documented study, Dorothy Ross (1991) shows how the version of economics that came to be dominant in the twentieth century was shaped by the specific US cultural context in which it was developed. This context favored an economics that was modeled on natural rather than historical sciences and was deeply imbedded in the classical ideology of liberal individualism. The upshot of this is that the culture of economists is to a large extent US culture. A step further along this line one can interpret economic thought not only as representative of a cultural setting but as a cultural system itself. The culture of economics, in that case, is seen as the culture built around the identity of being an economist. It has been shown that the community of economists has its own distinctive system of meanings, symbols and norms. McCloskey (1983, 1998) has highlighted some of these symbols, metaphors and norms employed by economists in debate, arguing that our economic knowledge is built on the shared usage of these devices (rather than on modernist scientific methods, as many an economist is prone to believe). More recently, Yonay and Breslau (2006) have taken this point further, producing a fascinating ethnography of the culture of mathematical economics. They argue that the economist's practice of building economic models is informed by a shared, unique understanding of how to mediate between reality and an analytical model. Models are based on a distinctive set of simplifications and assumptions that is deemed conventional and acceptable within the community. There are also shared beliefs about the meaning and purpose of economic models, as well as distinctive criteria regarding simplicity, elegance and motivation. All in all, economists hold a distinct set of views, practices, symbols and methods, guiding and giving meaning to their work.

Contributions such as these from McCloskey (1983, 1998) and Yonay and Breslau (2006) point at a distinctive culture of the community of economists. Others have exposed the distinctive behavioral patterns, norms and beliefs of economists through experiments. Marwell and Ames, in a paper with the revealing title "Economists free ride, does anyone else?" show that economics students differ significantly from others in actually behaving in accordance with economic theory (Marwell and Ames 1981). More specifically, they show that economic students are more prone to free-riding behavior than other students, have different, less clear ideas of what fairness entails, and are less likely to invoke fairness in their investment decisions. Colander and Klamer (1987) show that it takes a significant process of socialization to bring about these differences and make economists out of new students. On the basis of these studies, one might conclude that *homo oeconomicus* might in fact exist, but they are bound to be an economist.

What all these approaches have in common is that they all view economic thought as a social activity worthy of analysis itself. Economic thought is not only a description of the economy, it is also the product of activities of the community of economists within their social context. Moreover, these activities, being part of the social environment, also shape this environment. The norms, symbols and meanings that set out the culture of economics are therefore of interest to the social scientist. Studies like these show that, alongside the economy-and-culture, economy-as-culture and culture-as-economics perspectives, economics itself also has, and is part of, a culture.

Table 4.3. *Typology of approaches to culture in economics*

Combination			Integration		Reflection
Culture and economy			*Economy as culture*	*Culture as economics*	*The culture of economics*
Preferences	Constraints	Deviating outcomes	Geertz Polanyi	Becker Harris	Bourdieu McCloskey Yonay and Breslau
Inglehart Barro	*NIE* North Williamson	*Asian Exceptionalism* Fernandez			

4.6 Conclusion

In this chapter, we have discussed the various routes along which the connection between culture and economy can be studied. This has led to a categorization for discussing contributions to the culture and economy literature (Table 4.3). We have distinguished four categories of approaches. The culture-and-economy approach seeks to add culture to economic theory as it is, without trying to adapt either our conception of what economics is or our conception of culture. The economy-as-culture and culture-as-economics approaches go a step further by seeking to develop a single, integrative framework for studying culture in economy. The economy-as-culture perspective does so by rejecting economic theory altogether and analyzing everything from an exclusively cultural perspective. By contrast, the culture-as-economics approach of Gary Becker and, in a different way, Marvin Harris sees everything as reducible to economic principles. Finally, we identify a fourth position, which focuses on the practice of economics itself, reflecting upon it from a cultural perspective.

As we will discuss extensively in Part II, the current way mainstream economics has decided to include culture in economics resembles the economy-and-culture approach. As such this is not surprising, since the simple addition of culture to economic thinking requires the least adaptation of theory or methodology for economists. By contrast, the economy-as-culture approach, although popular among ethnographers and historians, tends to be too far removed from economic thought to still make a meaningful connection. The culture-as-economics perspective, from the other side, is, of course, easy to reconcile with economic theory, but does not address the very motivation for the resurgence of culture in economics: the widespread feeling that orthodox economic theory, while useful, has its limits. Studying the culture of economics, finally, offers interesting insights and is useful in making economists aware of some of their subconscious assumptions and dispositions, but is not a route towards new insights about culture and economy.

In the remainder of the book, we therefore limit ourselves to a discussion of approaches that broadly falls within the economy-and-culture approach. This literature makes up the bulk of contributions to the current debate about culture in economics and is therefore the most relevant in our discussion. However, despite the fact that contemporary economic research on culture includes culture mostly as an exogenous factor, the broader questions in the field as a whole also relate to the issues discussed in the other approaches. We are convinced that it is important to study the new cultural economics against this broader background. This chapter has positioned the current debate in economics in this broader framework. In order to complete our understanding of the role of culture in economics, the historical, conceptual and theoretical discussion in this chapter and the previous ones needs to be complemented with a closer discussion of associated methodologies. The next chapter discusses these different methodological approaches.

5 | *A methodological perspective on culture in economics*

5.1 Introduction

In this chapter, we discuss the main methodological issues associated with research into culture in economics. In this discussion, we limit ourselves to those topics that are specific to research into culture in economics, or at least those that play a larger role in this particular field. As in any type of social scientific inquiry, we have to find answers to questions about ontology and epistemology. Also, we face issues such as internal and external validity, and we have to deal with decisions about what kind of data to use or how to analyze them. None of these issues, however, is specific to research into culture and economics. For students interested in the arguments for and against the various positions, we refer therefore to more appropriate volumes discussing methodology in general.

In addition to methodology, this chapter reviews the most common methods to study the impact of cultural differences on economic performance: values surveys and cross-cultural experiments. Again, this is not to say that by discussing only these we have covered the whole range of methods used in cultural economic research. A brief look shows numerous examples of case studies, discourse analysis, historical analysis and even casual observation in the literature (e.g. Morishima 1982; D'Iribarne 1989; Maseland 2006; Landes 1998; Fallows 1994; Etounga-Manguelle 2000). However, none of these methods is typical for the study of culture in economics, as they are widely used elsewhere. For this reason, we do not discuss them here.

What kind of specific methodological problems do researchers of culture in economics face? On the basis of the previous discussion, we can identify at least three closely related key issues. First of all, culture deals with structures that are deemed given to the individual. Economists work from a model of reality in which behavioral patterns and outcomes are retraceable to individual, purposeful decision-making. As a result, economists studying culture face a challenge of aligning cultural structures to economic agency. Second, we note that the concept of culture refers to properties at the collective, macro-level while most economic theory operates at the level of the individual or is derived from the micro-economic behavior of individual agents (Hodgson 2007a, 2007b).[1] Hence, research into culture in economics encounters a problem in realigning the micro- and macro-level. These two problems are closely connected and we discuss them simultaneously in this chapter.

The third problem is of a slightly different nature, referring to the kind of knowledge that we, as economists, seek by conducting research into culture. Economists' focus on establishing universal insights and principles creates tensions with the idea of a diversity in cultural logics and perceptions of reality. This context specificity is hard to align with this basic assumption of universalistic behavior, because if, for example, rationality may be universal but the outcome of the rational decision-making differs in different cultures, the universal model of economic decision-making raises a methodological challenge.

This tension between universalistic and particularistic is related to the phenomenon of a cultural bias. Whereas this is a problem for all (social) scientific research, it is more apparent for studies into culture in economics. The pitfall of having one's cultural background dominating the analysis always looms large in economic studies of culture. In part, this problem is aggravated by the history of the field; as we have argued, the lines along which culture and the economic became separated fell to a large extent together with the division between "us" and "them." From this perspective, the very distinction between the economic – referring to allegedly universal structures of behavior modeled on West European and US self-images – and culture – referring to that which deviates from these structures – is already informed by an ethnocentric bias. If people's cultural background is deemed to be important for their behavior, this also goes for the cultural background

---

[1] Hodgson (2007a, 2007b) clearly shows that two interpretations of methodological individualism exist: (i) social phenomena should be explained entirely in terms of individuals alone, and (ii) social phenomena should be explained in terms of individuals plus relations between individuals. Hodgson suggests that both approaches should not be labeled as methodological individualism and he suggests thinking in terms of individuals and social structures.

of researchers. Researchers, like everyone else, have been conditioned to act and think in ways determined by their culture. In this sense, to a certain extent research is culturally specific and researchers have to deal with this fact in one way or the other.

The reason we believe these issues to be especially relevant for research into culture in economics should be obvious by now. These three challenges are in fact nothing but the methodological manifestations of the oppositions between the cultural and the economic perspectives summarized in Table 3.1. They follow directly from the elements of a culture definition discussed in Chapter 1. The structure–agency challenge follows from our understanding of culture both as an inherited, unquestioned given and as human-made. The aggregation challenge follows from applying economic analysis, approaching society from the perspective of individuals, to culture, conceived as having something to do with collective identity. The particularistic notion of culture implies that there are multiple ways to look at reality, eroding the confidence in objective, universal statements and unique optimal solutions.

Researchers of culture in economics have had to find ways to deal with these challenges. In the first section of this chapter, various responses to these methodological issues are discussed. It is up to us to decide how successful they are and, in cases where we decide they are not, how much we hold it against the research in question. The second section of this chapter deals with research methods. Here we discuss the advantages and problems of values surveys and cross-cultural experiments. The discussion of contemporary applications in the next part of this book serves as further illustration and in-depth study of these methodological challenges.

5.2 Methodological challenges when including culture in economics

5.2.1 From micro-agency to macro-structures and back

In the previous chapters, we have noted that researchers of culture in economics face the challenge of realigning two concepts that have become disconnected over time. A methodological aspect of the divide between the economic and the cultural is the fact that economic analysis starts out from individual decision-making, whereas culture is deemed to refer to collective structures, existing beyond the conscious actions of individuals but nevertheless informing and framing them (Licht 2008). Whereas economic theory confronts social phenomena as products of individual actions, the idea of culture as "that which is not economically rational" suggests a domain in which social structures autonomously determine the actions of individuals. The methodological individualism characterizing economic theory is at odds with the structuralism that seems to be implied in the notion of culture (at least, in much economic thinking about culture). Thus, we have a methodological problem of realigning structure and agency, or at a more practical, methodical level, how to connect analyses at the micro- and macro-levels.

To align micro- and macro-level at the theoretical level, three categories of answers have been given, analogous to the various ways in which authors have sought to realign culture and the economic. First, some researchers have approached all behavior as determined by structures. Theoretically, this corresponds to the economy-as-culture strategy for integrating culture and economy. Second, other researchers approach culture as a result of actions by individuals. In the approach of Gary Becker and others in the culture-as-economy group of literature, all social phenomena can be reduced to individual economic decisions. Third, there is a category of literature that does not really resolve this tension between structure and agency that dogs the study of culture in economics, but tries to bring the two together into a single theoretical model (corresponding to the culture-and-economics approach). The new institutional economics of Douglass North is a good example. Institutions and cultures, in this approach, are not products of conscious design by individuals but enter the model as structures which have a life of their own (*see also* Greif 2006 and Bowles 2004). They are nevertheless influenced by the unintended consequences of individual actions, just as they provide the structural background against which individuals can make decisions. At the theoretical level such a compromise between structure and agency might be satisfactory enough. However, the problem resurfaces when researchers stop theorizing and move on to "actual" empirical research.

Since our thinking about economics and culture operates at the individual and collective levels respectively, the question is what our level of analysis ought to be (Hodgson 2007b). In general, the level of data ought to conform to the level of theory; otherwise, analysis and interpretation of these data in accordance with the level of theory leads to erroneous conclusions (Robinson 1950; Klein *et al.* 1994). In this case, however, we have two levels of theory. If cultural theory implies we have to measure culture at the collective level, and economic theory implies we have to study economic behavior at the individual level, relating culture to economic behavior requires the translation of either one to the level of the other. To do this, there are basically two options. The first one is to go from macro to micro and translate the collective variable of culture to a factor in individual economic decision-making. For example, we can include the cultural background of an individual as a factor in the labor supply decisions of that individual. The second option is to do the opposite: we can aggregate and average findings and insights about economic behavior of individuals in order to come to characteristics of societies as a whole. An example of this is the use of national cultures as determinants in regression analyses of gross domestic product (GDP) growth rates.

For each route, methodological pitfalls lurk along the way. The main problem is that the level of analysis does not correspond to the level of theory and conceptualization of culture (in the case of option 1) or the level of theory and conceptualization of the economic (in the case of option 2). In the first case, in which we translate the variable at collective level – culture – into a variable at individual level, there is a so-called *ecological fallacy*, the mistake of inferring individual behavior from aggregate data (Robinson 1950). If one finds that Mexican society is Catholic, for example, it does not follow from this that each and every Mexican is Catholic. As long as the collective is not homogeneous, the translation of macro-characteristics to the micro-level is problematic. To assume that characteristics of individual members of a group are the same as the average characteristics of the group as a whole is to ignore the diversity within collectives and does no justice to the heterogeneity of agents.[2] Generally speaking,

---

[2] Note that even the alternative statement that every Mexican is living in a Catholic society is false, since many Mexicans are living in non-Catholic societies outside Mexico, and Mexico may consist of various sub-national regions, some of which might not be Catholic. The mistake is the same: one incorrectly attributes characteristics of Mexican society as a whole to individual Mexicans.

researchers of culture have long been aware of this problem and are seeking to avoid the error (e.g. Hofstede 1980; Sekaran 1983), usually by looking at relations at the collective level only.

Thus, we end up on the second route, translating economic variables to the collective level at which culture is conceptualized. Here, problems associated with aggregation come into play. The leap from micro to macro by simply aggregating individual data may not be legitimate if the aggregation procedure is affected by interaction effects between individuals (*see* Chapter 7 for a discussion of this problem with regard to the trust literature). Given that the behavior of individuals is dependent on the behavior of the group, this constitutes a problem for aggregation (Manski 2000). Even if the theoretical relation at the individual level holds, the collective might behave not in accordance with the theory, because the behaviors of individuals depend on each other as well. As Hofstede puts it: "Culture is no king size personality; cultures are formed through the interactions of different personalities, both conflicting and complementary, which create a whole which is more than the sum of its parts" (Hofstede 2001: 463).

The problems involved in moving from micro- to macro-level and vice versa are not easily solved, and we return to this issue in the final chapter. Tensions around methodological issues such as aggregation, ecological correlations and conceptual topics such as structure and agency have always provoked fierce debate among social scientists and will probably continue to do so. For the debate about culture in economics this implies that as long as culture and the economic are conceptualized as operating at two different levels, we have to live and deal with these tensions. Only those approaches which do not conceptualize culture and the economic at different levels – such as the interpretive approach or Becker's "everything is economics" approach – can manage to escape this discussion.

5.2.2 Universal vs. particular: idiographic and nomothetic approaches

A second class of methodological problems that is perhaps not specific to research about culture in economics but certainly plays a prominent role in this field revolves around the notion of universality vs. that of the particular. Adler (1983) has provided a helpful typology of management studies involving culture, which can be extended to studies of culture in economics (Table 5.1). This typology is based on the ways in which studies deal with their cultural perspective vis-à-vis other cultural perspectives. A key distinction that we make is that between idiographic and nomothetic research designs. Whereas the former studies economic behavior in its specific contexts only, the latter approach assumes that universal behavior exists or that universal dimensions of behavior exist (but societies may differ in their scores on these dimensions). The idiographic cluster consists of parochial, ethnocentric and polycentric approaches, differing in their research focus but sharing the practice of studying cultures on a case-by-case basis. The nomothetic cluster consists of comparative, geocentric and synergistic approaches. In contrast with the idiographic cluster, they share an assumption of universal structures of behavior, but differ in the way universality comes into being. Universality can be achieved by denying a role for culture at all (geocentric), by assuming that universal dimensions of culture exist and matter (comparative), or by focussing on the role of cultural differences and assuming that universal ways exist to deal with these differences (synergistic).

Idiographic approaches

First of all, there is research that simply does not take into account any role of cultural background. Researcher, research subject and audience all share the same cultural background, so that there is no strong awareness of the implications of cultural difference. As a consequence, research insights are often deemed applicable regardless of context, in spite of the fact that they have been developed in one cultural setting only. Such *parochial research*, as Adler calls it, thus assumes universality. The label of parochial research might be applied to much economic theory. Economic theory claims to deal with behavior and mechanisms that are universal even when it has mainly been a product of and applied to North American and European contexts.

The second category, *ethnocentric research*, transcends cultural boundaries, but only with respect to the research subject. It is acknowledged that there are different cultural settings and these are the object of study, but it is denied that they require different theories and perspectives. The perspective from which other cultures are addressed is the one developed in the researcher's own culture, which is deemed applicable regardless of context. Whereas researcher and audience

Table 5.1. Overview of methodologies to study culture (adapted from Adler 1983)

	Title	Culture	Approach to similarity and difference	Approach to universality	Type of study	Cultural backgrounds	Primary question
Idiographic research	PAROCHIAL RESEARCH	Home culture studies	Assumed similarity	Universality is not considered	Domestic studies of economic behavior	Researcher, audience & research subject of culture 1	What is the economic behavior of people and firms like? Study is applicable in only one culture and yet it is implicitly motivated by the assumption that it is applicable in many cultures
	ETHNOCENTRIC RESEARCH	Host culture studies	Search for similarity	Questioned universality	Application in foreign cultures of home-grown insights	Researcher and audience of culture 1, research subject of culture 2	Are behaviors and institutions in other cultures fitting home-country theories?
	POLYCENTRIC RESEARCH	Studies in many cultures	Assumed difference	Denied universality	Individual studies of behavior in specific foreign cultures	Researcher, audience and research subject of culture 2	How do economic agents behave and what do institutions look like in society X?

Nomothetic research						
COMPARATIVE RESEARCH	Studies contrasting and comparing many cultures	Search for both similarity and difference	Emergent universality	Studies comparing economic behavior in many foreign cultures	Researcher, audience and research subject of culture 1 and 2	How are economic behaviors and institutions similar and different across cultures?
GEOCENTRIC RESEARCH	Culture deemed irrelevant	Assumed similarity	Assumed and extended universality	E.g. international trade theory	Researcher and audience of culture 1, research subject of culture 1 and 2	What is the economic behavior of people and firms like?
SYNERGISTIC RESEARCH	Intercultural economic studies	Use of similarities and differences	Created universality	Studies of universal patterns of economic behavior across cultures	All above variants possible	What are the universal effects of cultural differences on international economic relations?

share the same cultural background, the difference with parochial research is that other cultures are under study.

An obvious variant of ethnocentric research is studies dealing with the question as to whether insights developed in culture A are valid within culture B as well. Popkin (1979), for example, seeks to show that Vietnamese peasants are behaving in an economically rational manner when choosing crops. Although the researcher does not just assume people in the other culture to behave "rationally," it is assumed that economic rationality is a relevant yardstick for investigating other cultures. In other words, the question is framed in terms of the theoretical perspective developed in the own cultural setting. It is, "Are they behaving like us?" instead of the more open, "What is their behavior like?" The same thing happens when we do the opposite: describing behavior in other cultures as dissimilar to the behavior described by the (culturally specific) theory. Popkin's attempt to show that rational choice can be extended to Vietnamese peasants can be seen as an attack of the (then) popular notion that people in developing societies are traditional beings to whom rational choice would not apply.[3] As in Popkin's research, this notion sets rational choice as the standard from which other cultures are assessed.

In general, applying single-culture standards to other cultures is an elusive and pervasive form of ethnocentrism in studies about culture in economics. While acknowledging the role of cultural differences in economic behavior and outcomes is arguably a way forward, many economists have a tendency to analyze differences between societies as differences in the degree to which each society corresponds to a theoretical benchmark. The attention for differences in institutions such as property rights has sensitized economists to cultural variation. However, in practice, institutional economics usually interprets property rights as unidimensional issues; variation is limited to the fact that they can be better or worse, or that a society can have more or less of them (e.g. Rodrik *et al.* 2004; Dollar and Kraay 2003). A single yardstick, based on a theory that has been formulated within a specific cultural context, is applied to all societies and there is scant attention

---

[3] In this sense, it fits within the more general movement in development economics at that time, in which it was argued that neoclassical economic insights were applicable in developing societies just as well (e.g. Lal 1983).

for differences in *types* of property rights between cultures. The danger in such an analysis is that one ends up comparing other societies on the basis of the degree to which they have the same institutions as one's own. Thus, the second culture is measured against the first rather than being described in its own terms.

Moving down in Table 5.1, we come to approaches that take cultural differences more seriously and acknowledge the potential cultural specificity of theories developed in one cultural setting. Rather than assuming universality in general, these approaches seek to establish which elements of behavior and institutions are culturally specific, and describe these in terms of their own culture while developing more general theory about the elements that are presents in all cultures. *Polycentric research* takes up one extreme position on the dimension of cultural uniqueness–universality. In polycentric research, institutions, behavior and meanings thereof are viewed as understandable only in terms of their own culture. Researchers seek to avoid ethnocentrism by limiting the domain of applicability of their statements solely to the context in which they have been developed. Hence, studies are written as if audience, research subject and – ideally – researcher are culturally the same in each case; we take inside views from within each culture.

Once one adopts this extreme position of cultural uniqueness, it becomes impossible to say anything transcending the culture under study. Cross-cultural comparative research of behavior and institutions is ruled out. Since each culture is fundamentally different from any other, there are no shared, universal structures or principles on the basis of which we can compare cultures. Not all researchers take such an extreme position, however. Many dispute the claim that there is absolutely no shared element of behavior among cultures, arguing that the polycentric view creates overly strict boundaries between cultures. While there are differences between cultures, there are also similarities. Some things are particular to a single culture (*emic*), others are alike in all cultures (*etic*). Therefore, analysis need not be limited to *idiographic research*, which describes only the uniqueness of one case, but can also take the form of *nomothetic research*, which seeks to establish general laws and principles about human behavior. Cross-cultural analyses and comparisons of human behavior and institutions are possible according to this argument.

Nomothetic approaches

One approach that specifically studies the general laws and principles of human behavior is *comparative research*. It is assumed that universal dimensions of human behavior exist and that cultural differences translate into different positions or "scores" on a dimension. However, this approach, developing insights about more than one culture, has to tread carefully if it is to avoid falling back into ethnocentrism. Any comparative research project is looking for both differences and similarities between cultures. Even if it is mainly looking for differences between culture A and culture B, in order to compare meaningfully it has to establish a common perspective on the basis of which one can compare. In establishing this common perspective, ethnocentrism is a real danger.

Let us take a closer look at what a cross-cultural comparison entails. A meaningful investigation into cultural differences requires two things. First, in order to identify cultural differences, we need to have a scale on which comparisons can be made, which has to be relevant to all the cultures in the study. Second, we need comparable units of culture.

To start with the latter, comparative research usually focusses on states as comparable units of culture. When we say we are comparing cultures, we are most of the time in effect comparing states (e.g. Hofstede 1980, 2001; Inglehart 1997; House *et al.* 2004; Guiso *et al.* 2006; Knack and Keefer 1997). Yet, a state has primarily geographical boundaries, not cultural ones. In order to be able to use states as comparable units in cultural research, we therefore have to assume that the geographical boundaries of a state coincide with cultural boundaries of a cultural community: one state, one culture. This is a rather strong assumption. Other units of culture could be constructed, such as language communities, ethnicity or religious communities. None of these, it should be noted, falls together with the borders of states.[4] In the light of the discussion above, we might note that the conception of a state falling together with one culture entails the idea of the nation-state, which has historical and cultural roots in nineteenth-century Europe. Taking states as comparable units of culture is thus potentially problematic, since (a) it might not be the most relevant

---

[4] To illustrate this, try to think of one European state within whose borders only one language is spoken that is not spoken in another European state.

unit of culture and (b) it suffers from a slight ethnocentric bias. However, we might note that these potential problems are a consequence of the comparative method rather than of the focus on states. Although research focussing on the nation level has been strongly criticized (e.g. McSweeney 2002a, 2002b), it is not clear how focussing on alternative units of culture would prevent the potential problems outlined here.

In the search for scales relevant to all cultures under study, the danger of ethnocentric bias is also present. Often, researchers have created categorizations of cultures and simply assumed these to be appropriate and relevant in other cultural settings. Religion, language, colonial heritage and family structure, for example, have all been used as categories on the basis of which to classify and rank cultures (e.g. Stulz and Williamson 2003; Lane and Ersson 2005; Todd 1985). While the universality of many of these categories may seem plausible on first sight, problems still crop up. Studies using religion as the source for categorization, for example, start out from the premise that religions are zero-sum variables: to belong to one religious community is to not belong to another. While this may be true (in principle) in the monotheistic Abrahamic tradition (Judaism, Islam and Christianity) in which most researchers have been raised, it does not hold for many other faiths such as Taoism, Buddhism and Confucianism.[5] Moreover, the implicit assumption that religions are internally homogeneous is also problematic. Most religions can be broken up into various denominations with different views. Even if researchers take into account such differences, they are usually more aware of them within their own religious context than outside it (Lane and Ersson (2005), for example, break up Christianity into an Orthodox, Protestant and Catholic faith, while Islam is included as a single category). Moreover, even people of the same denomination exhibit very different beliefs and moral values when it comes to topics outside the core of their religious thought. Catholicism ranges from conservative Opus Dei to radical liberation theology; views of evangelical Christians in the US on the ideal economic system range from very free market-oriented to a flat rejection of capitalism in favor of socialism (Iannaccone 1992a).

What this shows is that even a seemingly basic categorization like religion to some extent mistakes the own, culturally specific,

---

[5] Confucianism, moreover, while often included in studies focussing on religion, is not a religion but a philosophy.

interpretation for a common perspective. In order to prevent such problems, some authors recommend that comparative studies should be carried out by multicultural research teams only (Triandis 1972; Chinese Culture Connection 1987; Bond and Chi 1997; House *et al.* 2004; Hofstede 2006). In this set-up, researchers and subjects under study share a cultural background, but the audience is intended to be global.

Others doubt that such a move would be enough, arguing that it would be naïve to think any research project is able to overcome all bias toward the own cultural perspective. All methods claiming not to be culturally biased at all are suspect, as they are likely to be simply blind to the kind of cultural bias plaguing them. Cultural biases are unavoidable, so that perhaps the most one can do is to try to balance them by presenting accounts from different perspectives at the same time.

This is the idea behind the alternative method for comparative research that can be extracted from the work of Anderson (1991, 1998, 2005). It maintains the idea in normal comparative research that a comparison requires a common perspective applicable to both settings in the comparison. However, it also takes over the idea of cultural uniqueness from polycentric research. Combining the two ideas results in the position that any cross-cultural comparisons entail the application of culturally specific but universalizing frameworks to the various cultural settings under study. The framework is not universally relevant and appropriate, but we treat it as such. This implies that any cross-cultural comparison entails a kind of double vision: one looks at one culture while simultaneously seeing it from the perspective of another culture. In order to avoid privileging one region over the other as grounds for comparison, Anderson describes how one might not only look at Indonesia from a Eurocentric perspective – as most research has done – but also look at Europe from an Indonesian perspective. Seeing Europe as through an inverted telescope miniaturizes and distances the image, so that one becomes aware of how others might see one's own cultural background. Thus, one can include this other side of the comparison in the analysis. A German researcher seeking to conduct a comparative research project about the Philippines and Cuba, for example, might not only look at both nations from a German perspective but also try to look at Germany from a Philippine and Cuban perspective. A more balanced and insightful view emerges from such a procedure. Anderson (2005) shows that not only is it illuminating to "look back" from a culture under study to the own culture, it is also useful trying to look at the Philippines from a Cuban perspective and vice versa. In terms of the typology, this form of comparison does not assume the existence of universal structures of human behavior. Moreover, in contrast to comparisons by multicultural research teams, in this form of comparative research, researcher and research subject are never of the same cultural background – that would preclude the double vision needed for comparison – but subject and researcher are constantly switching in cultural perspectives.

If we move further down Table 5.1, in many ways we move back toward where we started. Geocentric research, like parochial research, is characterized by a neglect of the role of cultural background in research. Culture is deemed to be irrelevant to the applicability of researchers' insights. The difference with parochial research, however, is that the focus of geocentric research is – as the term already indicates – processes on a world scale rather than individual behavior. In geocentric research, researcher and audience share the same culture, so that there is no problem of cultural translation. Yet, the research subject is global – international trade, foreign direct investment (FDI), behavior of multinationals, etc. The fundamental assumption is, however, that culture is irrelevant in studying these aspects of economic behavior of firms and/or individuals.

The last category in the typology, *synergistic research*, is really not a different way of dealing with the role of cultural backgrounds in research, but is about a change of research question. Rather than studying a single culture or comparing a number of them, synergistic research has cultural differences as its subject. The fundamental characteristic it shares with the comparative and geocentric research is its nomothetic approach toward culture: it is about the *universal* effects of cultural differences. The question it seeks to address is how people and institutions behave in interaction with other cultures. With this research subject, several different sub-approaches could be distinguished. For example, one could try to find general laws about cross-cultural interaction on the basis of analysis of the behavior of people from the researcher's culture in such interactions (analogous to a parochial approach). Alternatively, one could analyze cross-cultural behavior by people from other cultural backgrounds from the own perspective, which would result in ethnocentric synergistic research. Polycentric and comparative synergistic research is also possible. In fact, Anderson's double-vision comparative method could also be seen as a synergistic approach. It makes use of the fact that to compare between different cultures itself is a form of cross-cultural interaction. Comparative research provides not so much knowledge about another culture as an account of how someone from culture A sees culture B and (ideally) vice versa. In this conception of knowledge about cultures, synergistic and comparative research questions blend together.

This typology of ways of dealing with cultural specificity of research shows two things. First, there is a tension between universalistic and particularistic approaches, and second, cultural bias is a pervasive problem in cultural research projects. Awareness of the problem and, equally important, of the ways in which cultural bias can creep into one's research project at different levels is crucial. In order to bring this point home more clearly, we now descend in level of abstraction and discuss research methods used in cultural economic research.

5.3 Research methods

Having discussed the main methodological issues that are specific to research into culture in economics, we can now direct our attention toward research methods. Within the field of cultural economics, the whole usual range of research methods is available. However, there are some methods that are more or less specific to cultural studies or have particular characteristics in this case. One example is the use of cross-cultural *comparative experiments*. Another is the employment of cross-country regressions on quantified data about culture. Often these data come from large-scale, international *values surveys*. Without denying the importance and relevance of other possible research methods such as case-based research, we limit our discussion to a description and assessment of these two methods.

5.3.1 Comparative experiments

The use of experiments in economics has been increasing in recent decades. Like the turn toward culture, it is driven by a desire to develop an economics that focusses less on stylized models based on assumed patterns of behavior and is more attuned to actual behavior and social practices of agents (Bowles 2004). Experiments have been especially popular in showing deviations from the rationality assumption. People have been shown to be more cooperative and less opportunistic than assumed in mainstream theory so far. Given this background, it is no surprise that experiments have also been employed in research seeking to show the impact of culture on economic behavior.

The set-up of such experiments is generally as follows. People with various cultural backgrounds are asked to play an experimental game. Roth *et al.* (1991), for example, ask participants to play a so-called ultimatum game. In an ultimatum game, player 1 has to make a proposal to player 2 about how to divide a given sum of money. Player 2 can either reject the proposal, in which case neither party gets anything, or accept it, in which case both parties receive the agreed amount. After this, the game is finished. The *homo oeconomicus* would make low offers and (expect the other to) always accept any offer, since any money is better than none. In experiments, results are usually different, however. Roth *et al.* (1991) find that offers are generally quite equitable and that grossly inequitable offers are typically rejected. When comparing results cross-culturally, he finds no substantial differences across developed economies.

Henrich (2000) and Henrich *et al.* (2006) follow a similar procedure, applying it to a more diverse sample of participants, coming from both developed and developing societies of various continents. In these studies, substantial differences in proposals as well as acceptance and rejection tendencies were found. Henrich (2000) compared adult Machiguenga (a tribe from the tropical forests of the Peruvian Amazon) with graduate students from the University of California, Los Angeles (UCLA). It is shown that the Machiguenga offered substantially less and were more willing to accept low offers than students from UCLA (the Machiguenga were thus behaving more like the *homo oeconomicus*).

Studies comparing such experimental results across cultures have taken off in recent years (e.g. Buchan *et al.* 2002; Gächter *et al.* 2005; Gächter and Herrmann 2009; Gintis 2008; Herrmann *et al.* 2008). A number of overview books have been published on differences in habits, habit formation, institutions and economic behavior using experimental methods (e.g. Camerer 2003; Greif 2006; Henrich *et al.* 2004; Ostrom 2005). The main findings of this literature, according to Samuelson (2005), are that the results of ultimatum games played in various societies differ considerably. What is more, the variation in behavioral outcomes observed in these games is significantly related to the society in which experiments are conducted. Meanwhile, intra-group differences such as sex, age and gender are shown to have only marginal explanatory power. Finally, clear links are established between experimental behavior and everyday life, providing a view on preferences as being shaped by one's culture and way of life (among other geographical circumstances). Findings like these led Henrich *et al.* to conclude that "preferences over economic choices are not exogenous as the canonical model would have it, but rather are shaped by the economic and social interactions of everyday life" (Henrich *et al.* 2001: 77). In other words, culture matters.

The methodological problems of aggregation/disaggregation and cultural bias are clearly present in experiments of this design, especially if one is using them to show cultural differences between societies. To start with the first, experiments take place among individuals and involve individual behavior. Culture, meanwhile, exists at the level of the collective. In order for experiments to tell us something about culture, we need to assume that the behavior of the individuals in the experiment is representative of the behavior of the pre-defined collective. While the issue of the representativeness of the sample of individuals is present in behavioral experiments in general, this becomes problematic if the experiment is used to show cultural differences. In that case, for the experiment to be valid, we need a sample of individuals that is representative for the culture as a whole. At the same time, the fact that there is cultural behavior specific to the group as a whole is what the experiment is supposed to show in the first place. The Henrich (2000) experiment with a number of Machiguenga participants cannot be taken to tell us something about Machiguenga culture as a whole. Most obviously, this is because the participants cannot simply be assumed to be representative of Machiguenga culture. On a deeper level, this is because we cannot assume a distinctive Machiguenga culture to exist in the first place, since that would amount to assuming what we seek to show. What is more, even if individuals were representative for their culture, individual behavior cannot be simply added up to get to collective structures. The tendency of Machiguenga participants to share in a certain manner among themselves tells us nothing about the tendency to share at the collective level of Machiguenga culture. Perhaps Machiguenga tend to form small groups in which members cooperate. If these groups do not cooperate, Machiguengan culture is characterized by a lack of cooperation at the collective level (what we will label generalized morality in Chapter 7). What this shows is that experiments have a problem with revealing characteristics of the collective (culture) because they focus on characteristics of individual behavior.

With regard to cultural bias, on the most basic level, it is assumed that the game is relevant across cultural settings. Since this is a pretty obvious problem, designers of experiments usually take note of it and attempt to address it. As with the aggregation/disaggregation issue, however, less obvious problems lie underneath this. A deeper-rooted, potentially ethnocentric assumption of cross-cultural experiments is that the relation between playing games and behavior in daily life is the same across societies. However, in some societies playing games might be a clearly demarcated type of behavior, so that games are governed by other rules than public life. Games, in contrast to other forms of social interaction, might be simply about winning, encouraging opportunistic behavior not acceptable in public life. In other societies, games might be an integrated part of social life and follow the same rules as other behavior. The meaning of playing games is likely to differ between cultures, making cross-cultural comparison between outcomes of games problematic. In a similar vein, differences in results of ultimatum games might not so much say something about differences in tendencies to cooperate or trust each other as say something about differences in embeddedness of the market (remember Polanyi's analysis on pages 98–101). Societies which separate the market sphere very clearly from the rest of society are likely to portray more opportunistic behavior when it comes to playing money-distributing games than societies in which the market is an integrated part of social life in general.

We thus do not know how representative market behavior (and game behavior) is for social interactions in general. In a methodologically interesting study, Danielson and Holm (2005) compared results of a survey and an experiment among students in Sweden and Tanzania. They found that survey questions on trust corresponded with trusting behavior in the experimental game for Swedish students, but not for Tanzanians. One possible explanation for this is that the setting of an ultimatum game is probably much closer to the general institutional setting of a developed market society like Sweden than to the institutional setting of a developing society, in which the market sphere is a much more marginal aspect of social reality. Hence, where cross-cultural experiments assume experiments to capture the same aspect of public life in all societies, the representativeness of experiments for general behavior might differ among societies. As with any comparison, cultural bias lurks not only in the content of claims and interpretations but in the very structure of the comparison itself. We encounter the same problem in cross-cultural values surveys.

5.3.2 Values surveys and dimensions of culture

By far the most popular method for comparing cultures is on the basis of cross-cultural values surveys (Hofstede 1980, 2001; House *et al.* 2004; Inglehart 1997; Schwartz 1994, 2006; Trompenaars 1994). The most prominent sources of values survey data include the datasets developed by Hofstede, Schwartz, the European Values Survey (EVS)/World Values Survey (WVS) and, more recently, the Global Leadership and Organizational Behavior Effectiveness (GLOBE) project.[6] In all these projects, surveys are conducted in various countries, measuring the inclinations of people toward a broad range of objectives. The items in these surveys are constructed into dimensions on which various cultures can be scored. The score of a particular culture is determined by aggregating and averaging individual values. So we learn that Sweden is more feminine than Japan, or that Albania is more assertive than Kuwait (Hofstede 2001; House *et al.* 2004).

Since values surveys are a form of comparative research, they require a scale to be constructed which is applicable cross-culturally (Hult *et al.* 2008). Two routes have been taken to this end – since it is tricky to simply assume categories to be universally relevant, some researchers have taken the route of deriving scales empirically; others have sought to derive scales theoretically.

---

[6] We exclude Trompenaars (1994) from our discussion here, as it is not used in the academic literature to the same extent as Hofstede, Schwartz, WVS/EVS and GLOBE. It is a popular reference in more practice-oriented inter-cultural management courses.

Hofstede's IBM project, Schwartz's response and the GLOBE initiative

Without any doubt, Geert Hofstede has been the personification of cross-cultural research for many (business) economists. The importance of his work is reflected in the large number of citations – he is by far the most cited Dutch economist. Originally trained as an engineer, he obtained a Ph.D. in Psychology from the University of Groningen in the Netherlands. His most prominent work can be found in two books: *Culture's Consequences* was first published in 1980, with a new edition in 2001, and *Cultures and Organizations* was first published in 1991, then revised in 1997 and 2005.

Working at IBM in the 1960s, Hofstede developed a large database on attitudes and beliefs of IBM employees all over the world. He found that people working for the same organization showed a tendency to respond similarly depending on their national background, or alternatively that societies could be ranked in a consistent way according to several unique dimensions. Developing his work further, Hofstede devised his famous set of four cultural dimensions: power distance, uncertainty avoidance, individualism (vs. collectivism) and masculinity (vs. femininity).

1. Power distance, which refers to the extent to which people believe that power and status are distributed unequally and the extent to which they accept an unequal distribution of power as the proper way of organizing social systems.
2. Uncertainty avoidance, which refers to the extent to which people are uncomfortable with uncertain, unknown, or unstructured situations.
3. Individualism vs. collectivism, which reflects the degree to which a society emphasizes the role of the individual as opposed to that of the group.
4. Masculinity vs. femininity, which refers to the extent to which a society emphasizes traditional masculine values such as competitiveness, assertiveness, achievement, ambition and the acquisition of money and other material possessions, as opposed to feminine values such as nurturing, helping others, putting relationships with people before money, not showing off and valuing the quality of life.

Hofstede and Bond (1988) later uncovered a fifth cultural dimension, called long-term orientation. Unfortunately, the scores on this dimension are available for only a limited number of countries, thus reducing its empirical applicability. Moreover, scholars have questioned its added value, as it has been argued to reflect the same underlying cultural values as the individualism dimension (*see* Barkema and Vermeulen 1997). Hofstede assigned each country a score on each cultural dimension that varied between zero and 100 to indicate how people from different cultures feel about the above societal issues. Throughout the years, these scores have extended to an increasing number of countries.

Hofstede's work has been confirmed in replication studies (for example, Van Oudenhoven 2001; Merritt 2000; Søndergaard 1994), but it also received a considerable amount of criticism (*see* Drogendijk and Slangen 2006 for a succinct overview). Schwartz, in particular, has criticized Hofstede on a variety of methodological grounds, more specifically the supposed lack of a theoretical framework and the need to use value measures that have equivalent meaning across cultures at the individual level (Schwartz 1994, 1999, 2004, 2006; Licht *et al.* 2007). Schwartz has, however, also developed an alternative culture framework, incorporating most of his criticism. Starting from a theoretically derived number of culture dimensions, Schwartz recognized fifty-six individual values that could be further reduced to forty-five that have identical meaning across cultures. Using a survey on school teachers and college students from sixty-seven countries between 1988 and 1998, he acquired information on values and value differences (Schwartz later extended his framework to seventy-three countries). He defined three basic issues that confront all societies and derived three corresponding value dimensions (Schwartz 1994, 1999, 2004, 2006):

1. Embeddedness/Autonomy: this dimension incorporates the desirable relationship between the individual and the group. Embeddedness refers to a cultural emphasis on the person as embedded in the group, while autonomy refers to a view on individuals as autonomous, independent persons. Schwartz distinguishes between two types of autonomy. Intellectual autonomy refers to the extent to which people are free to independently

pursue their own ideas and intellectual directions. Affective autonomy does the same but then with respect to their affective desires.

2. Hierarchy/Egalitarianism: this dimension refers to the ideal way to elicit cooperative, productive activity in society. Hierarchy denotes the extent to which it is legitimate to distribute power, roles and resources unequally. Egalitarian commitment refers to the extent to which people are inclined to voluntarily put aside selfish interests to promote the welfare of others.

3. Mastery/Harmony: this dimension is supposed to reflect the relation of humankind to the natural and social world. Mastery expresses the importance of getting ahead by being self-assertive. Harmony denotes the importance of fitting harmoniously into the environment.

An important initiative parallel to Hofstede's and Schwartz's work on culture dimensions is the most recent culture and practices project by the international research GLOBE team founded by Robert J. House of the Wharton School at the University of Pennsylvania. The researchers of the GLOBE project were particularly interested in identifying leadership attributes and organizational practices that were culturally endorsed. One hundred and fifty social scientists from sixty-one cultures were involved in this long-term programmatic series of cross-cultural leadership studies. The overall goal of GLOBE is to develop an empirically based theory to describe, understand and predict the impact of specific cultural variables on leadership and organizational processes and the effectiveness of these processes (House *et al.* 2001: 492). The GLOBE team has developed nine dimensions of culture:

1. Power distance: the degree to which members of a collective expect power to be distributed equally.
2. Uncertainty avoidance: the extent to which a society, organization or group relies on social norms, rules and procedures to alleviate unpredictability of future events.
3. Humane orientation: the degree to which a collective encourages and rewards individuals for being fair, altruistic, generous, caring and kind to others.

4. Collectivism I: the degree to which organizational and societal institutional practices encourage and reward collective distribution of resources and collective action.

5. Collectivism II: the degree to which individuals express pride, loyalty and cohesiveness in their organizations or families.

6. Assertiveness: the degree to which individuals are assertive, confrontational and aggressive in their relationships with others.

7. Gender egalitarianism: the degree to which a collective minimizes gender inequality.

8. Future orientation: the extent to which individuals engage in future-oriented behaviors such as delaying gratification, planning and investing in the future.

9. Performance orientation: the degree to which a collective encourages and rewards group members for performance improvement and excellence.

These nine dimensions and the underlying methodology are well described in House *et al.* (2004). Of all the different culture dimensions projects, it should be noted that Hofstede especially has made his way into economics (certainly in international business, *see* Chapter 8). Schwartz and GLOBE are not used as extensively as Hofstede in economics, but are considered by some scholars to be superior to Hofstede in certain areas such as cross-cultural psychology and international management because of their theoretical starting point and associated cross-cultural methodology.[7] We think this lack of usage of the latter two is caused by an absence of familiarity, and with the current surge in cultural economics, we may well expect economists to start using Schwartz and GLOBE data more in the future. More information on the culture dimensions can be found in the books referred to above and at www. geerthofstede.com and www.thunderbird.edu/wwwfiles/ms/globe.

---

[7] This assessment of GLOBE as superior is not shared unanimously. In a recent issue of the *Journal of International Business Studies*, a fierce debate ensued after Hofstede criticized GLOBE on a wide range of methodological and conceptual issues, including the charge of "US centeredness (Leung 2006)." He concludes that GLOBE's "questionnaire items may not have captured what the researchers supposed them to measure" (Hofstede 2006: 885). In a reply to these comments, the GLOBE team (Javidan *et al.* 2006) argues that Hofstede's approach is the one likely to be US biased, since it is based on employees from IBM, a US multinational. Moreover, Hofstede's study is criticized for suffering

In both Hofstede's (1980, 2001) and Inglehart's (1997) approaches, the scales on which cultures can be ranked are emerging out of the research data. Values surveys are conducted, consisting of items that are still assumed to be relevant and appropriate in all cultures, but these items themselves are not used as the basis for comparison. Through data-reduction methods such as factor analysis, respondents' scores on this broad range of items are replaced with a smaller number of new variables (factors). Items that co-vary highly are grouped together. The guiding principle for data reduction is to maximize explanation of the total variance in the original matrix, while minimizing the number of factors (Hofstede 2001: 31–32).[8] Hofstede (1980) thus identified his four initial dimensions of culture. In a similar way, Inglehart identified the dimensions well-being/survival and secular–rational/traditional authority. These dimensions have been used regularly in empirical research into culture in economics (e.g. De Jong 2002; Franke *et al.* 1991; Granato *et al.* 1996; Inglehart and Carballo 1997; *see* Part II for a more extensive discussion of the literature).

Hofstede's methods of deriving scales empirically have not been free from criticism (House *et al.* 2004: 123). Whereas from the perspective of preventing ethnocentric bias an argument might be made in favor of having concepts and dimensions emerging from the data rather than them being imposed, from the perspective of theory development it is problematic. It is difficult to determine the actual construct measured by empirically developed scales. Moreover, since the original survey was not designed to measure the construct of interest, certain biases in the items cannot be corrected. Hence, from this perspective one could argue that the most Hofstede could claim on the basis of his research is that he has identified four dimensions, not that these dimensions reflect the concepts uncertainty avoidance, individualism, power distance and masculinity/femininity, nor that they are

from empiricism, as it is not based on a clear theoretical framework that was developed *before* his data collection started. Reviewing both the GLOBE and the Hofstede projects, Smith (2006) tries to strike a middle ground between what he calls the two elephants that when fighting may trample the grass. In yet another round of debate, Maseland and van Hoorn (2009, 2010) suggest that both GLOBE and Hofstede's approach measure not so much absolute preferences as marginal preferences, an argument that can be found in Schwartz (2006: 143) as well.

[8] Similar methods include cluster analysis, multidimensional scaling and smallest-space analysis.

universally appropriate. Because of these problems, many researchers have advocated a more theory-driven approach to develop quantitative scales of culture. Schwartz, for example, has scrutinized the literature and identified several values he deems universally relevant, which he groups into categories. Empirical research served to validate this proposition, while attention was being paid to potential biases, such as having items relevant to only one culture (Schwartz 1994, 2006). A more recent study conducted by GLOBE followed a similar procedure (House *et al.* 2004). Their differences notwithstanding, both these studies came up with a number of dimensions that were more or less comparable to the ones identified by Hofstede.

World and European Values Survey

The European Values Study is a large-scale, cross-national and longitudinal survey research program on basic human values, initiated by the European Value Systems Study Group (EVSSG) in the late 1970s, at that time an informal grouping of academics at the Faculty of Social Sciences of Tilburg University (the Netherlands) and the Catholic University of Leuven (Belgium). The founding fathers were Jan Kerkhofs (Leuven) and Ruud de Moor (Tilburg). Now, the program is carried on in the setting of a foundation, using the name of the group European Values Study (EVS). The first wave of research was carried out in 1981, covering sixteen mainly Western European countries, the second one in 1990 covering more than thirty countries (including a couple of Central and Eastern European countries) and the latest one in 1999/2000. One of the reasons explaining the popularity of the EVS is the fact that for participation in the survey, each country has to have at least 1,000 respondents who as a collective could be considered a representative sample of the broader society.

Out of this pioneering group of mainly sociologists, Ronald Inglehart started the World Values Survey (WVS) in the 1990s. The WVS aims at a better coverage of non-Western societies and explicitly includes the analysis of the development of a democratic political culture in emerging democracies. The majority of the survey questions in the WVS and the EVS are similar, which is logical given the fact that the WVS emerged out of the EVS. The two research groups now work closely together, allowing researchers to study more countries over a longer period of time. The database contains hundreds of questions on four broad topics: family, religion and morality, work/leisure and broader societal issues. The WVS/EVS question that has been used most often in economics is the famous question on trust: "Generally speaking, do you think that most people can be trusted, or that you cannot be too careful?" (*see* more in Chapter 7).

The name most closely associated with the WVS is Ronald Inglehart, a political scientist at the University of Michigan. Supported by data from the WVS, Inglehart has extensively described and empirically analyzed the relationship between cultural values and economic development (Inglehart 1990, 1997, 2006). He writes that "in marked contrast to the growing materialism linked with the industrial revolution, the unprecedented existential security of advanced industrial society gave rise to an intergenerational shift towards postmaterialist and postmodernist values" (Inglehart and Baker 2000: 21). Industrialization is linked with an emphasis on economic growth at almost any price, whereas in affluent societies elements such as the quality of life, environmental protection and self-expression are emphasized. As Bell (1973) wrote, industrialization brought less dependence on nature and the world became mechanical, bureaucratic and rationalized. In sum, the shift from industrial to service economies goes together with a shift in value priorities from an emphasis on economic and physical security toward an increasing emphasis on subjective well-being and quality of life.

Inglehart's central thesis correlates strongly with modernization theory as discussed earlier: economic development has systematic, and to some extent predictable, cultural and political consequences. According to Inglehart, these consequences are not iron laws of history but probabilistic trends, a thesis that he illustrates through WVS data. In other words, the probability is high that certain changes will occur as societies develop economically, but it also depends on the specific cultural and historical context of the society in question.

In operationalizing his theoretical ideas, Inglehart uses WVS/EVS questions reflecting his two main dimensions, which are traditional vs. rational and survival vs. self-expression. Traditional values emphasize the following (rational values emphasize the opposite):

- God is very important in respondent's life.
- Respondent has a strong sense of national pride.
- Respondent favors more respect for authority.
- Divorce is never justifiable.
- Respondent almost never discusses political matters.

Survival values emphasize the following (self-expression values emphasize the opposite):

- Respondent gives priority to economic and physical security over self-expression and quality of life.
- Respondent describes him/her self as not very happy.
- Respondent describes him/her self as not very satisfied with life.
- Homosexuality is never justifiable.
- Respondent feels one has to be very careful in trusting people.

For the exact procedure of calculating the two dimensions, we refer to Inglehart's work. More information on both the WVS and the EVS can be found at www.europeanvalues.nl and www. worldvaluessurvey.org. The EVS in particular has a substantial amount of information on background and underlying methodology. An overview of main findings, key explanations and reflections from the EVS was published in 2003 (Arts *et al.* 2003).

An extensive comparison of Schwartz' and Inglehart's frameworks can be found in Schwartz (2006) and one of the (updated) Hofstede dimensions and GLOBE in Tang and Koveos (2008). A comparison of the frameworks developed by Schwartz, Hofstede and GLOBE can be found in Smith, Bond and Kagitcibasi (2006). Despite all these different approaches to and measures of cross-cultural values, it is interesting to observe that countries cluster together in (more or less) similar cultural zones, whatever method is applied (Schwartz 2006: 157, 177).

Whether empirically or theoretically driven, values surveys, and in particular their employment in deriving dimensions of culture, have not been safeguarded from criticism. One problem they have to deal with is the fact that values surveys produce data on the micro-level. These are averaged and aggregated in order to come to measures of national culture. Apart from the question of whether a focus on the nation is appropriate, the move from micro to macro is always a tricky one, especially if values surveys dimensions are subsequently used to explain phenomena at a lower level (Davis and Davenport 1999; Haller 2002; McSweeney 2002a, McSweeney 2002b; Silver and Dowley 2000). With regard to the identification of dimensions, there is an ongoing discussion about the appropriate number of dimensions (Flanagan 1982a, 1982b; MacIntosh 1998), since this is basically a subjective decision by the researcher (more so in the case of empirically derived scales). Another issue is whether questions in values surveys succeed in measuring cultural values, or that they are more prone to capture what respondents have on their mind at the time of the survey; whatever is in the news around the time, they report as important (Flanagan 1982b; Clarke *et al.* 1999).

Questions can also be asked about the relation between values, as measured in values surveys, and economic outcomes. Hofstede assumes values to be the basis for practices resulting in (economic) outcomes (Hofstede 2001: 11). Values thus explain outcomes, not vice versa; they are stable and for all purposes exogenous. As we have seen, however, this view of culture as a more or less immutable variable is at odds with recent anthropological insights (e.g. Appadurai 1996) or developments in economics (there is a small but increasing literature on the endogeneity of preferences, e.g. Bowles 1998, 2004). From a different angle, Maseland and van Hoorn (2009, 2010) also challenge the idea of values as measured in values surveys being independent from outcomes. They claim that values surveys are likely to measure people's marginal preferences rather than their underlying values. As such, values surveys scores are expected to be negatively influenced by increases in satiation of the objectives they refer to; more freedom in practice means a lower valuation of freedom. After all, people's marginal valuation of something falls when they have more of it. Citing evidence from the GLOBE study, Maseland and Van Hoorn show that societal values and practices are generally negatively correlated, which supports the interpretation of values surveys as eliciting marginal preferences rather than values. This would cast doubt on the use of values surveys in culture studies.

Leaving aside such issues, one could ask the even more fundamental question of whether culture is something that is quantifiable in the first place. Of course, one's view on this issue depends on one's definition of culture as well as one's methodological inclinations in general. Polycentric researchers will dismiss the idea of cultural dimensions as being a form of cross-cultural comparison. A holistic view of culture focussing on the *emic* precludes the kind of analysis conducted in values surveys. Interpretive researchers are likely to see values surveys as hopelessly simplistic and doing no justice to the complex reality. Since the values surveys approach is thus symptomatic of a wider perspective on good social science, it has borne the brunt of many a critic not sharing this perspective; the idea of cultural dimensions has been vehemently attacked ever since their first appearance. In spite of this, it is still one of the most popular research methods in economics to include culture. Perhaps this only goes to show the importance of cultural differences and the problems they create for cross-cultural communication. Surely, quantifying culture makes more sense from within the quantifying cultures of psychology and economics than in the writing cultures of anthropology and history.

5.4 Conclusion

In this chapter we have discussed the various methodological concerns when incorporating culture in economics. Many of the problems, such as endogeneity of variables, validity issues and sample representativeness, hold for social science and (applied) economics in general, but three main issues stand out when discussing the role of culture: the structure–agency issue, the micro–macro issue and the universality–context specificity issue. With respect to the first we discussed the methodological challenges in aligning structure and agency, as well as the methodical problems related to aggregation and the ecological fallacy. Regarding the latter, we explicitly discussed the need to be aware of the danger of ethnocentrism or a cultural bias when investigating cultural aspects of economic behavior. We return to these two issues in the final chapter, including specific examples of the contemporary applications that we will discuss in the next part of the book. Embedded in a taxonomy of culture research, we also discussed the frequently used methods of comparative survey research. We mentioned the role of databases developed by Hofstede, Schwartz, GLOBE and the World and European Values Surveys containing quantitative data on culture. Having done so, this chapter concludes the first part of the book. Complementary to this first part, in which we extensively discussed historical developments, and theoretical and the associated methodological aspects of culture in economics, the next part of the book contains four applications. We deal with the theoretical and methodological strengths and weaknesses, and the empirical findings of research on entrepreneurial culture, trust, international business and comparative corporate governance.

PART II

Contemporary applications

Introduction to Part II

In the first part of this book we discussed the historical, theoretical and methodological background of the debate about culture in economics. Our main argument was that the history of this debate continues to shape today's research and theory development. By the beginning of the twentieth century, cultural studies and economics had become conceptual opposites. Whereas culture referred to inherited structures inherent to particular collective identities, economics was concerned with the decision-making process of universal, rational individuals.

The implication of this opposition is that researchers seeking to address culture and economics together face a daunting task, both theoretically and methodologically. Cultural studies and economics have fundamentally different ways of looking at social reality. Viewing the world as a multitude of structurally different collectives tends to obscure the agency and rationality that drive behavior. Moreover, it is hard to obtain general insights and principles if every insight is context-specific. However, interpreting social reality as the outcome of a universal rational choice made by individuals ignores the societal diversity and irrationality (in the economic sense) that characterize our world. Introducing culture into the economic model therefore brings the challenge of methodologically aligning the cultural and economic perspectives.

As we summarized in Table 3.1 – reproduced and extended below – this challenge consists of several related key dimensions: (i) exogenous structures vs. rational agents, (ii) collectives vs. individuals and (iii) context-specific insights vs. universal principles. In Chapter 4 we discussed the different ways to include culture in economics. We argued that most scholars take a culture-and-economics approach in which culture is added as an exogenous factor, which highlights the challenge of aligning the cultural and economic perspectives. Alternative

Table 6.1. *Culture and economics in this book*

Part I

Culture is:	Cultural perspective:	Economic perspective:
Inherited and unquestioned	Exogenous structures	Rational agents
Related to collective identity	Collectives	Individuals
Worldviews influencing behavior	Context-specific insights	Universal principles

Translates into →

Part II

	Chapter 6: Entrepreneurial culture	Chapter 7: Trust	Chapter 8: International business	Chapter 9: Comparative corporate governance
Infinite regress	○	●	○	●
Structure agency tension	●	◐	○	○
Multi-level issues	●	●	◐	○
Optimality of culture	●	○	●	●
Cultural bias	◐	◐	◐	●

ways to deal with this tension are also discussed in Chapter 4. Chapter 5 followed up on this by offering a discussion of methodological approaches typically taken in the culture-and-economics approach. We discussed the different values survey approaches, the problem of aggregating individual survey responses, the strengths and weaknesses of comparative experiments and the role of context specificity.

As summarized in Table 6.1, the second part of this book shows how these problems are encountered and dealt with in practice. Chapter 6 discusses the literature about entrepreneurial culture, in which we are confronted with the problem of linking individual attitudes to outcomes at the societal level. This not only yields a multi-level issue but triggers questions on the relation between structure and agency. Chapter 7 focusses on the trust debate, which highlights the tension between exogenous, culturally determined and individual, rational and calculative aspects of trust. In Chapter 8, we deal with the ways in which culture has been addressed in international business. In this chapter, we show how the challenge of dealing with diversity has been addressed in this literature. Chapter 9 discusses the role of culture in corporate governance. In this literature we encounter problems of cultural exogeneity as well as problems related to the "optimality" of culture. In all four chapters the problem of a cultural bias lurks in the background to some extent, most prominently in Chapter 9. The purpose of these chapters is to show that the methodological and conceptual challenges we have identified on the basis of the historical and theoretical discussion in the first part are very much dominating the research about culture and economics in practice.

6 | *Entrepreneurial culture*

6.1 Introduction

The rationale for including a chapter on entrepreneurship can perhaps best be illustrated by the following quote from one of the authors of this book:

"For a couple of years I have been teaching a course on industrial economics that was attended by both continental European students and students from the United States. Every year, when I discussed the economics of entrepreneurship I posed my students the same question, which was: 'Suppose you had to hire someone for your firm, and you had the choice between two individuals who are completely identical except for one aspect: person A had started his own firm, but this venture turned out to be unsuccessful, and he had to close it within a year, and is now looking for a new job, and person B who did not start his own firm. Whom would you hire?' Interestingly enough, I got the same pattern of answers every single year. Whereas the students from the United States would choose person A because he had shown initiative, the European students would pick person B, because person A had clearly failed."

This phenomenon is not unique and has been observed by others. At a more scientific level, Grilo and Thurik (2006) use Eurobarometer survey data for twenty-five EU countries and the US in 2004, and while controlling for individual-level differences, they show that European citizens have a lower preference for self-employment compared with US citizens. If this is indeed true (and there is no reason to question their analysis), this may have major consequences for the rates of entrepreneurship and the dynamics required for an economy to grow. Moreover, it puts a new perspective on the political discussion on fostering entrepreneurship.

Entrepreneurship has been a topical issue for some years now. One reason for the interest in entrepreneurship is that it is seen as an important vehicle to create jobs (Fölster 2000; OECD 1998, 2000) and dynamize the economy through innovative action (Robbins *et al.* 2000). Wennekers and colleagues (Wennekers 2006; Wennekers *et al.* 2005) have found that rates of entrepreneurship differ over time and by country *and* that societies differ in their orientation toward entrepreneurial activity. Whereas some countries score consistently high on indicators of entrepreneurial activity (e.g. the US), others remain in a backward position (Reynolds *et al.* 2002; Freytag and Thurik 2007). A number of authors have suggested that irrespective of the economic and environmental conditions, a society's cultural orientation toward entrepreneurship may play an important role in this respect. "While intertemporal differences can be attributed to economic effects such as per capita income and to technological developments, contemporaneous differences are of a mainly institutional or cultural nature" (Freytag and Thurik 2007: 118). Certain societal values may be conducive to start-up activity and economic dynamism. Not surprisingly, the relatively high levels of entrepreneurship in the US have been related to cultural values such as freedom, independence, achievement, individualism and materialism (Morris *et al.* 1994; Spence 1985).

In this chapter we take issue with this anecdotal evidence on the role of entrepreneurial culture. We focus on the main contributions and sketch their strengths and weaknesses while critically examining their methodological foundations. After a brief discussion of the role of the entrepreneur in economic theory and the way entrepreneurial culture has been addressed, we continue with the author we consider to be the first and most frequently cited in this respect: McClelland (1961) and his often used concept of "need for achievement," also referred to as *N* achievement. Following McClelland's typical approach, we discuss contemporary approaches basically following the same "aggregate psychological trait" route from psychological traits of entrepreneurs to aggregate cultural characteristics, subsequently linking the latter to measures of (national) economic success. We describe these more recent approaches and provide a critical reflection. Implications for the broader discussion on the role of culture in economics are discussed. In doing so, we focus on this interplay between individual characteristics and aggregate outcomes.

6.2 How to theorize on the entrepreneur and entrepreneurial culture

6.2.1 The entrepreneur in economics

The claim that differences in national and regional economic success are related to the presence or lack of an entrepreneurial culture is not new (Hoselitz 1957; Baumol 1968; Leff 1979; Soltow 1968). Despite the generally acknowledged (often implicit) argument that there may be a fundamental relationship between economic development and the presence of an entrepreneurial spirit, there is no well-developed theory on how entrepreneurial culture (however defined) may affect national or regional economic development processes. Several attempts have been made to either formally model the role of the entrepreneur (Lucas 1978; Kihlstrom and Laffont 1979; Schmitz 1989; Jovanovic 1994; Braunerhjelm *et al.* 2009) or provide conceptual frameworks (Leibenstein 1968; Kirzner 1997). Empirical studies either are case based (Saxenian 1994), limiting the scope for generalization, or – in the occasional case of large samples – entrepreneurial culture is "measured" by the residual or a fixed effect (Davidsson 1995; Georgellis and Wall 2000; Guerrero and Serro 1997; Wagner and Sternberg 2002). There are few attempts at actually measuring entrepreneurial culture.

This lack of a sophisticated framework is at least partly caused by the fact that mainstream (neoclassical) economic theory does not leave much room for the role of the entrepreneur (Leibenstein 1968; Baumol 1968, 1993; Kirzner 1997; Casson 2003 [1982]; Licht 2010). According to Leibenstein (1968), the main difficulty of the misfit of the entrepreneur in mainstream (neoclassical) thinking is caused by the conventional theory of the production function, in which the complete set of inputs is specified, known and has a fixed relation to output. In his view, the entrepreneur is someone who extends the production function by broadening the existing set of inputs. This "input-completing capacity" of the entrepreneur implies that the entrepreneur has to employ ill-defined inputs which are vague in their nature and whose output is indeterminate (and the fact that the outcome is unknown and entrepreneurs bear a non-calculable risk is a key issue in Knight's 1921 view). The capacity to reorganize these ill-defined inputs is not uniformly distributed and the ability and willingness for such a risky process of gap-filling and input-completing can be considered a scarce talent. According to Leibenstein, the entrepreneur as a gap-filler and input-completer is the prime mover of the capacity-creation part of the economic growth process (Leibenstein 1968).

Entrepreneurship is associated not only with the formation of new firms but with entrepreneurial action in the sense of starting something new. It is a process that often leads to new business formations, but it may very well include innovative and enterprising behavior inside existing organizations (Cromie 2000). Intrapreneurship or corporate entrepreneurship plays an important role in the process of strategic renewal of existing firms. It can be associated with alertness, finding new product-market combinations and innovation (Wennekers and Thurik 1999). Entrepreneurs are important for the growth of firms since they provide the vision and imagination necessary to carry out opportunistic expansion (Penrose 1959; Casson 2003). Entrepreneurial activity shakes up existing business routines (Schumpeter 1934, 1951). And in the long run, it is expected to positively affect firms' competitiveness (Leibenstein 1968).

6.2.2 Three perspectives on culture

Uhlaner and Thurik (2007) describe three approaches to theorizing on the relation between cultural values and entrepreneurial activity. "Hypotheses on the relationship between cultural indicators and entrepreneurship differ, depending upon whether one chooses to view the relationship from one of the 'pull' perspectives, such as the *aggregated psychological traits* perspective or *social legitimation* perspective, or, by a 'push' perspective such as the *dissatisfaction* perspective" (Uhlaner and Thurik 2007: 165). The aggregated psychological traits perspective seeks to explain rates of entrepreneurship on the basis of an individualistic view of culture. It argues that if there are more people with entrepreneurial values in a country, there will be an increased number of people displaying entrepreneurial behaviors (Davidsson 1995). For example, the Europeans' lower propensity to hire an unsuccessful entrepreneur in the example of US and European students is rooted in a lower valuation of initiative and risk-taking in this perspective. The legitimation perspective explains differences in entrepreneurial activity by societal differences in the social status of entrepreneurs, the attention paid to entrepreneurship in the educational system, and the tax incentives for entrepreneurship. Following this line of reasoning, European students might be less inclined to hire an unsuccessful entrepreneur not because they do not value risk-taking initiative but because they might see entrepreneurial activity as undignified and overtly materialistic, or because they view entrepreneurs as difficult people to work with. Finally, the dissatisfaction perspective explains entrepreneurship as a clash between the population at large and potential entrepreneurs driving the latter group into self-employment. In this perspective, European students' lower estimation of entrepreneurs might be due to an institutional setting in which mainly those who fail to get regular employment become entrepreneurs. Empirical "evidence" for the dissatisfaction hypothesis is mainly indirect, for example by showing that countries that score highly on Hofstede's uncertainty avoidance have lower levels of entrepreneurship (Noorderhaven *et al.* 2004). Although the above theoretical explanations differ, most empirical applications cannot distinguish between these perspectives. In general, though, we can safely say that most approaches relating aspects of culture or something called entrepreneurial culture to economic success seem to follow the aggregate psychological traits perspective.

It is for this reason that we start with a critical discussion of McClelland's work on *N* achievement. We do so not only because he is generally considered the first author who specifically studied and measured entrepreneurial culture but especially because his approach is typical for many contemporary studies, i.e. entrepreneurs have different value systems and any understanding of entrepreneurial culture starts with understanding entrepreneurs. It is mostly in the second stage that economists enter the scene, when entrepreneurial culture is related to aggregate economic outcomes such as growth or levels of entrepreneurship.

6.3 McClelland's seminal study on *N* achievement

The concept of need for achievement, originally developed by Murray in 1938 and popularized by McClelland in 1961 in his seminal work *The Achieving Society*, has been argued to be crucial for economic development (McClelland 1961). As (part of) the critique on his study still holds for contemporary studies on (entrepreneurial) culture and economic growth, we discuss his study extensively. First we describe his core idea of N achievement.

6.3.1 McClelland's approach

McClelland's idea on N achievement was not new. In 1953 Winter-bottom had already pointed to a possible link between achievement motivation and economic development by studying the behavior of mothers when raising their sons. She did so by first interviewing a group of 2–9-year-old boys to obtain N achievement scores and then conducted interviews to determine whether mothers had different attitudes toward raising children. She found that mothers of sons with high N achievement scores had set higher standards for their sons. Similar arguments can be found in Weber's thesis on the Protestant ethic. Despite these early contributions, McClelland is widely seen as the person who coined this idea.

In several earlier works McClelland and colleagues had studied different motives. Motives are relatively stable and enduring personality traits. They did so through responses to standardized picture tests carried out by children and students. *The Achieving Society* extends his early work by applying the idea of N achievement to distant and contemporary societies. In this book McClelland measured N achievement levels for both contemporary and preliterate societies. The method of determining the N achievement level of a preliterate culture relies on the analysis of the content of folk tales widespread in a culture (McClelland 1961: 63–70). Measurement of N achievement in contemporary societies was based on schoolbooks used by second- and fourth-grade children. These are assumed to be "projective" and reflect the motives and values of the culture in the way they are told or in their themes or plots. Since textbooks are widely standardized in most countries, they represent popular culture and not just a social class, according to McClelland.[1]

---

[1] The sample of countries pertained to countries outside the tropics and did not include the very small or inaccessible (at that time) nations such as Kuwait, Liechtenstein or Iceland. This yielded twenty-three countries in 1925 and forty-one countries in the period around 1950. For each country, twenty-one stories were chosen, between 50 and 800 words in length. In order not to reveal the identity of the country, all characters were given similar names (Mary, Jane and Judy for girls, Peter, Bob and John for boys). In countries with more than

Given the information on *N* achievement scores in countries, the hypothesis could be tested that *N* achievement levels in them [the stories] would *predict* subsequent economic growth (McClelland 1961: 71). McClelland correlated *N* achievement with measures of growth in electricity production per capita. He showed that for a sample of twenty-three countries, the 1925 scores on *N* achievement were correlated ($+.53$, $p < .01$) with growth-beyond-expectation during the subsequent twenty-one-year period. Replicating this with national income data yielded a non-significant positive correlation ($+.25$). When averaging both measures he obtained a significant positive correlation ($+.46$, $p < .05$). This finding is the basis for his thesis that countries characterized by high levels of *N* achievement have higher levels of economic development.

6.3.2 Critique on McClelland

Although many scholars (including McClelland himself) were quite critical at the time regarding the potential methodological flaws in his book, *The Achieving Society* was generally regarded as an important step forward in the field of economic psychology and the relation between culture and economic development in general (Cochran 1960; Crockett 1962; Brewster-Smith 1964). As Katona puts it, "future

one linguistic group (for example, Switzerland, India, Pakistan, Canada), McClelland tried to perform the analysis for all subgroups. More than 1,300 stories were collected ($23 \times 21 + 21 \times 41 = 1,344$), mixed together and coded. Examples of stories can be found in the appendix of *The Achieving Society*. Two judges scored the stories for three motivational variables. Their reliability coefficients for samples of thirty stories ranged between .92 and .98, suggesting a high degree of agreement. To get a total score for a country, each achievement-related story was given a score of $+2$, each possibly achievement-related story a score of $+1$ and each unrelated story a score of 0. McClelland's team found that the stories from a given country scored persistently high or low in *N* achievement. The mean *N* achievement scores reflected the sum of achievement characteristics per story for each country divided by the total number of stories ($=21$). The assumption was that "a simple count of the number of such achievement related ideas in stories written under normal testing conditions could be taken to represent the strength of a man's concern with achievement. The count has been called the score for *N* achievement (abbreviation for 'need for achievement')" (McClelland 1961: 43). For the exact procedure we refer to McClelland *et al.* (1953). It should be noted, however, that it is virtually impossible to exactly replicate the scoring system McClelland applied when calculating his *N* achievement story.

studies of economic development cannot disregard what has been presented by McClelland" (Katona 1962: 583). Nevertheless, over time a number of critical remarks have been made (Frey 1984). Not surprisingly, a major point of critique concerns his measurement of *N* achievement and the method applied in relating it to economic success.

Rubin's (1963) critique concentrates on the method of analysis. First, Rubin mentions McClelland's simplicity in trying to come up with one single measure for motivational level (given the diversity of occupational and social groups in society). The motivational level of small but crucial groups may be far more important for economic growth than the motivational level of the entire population. Moreover, according to Rubin, it is too presumptuous to relate something as complex as economic development to a single personality characteristic. Therefore, Rubin questions the rationale for the correlations. He challenges the added value of this for the development of a theory of social change and he feels that the problems of "measurement are 'solved' in an amazingly cavalier manner" (Rubin 1963: 119). This leads Rubin to conclude that *The Achieving Society* is "one of the most fascinating and irritating, one of the most valuable and misleading books I have ever had the pleasure and displeasure of reading" (1963: 118). More specifically, Rubin points to the disturbing method and irritating tone, especially regarding McClelland's underestimations of the achievements of economists (p. 120). In his eyes McClelland claims too much.[2]

Schatz (1965, 1971) criticizes McClelland for being inconsistent in his units of measurement when he uses per capita values of national income and electricity before 1950 but log of total values of electricity for post-1950 growth. Schatz points to a number of arbitrary assumptions, which lead to an overestimated relationship between *N*

---

[2] As an example of this, Potter (1962) cites the following passage from McClelland: "It may come as something of a shock to realize that more could have been learned about the rate of future economic growth of a number of these countries in 1925 or 1950 by reading elementary school books than by studying such presumably more relevant matters as power politics, wars and depressions, economic statistics, or governmental policies governing international trade, taxation or public finance" (McClelland 1961). Potter rightfully questions whether such generalizations are warranted.

achievement and economic development. Moreover, Schatz (1965) questions the causality and the proof for it and argues – similarly to Rubin (1963) – that McClelland's findings are in conflict with what economists know about economic growth. Interestingly, in a reply to Schatz's critique, McClelland (1965) defends his choice for data on the basis of availability and the argument that economists' standard measures of economic development are poor and conceptually inadequate. He challenges the critique of economists by writing that the argument to dismiss his findings is based on the grounds that "it just isn't done that way, my boy!" (McClelland 1965: 245).

Similar comments on the unorthodox measures have been made by Hoselitz (1962), Potter (1962), Weisskopf (1962) and Brewster-Smith (1964). Weisskopf especially criticizes the supposed circular reasoning. He argues that correlational analyses are not suitable for proving both causal interconnections and the correctness of the measurement. Moreover, the underlying theoretical question as to why a high psychological need for achievement in general leads to higher achievement in the economic sphere is never raised or answered. Weisskopf concludes that the evidence for McClelland's thesis seems to be derived from *post hoc ergo propter hoc* (because one thing follows the other, it was caused by the other). Other scholars have questioned non-technical aspects of McClelland's work. Katona (1962) has criticized the role of the larger number of entrepreneurs in a society (B) of which McClelland argues that these form the link between N achievement (A) and economic growth (C). According to Katona (1962), McClelland is much more successful in demonstrating the link between A and C than between either A and B or B and C. Moreover, Katona criticizes McClelland for holding all forms of entrepreneurship in such uncritical esteem.[3] Finally, scholars have taken issue with the limited

---

[3] More recently, in two related papers, Wong *et al.* (2005) and Van Stel *et al.* (2005) take issue with this complexity and hypothesize that the influence of entrepreneurship may differ in developed vs. developing countries. Their argument is that high entrepreneurial activity in developing countries may not necessarily lead to higher economic growth, because it is not reflected in high growth-potential businesses. Entrepreneurship in these countries is motivated by so-called "shopkeeper" or "refugee" arguments. This implies that entrepreneurship is not driven by (expected) opportunities but rather is used as a "last resort" of (self-)employment. This in turn may lead to an insignificant or even negative influence of entrepreneurship on economic growth. In developed

possibilities to develop and promote N achievement (Erasmus 1962; Rubin 1963).

Despite all these comments and even explicit opponents of his thesis, few will be able to deny the power of McClelland's case and none will be able to completely refute the assertion that N achievement may be one of the principal factors in economic growth (Hoselitz 1962). In order to substantiate his thesis, Erasmus demands further empirical testing in order to increase general acceptance (Erasmus 1962).

6.3.3 Empirical tests of McClelland's thesis

Empirical tests of McClelland's thesis do exist. In 1976, Finison related N achievement scores to more recent data than McClelland used. McClelland showed a positive correlation between N achievement (1925) and growth in electricity production (1925–1950). Finison uses more recent data and shows a *zero* correlation between N achievement (1950) and growth in electrical production (1950–1971). Moreover, he finds a *negative* correlation between N achievement (1950) and national income growth (1950–1971). A similar test was performed by Mazur and Rosa in 1977. In addition to correlations, these authors perform regression analysis in which they relate N achievement (1950) to predict national income in 1971 and total energy production in 1971 (Mazur and Rosa 1977). They do control for initial level of income in 1950 or electricity production in 1950. Like Finison (1976), they find a negative relationship between N achievement 1950 and national income growth. Their results do not provide support for McClelland's thesis. Frey (1984) takes issue with the causal link McClelland proposed. Using regression analysis, he showed partial support for the thesis that N achievement is a cause of economic growth and not the result. Frey (1984) also showed that the estimated effect size is relatively small, leading him to conclude that McClelland may have overstated his initial results. A more recent test of McClelland's argument is Gilleard (1989). Using GDP per capita from the World Bank for different periods after the Second World War, Gilleard regressed

countries, however, entrepreneurship is primarily driven by (expected) opportunities in high-growth-potential industries. Accordingly, in these countries entrepreneurship will have a positive influence on economic growth. Both papers present (partial) empirical evidence for this hypothesis.

growth differentials on initial level of GDP per capita and N achievement. For the period 1950–1970 and 1950–1975 he obtained significant results, though negative. For the period 1950–1960 he obtained a negative relationship, though insignificant. The most recent and extensive test of McClelland has been performed by Beugelsdijk and Smeets (2008). Applying standard Barro (1991) growth models, these authors test McClelland's thesis by performing a range of regression analyses. In addition to their own growth model, Beugelsdijk and Smeets (2008) benchmark their results against three major, generally accepted empirical growth studies. These benchmark studies are Mankiw *et al.* (1992), Zak and Knack (2001) and Granato *et al.* (1996). Beugelsdijk and Smeets (2008) find no support for McClelland's main thesis.

In sum, empirical tests of McClelland's hypothesis have so far failed to find support for his original thesis. Most of them report insignificant or weak relationships, some even negative. Most of the theoretical critiques concern the lack of theory and the methodology (both measurement and testing) applied. Interestingly enough, despite the lack of empirical support, contemporary approaches start from the same premise: a concept such as entrepreneurial culture exists and matters; and many of these more recent contributions have embedded their aggregate measure for entrepreneurial culture in micro-level studies of entrepreneurs. Instead of using children's stories, these studies start from a micro-level personality trait analysis.

6.4 Entrepreneurial trait research: unique personality of entrepreneurs

As explained before, the aggregate psychological trait explanation is based on the view that if there are more people with entrepreneurial values in a country, there will be more people displaying entrepreneurial behavior (Uhlaner and Thurik 2007). An entrepreneurial culture is in this case perceived as a collective programming of the mind (Hofstede 2001) in which the underlying value system is oriented toward entrepreneurial behavior and the distinguishing personality traits typically associated with entrepreneurs. In order to "measure" something like entrepreneurial culture, it is therefore necessary to first understand the individual-level characteristics of entrepreneurs.

6.4.1 Entrepreneurial traits

One of the first economists explicitly focussing on entrepreneurship was Joseph Schumpeter (1934). When describing entrepreneurs, Schumpeter noticed that entrepreneurial action requires aptitudes that are present in only a small fraction of the population. Entrepreneurship calls for a specific type of personality and conduct that differ from the rational conduct of economic man. According to Schumpeter, the entrepreneur is a leader, willing to break through ordinary constraints (cf. Leibenstein's input completing capacity). Entrepreneurs are characterized by an autonomous drive to achieve and create for its own sake. When discussing the "psychology of the entrepreneur," Schumpeter argues that "there is the dream and the will to found a private kingdom, usually, though not necessarily, also a dynasty. (. . .) Then there is the will to conquer: the impulse to fight, to prove oneself superior to others, to succeed for the sake, not of the fruits of success, but of success itself. (. . .) Finally, there is the joy of creating, of getting things done, or simply of exercising one's energy and ingenuity" (Schumpeter 1934: 93).

Since Schumpeter's contribution to the field of entrepreneurship, several authors have studied the personality characteristics of entrepreneurs. The field of (economic) psychology has a long history of measuring traits of entrepreneurs (Brockhaus and Horovitz 1986; McClelland 1961; Rotter 1966; Timmons 1978; Davidsson 2004; Shane 2003). Studies at this individual level have focussed on a wide range of issues, such as age, educational profile, professional background and motivations to become self-employed (for a succinct overview, *see* Licht and Siegel 2006).

At least two major methodological challenges arise when studying entrepreneurial traits. First, it is important to distinguish between motivations to become self-employed and the general value pattern of entrepreneurs (a clear distinction must be made between values and motivations). Second, by comparing different motivations to become self-employed in a sample of self-employed, we do not know anything about the difference between self-employed people and those who are not self-employed. Ideally, we would be able to study a panel of potential entrepreneurs and compare those who decided to start their own business with those who decided not to do so. Otherwise we create an endogeneity problem at the individual level because it is unknown whether the entrepreneur's value pattern was influenced by his decision to become self-employed. How does his personality look *ex ante* and *ex post* the decision to start his own firm? Despite these methodological challenges, a relatively small but focussed literature on entrepreneurial trait research exists in economic and social psychology. Reviewing this literature on entrepreneurial trait research, a range of specific personality characteristics of entrepreneurs emerges. Central to the trait research is the notion that entrepreneurs are different.

As discussed earlier, McClelland (1961) showed that entrepreneurial behavior can be associated with personality characteristics such as a high need for achievement, moderate risk-taking propensity, preference for energetic and/or novel activity, and the tendency to assume personal responsibility for successes or failure. Brandstätter (1997) studied Austrian entrepreneurs and found risk-taking, extraversion, social recognition and readiness for change to be distinguishing characteristics which entrepreneurs displayed more than the general Austrian population. In a comparison of managers and entrepreneurs, Fagenson (1993) found that these groups had different value systems. In contrast to managers, entrepreneurs want to be free to achieve and to actualize their potential. Brockhaus (1982) identifies three attributes consistently associated with entrepreneurial behavior: need for achievement, internal locus of control and a risk-taking propensity. Thomas and Mueller (2000) find similar personality characteristics. Sexton and Bowman (1985) conclude that entrepreneurs need autonomy, independence and dominance. Chell *et al.* (1991) associate entrepreneurs with traits such as opportunistic, innovative, creative, imaginative, restless and proactive, and perceive them as agents of change. Comparing Canadian entrepreneurs with senior managers who decided not to start ventures, Amit *et al.* (2001) found that wealth attainment was significantly less important compared with issues such as power, vision, leadership and independence.

In an attempt to summarize the personality trait literature, Cromie (2000) concludes there are (at least) seven characteristics distinguishing entrepreneurs or business owners from non-entrepreneurs. Although the differences are not equally strong for *all* groups of non-entrepreneurs (e.g. he found that managers or university professors score equally highly on some of the seven dimensions), he lists the following seven. First, he mentions "need for achievement" (cf. McClelland 1961). This reflects a person's need to strive hard to attain success. According to Cromie, "high achievers set demanding targets for themselves and are proactive and bold in setting about accomplishing objectives" (Cromie 2000: 16). Second, he mentions locus of control (cf. Rotter 1966; Brockhaus 1982). The concept of locus of control refers to the perceived control over events. Internal locus of control implies the individual's belief that they have influence over outcomes through ability, effort or skills. At the other end of the spectrum, external locus of control means the individual believes that forces outside their control determine the outcome. Obviously, individuals with an internal locus of control are more likely to be entrepreneurs. The third aspect Cromie (2000) mentions is risk-taking. Despite the complexity of the concept of risk, entrepreneurs are generally considered to have a greater propensity to take risks. Fourth, Cromie mentions creativity. Enterprising individuals develop new ideas, spot market opportunities and recombine existing inputs in order to create added value (cf. Leibenstein 1968). Finally, he mentions need for autonomy, tolerance for ambiguity, and self-confidence (*see also* Blanchflower and Oswald 1998; Blanchflower *et al.* 2001). Need for autonomy refers to the ability and will to be self-directed in the pursuit of opportunities (Lumpkin and Dess 1996). Tolerance for ambiguity is related to the uncertainty inherent in entrepreneurial action. Entrepreneurs are associated with the ability to deal effectively with situations or information that is vague, incomplete, unstructured, uncertain or unclear, without experiencing psychological discomfort (Scheré 1982). Self-confidence, finally, is related to self-efficacy (Chen *et al.* 1998), which can be defined as an individual's cognitive estimate of their "capabilities" to mobilize the motivation, cognitive resources and courses of action needed to exercise control over events in their lives (Wood and Bandura 1989).

Obviously, personal attributes are important but not all-pervading determinants of behavior (Cromie 2000: 25). The economic environment, family background, employment history, organizational experiences, social networks, national culture and personality traits all affect the probability that someone will act entrepreneurially (Rauch and Frese 2000). McGrath *et al.* (1992) have pushed trait research even further by investigating whether this supposed set of entrepreneurial characteristics transcends cultures. In other words, do entrepreneurs have a predictable set of values different to those of non-entrepreneurs regardless of the home culture? To answer this question, McGrath *et al.* (1992) and McGrath and MacMillan (1992) use Hofstede's four-dimensional cultural framework to compare the value orientation of non-entrepreneurs and business owners in a sample of eight, respectively nine countries. They find that entrepreneurs have a persistent and characteristic value orientation, irrespective of the values of their national culture.

6.4.2 From individual traits to national culture

Based on the assumption and empirical support for the thesis that entrepreneurs have different value patterns than non-entrepreneurs, scholars have subsequently argued that societies characterized by such values can be expected to experience higher rates of entrepreneurship and economic growth. In a way, this coincides with Leibenstein's view, in which the set of individuals with gap-filling and input-completing capacities is exogenous and the personality characteristics of these entrepreneurs are important. In a similar vein, the Austrian School has argued that it is this relatively scarce willingness to take risks that allows an economy to develop and grow (Kirzner 1997; Rosen 1997; Yeager 1997). Hence, following the aggregate psychological trait perspective, if more people possess these entrepreneurial traits, it can logically be argued that this results in increased economic dynamism and economic growth in the end (Davidsson 1995; Uhlaner and Thurik 2007). In other words, entrepreneurship, innovation and economic growth are logically linked through the recognition and exploitation of opportunities in economic and social arenas (Drucker 1985; Schumpeter 1951). Despite the intuitive attractiveness of Leibenstein's concept of the entrepreneur and the Austrian School, their abstract concepts of the entrepreneurial process only indirectly allow for theorizing on the relationship between entrepreneurial culture and economic growth.

With the exception of the Achievement Motivation Index developed by McClelland (1961), the "favorable attitude" index developed by Morris and Adelman (1988) and Lynn's (1991) analysis of the entrepreneurial orientation of students in forty-one countries, to our knowledge there have been no large-scale empirical attempts to actually measure entrepreneurial culture and relate it to economic development. Although most recently several scholars have provided valuable insights regarding the relationships between entry and exit rates, new business formation and regional economic growth (Audretsch and Keilbach 2004; Fritsch 2004), only few initiatives exist that focus on the role of entrepreneurial *culture* specifically (Akçomak and Ter Weel 2009; Suddle *et al.* 2006, 2010; Beugelsdijk 2007). It remains to be seen whether these recent, relatively small-scale attempts to operationalize entrepreneurial culture will be picked up.

Moreover, and perhaps complicating matters even more, in order to measure a concept such as entrepreneurial culture, one has to combine different strands of literature in the field of entrepreneurship, thereby crossing disciplinary boundaries (Acs and Audretsch 2003). The field of entrepreneurship is scattered across different paradigms (Stevenson and Jarillo 1990; Suarez-Villa 1989). Economists are mainly concerned with the effects of entrepreneurship, while social psychologists are more interested in the origins of entrepreneurship. Measuring entrepreneurial culture requires one to incorporate insights from the social psychological literature, more specifically entrepreneurial trait research (McClelland 1961; Rotter 1966; Brockhaus 1982; Cromie 2000; McGrath *et al.* 1992). And in order to assess its economic significance, one has to relate to the empirical economic growth literature (Barro 1991; Mankiw *et al.* 1992; Barro and Sala-I-Martin 1995).

This lack of a well-developed unified framework has not stopped scholars from developing and/or testing hypotheses on the relationship between entrepreneurial culture and economic success. A number of authors have argued that entrepreneurial culture may affect certain aspects of economic performance, such as innovation (Shane 1993) or economic growth in general (McClelland 1961; Freeman 1976; Suarez-Villa 1989; Lynn 1991). Without specifying the causality – for example, via the production function (Leibenstein 1968) – the core idea is that entrepreneurial culture is beneficial for economic performance. The positive effect of entrepreneurial culture on economic growth has been argued to be caused by the mediating effect of entrepreneurship (Wennekers and Thurik 1999). Building on various perspectives such as macro-economic growth theory, historical views on entrepreneurship, industrial economics (mainly Porter's view) and evolutionary economics, Wennekers and Thurik synthesize these insights to provide a broad picture of how economic growth is linked to entrepreneurship. In their view, entrepreneurship is a behavioral characteristic. Therefore, "linking entrepreneurship to economic growth means linking the individual level to the aggregate level" (Wennekers and Thurik 1999: 46). And this view on entrepreneurship as a mediator between culture and growth corresponds with the aggregate psychological traits perspective.

6.5 Economic Consequences of Entrepreneurial Culture

6.5.1 Entrepreneurial culture and economic growth

In their seminal work on comparative patterns of economic development between 1850 and 1914, Morris and Adelman (1988) develop a measure reflecting the "favorableness of attitudes toward entrepreneurship." Their classification scheme has six classes, where the top category A contains countries where non-elite businessmen could achieve social recognition in their lifetimes through mercantile or industrial successes. The bottom category F contains those countries where social recognition of capitalist entrepreneurship by the established social elite was not common. Countries in category A are, for example, Australia, Sweden, Switzerland and the United States, whereas countries such as Egypt, India, China and Spain can be found in category F (*see* appendix of their book, pp. 424–426). The classification of countries was based on informed judgements concerning the attitude of established social elites toward entrepreneurial success. Morris and Adelman (1988) were able to develop such a measure for a broad range of countries for the period 1850–1890. Using principal components analysis on this measure and a range of other variables associated with the process of economic development, they show that this measure correlates well with a range of other aspects of economic development, but for different groups of countries in different ways. This would suggest that different growth paths exist and that entrepreneurial culture plays a different role in these various patterns of economic development.

Despite the conceptual attractiveness of these claims relating (aspects of) an entrepreneurial culture to economic growth and development, empirical evidence is limited. Thirty years after McClelland's seminal work, Lynn (1991) made a similar attempt by scoring the value systems of students in forty-one countries and combining these into one national indicator of entrepreneurial attitude. Lynn compares the four psychological theories of economic growth (Weber's work ethic,

Schumpeter's competitiveness, McClelland's achievement motivation and Wiener's status of the land owner[4]) and finds that differences in attitudes toward competitiveness best explain variation in economic growth rates across societies. Competitiveness can be defined as the drive to win against others and to obtain some form of dominance over them through winning. This drive was identified by Schumpeter as one of the major motivations of the entrepreneur (Lynn 1991). Again, though, just like McClelland, Lynn does not use economic models to test for alternative explanations; his finding that a society's orientation toward competitiveness is related to economic growth rates is interesting. More recently, Granato *et al.* (1996) used the World Values Survey to develop an achievement motivation indicator and to relate this to economic growth. Their measure is based on four questions on people's opinion regarding the importance of thrift, determination, obedience and faith as four qualities which children can be taught at home. Granato *et al.*'s achievement motivation index is then calculated as the percentage of respondents emphasizing thrift and determination as important qualities, minus the percentage emphasizing obedience and faith. Although their analysis is embedded in a modern economic growth framework, reinterpretations suggest their main finding on the positive role of an entrepreneurial culture for economic growth is based on weak measures and omitted variables (Beugelsdijk and Smeets 2008).

A more advanced empirical approach can be found in Beugelsdijk (2007). His empirical approach consists of several steps. First, he constructs a micro-based measure of entrepreneurial culture by comparing the value pattern of entrepreneurs and non-entrepreneurs. Based on the distinctive pattern of entrepreneurs at this individual level, the average score of a population on these entrepreneurial characteristics is calculated. As his analysis is based on the EVS dataset which is available only for Europe, Beugelsdijk (2007) subsequently calculates the "entrepreneurial culture" score for fifty-four European regions. He relates this micro-embedded measure of entrepreneurial culture to regional innovation patterns (using patent data) and economic growth.

---

[4] Wiener's (1981) thesis is that anti-industrial values account for the explanation of the British relative industrial decline after 1850. The argument regarding land ownership is that it affects businessmen by making them indifferent, indolent and unenterprising individuals.

He finds that entrepreneurial culture affects the number of patents developed in a region and that the effect of entrepreneurial culture on regional economic growth is mainly indirect, i.e. through increased innovativeness.

This supposed indirect link of entrepreneurial culture on growth through innovation brings us back to the second important stream of literature in this area. A society characterized by an entrepreneurial culture may lead to higher levels of entrepreneurship (Suddle *et al.* 2006), subsequently triggering a process of economic dynamism and resulting in economic growth (Carree and Thurik 2003).

6.5.2 Entrepreneurial culture and entrepreneurship

Instead of relating entrepreneurial culture directly to economic growth, a limited number of authors have related societal values to indicators of entrepreneurship. Wennekers and Thurik (1999) single out two major roles for entrepreneurship in relation to economic growth. The first has to do with the start-up rate of new firms. In the second case they think of enterprising individuals (including so-called intrapreneurs or corporate entrepreneurs), who undertake entrepreneurial action without necessarily founding a new firm. Empirical studies linking measures of entrepreneurial culture to entrepreneurship have mostly focussed on the first, i.e. start-up rates.

In an empirical analysis of the effects of regional characteristics on new firm formation in Finland, Kangasharju (2000) introduces the concept of "entrepreneurial ability" in explaining the probability of firm formation. A regional analysis of entrepreneurship in Sweden showed that regional rates of new firm formation depend partly on entrepreneurial values (Davidsson 1995). Georgellis and Wall's (2000) study of rates of self-employed across British regions suggests that the "entrepreneurial human capital" of a region is an important explanatory factor. More recent research on Florida's idea of creative classes suggests a positive link exists between the regional existence of creative classes and firm formation rates (Florida 2002; Lee *et al.* 2004). Entrepreneurial culture is included in these studies as some kind of region-specific fixed effect (Guerrero and Serro 1997; Wagner and Sternberg 2002). The link between entrepreneurial values and aggregate economic outcomes is an indirect one. One obvious method for going beyond such fixed-effects approaches is to use existing values surveys and relate the cultural dimensions as developed in these surveys to measures of entrepreneurship.

Hofstede's (2001) seminal work on culture's consequences triggered a number of studies relating his four cultural dimensions to entrepreneurship and entrepreneurial activity. In addition to the studies mentioned earlier by McGrath and colleagues, Shane (1992) has developed a theoretical framework and tested the relationship between national cultures and rates of innovation (Shane 1993). Morris *et al.* (1994) relate one of Hofstede's dimensions – individualism/ collectivism – to corporate entrepreneurship. They focus on individualism as it has been linked to the willingness of people to violate norms and their level of achievement motivation (Hofstede 2001), both of which are associated with entrepreneurship. They show that entrepreneurship declines the more collectivism is emphasized (Morris *et al.* 1994). Though it was also found that dysfunctional (high) levels of individualism exist, this result suggests that in cultures in which group thinking may outweigh individual initiative, few individuals would put their (perhaps latent) entrepreneurial ambitions into action. Despite their conceptual attractiveness and availability for a large number of countries, the Hofstede dimensions reflect general cultural characteristics and have not been developed to score and rank societies in terms of their (lack of) entrepreneurial culture, as, for example, McClelland's index has.

Taking this criticism as a starting point, Wennekers *et al.* (2005) and Suddle *et al.* (2010) have tested a model in which they explain levels of entrepreneurship in a sample of thirty-three countries by a composite indicator of entrepreneurial culture of which the underlying items relate to core concepts of entrepreneurial trait research. According to Suddle *et al.* (2006), advantages of this approach over the existing literature are the facts that their measure is a) not a general cultural indicator (like the Hofstede individualism dimension) but relates specifically to entrepreneurial culture, and b) it is embedded in micro insights of literature on entrepreneurial trait research. Using the 1999 WVS, Suddle *et al.* (2010) operationalize entrepreneurial culture by a composite factor consisting of three underlying indicators derived from this WVS database. The three questions used to calculate the composite measure are based on the fraction of respondents providing the following answers to three questions: i) Question: Which aspects of a job do you think are important? Answer: An opportunity to use initiative; ii) Question: Which aspects of a job do you think are important? Answer: A job in which you can achieve something; and iii) Question: Why are there people in this country who live in need? Answer: Because of laziness and lack of willpower. The national scores reflect the percentage of respondents answering the indicated categories on these questions. As these underlying variables relate to "initiative," "achieving" and "personal influence," which are key constructs in trait research, Suddle *et al.* (2006, 2010) claim that they have a strong theoretical base. "Initiative" corresponds with one of the key meanings of entrepreneurship, namely "to take in hand" (Wennekers 2006). "Achieving" is another relevant variable, as many studies have researched the cultural dimension of entrepreneurship, most notably McClelland (1961). Finally, "personal influence" represents the internal locus of control (Rotter 1966). Applying principal components analysis yields one variable representing entrepreneurial culture. To corroborate their measure and findings, Suddle *et al.* (2010) also use alternative existing indicators of entrepreneurial culture, such as McClelland's *N* achievement index, Lynn's attitude scores, Granato *et al.*'s achievement motivation index and the performance-orientation measure of the GLOBE database (*see* Chapter 5).

Using nascent entrepreneurship from the Global Entrepreneurship Monitor as an indicator of entrepreneurial activity, Suddle *et al.* (2010) test the hypothesis that entrepreneurial culture positively affects nascent entrepreneurship based on the above set of alternative indicators. Controlling for a range of variables, among them level of economic development, tax level, social security system and demographic characteristics, they find that except for the composite measure of entrepreneurial culture based on the three WVS items, the other four indices are not significantly related to nascent entrepreneurship. In fact, Granato *et al.*'s achievement motivation index (1996) is even significantly negative.

Parallel to these economic approaches linking proxies for entrepreneurial culture to rates of entrepreneurship, there is a stream of research trying to understand the decision to start one's own venture from a social cognition perspective and attempts to relate that to cross-national differences in start-up rates. For example, based on the conceptual framework by Busenitz and Lau (1996), in which social, cultural and personal variables are related to cognition and cognition to outcomes such as the venture creation decision, Mitchell *et al.*

(2000) build and test a cross-cultural model of venture creation. In their study, they carefully collected information on 753 individuals from seven countries that either decided to start a venture or decided not to do so. Comparing these two groups, Mitchell *et al.* find that some of the individual-level drivers of the decision to create a venture are moderated by cultural values, specifically in Hofstede's individualism or power-distance index. This complements the studies by McGrath and colleagues, referred to earlier, in which it was shown that entrepreneurial traits transcend cultures. In fact, it suggests that although the entrepreneurial traits are culture-independent, the decision to create a new venture depends on a range of individual factors, of which some are moderated by cultural characteristics. These types of approaches, in which individual- and nation-(including culture-)level factors driving the decision to become an entrepreneur are simultaneously taken into account, seem to be gaining ground. Recent studies by Grilo and Thurik (2006) and Thurik and Grilo (2007), for example, study individuals and include country-specific effects by dummies. As a next step (e.g. Freytag and Thurik 2007) their goal is to explain these "individual-level corrected country dummies" by regressing them on a range of cultural and institutional variables. Although such a multi-level approach looks promising, it has not resulted in many publications yet, although it seems to be a positive path for the near future.

In sum, despite the lack of strong empirical evidence, entrepreneurial culture is argued to influence economic growth in several ways. First, value patterns conducive to entrepreneurship may increase the start-up rate of new firms. Second, culture may positively affect intrapreneurial activities that subsequently yield efficiency advantages within existing firms. Hence, "wherever entrepreneurial employees reap the benefits of their abilities, within the firm or in a spin-off, their activities are likely to enhance growth at a macro-level" (Wennekers and Thurik 1999: 45). Despite the conceptual attractiveness of this type of reasoning, there is no robust empirical evidence (yet) supporting the thesis that entrepreneurial cultures explain national or regional differences in rates of entrepreneurship, nor is there strong evidence of a fundamental empirical relationship between entrepreneurial culture and economic growth. Part of the explanation for these mixed findings is related to the complex relationship between entrepreneurial activity as such and economic growth. Another reason is the fact that linking entrepreneurship and economic success implies linking the individual level and the collective level, which poses a major methodological challenge.

6.6 Discussion: linking the individual and the collective

Scholars trying to explain differences in economic growth or rates of entrepreneurship by referring to the lack or presence of a so-called entrepreneurial culture are on slippery ground. As we have described in this chapter, the field is scattered with conceptual, methodological and methodical problems. Given the misfit of the entrepreneur in economic theory, there is no well-developed, overarching theoretical framework to analyze the antecedents and consequences of an entrepreneurial culture. However, just pointing to the position of the entrepreneur in economic theory in general does not solve the problem. We think there are at least four general issues when studying entrepreneurial culture.

First, as we will discuss in more detail in the next chapter on trust, severe methodological problems may arise in multi-level settings in which individual-level phenomena are nested in higher-level phenomena. In the case of entrepreneurship, the entrepreneurial culture literature is clearly embedded in the aggregate psychological trait perspective. On the basis of individual-level trait analysis, researchers have come up with a range of individual personality characteristics of entrepreneurs. In their analyses of an entrepreneurial culture, many scholars have aggregated these individual characteristics to reflect a nation-level characteristic. The methodological question arises as to whether the aggregation of individual-level characteristics is indeed equal to the grand total. In other words, is the sum of the items similar to the aggregate, i.e. is culture really the sum of the personality characteristics? Or is this a way of redefining structure as agency?

Moreover, the motivational level of small but crucial groups may be far more important for future economic growth than the motivational level of the entire population. In other words, for some phenomena of interest (and entrepreneurship is one of these), it is not so much the value pattern of society at large but of certain subgroups. As far as we know, it is only Morris and Adelman (1988) who have taken this into account by measuring the attitude of the established social elite toward entrepreneurial success. The role of power relations is an area worth further scrutiny. In addition to the question as to whether it is allowed to simply aggregate individuals, there is the question that has to do with the issue of who to include in the aggregation procedure.

Second, the question arises as to whether we need to distinguish between a theory of general dimensions of (national) cultures and a theory based on a specific concept that can be labeled entrepreneurial culture. This is of great importance for the hypotheses developed and the methodology applied to test these hypotheses. In the first case, the nature of the argument would be something along the lines of Hofstede's cultural consequences; cultures can be measured and mapped on a multidimensional scale and some of the dimensions can affect rates of entrepreneurship. In case one opts for an entrepreneurial culture concept, the assumption is that a universal (culture-independent) concept exists and that societies can be ranked on this single index. This is the typical approach taken by McClelland and scholars following the aggregate psychological trait perspective. It does not so much assume that general cultural characteristics can be related to rates of entrepreneurship or growth, but it starts from the premise that a new measure can and needs to be developed that defines the extent to which a society is characterized by entrepreneurial values, however defined. The choice between a single entrepreneurial culture measure or general cultural dimensions is a fundamental one, and at minimum the choice between the two approaches should lead to different research questions. In a way, the choice also boils down to a difference between an inductive approach, in which empirical dimensions of culture have been established, and a deductive approach, in which the starting point is a theoretical concept "entrepreneurial culture." The problem of the latter approach is that those definitions of entrepreneurial culture that are directly derived theoretically from entrepreneurship are definitions that border on the propensity to engage in entrepreneurial activity. For example, entrepreneurial activities are risky and achievement oriented, so risk preference and achievement orientation are (part of) entrepreneurial culture. Research arguing that the higher scores of such entrepreneurial cultures are associated with higher rates of entrepreneurship runs the risk of developing and testing a tautological argument.

The cultural-dimensions approach is not risk-free either. The route to regress a number of general cultural characteristics (e.g. Hofstede's dimensions) on start-up ratios or growth seems too easy and theoretically superficial. Any relationship between culture and any other outcome variable can be "tested." But is this really theoretically challenging? At the minimum we would suggest taking a multi-level perspective by theorizing and testing the cross-level interactions between individual-level drivers of the choice to become self-employed and the way someone's cultural heritage affects these individual drivers. There is still substantial room for theoretical advancement given the current lack of a well-developed framework.

Third, methodical problems exist. Empirical tests are fraught with difficulties such as endogeneity, omitted variable bias and other measurement and validity issues. Moreover, it is difficult to compare and understand the empirical results because (almost) none of the indicators used is similar and no convergence in terms of how to measure entrepreneurial culture can be observed or expected in the short run. This makes it very difficult, if not impossible, to generate a stock of knowledge on the basis of which converging insights emerge.

Finally, so far we have discussed the role of (entrepreneurial) culture in a rather exclusionary way, as if culture can be separated from all other factors affecting rates of entrepreneurship and economic success, most notably institutions. But theory can be improved if we include the broader role of institutions, especially because formal institutions are of great importance for understanding entrepreneurship. An example of such a broader approach could be Kostova's (1997) three-dimensional country institutional profile. This framework can be used to study and explain how a country's government policies (constituting a regulatory component), widely shared social knowledge (the cognitive component) and value systems (the normative component) affect domestic business activity. However, as Kostova (1997) argued herself, these institutional profiles lose meaning if they are generalized across a broad range of issues and they must be measured with regard to specific domains. Kostova (1997) focuses on the institutional factors, which is attractive because in understanding the country-level differences in entrepreneurship, such an institutional explanation still seems to be a promising part of the unexplained variance in cross-national start-up rates. Moreover, institutions and cultural characteristics co-develop and formal legal rules and regulations regarding the setting up of your own business are closely related to a country's belief system.

At the start of this chapter we referred to the anecdote on students from the United States and Europe regarding their personnel hiring preferences. Having discussed so much material regarding the role of culture and its effect on entrepreneurship and economic growth, we do feel that we have de-mystified part of this real-world phenomenon. But much more work needs to be done. In doing so, we think a multi-level approach is a suitable and promising method to explore how culture affects the decision to start a venture and how culture affects the individual-level drivers of this decision. Given that (i) entrepreneurial trait research has shown that entrepreneurs are different from non-entrepreneurs, irrespective of the cultural characteristics in which these individuals operate, and (ii) that some of the individual-level factors affecting the choice to become self-employed are moderated by certain cultural dimensions, the challenge is not so much to explain or show that culture matters but to push the research frontier by understanding which cultural dimensions matter when and how by specifically linking the individual and aggregate level of analyses.

7 | Trust

7.1 Introduction

An important part of the current discussion on the relationship between culture and economic development is embodied in the concept of social capital, of which trust is seen as one of its most important dimensions (Fukuyama 1995; Zak and Knack 2001; François 2002; Uslaner 2002). This is reflected in the definition of social capital. It relates to the willingness of citizens to trust others, including members of their family, fellow citizens and people in general (Whiteley 2000: 450). Social capital is the study of network-based processes that generate beneficial outcomes through norms of trust (Durlauf and Fafchamps 2004). The importance of social capital and trust for the debate on culture and economic development is not to be underestimated. According to Guiso *et al.* (2006: 29), the opening through which culture entered the economic discourse was the concept of trust. This was reflected in two consecutive presidential lectures at the yearly meeting of the European Economic Association by Tabellini (2007a) and Fehr (2008). Using the culture label, they both discussed the importance of trust for economic interaction. Trust was also a topic in the 2009 presidential lecture at the American Economic Association by Dixit (2009), which dealt with formal and informal governance institutions. Given this interest in trust and the perception of many economists that trust proxies for culture, we devote this chapter to it. Our ambition is not to provide a state-of-the-art overview of the trust literature – something that is impossible to achieve in just one chapter – but to critically evaluate "the position of trust" in the broader debate on culture and economics. We do not attempt to categorize all existing theories on trust, or provide a new theoretical framework. What this chapter seeks to do is to address the main issues we think are necessary to properly understand why trust has emerged in the context of the debate on the role of culture in economics, and to show what we can learn from this.

This chapter is structured as follows. In the next section we define trust and show why and how trust and culture are related. In Section 7.3 we take a closer look at the sources of trust, after which we turn to studies on the economic effects of trust (Section 7.4). Because culture relates to aggregate entities such as nation-states or regions, the vast majority of empirical studies on trust concerns macro studies. To operationalize trust at this level, many scholars have used the trust question as found in the World or European Values Survey. We discuss not only the results of these empirical studies, but also relevant methodological aspects (Section 7.5). Based on our evaluation in Section 7.6, we conclude that studies of trust have yielded new and important insights, but major identification problems exist concerning the effects of trust, culture and institutions, and their interrelationship. Specifically, some of the antecedents and consequences of trust frequently coincide, complicating matters considerably. Based on our evaluation of the culture–trust literature, we come up with a number of suggestions on how to proceed in the field of trust and what this means for our study of culture.

7.2 Trust as a proxy for culture

The literature on trust is extensive. To cope with this, as a starting point we need to distinguish between levels of trust, the scope of trust and the sources of trust. What we call the level of trust refers to the level of measurement. Are we looking at trust among individuals or at trust within society in total? The scope of trust refers to the question of who is trusted: are people inclined to trust society in general, or only a small circle of familiar individuals? With regard to the sources of trust, we can distinguish between trust stemming from general norms and inclinations present in a particular society and trust as the product of bounded rational decision-making.[1] In all three aspects of trust, we can see a micro–macro distinction. With regard to levels, we can measure

---

[1] This is not to say that following certain societal norms is irrational. In fact, most theoretical models start from this assumption. The point is that sources may stem from (non-calculative) norms and values (which may have been developed themselves in a rational evolutionary process) and from a calculative decision-making process.

trust at the micro- or the macro-level. With regard to scope, a person's trust can cover the micro- or the macro-level. Finally, trust can stem from micro- or macro-sources. Where the literature speaks of trust, this can therefore mean several things, often depending on the specific scholarly background of the researcher. The distinction between micro- and macro-scope of trust is made by many scholars from different backgrounds (Luhmann 1979; Misztal 1996; Rousseau *et al.* 1998; Putnam 2000; Paxton 1999); Luhmann's (1979) distinction is shared by many. According to Luhmann, the micro-level is based on the emotional bond between individuals, which is more characteristic of primary and small group relationships. The macro-level concerns more abstract relationships where trust is related to the functioning of bureaucratic systems (e.g. legal, political and economic). Paxton (1999) distinguishes between concrete and abstract trust (a perception of the trustworthiness of the "average" person). She claims that "while trust in specific others may be important at more micro-levels of social capital, generalized trust is the important feature of national-level social capital" (Paxton 1999: 99).

7.2.1 Typologies and sources of trust

Trust is often defined as a property of individuals or characteristic of interpersonal relationships and is mostly seen as the perception and interpretation of the other's expected dependability. Trust refers to the confidence that a partner will not exploit the vulnerabilities of the other (Barney and Hansen 1995). As Zaheer *et al.* (1998) summarize, the concept of trust may be framed as an expectation of a partner's reliability with regard to their obligations, predictability of behavior and fairness in actions and negotiations while faced with the possibility to behave opportunistically. Hence, trust has to do with signaling that the actor will not play one-shot games and behave opportunistically (Ben-Ner and Putterman 2009; Puranem and Vanneste 2009).[2]

Notwithstanding this general notion of trust, numerous typologies of trust have been developed. This is a reflection of both the

---

[2] Despite this crucial role of opportunistic behavior, it is only recently that management scholars have specifically addressed the question of how to *repair* trust in cases of opportunistic behavior (*see* Gillespie and Dietz 2009; Kim *et al.* 2009; Tomlinson and Mayer 2009; Ren and Gray 2009).

richness of the concept and the lack of convergence (McKnight *et al.* 1998; Rousseau *et al.* 1998). One of the most commonly accepted typologies of trust is calculus-based trust, knowledge-based trust and identification-based trust (Lewicki and Bunker 1996). Calculus-based trust has to do with the fear for the consequences of not doing what one promised or said they would do. Rational arguments drive the choice for individuals to trust or not (Coleman 1990; McKnight *et al.* 1998). Knowledge-based trust is grounded in the predictability of the other's behavior, either experience-based or established through reputation. Identification-based trust is based on the perceived similarity between partners yielding empathy and trust.[3] Nooteboom (2002) distinguishes between rational reasons and psychological causes. Reasons arise from a rational evaluation of the trustee's trustworthiness. This can be based on knowledge of the trustee inferred from reputation, records, norms and standards, or from one's own experience. A psychological cause is empathy. This is the ability to share another person's feelings and emotions as if they were one's own, thereby understanding the motives of the other's actions. Empathy affects both one's trustworthiness, in the willingness to make sacrifices for others, and one's trust, in the tolerance of behavior that deviates from expectations. Since one can identify with the other, one may sympathize with their actions, seeing perhaps that these actions were in fact a just response to one's own previous actions (Nooteboom 2002: 81).

This combination of calculative (rational) and psychological aspects of trust may help us understand why many economists use the concept of trust as a vehicle to discuss the role of culture. Trust as explained above is compatible with the notion of calculativeness and rationality as commonly applied in (micro) economic (game) theory. Using trust as a proxy for culture therefore provides the opportunity to discuss and theorize upon the micro-foundations of culture. But trust also contains the notion of a shared identity that lifts the role and meaning of trust beyond the level of the individual. It is this – in Nooteboom's terminology – empathic aspect that partly explains the non-calculative behavior observed in games. Because – as we have described in previous

---

[3] In addition to this classification, many more types of trust can be found in the literature, e.g. deterrence-based, knowledge-based and identification-based, fragile trust vs. resilient trust, cognition-based vs. affect-based trust, goodwill trust and competence trust (Das and Teng 2001). The adjectives used refer to the source of trust.

chapters – culture has often been interpreted in terms of the irrational residual explanation of economic behavior, it is not surprising to observe that trust is often presented and used to study culture (e.g. as used by Tabellini and Fehr in their agenda-setting presidential lectures referred to in the introduction of this chapter). Hence, the very nature of trust, and its micro-foundations, make it indeed an attractive candidate to proxy for culture.

7.2.2 Scope of trust: from micro to macro

As discussed in previous chapters, culture is a societal characteristic of aggregate entities such as nation-states or regions. Trust may be an attractive and logical proxy for culture because of the possibilities it generates to develop theory that is based on micro-foundations. But in order to relate trust (and hence culture) to macro-economic outcomes, inevitably one must shift the theoretical lens from the individual micro-level to the societal macro-level.[4] Because culture is a societal or macro-phenomenon by definition, the macro-level is where the core of the trust–culture–economic performance reasoning can be found. Although earlier studies exist, this started off with Putnam *et al.*'s (1993) study of Italian regions (Fine 2001). In his study on northern and southern Italian regions, Putnam (1993) argues that the critical factor in explaining effectiveness of regional governments and economic performance in Italy is to be found in regional differences in social structure. Putnam argues that in regions where social relationships are more horizontal, based on trust and shared values, social capital is higher and the regional economies are more efficient. Although the discussion of trust in the context of regional economic performance forms only one chapter of Putnam's book, it triggered an impressive number of follow-up studies trying to relate trust, and more broadly

---

[4] This multi-level challenge also pertains to the risk of ecological fallacies, in which global phenomena or data aggregates that are actual representations of lower-level phenomena cannot be generalized to those lower levels (Robinson 1950). The ecological fallacy consists in inappropriately inferring an individual-level behavioral relationship from an analysis of aggregate-level data: if countries with more Protestants tend to have higher suicide rates, then Protestants must be more likely to commit suicide (Freedman 2001). In other words, ecological correlations are unreliable indicators of individual correlations, which makes it difficult to draw individual-level inferences from aggregate data (Hofstede 2001).

social capital, to regional or national economic performance (more on that later).

Theoretically, this step from the micro- to the macro-level is challenging. One way to deal with this micro–macro problem – though not presented in that way – has been followed by Tabellini (2008a, 2008b) and Karlan *et al.* (2009). Embedded in an impressive literature in social sciences, they distinguish between generalized and limited group morality. This is not new (and they do not claim it to be new) and such a distinction can, for example, already be found in Platteau's works (1994, 2000) on development economics. Limited group morality refers to the societal phenomenon that codes of good conduct and proper behavior are confined to small circles of friends, family and clan members. Outside of this small network, opportunistic behavior is the prevalent code of conduct. A society characterized by a generalized morality does not distinguish between insiders and outsiders. A core element in these approaches is the concept of (generalized) reciprocity: "a society that relies on generalized reciprocity is more efficient than a distrustful society, for the same reason that money is more efficient than barter. Honesty and trust lubricate the inevitable frictions of social life" (Putnam 2000: 135). And "when each of us can relax her guard a little," transaction costs are reduced (Fukuyama 1995). Or as Arrow writes: "It is useful for individuals to have some trust in each other's word. In the absence of trust, it would become very costly to arrange for alternative sanctions and guarantees, and many opportunities for mutually beneficial co-operation would have to be foregone" (Arrow 1971: 22). Both the micro-economic function of trust as a lubricant of economic transactions and its substitution effect for (lack of) legal norms are used as theoretical arguments (more on that later). As Tabellini (2008b) writes while referring to Weber (1992 [1930]), it is this emancipation of the individual from feudal arrangements that has typically been associated with a diffusion of generalized morality (Banfield 1958; Putnam *et al.* 1993). This distinction between a limited group morality and a generalized morality is important for our understanding of why generalized trust may have economic functions that materialize at the aggregate level (Platteau 1994). It is here where the role of an anonymous state and confidence in government become important, as they may provide a source of trust for interaction with anonymous parties (Zucker 1986; Greif 1994, 2006). The willingness to trust strangers promotes civic engagement and community building and may help overcome the problems of collective action, a phenomenon carefully described by Putnam *et al.* (1993) in their Italy study. As a result, societies with a generalized morality and associated high levels of trust can be expected to be more successful in economic terms.[5] It is this reasoning that has formed the core hypothesis in many contemporary empirical studies. The concept of generalized morality, and its relation with trust, are key elements in the discussion on the role of culture in economic development (Tabellini 2007b, 2008a, 2008b).

7.2.3 Trust as culture

Although this is not a deliberate and conscious development, and much more the result of an ad-hoc process of interacting scholars from different fields of research, a certain latent logic does exist as to why trust is often seen as a proxy for culture. The fact that the micro-foundations of trust fit many of the commonly used frameworks in economics forms part of the explanation. It requires no fundamental shift of paradigm but incremental improvements of existing models to include trust in these models. At the same time, trust as an object of study also fits the (recent) behavioral turn in economics because trust has psychological (behavioral) aspects (Fehr 2009). Finally, the opportunity to lift trust from a micro-construct to a macro-phenomenon has allowed for the development of hypotheses at the societal level. This is important because culture is a societal phenomenon as well. The fact that these theoretically derived hypotheses coincide with real-world observations made by Putnam *et al.* (1993), Banfield (1958) and Greif (1994, 2006)

---

[5] Using a different terminology, other scholars have used the distinction between particularized and generalized trust (Uslaner 2002; Bahry *et al.* 2005; Berggren and Jordahl 2006) to get to grips with the concept of macro-trust. According to Bahry *et al.* (2005), generalized trust entails norms of reciprocity and cooperation that underpin civic society. Particularized trust refers to deeper ties between people from a relatively closed circle, such as family members, friends and others with similar backgrounds. Uslaner (2002) interprets generalized trust as the willingness to consider strangers as part of one's own moral community. Generalized trust links us to people who are different from ourselves, whereas particularized trust is based on the in-group. As Fukuyama puts it: "The ability to associate depends, in turn, on the degree to which communities share norms and values and are able to subordinate individual interests to those of larger groups. Out of such shared interests comes trust, and trust, as we will see, has a large and measurable economic value" (Fukuyama 1995: 10).

has further strengthened both the credibility and the importance of the study of trust.

Now that we analyzed why trust studies are frequently perceived and presented as "culture" studies, it is time to discuss the antecedents and consequences of trust in more detail. In the next section we look at the antecedents of trust and in the subsequent section we elaborate on the literature that has dealt with the economic effects of trust. Whereas economists have focussed mainly on the growth effects of trust, sociologists have used trust as a dependent variable and try to explain why trust levels differ between countries. It is important to discuss trust from both angles because – as we argue in the final section – major identification problems exist concerning the causal linkages between trust, its sources and its effects.

7.3 Antecedents of trust

Whereas economists show a natural tendency to perceive trust as a factor driving economic phenomena, most sociologists tend to reverse causality. Trust is studied as a dependent variable and a range of scholars (incidentally also economists) has concentrated on the sources of trust. Delhey and Newton (2005) describe several theories that have been related to trust and its development over time. Their categorization specifically includes a discussion on how institutions affect levels of generalized trust. From this literature a picture emerges in which (well-functioning) institutions and cultural characteristics such as religious values are argued to drive cross-country differences in generalized trust. In categorizing this literature, Delhey and Newton (2005) list five different (but related) sources of trust. We discuss each of these sources.

7.3.1 Social distance

The first factor Delhey and Newton (2005) put forward as an explanatory phenomenon concerns the presence of societal division and cleavages. These fractionalizations can be along class, religion, language, income or ethnicity. The point is that social divisions are generally associated with low levels of generalized trust. This reasoning fits the earlier references to Platteau's and Tabellini's limited vs. generalized group morality. Societal cleavages are expected to generate a high level of in-group trust, but low levels of generalized trust. The trust radius is short (Fukuyama 1995).

Empirical tests of this hypothesized negative relationship are abundant. In their paper on social capital and economic growth, Knack and Keefer (1997) estimate the effect of ethnic homogeneity on levels of generalized trust in a sample of twenty-eight countries. They find that with each three-point increase in the percentage belonging to the largest ethnic group, trust rises by one point. Similar conclusions have been obtained by Knack (2003). Zak and Knack (2001) not only explain generalized trust from differences in ethnic homogeneity, but also look at the effects of income and inequality. They find that trust declines continuously as social distance increases, and find a U-shaped relationship between ethnic homogeneity and trust, with trust first increasing and then decreasing as ethnic homogeneity increases. This latter finding suggests that trust is highest in societies characterized by medium levels of homogeneity. Zerfu *et al.* (2009) complement this ethnicity argument by showing for a sample of eight African countries that the interaction of ethnicity with ethnic nepotism has a self-reinforcing negative effect on generalized trust. According to Rothstein and Uslaner (2005), (in) equality pertains not only to economic aspects but also to equality of opportunity. They see "the distribution of resources and opportunities in a society as the key to the other parts of [their] story – honest government, generalized trust, and social welfare regimes." With equal opportunity, Rothstein and Uslaner (2005) point to the role of universalistic social welfare programs.

The inequality finding has been tested and confirmed at the local level as well. Alesina and Ferrara (2000, 2002) show that the presence of diverse local communities negatively affects the level of generalized trust. Combining experimental-based trust measures with survey-based trust measures, Glaeser *et al.* (2000) find that trustworthiness declines when partners are of different races. In a similar vein, Fershtman and Gneezy (2001) have tested and found that ethnic fractionalizations are associated with discrimination and mistrust. Empirical evidence based on multi-level techniques seems to suggest that differences exist between the US and Europe on the negative effect of ethnic diversity on generalized trust (Hooghe *et al.* 2006). Using twenty-six different indicators of ethnic diversity in a sample of European countries, including several dynamic measures, only a couple of them show a negative significant relationship with social cohesion and only the influx of foreign workers was found to be negatively related to individual scores on the generalized trust question (Hooghe *et al.* 2006).

Ethnic fractionalization has not only been shown to affect aggregate trust scores, it has also been argued to impede the process of economic development (Hodgson 2006). Analyzing a cross section of countries, Easterly and Levine (1997) find that ethnic heterogeneity promotes corruption (*see also* Mauro 1995) and rent-seeking, and leads to a lack of financial institutions, inefficient policies and low educational achievement. Their estimations suggest that a one-standard-deviation decrease in ethnic heterogeneity increases economic growth by a third of a standard deviation. All in all, their results point to a gap of more than 2 percent between the growth rates of the most homogeneous and most heterogeneous countries, which leads them to conclude that ethnic heterogeneity is the main source of economic backwardness of African countries. Similar negative effects of ethnic fractionalization have been found regarding the provision of collective goods such as local public spending on education (Poterba 1997), voter turnout (Costa and Kahn 2003) and support for redistributive welfare spending (Luttmer 2001; Goldin and Katz 1999). Polarization along racial lines has even been put forward as an explanation of lower levels of city growth (DiPasquale and Glaeser 1996).

But societal division does not only take place along racial or ethnic lines. Economic inequality is an important aspect of social classes. Empirical evidence suggests that income inequality lowers civic participation and community expenditure (La Ferrara 2002; Lindert 1996). Knack and Keefer (1997), Zak and Knack (2001) and Knack (2003) find strong negative effects of income inequality on levels of trust in samples of twenty-eight, thirty-six and thirty-nine countries. Similar results hold for individual-level analyses in the US (Costa and Kahn 2003) and Europe (Hooghe *et al.* 2006). Controlling for individual characteristics such as age, sex, race, gender, etc., Costa and Kahn (2003) found that rising levels of income inequality in the US explain about one-third of the decline in civic participation and trust among people between twenty-five and fifty-four years old in the period 1972–1998. You (2005) applies hierarchical linear models to individual-level data and finds that income levels are unimportant, but when income distribution is skewed, social solidarity decreases. All these results lead Costa and Kahn (2003) to conclude that "more homogenous communities foster greater levels of social capital production" (Costa and Kahn 2003: 103). More generally, this conclusion on the (negative) role of heterogeneity in the production of trust fits the remark by Gradstein and Justman that "the absence of a common culture inhibits the ability of economic agents to interact with each other and undermines the efficiency of production and exchange" (Gradstein and Justman 2002: 1192). All in all, there seems to be a general acceptance among social scientists of the existence of a negative relationship between the presence of societal cleavages and low levels of generalized trust.[6]

7.3.2 Modernization

The second source of generalized trust mentioned by Delhey and Newton (2005) is related to the first and concerns economic development and modernization. Referring to classical (European) sociological theories, it is argued that modernization implies the development of a rational–legal and bureaucratic society that generates alienation (Weber 1921; Simmel 1950; Tönnies 2001 [1887]). This process of alienation and its linkages to the development of certain types of trust has been vividly described by Zucker (1986). In her historical overview of the development of US business at the end of the nineteenth and the beginning of the twentieth centuries, she describes the important role of institutions-based trust in an impersonal environment without familiarity and similarity. Third-party certification (regulations, laws) and escrows (e.g. insurance companies) are important sources of institutions-based trust and were required as internal migration eroded or put severe limits on the particularized interpersonal sources of trust (character-based or process-based). Zucker's (1986) analysis complements Greif's (1994, 2006) game-theoretical analysis on traders in medieval Europe. The main point of Greif's analysis – in a way similar to Zucker's (1986) argument – is that both a collectivist and an individualist system exist to reduce uncertainty in overseas trade relations. But it is the individualist one that is more suitable for the process of economic development. The collectivist system – used to describe the

---

[6] Interestingly enough, Putnam (2000) argues that the rising inequality levels in the US are a potential explanation for the decreasing levels of social capital, yet none of his policy prescriptions refers to inequality.

system of the Maghribi traders – is characterized by a segregated social structure in which kinship, family or clan relations are important and contract enforcement is achieved through informal norms and group pressure. Bilateral and multilateral reputation mechanisms are crucial for the reduction of the incentive to engage in opportunistic behavior (Platteau 1994). The individualist system – used by Greif to describe the Genoese traders – is characterized by an integrated social structure, where contract enforcement is achieved through specialized courts. As discussed before, Platteau (1994) and Tabellini (2008a) frame this distinction in terms of limited group morality (collectivist) versus generalized morality (individualist). According to both Greif (1994) and Platteau (1994), it is the latter system which is more suitable for the organization of economic transactions outside the closed social circle. In the end, this system in which institutions of third-party enforcement are developed is more suitable for expanding markets. And this conclusion is exactly in line with Zucker's (1986) historical description. The Zucker–Greif–Platteau–Tabellini framework basically argues that a successful expansion of markets and the associated process of economic development coincide with an evolution in which the source of interpersonal trust shifts from being character or process based to institutions based, allowing for economic transactions with anonymous parties.[7]

A problematic aspect of the relationship between trust and modernization concerns the measurement of trust. Theoretically, it is clear that less developed economies may have relatively low levels of generalized trust. Trust is based on a limited group morality and the associated bilateral and multilateral reputation mechanisms. This does not imply there is a lack of trust, however. In fact, the source of trust may differ, but the argument on the reduction of transaction costs in economic interactions may still hold. Developed economies with well-functioning institutions, allowing for transactions with anonymous parties, may have higher levels of generalized trust. In developing countries, trust is present, but not the generalized type associated with well-functioning

---

[7] This role of modernization and its relationship with trust has been a key issue for sociologists. Simmel (1950), for example, also sees trust as one of the most important drivers toward the development of a modern society. Tönnies (2001 [1887]), meanwhile, has argued that the modernization process from a *Gemeinschaft* (cf. Platteau's limited group morality) to a *Gesellschaft* is associated with a decrease in trust.

institutions. The point is that in the absence of generalized trust there are boundaries of the growth of the collectivist system, and to grow beyond these boundaries and make the leap toward an individualist system characterized by a generalized morality, well-functioning institutions such as a state or legal system are needed (cf. Greif 2006). Hence, the argument on transaction costs is incomplete for less developed countries with poor-functioning aggregate institutions.

7.3.3 Democracy and political institutions

Third, Delhey and Newton (2005) mention democracy and what they call "good government" as a source of trust. Their argumentation is based on the premise that if "trust is a collective property it is likely to be influenced by social institutions and structures, particularly those of the government and the public sector" (Delhey and Newton 2005: 313). Two (partly) conflicting theoretical traditions exist regarding the relationship between trust and political institutions (Mishler and Rose 2001; Rainer and Siedler 2009). On the one hand, it has been argued that generalized trust is exogenous, embedded in cultural traditions and communicated through socialization processes, creating a civic culture (Almond and Verba 1963; Putnam 1993; Inglehart 1997). On the other hand, the institutional tradition stresses the endogeneity of generalized trust. Trust emerges in a rational process in which expectations on the performance of political institutions form the basis of trust or, in the case of untrustworthy institutions, distrust (North 1990). Not surprisingly, it is especially this institutional approach with which most economists feel most comfortable. Although these two different orientations are the two ends of the endogeneity continuum, most of the (empirical) studies cannot be structured neatly along this line and the majority of the studies argue that culture can have conditioning effects, but that generalized trust is affected by perceived institutional performance (Dixit 2009).

This institutional argument is obviously closely related to the previous modernization argument. If the development of rational–legal institutions and the associated development of generalized trust holds, then a positive relationship can be expected between the quality of a country's institutions and the level of generalized trust. Zak and Knack (2001) find strong positive and significant effects of a range of World Bank measures of the quality of institutions on trust. As argued before, such positive associations have been observed by others as well (LaPorta *et al.* 1997; Knack 2003; Berggren and Jordahl 2006). The problem of these findings is that the nature of the relationship, particularly the direction of causality, is unknown (Knack and Keefer 1997: 1279). It seems likely that democratic institutions are conducive to interpersonal social trust, as well as trust being conducive to democracy (Inglehart, see p. 5 of Rothstein 2003). Paxton (2002) explicitly tests the nature of the relationship between democracy and social capital measured as generalized trust and associational membership. She finds support for a reciprocal relationship between trust and democracy. More associations are expected to arise in democratic regimes. However, theory also prescribes that participation in trusting associations allows individuals to experience differences and changes in values and preferences which increases democratic participation. The "presence of associations provides further resources to collectively mobilize and pursue specific goals in a large society" (Paxton 2002: 259). Using data from the World Values Survey, she shows not only the existence of such a reciprocal relationship but also that connected (trust-building) associations have a strong positive influence on democracy, while isolated types of associations have a strong negative effect on democracy. In a quasi-experimental set-up, Rainer and Siedler (2009) compare trust levels between East and West Germany and test whether levels have changed since the country's reunification. They distinguish between social trust (trust in other people) and institutional trust (trust in legal and political institutions) and find that both types are lower for people who lived under communism than for West Germans. Interestingly, they also find that reunification has not led to higher levels of social trust, but did lead to convergence of institutional trust in the post-reunification period. Rainer and Siedler (2009) show that the persistent low level of social trust can be explained by the economic and social problems that persisted in East Germany after reunification.

According to Rothstein, it is not only the quality of the government institutions but also the type of government institutions, especially the structure of the welfare state, which is important for understanding the different levels of social capital found in developed countries. Rothstein explicitly links the special position of Scandinavian countries – traditionally characterized by the highest trust scores – with the design of the welfare state in these countries (Rothstein 2003; Kumlin and Rothstein 2005; Rothstein and Uslaner 2005). Using Swedish and US data, he tests the hypothesis that universal welfare state institutions tend to increase social trust, while experiences with needs-testing programs undermine it. The latter refers to public service that is provided only after an individual's needs test. Individual citizens must meet certain conditions to qualify for a benefit or service. These needs testing-based programs leave a greater scope for bureaucratic discretion and hence may give rise to suspicions concerning poor procedural justice and arbitrary treatment. The alternative, being universal welfare programs, may be associated with a sense of equal treatment and principles of fairness. "When people do not see themselves as part of the same moral community with a shared fate, they will not have the solidarity that is essential for building up social trust" (Rothstein and Uslaner 2005: 61). According to Rothstein, the universal nature of the Scandinavian welfare state may at least partly explain the high levels of generalized trust in these countries. Needs testing stigmatizes the poor, in his view. His argument is based on the concept of procedural justice. The legitimacy of the institutional/political system depends (partly) on the system's ability to create procedural justice in concrete encounters between citizens and public institutions. The causal link Rothstein puts forward runs from trust in the impartiality of government institutions responsible for the implementation of public policies to trust in "most people." In his words: "It makes no sense to trust 'most people' if they are generally known to bribe, threaten or in other ways corrupt the impartiality of government institutions in order to extract special favors. One reason 'most other people' may be trusted is that they are generally known to refrain from such forms of behavior" (Rothstein 2003: 18). Empirical tests of this argument strongly support his thesis (Kumlin and Rothstein 2005; Rothstein and Uslaner 2005). In a similar vein, but based on a sample of post-communist countries, Mishler and Rose (2001) find that aggregate corruption erodes trust in political institutions, but only to the extent that individuals perceive corruption, a conclusion that fits the procedural justice argumentation.

7.3.4 Associational activity

Fourth, Delhey and Newton (2005) list the presence of voluntary organizations and civil society as a frequently cited source of generalized trust. Although the interest of economists in group membership is only recent (Hargreaves Heap and Zizzo 2009), theoretical arguments have a long history dating back to political philosophers Tocqueville and Mill. Referring to the work of Alexis de Tocqueville, Putnam (2000; Putnam *et al.* 1993) maintains that these civil associations contribute to the effectiveness and stability of a democratic government because of their "internal" effects on individual members and their "external" effects on the wider polity. According to Putnam, "associations instill in their members a habit of cooperation, solidarity and public-spiritedness. [. . .] Participation in civic organizations inculcates skills of cooperation as well as a sense of shared responsibility for collective endeavors. Moreover, when individuals belong to 'cross-cutting' groups with diverse goals and members, their attitudes will tend to moderate as a result of groups interaction and cross-pressures" (Putnam 1993: 89–90). Externally, a dense network of associations may enhance "interest articulation" and "interest aggregation," thereby contributing to effective social collaboration and trust building.

Empirical evidence points to a two-way relationship. Brehm and Rahn (1997) use data from the US General Social Survey and show that membership in groups and generalized trust are strongly related, with causation running both ways. Although Stolle and Rochon (1998) do not test for reverse causality, they find that membership is positively related to trust in a sample of the US, Swedish and German citizens. A number of country-level studies exist as well. Using data from the WVS survey 1990 and 1995, LaPorta *et al.* (1997) and Knack (2003) find a strong positive relationship between group membership in voluntary organizations and generalized trust. Knack (2003) differentiates between types of associations. He distinguishes so-called Putnam and Olson groups. As already discussed, Putnam (1993) argued that the economic success of northern Italian regions can be attributed to richer associational life because associations "instill in their members habits of cooperation, solidarity, and public-spiritedness" (1993: 89). Olson (1982), meanwhile, observes that associational activity may hurt growth because of rent-seeking activities. According to Olson, many of these associations may act as special interest groups lobbying for preferential policies that impose disproportionate costs on society (*see also* Knack and Keefer 1997 and Knack 2003). Moreover, strong feelings of group membership are associated with negative discrimination against outsiders reducing generalized trust (Hargreaves Heap and Zizzo 2009). In sum, whereas Putnam groups may be evoking positive effects, these may be reduced by harmful effects of the Olson groups. In operationalizing these two types, Knack (2003: 345) defines Putnam groups as membership of associations related to education, arts, music and cultural activities, youth work, local community action and sports or recreations. Olson groups are defined as membership of professional associations, trade unions and political parties or groups. Knack (2003) finds a positive and significant correlation between Putnam groups and generalized trust, while the estimated coefficients for the Olson groups are insignificant. Interestingly, Knack and Keefer (1997) report the opposite result: Olson groups being positively related to trust levels and Putnam groups having no statistical relation with trust. Other studies at the country level report mixed results on the membership–trust relationship as well (Delhey and Newton 2005).

One reason for these mixed findings may be related to the internal validity of these associational activity measures. Finding associations that proxy the supposed theoretical links may differ between countries and regions, because of their context specificity (cf. Yoo and Lee 2009). For example, from a practical point of view, it may make no sense to look at membership of unions in the United Arab Emirates, where they are forbidden, as well as in Denmark, where membership is obligatory for some professions. The role of hunting associations may be relevant in Finland, but not in central Amsterdam. Moreover, what is social capital in one context may be unsocial capital in another. In this context, Krishna and Schrader (1999: 5 in Casey 2004: 104) write: "The Church that supports brotherhood and peace in one context may become a forum for armed militancy in another. Unions that may promote coordination and cooperation with the state in a corporatist context can wage bitter confrontation in another context." In other words, the internal validity of the measures used may be relatively low, or are at minimum sample or context specific.

Another reason for the mixed findings between associational activity and trust may be the presence of omitted background variables at the individual level. Participating in all kinds of associations may have many effects, but it does not appear to increase trust in other people (Rothstein 2003). Individual-level analyses seem to indicate that "the correlation between participation and social trust is created in a self-selection process where people who are already high social trusters are more likely to join and become active in organizations/networks. However, the actual participation itself does not seem to increase people's tendency to trust others" (Kumlin and Rothstein 2005: 11). Finally, "particularized trusters may be as involved in civic life as generalized trusters, but they will restrict their activities and good deeds to their own kind" (Rothstein and Uslaner 2005: 45). Again, the problem arises that these social capital measures suffer from a lack of internal validity. All the above factors complicate the theoretical and empirical relationship between generalized macro-trust and associational activity.

Because of these measurement problems, Owen and Videras (2009) apply a latent class analysis on social capital. Starting from the idea that social capital is an unobservable, multidimensional construct, their latent class approach allows them to classify individuals into distinct *types* of social capital using both memberships and trust indicators. Instead of the number of voluntary organization memberships, they focus on network type and show how different socio-economic determinants sort individuals into different types of social capital classes (e.g. high trust, low membership; low trust, low membership, etc.). Such a latent-class approach is interesting because it opens the complex web of linkages between (types of) associational activity and trust.

7.3.5 Religion and religious culture

Finally, Delhey and Newton (2003) describe the role of religious cultural traditions as a source of trust. According to Fukuyama (1995), traditional religions constitute the major institutionalized sources of culturally determined behavior. The argument as to why religious traditions may affect trust basically relates back to Weber and his Protestant Ethic (Weber 1992 [1930]). Next to the Protestant heritage, scholars have pointed out that the Confucian tradition may fulfill similar functions and can be associated with higher levels of generalized trust (Delhey and Newton 2003). Although there is no single uniform Protestant tradition and more types of Confucianism exist[8] (for example, Chinese and Japanese, *see* Fukuyama 1995: 343–347), religion

---

[8] Confucianism is not an exclusive category, i.e. people are both Confucian and Buddhist or Taoist.

and religious traditions are often operationalized in terms of dummies in cross-country regressions.

Putnam *et al.* (1993) argue extensively that the Catholic Church, through its hierarchical structure and the permanent imprint this made on society, has discouraged the formation of trust, for which horizontal networks are more important. "Despite the reforms of the Second Vatican Council and the flowering of many divergent ideological tendencies among the faithful, the Italian Church retains much of the heritage of the Counter-Reformation, including an emphasis on the ecclesiastical hierarchy and the traditional virtues of obedience and acceptance of one's station in life. Vertical bonds of authority are more characteristic of the Italian Church than horizontal bonds of fellowship" (Putnam *et al.* 1993: 107). Putnam is not unique in this reasoning; Seligman has also made the argument that trust cannot take root in hierarchical cultures (Seligman 1997: 36–37). In fact, Guiso *et al.* (2003) claim to have shown that the more liberal doctrine after the Second Vatican Council in 1962 has positively affected the trust levels of later generations raised under this new doctrine.

LaPorta *et al.* (1997) have applied this conceptual idea to all religions and distinguish between hierarchical religions (being Catholicism, Eastern orthodox and Islam) and non-hierarchical religions. They find a strong negative correlation of the former with trust (–.61), confirming the idea that hierarchical religions are associated with lower levels of generalized trust. They also note that this negative correlation is mostly driven by Catholicism and trust, a result obtained by Zerfu *et al.* (2009) as well. Following LaPorta *et al.* (1997), Berggren and Jordahl (2006) regress religious denomination on trust levels. They find a strong negative effect of Catholics, Muslims and followers of the Orthodox Church as compared with Protestant countries. According to Guiso *et al.* (2003), religious affiliation may increase general trust levels.

In this context it is not surprising that the Scandinavian countries with a clear Protestant heritage obtain the highest score on generalized trust in all the different waves of the World and European Values Survey. This Nordic effect (Delhey and Newton 2005) has led Van Oorschot *et al.* (2006: 161) to write that "Scandinavians seem to be the social capital champions of Europe." Moreover, they find that any country with a Protestant tradition – even controlling for Scandinavia-specific effects – has significantly higher generalized trust scores. Similarly, Rothstein and Uslaner (2005) explain the (country) level of trust by the share of the Protestant population and find a positive and significant effect.

Explaining government performance in fifty US states by levels of social capital (a composite index of generalized trust, associational activity and census response rates), Knack (2000) applies an instrumental variable approach. In his first-stage regression, social capital is instrumented by various religious denominations. He includes the fraction of mainline Protestants, evangelical/fundamentalist Protestant, African American Protestant, Catholicism, Eastern orthodox, Mormon Churches and Jewish Americans. First, he finds that religious composition of US states explains most of the cross-state variation of the social capital index. He also finds that mainline Protestants are strongly associated with higher levels of social capital. Interestingly, the percentage of the state population with Scandinavian ancestry is positively and significantly related to the level of social capital. In line with the earlier discussion on inequality, a significantly negative effect is found for GINI income inequality and US state level of social capital. Despite these clear country-level findings on the positive and significant effect of Protestant tradition, this effect disappears in individual-level analysis once controlling for country-specific effects (Rothstein and Uslaner 2005).

Finally, Delhey and Newton (2005) not only list these five theories on the potential sources of trust,[9] they also test their ideas empirically. Regressing degree of ethnic fractionalization and GINI income inequality (I), composite indicators of modernization (II) and good government (III), associational activity (IV) and dummies for (Protestant) religious tradition (V) on generalized trust in a sample of sixty countries, they find confirmation for the negative role of (I) and the positive role of (III) and (V). Their test on the origins of generalized

---

[9] In addition to these five potential sources of trust, Delhey and Newton (2003) mention the disruptive role of conflicts such as civil wars. Rapid social change, persistent social strain and disruption are expected to produce an increase in distrust. This is empirically confirmed by Rothstein and Uslaner (2005) and Guiso *et al.* (2009). However, opposition to an external enemy may also draw society together and increase trust (cf. Greif 2006). Although we do not think this sixth factor is irrelevant, we feel the five phenomena listed above are more structural. In a way, social disruption has similar theoretical effects to the earlier mentioned effects of high social distance.

trust fits the findings of Knack and Keefer (1997) and Berggren and Jordahl (2006). An overview of a large number of empirical studies attempting to explain generalized trust (operationalized as the "generally speaking" question discussed before) can be found in Table 7.1.

7.4 Trust–growth studies

Having discussed the background against which the scholarly interest in trust has developed and the different sources of trust, we now turn to the literature that studies the effects of trust. Specifically, we discuss the literature that addresses the link between trust and economic growth. We first elaborate on the theoretical arguments typically found in these studies, then turn to the empirical and methodological part of these trust–growth studies.

7.4.1 Arguments

The argumentation as to why generalized trust may yield macroeconomic benefits builds on direct and indirect linkages. The direct effect of high levels of trust concerns the reduction of transaction costs (Gulati 1995, 1998; Roth 2009). The trust literature (especially in management and strategy) has provided a number of arguments as to why trust reduces transaction costs (Barney and Hansen 1995; Lane and Bachmann 1998; Mayer *et al.* 1995; McAllister 1995; Nooteboom 2002). We mention the most important ones. First, through third parties, trust provides options for control in social networks. Second, trust is linked with the facilitation of highly uncertain transactions. It reduces the uncertainty of these kinds of transactions, especially the relational risk involved. Uzzi shows that "trust facilitates the exchange of resources and information that are crucial for high performance but are difficult to value and transfer via market ties" (1996: 678). The third function of trust is related to its information function (Karlan *et al.* 2009; Gulati 1998; Sako 1992). Another benefit of trust as a vehicle in forming alliances is the reduction of search costs for alliance partners. Firms in social networks of trusting relationships can ally with someone they already know (Gulati 1995: 107). Ring and Van de Ven (1992) have shown that informal, personal connections between and across organizations play an important role in determining the governance structures used to organize transactions. Repeated ties between

Table 7.1. *Determinants of generalized trust – overview of empirical studies*

Study	Sample	Significant negative	Significant positive	Remarks
1 Knack and Keefer (1997)	28 countries, cross-country regression	GINI income inequality Ethnic heterogeneity	Associational activity: Olson groups Protestantism Institutional quality: independence of courts GDP per capita	
2 LaPorta *et al.* (1997)	40 countries, cross-country regression	Inflation	Institutional quality: * efficiency of judiciary * lack of corruption * bureaucratic quality * tax compliance Associational activity: * civic participation * participation in professional organizations	
3 Knack (2000)	50 US states, cross-state regressions	GINI income inequality	Protestantism Scandinavian ancestry Home ownership	The dependent variable is a composite measure including generalized trust
4 Mishler and Rose (2001)	Individuals (N=9,976), cross-section regression	* Education level * Perceived corruption * Aggregate corruption	* Age * Gender (female) * Household income * Economic prospects	Trust is measured in "people who you meet" on a 7-point scale

5	Zak and Knack (2001)	36/41 countries, cross-country regression	GINI income inequality GINI land inequality Ethnic heterogeneity	Institutional quality: * economic discrimination * lack of corruption * contract enforceability * investor rights
6	Alesina and La Ferrara (2002)	Individual panel analysis, sample of >7000 US citizens	Individual level: * female * divorced * unemployed * black minority member State level: * racial fragmentation * GINI income inequality (but racial heterogeneity stronger effect)	Individual level: * education level (for age >16) * income * age (U-shaped)
7	Delhey and Newton (2005)	60 countries, cross-country regression	Ethnic heterogeneity GINI income inequality	Quality of government (composite indicator of various aspects of government quality) Protestantism Nordic/Scandinavian effect
8	Knack (2003)	39 countries, cross-country regression	GINI income inequality	Associational activity, especially Putnam groups

(cont.)

Table 7.1. (*cont.*)

Study	Sample	Significant negative	Significant positive	Remarks
9 Rothstein (2003)	Individual analysis, Swedish sample of N between 1707 and 2586		* Education level * Income level * Expressed interest in politics * Trust in police * Trust in courts * Associational activity	
10 Berggren and Jordahl (2006)	51 countries, cross-country regression	Ethnic fractionalization GINI income inequality Non-Protestant religions (esp. Catholicism, Muslims and Orthodox Church)	Economic Freedom index, especially the sub-indices: (a) Legal structure and security of property rights (b) Access to sound money	
11 Hooghe *et al.* (2006)	Multi-level analysis, 36,617 individuals and 20 European countries	Country level: * influx of foreign workers * GINI coefficient Individual level: * unemployed * born abroad	Country level: * GDP per capita Individual level: * age * female * education level * religious involvement	

	Study	Method/Sample			Notes
12	Kumlin and Rothstein (2005)	Individual-level analysis, cross-section regression, Swedish sample of 2543 persons	* Needs-tested welfare program contacts * Unemployed * Right-wing ideology	* Universal welfare program contacts * Age * Education level * Involvement in civic associations * Family income	Trust is not measured by the binomial question, but on a scale of 0–10
13	Rothstein and Uslaner (2005)	63 countries, cross-country regression	* GINI income inequality * Civil war * Former communist nation	* Protestant share of population	
14	Rothstein and Uslaner (2005)	Individual-level, US national election study 1992 (N=1753)	* Receipt of needs-tested welfare benefits * In-group trust * Have no say in politics	* Talk to neighbors * Income * Education level * Age	
15	Van Oorschot et al. (2006)	Individual-level analysis, N=28,894 from 24 countries	* Unemployed * Gender: female * Catholic	* Education level * Household income * Scandinavia/Nordic effect * Church attendance	
16	Björnskov (2007)	73–76 countries, cross-country analysis	* GINI income inequality * Former communist nation * Catholicism and Islam	* Monarchy	

(cont.)

Table 7.1. *(cont.)*

	Study	Sample	Significant negative	Significant positive	Remarks
17	Algan and Cahuc (2010)	Individual-level analysis of second-generation US citizens 1977–2002 (N=1808)	* Female	* Age * Education level * Scandinavian ancestry * Trust level of migrant's home country	
18	Rainer and Siedler (2009)	Individual-level analysis; East and West Germany (N=4582)	* Gender: female * GINI income inequality * East German	* Education level * University degree * Household income	
19	Zerfu et al. (2009)	Individual level in sample of 8 African countries (N=7787)	Individual level: * ethnicity * size of town * orthodox religion * Catholic * ethnic nepotism Country level: * ethno-linguistic fractionalization	* Age * Islamic * Education (U-shaped)	

firms yield trust that is manifested in the form of the less specified contracts used to organize subsequent alliances (Gulati 1995). In this case, trust serves as a substitute for contractual safeguards and reduces transaction costs.[10]

The indirect effect relates to the improved government performance which subsequently affects economic growth. This latter argument is the core of Boix and Posner's (1998) reasoning why social capital may generate macro-level benefits. Social capital contributes to effective governance by facilitating the articulation of citizens' demands: "sophisticated voters make the elected more representative and accountable" (Fine 2001: 113). Social capital reduces the need to secure compliance by creating complex and costly mechanisms of enforcement. It reduces transaction costs in the arena of citizen–government relations because social capital shapes the expectations citizens have about the behavior of others. Finally, social capital encourages the articulation of collective demands that are to everyone's benefit. According to Boix and Posner, this all leads to the conclusion that social capital reduces the probability of individuals engaging in opportunistic behavior and the resources devoted to monitoring agents' performance can be invested in more productive ways.

This improved government-based performance argument closely relates to Putnam *et al.*'s (1993) original thesis and also dates back to Almond and Verba's (1963) argumentation relating civic virtues to government performance. A similar reasoning can be found in Knack (2000). In his view, social capital affects government performance in three ways. First, it can broaden government accountability. Greater trust and more civic-minded attitudes can improve governmental performance by affecting the level and character of political participation, reducing rent seeking and enhancing public-interested behavior (Knack 2000: 3). Second, it may facilitate agreement where political preferences are polarized. In the case of high trust, the public spiritedness may serve as a type of glue in case of conflicts. The willingness to compromise is greater when there is a shared interest in the public domain (Putnam 2000). Third, Knack argues that social capital may

---

[10] Many of these studies can be seen as a critique or extension of Williamson's (1975, 1985, 1998) transaction cost theory. Puranem and Vanneste (2009) and Carlin *et al.* (2009) discuss the conditions under which trust serves as a substitute for formal governance mechanisms.

improve innovation in policy making in the face of new challenges. This argument is based not so much on theory but on Putnam *et al.*'s (1993) observation that the more civic regions in Italy were more successful in responding to newly identified problems such as day-care programs, family clinics, etc. Theoretically, this may be related to the resistance to policy changes in areas with low levels of social capital, low trust, a lack of public spiritedness and clientilism. Knack (2000) finds that social capital, measured as an index of trust, associational activity and census response rates, is positively and significantly related to governmental performance in US states. (Performance is measured by surveys and interviews of budget officers, public managers and auditors and included thirty-five criteria. These criteria concerned topics such as financial management, accountability, strategic planning and communication.)

The indirect trust–government–growth route is most often taken by political scientists and sociologists. Economists generally feel more comfortable with a more direct approach relating trust to growth by building on the concept of (generalized) morality (Tabellini 2008a, 2008b). The underlying argument on *why* societies characterized by trust are economically more successful is mostly based on micro-level arguments deduced from either transaction costs theory or game theory (Axelrod 1984; Gambetta 1988; Glaeser *et al.* 2000; Ostrom and Walker 2003; Büchner *et al.* 2004; Bjørnskov 2009). We list the arguments frequently found in studies directly linking trust to economic growth in Table 7.2. In general, trust is argued to reduce transaction costs and principal–agent problems, increase (the efficiency of) investments in physical and human capital, and promote innovation.

The basic theoretical logic in most of the empirical studies on trust and growth contains a mix of the direct and indirect arguments. And most of the theoretical arguments found in studies by economists are derived from micro-level theories. Efficiencies of trust at the micro-level are aggregated. In a cross section it is therefore expected that countries having a "culture" characterized by high levels of trust grow faster. However, the leap from micro- to macro-functioning is not easy and may even be illegitimate, because what may be true for individuals may not be true for the society as a whole (Fine 2001). Measures of an individual-level construct cannot always simply be aggregated and assumed to be a veridical representation of its counterpart (Morgeson and Hofmann 1999: 260). We return to this multi-level issue in

Table 7.2. *Theoretical arguments linking trust to economic growth*

1. High levels of trust reduce transaction costs, especially the contract and control costs associated with economic transactions.
2. High levels of trust make a society less dependent on formal institutions, as trust is an (imperfect) substitute for a legal system. Trust allows for low-cost enforcement of contracts. This is especially the case in principal–agent settings when a principal has to trust the agent to deliver goods or services, but cannot supervise the quality or effectiveness of their work (without incurring high costs). Trust is an efficient enforcement mechanism. At the aggregate level, trust is argued to reduce the levels of fraud and crime in a society.
3. High levels of trust reduce the costs of defecting in prisoner dilemma situations. Bilateral and multilateral reputation mechanisms lead to potential punishment, such as loss of reputation and ostracism.
4. High levels of trust and social capital enable actors to solve collective-action problems in an efficient way. Related to the transaction costs argument, the Coase theorem is put forward as part of the explanation. The Coase theorem holds that when transaction costs are low, actors will be able to negotiate solutions to collective-action problems more efficiently than could be achieved by outside regulation (Whiteley 2000; Coase 1990).
5. High levels of trust trigger investment because trust is associated with long-time horizons beneficial for risky investments. According to some authors (e.g. Whiteley 2000), high levels of trust are associated with low levels of risk averseness, which will be beneficial for innovative investments. Empirical evidence for this argument is lacking, however.
6. High levels of trust make investments in education more efficient because the returns on the accumulation of human capital are assumed to be higher (cf. Bjørnskov 2009). According to Whiteley (2000: 451), "educational investment may not work effectively in a low trust society if employment practices are strongly influenced by ascriptive criteria such as kinship and ethnicity."

Section 7.5.3 and in the concluding section. First we discuss the results obtained in these trust–growth studies.

7.4.2 Results

Empirically, the majority of the contributions assess international differences in trust by means of the WVS question "generally speaking,

do you think that people can be trusted?" (Inglehart 1997; Knack and
Keefer 1997; Whiteley 2000; Zak and Knack 2001; Uslaner 2002),
to which the answer is a binomial choice between "most people can
be trusted" and "can't be too careful." Trust is measured as the percentage of respondents in each country that replied "most people can
be trusted." Of these macro-studies, Knack and Keefer's 1997 contribution has been the most influential.[11] In this paper, they investigate
whether social capital has an economic payoff by studying a cross section of twenty-nine market economies. In their empirical analysis, they
focus primarily on the role of trust as they feel it is the most important
indicator of social capital. Their results point to a statistically significant effect of trust on growth. They state that "the coefficient for
trust (. . .) indicates that a ten percentage point rise in that variable
is associated with an increase in growth of four-fifths of a percentage point" (Knack and Keefer 1997: 1260). In a follow-up analysis,
Zak and Knack (2001) extend the analysis by adding twelve countries
to the Knack and Keefer sample. On the basis of their analysis for
forty-one countries, Zak and Knack also conclude that trust – again
measured by the "generally speaking" question – has a positive and
significant impact on economic growth. With the exception of Roth
(2009), who established a curvilinear relationship between trust and
economic growth, all other studies we are aware of report a non-
negative effect of trust (*see* Berggren and Jordahl 2006 and Durlauf
and Fafchamps 2004 for overviews).

Analyzing regional growth differentials in Italian regions, Helliwell
and Putnam (1995) found that levels of social capital are positively
related to growth. However, they do not include generalized trust in
their composite measure of social capital. A European analysis of trust
and economic growth between 1980 and 1996 in fifty-eight regions
suggests trust (based on the Eurobarometer, not the WVS) is negatively and significantly related to growth (Schneider *et al.* 2000). Casey
(2004) ranks the scores of eleven British regions on the generalized
trust question and argues that this ranking coincides with the ranking
of level of regional economic development (Casey reports a correlation of .47). In a sample of fifty-four European regions, Beugelsdijk

---

[11] Because of our interest in culture, we focus only on macro-studies. It is beyond
the scope of this book to discuss studies addressing the effect of trust on
individual economic performance. For a recent individual-level analysis of the
effect of trust, we refer readers to Butler *et al.* (2009).

and Van Schaik (2005a) regress social capital, of which generalized trust forms an important component, on economic growth in these regions controlling for initial level of welfare. They find a positive and significant effect. However, using a more elaborate empirical growth model, controlling for country-specific effects and applying extensive robustness analysis, Beugelsdijk and Van Schaik (2005b) find no significant effect of trust in the same sample of fifty-four regions. Analyzing 102 European regions, Akçomak and Ter Weel (2009) show that trust has no direct effect on regional growth but does affect growth *indirectly* by affecting regional innovativeness (cf. Beugelsdijk 2007). In sum, the few regional-level studies there are do not show unambiguous positive and significant effects of trust on economic growth. The only exception is Tabellini (2008b). However, he does not specifically study generalized trust, but considers it as an element of a broader concept of culture. In his paper dealing specifically with European regions, Tabellini (2007b) uses within-country variation to explore the link between historical institutions, culture (proxied by trust) and economic development. In a sample of sixty-nine regions from eight countries, Tabellini's main contribution is perhaps not the use of trust at the regional level but the idea to perform an instrumental variable technique (two-stage-least-squares) in which level of economic development in 2000 is explained by culture in 1995–1997 (proxied by trust amongst others), which is subsequently explained by historical institutions proxied by literacy rates around 1880 and political institutions (constraints on the executive power) in 1600, 1700, 1750, 1800 and 1850. Although his paper contains several rich details, the main finding is that early political institutions shape current cultural traits that subsequently explain a large part of the differences in current levels of regional economic development. In his follow-up paper, Tabellini (2008b) uses similar proxies for culture (including trust)[12] and an even more inventive instrument for culture, which is the structure of a country's language (the use of pronouns or not and the type of pronouns,

[12] To be precise, Tabellini (2007b) uses the generalized trust question as a component of a four-item culture measure also including data from the World/European Values Survey regarding the extent to which people feel they control their lives, and two items that respondents can choose when confronted with a list of qualities that children can be encouraged to learn at home, being respect for others and obedience. Tabellini (2008b) uses trust and respect and drops the other two items.

such as *tu* and *vous* in French).[13] He finds strong support for these instruments and the two-stage procedure explaining current levels of economic development. In the regional analysis, Tabellini cannot use language as an instrument because of data unavailability, but again builds on past political institutions as an instrument. Although minor differences in control variables exist, Tabellini basically reconfirms his earlier (2007b) results.

Because of the mixed findings obtained in studies on the growth effects of trust, Beugelsdijk *et al.* (2004) have performed an econometric robustness analysis. Building on the datasets as used in the seminal contribution by Knack and Keefer (1997) and the follow-up article by Zak and Knack (2001), these authors assess the robustness of the relationship between growth and trust along several dimensions. Starting with the sample of twenty-nine countries in Knack and Keefer (1997), they investigate the effect of the twelve countries added in Zak and Knack (2001) on the robustness of trust in terms of significance and effect size. Their robustness analysis of the Knack and Keefer sample of twenty-nine countries indicates that trust is significant in only 4.5 percent of all relevant regression models, a result that cannot be considered to be robust. The most interesting conclusion, however, is the fact that by adding the twelve mostly less developed countries (LDCs), as Zak and Knack (2001) did, the estimated coefficient increases (in fact the effect size doubles) and the robustness in terms of fraction of significant results increases. They find that adding low-trust countries – mainly LDCs – seems to be crucial for obtaining a robust result on trust. Moreover, the estimated effect of trust is larger in samples containing a substantial number of LDCs. Results of this robustness test indicate the importance of the sample structure for obtaining significant effects. Using a different method, Beugelsdijk (2006) finds additional support for the hypothesis that the inclusion of less developed – low-trust – countries is crucial for a significant effect of the trust variable on economic growth. An explicit attempt to take into account the endogeneity of trust and institutions displays a similar pattern. Ahlerup *et al.* (2009) show that the marginal effect of trust on economic growth decreases with institutional strength, a finding they

---

[13] The use of language as an instrument for culture is based on the fundamental relation between the structure of society's language and a society's value system and is also referred to as the Sapir–Whorf hypothesis (Licht *et al.* 2007).

interpret as evidence of the non-linearity of trust. Trust serves as a substitute for formal institutions in developing countries and "almost ceases to matter when institutions are strong" (Ahlerup *et al.* 2009: 13). One problematic aspect of such reasoning is the assumption that trust scores as measured by the "generally speaking" question can be meaningfully compared between developed and developing countries. Recent critique has focussed on the validity and methodology of the trust question used in many of these empirical studies.

7.5 Methodology of the generalized trust question

Given the increased interest in social capital and trust, it is not surprising that the number of critical papers has been rising in the slipstream of the introduction of the concept. The critique is extensive and has started with a critique on Putnam's 1993 and 2000 books. Critics have not only pointed to the neglect of negative effects of social capital, the lack of a theoretical mechanism between social capital and economic growth, but also criticized the research method that Putnam has used (Jackman and Miller 1996; Tarrow 1996; Dekker *et al.* 1997; Harris and DeRenzio 1997; Paxton 1999; Torsvik 2000; Boggs 2001; Fine 2001; Sobel 2002). In contrast with Putnam, Jackman and Miller (1996) find little empirical proof that indicates a systematic relationship between culture and political and economic performance. They show that the strong correlation between the overall measure of culture and the institutional performance of Italian regions is an artifact of Putnam's application of the principal components analysis. According to Boggs (2001: 290), Putnam's explanatory framework rests upon a foundation of pseudo empiricism, with all the assembled data, charts and graphs telling us little about the conditions underlying historical change. The critique is broader than just responses to Putnam's work (Durlauf 2002a, 2002b), but here we focus on trust. We concentrate on three key issues. First, trust is related to institutions and this yields an identification problem. Second, some have argued that the generalized trust question used to operationalize trust lacks internal validity. Finally, it has been argued that the micro-level arguments on a reduction of transaction costs cannot be aggregated to the macro-level by simply arguing that high macro-trust increases economic growth, especially because of the earlier mentioned identification problem regarding the role of institutions.

7.5.1 Identification problems

As argued in the previous section, some trust scholars have claimed that the structure of the sample determines the statistical robustness of the trust–growth relationship. They argue that the inclusion of less developed countries is crucial for the statistical finding that trust is significantly and positively related to economic growth. Trust becomes significant in these country-level studies only once countries are included in the sample that score low on institutional quality. Though circumstantial evidence, this does suggest a fundamental relationship exists between the trust measure and the institutional quality of the countries included in the test. More direct evidence for such a hypothesis exists as well. Van Oorschot *et al.* (2006) report a positive and significant correlation of .627 between trust in institutions and generalized trust. Berggren and Jordahl (2006) report a correlation of .58 between aggregate trust and the Economic Freedom Index. Moreover, as summarized before, a number of scholars perceive well-functioning institutions to be a source of trust. Finally, Beugelsdijk (2006) performs a factor analysis on the generalized trust measure and a range of variables all measuring institutional quality. He finds that trust clusters together with several measures of institutional well-functioning, i.e. "contract enforceability," the "Transparency International corruption index," the "black market premium," "revolutionary coups," "rule of law," "capitalism" and "social infrastructure." All these variables measure aspects of institutional strength. This factor analysis suggests that generalized trust is closely related to institutional well-functioning.

One strategy typically followed by economists in case of endogenous variables is to apply instrumental variable approaches and use exogenous instruments in a two-stage procedure. Typical exogenous variables that have been used are, for example, literacy rates and historical political institutions (e.g. Tabellini 2007b, 2008b; Akçomak and Ter Weel 2009), ethnic/linguistic homogeneity (e.g. Knack and Keefer 1997), trust in migrants' home countries (Algan and Cahuc 2010) or common religion (e.g. Guiso *et al.* 2009). However, the problem with all these supposedly exogenous variables as instruments for trust is that there are also plausible arguments supporting a direct impact on the economic outcome of interest, or in other words, "they are not exogenous to the error term beyond doubt" (Fehr 2009: 258).

Given the problems of finding true exogenous variables, it is interesting to look at studies that have taken a sub-national perspective, because if generalized trust is indeed related to institutions, it is better to control for country-specific institutions by studying sub-national entities. Given that institutions like a legal system are often country-specific, regional trust studies are interesting because country-specific institutions are controlled for.[14] Interestingly, as discussed in the previous section, not all regional studies using trust to explain regional economic growth report a significant relationship between trust and growth (e.g. Beugelsdijk and Van Schaik 2005b). Country-level studies suggest the results obtained depend on the structure of the sample, and an analysis of trust in relatively well-developed European regions yields no significant result of trust on growth. Although this may be caused by poor empirical set-ups and lack of good proxies for trust (*see* next section), these results suggest that the effect of trust depends on the underlying sample, specifically the inclusion of entities with poor functioning institutions. Hence, the question arises as to whether trust reflects generalized morality, as seems to be the starting point for many scholars. Or does it simply proxy for institutional quality? These questions have triggered fierce debates (*see*, for example, the debate between Uslaner (2008) and Beugelsdijk's (2008) reply). At a minimum we can conclude that an identification problem exists regarding the economic effects of trust and those of the quality of institutions.

7.5.2 Validity problems

According to Miller and Mitamura (2003), the "generally speaking" question on trust was first used in a paper in the *American Sociological*

---

[14] In addition to this "institutional control" argument, regional studies are attractive for other reasons. The set of regions is relatively homogeneous compared with studies on culture and economic development that incorporate countries such as Taiwan and Germany or Japan and the United States in the same regression analysis. Temple's (1999) critical comment that countries differing widely in social, political and institutional characteristics are unlikely to fall on a common surface is heeded by taking a relatively homogeneous set of European regions (Beugelsdijk and Van Schaik 2005b) or US states (Knack 2000). This is especially relevant since it has been shown that countries may differ in terms of relevant proxies for social capital. Moreover, by comparing *national* cultures, "we risk losing track of the enormous diversity found within many of the major nations of the world" (Smith and Bond 1998: 41). By studying regions and regional differences, this risk is limited.

Review (Rosenberg 1956). It was part of a five-point scale that Rosenberg called "faith in people." Gradually this dichotomous variable became a stand-alone measure. Nevertheless, despite (or because of) its popularity, some scholars claim that the "generally speaking" question suffers from a number of validity problems. First, Uslaner (2002) and Smith (1997) claim that the responses to the survey question on trust depend on where in the survey the question is asked. Moreover, the actual meaning of the responses has been questioned (Moore 1999). When discussing this "generally speaking" question, Putnam (2000: 137–138) argues that the meanings of the responses remain murky in one respect. "If fewer respondents nowadays say, 'most people can be trusted' that might mean any of three things: 1) the respondents are actually reporting that honesty is rarer these days; or 2) other people's behavior hasn't really changed, but we have become more paranoid; or 3) neither our ethical demands nor other people's behavior have actually changed, but now we have more information about their treachery, perhaps because of more lurid media reports." Moreover, there is some ambiguity about what is meant by "most people" (Delhey and Newton 2005). This term may refer to a wide range of people such as family, friends, neighbors, and it is unknown how far this circle extends (Hardin 2002). Moreover, when people say that they trust the government, they do not mean anything closely analogous to what they typically mean when they say they trust another person (Hardin 2002, Chapter 1).

The validity of the "generally speaking survey trust measure" has been the key issue in the contribution of Miller and Mitamura (2003). They argue that the generalized trust question contains ambiguous meaning, which has negative consequences for its internal validity and interpretative meaning. Their basic argument is that the survey question does not constitute one scale, but consists of two discrete items, being trust and caution, instead of what ideally would have been (and most people interpret as) trust and distrust. The problem is that trust and caution are not opposites. Measures of trust and measures of prudence create separate factors, suggesting that caution does not correlate with distrust. Experiments in a sample of US and Japanese students show that when caution is removed and trust is measured on a separate scale, Americans appear to have higher levels of generalized trust than do Japanese. At the same time, the 1997 WVS measure of generalized trust is 43 percent for the Japanese and 36 percent for the Americans. Miller and Mitamura's (2003) analysis suggests that the binomial "generally speaking" question lacks substantial internal validity and is biased. This finding has consequences for the possibilities for cross-country comparisons of trust levels. If caution is more necessary in one society than in another, the trust scores are biased. If a person might score high on a generalized trust scale but is risk averse, that person might choose caution over trust when faced with a binomial choice between only these two. Hence, in countries in which people live in a closed and safe environment, associated with low levels of caution, the "generally speaking" trust measure may overestimate true trust; true levels of trust may be lower than measured by the survey.

Experimental approaches toward trust have yielded ambiguous results as well. Glaeser *et al.* (2000) have shown that the trust question used in the WVS-based research actually measures trustworthiness and not trust (*see also* Bellemare and Kroger 2007). They suggest developing alternative instruments to measure trust. The predictive power of survey trust questions – as compared with experiments-based trust questions – has also been shown to differ between countries. In comparing trust scores between Tanzania and Sweden, Danielson and Holm (2005) find that whereas the survey indicates that 74 percent of Swedes say that most people can be trusted and only 41 percent of Tanzanian subjects did so, experiments indicate their actual trust game behavior is remarkably similar. Danielson and Holm (2005: 530) deduce from this that aggregate-level survey trust answers reflect something that is at least partly different from trust behavior. Fehr (2009) has recently initiated a research line trying to decompose trust into its different components, more specifically the extent to which trust reflects risk taking and the extent to which it reflects social preferences (betrayal aversion and altruism). Embedded in behavioral economics, Fehr and his colleagues try to disentangle the endogenous and exogenous determinants of trust, a route that seems highly promising (*see* Croson and Konow 2009: 239, in the context of dictator games). In line with the conclusion of Miller and Mitamura, Fehr (2009: 239) writes that "the answer to the GSS and the WVS question is not only shaped by people's beliefs about others' trustworthiness, but also by their own preferences towards taking social risks." Fehr concludes that survey measures of trust reflect a composite of preferences and (rational) beliefs, a finding which can be extended to behavior in experimental trust games (Fetchenhauer and Dunning 2009).

7.5.3 Level problems

Most of the arguments in the trust–growth studies are derived from micro-level insights regarding the reduction of transaction costs. This seems powerful from a theoretical perspective, but empirical studies at the firm or the nation level use completely different measures of trust. Trust at the micro- and macro-level are operationalized in totally different ways. At the aggregate level, international differences in trust are measured by means of the WVS question "generally speaking, do you think that people can be trusted?" (Inglehart 1997; Knack and Keefer 1997; Whiteley 2000; Zak and Knack 2001). As explained before, trust is then measured as the percentage of respondents in each country that replied "most people can be trusted." At the micro-level, trust has been operationalized in numerous ways. Mostly it is measured as a multi-item scale consisting of questions that interviewees are asked to respond to when discussing certain (specific) partners or individuals (Moorman *et al.* 1992; Ganesan 1994; Brock Smith and Barclay 1997). Mostly these refer to degree of trust (on a Likert scale of 1–5 or 1–7) in expertise, keeping of promises and provision of trustworthy information (Ganesan 1994; Johnson *et al.* 1996; Beugelsdijk *et al.* 2006). In relationship marketing, trust is perceived as a component of a broader set of relational norms affecting the nature of inter-firm relationships (Heide and John 1992; Achrol 1997).

Building on multi-level theory, this has led Beugelsdijk (2006) to conclude that the "trust" that figures prominently in firm-level studies is not the trust of the macro-economic literature. The reduction of transaction costs because of a trusting relationship cannot simply be translated into the statement that high interpersonal trust reduces overall transaction costs in an economy, which positively affects GDP growth (Fine 2001). The distinction between micro- and macro-trust "gives an additional flavour to the notorious micro/macro distinction that is so difficult to handle in empirical research. We know perfectly well how to come down from the macro-level to the micro-level, considering the impact of societal structures and changes on individual attitudes. It is much more difficult to ascend again and to speculate about the effects of an aggregation of individual attitudes on macro phenomena" (Luhmann 1988: 105). As mentioned earlier, the leap from micro- to macro-functioning may be illegitimate, because what may be true for individuals may not be true for the society as a whole

(Fine 2001). Multi-level theory argues that measures of an individual-level construct cannot always simply be aggregated and assumed to be a veridical representation of its counterpart (Morgeson and Hofmann 1999: 260). According to Moore (1999), the assumption that trust is a generic phenomenon similar in all domains does not necessarily hold.

Part of the critique on the "generally speaking" question concerns the complexity in translating insights from micro- to macro-levels. The theoretical reasoning that lies behind the supposed effect of trust in these aggregate studies does not correspond fully with the way trust is operationalized in these studies. Moreover, if trust is related to institutions (as shown in the previous section on antecedents of trust), it is problematic to interpret the results of these trust studies unambiguously. For example, the fact that this question results in lower scores on trust in poorer countries than in richer countries does not necessarily imply that high levels of trust are important for economic development. It does not, because it does not do justice to the distinction between micro- and macro-trust. Of these two types of trust, the WVS "generally speaking" question comes closest to the latter. Given the interrelationship between trust and institutions, a low score on this variable need not imply a lack of interpersonal trust in poor countries but may also point to a lack of well-functioning institutions (cf. Danielson and Holm's (2005) results referred to earlier). Hence, both theoretically and empirically, this specific aggregate trust measure is strongly correlated with measures of well-functioning institutions, resulting in a serious identification problem. This identification problem becomes even more pressing because institutions and societal characteristics such as social distance have been argued to drive cross-country differences in trust levels. Put differently, trust serves as a proxy for culture in a large part of the literature, but cultural characteristics have also been found to affect levels of trust in a society. This creates a complex web of causal linkages between trust, culture, institutions and economic development.

7.6 Discussion: from well-tossed spaghetti to multi-layered lasagna

If there is one thing this chapter has shown, it is that both theoretically and empirically, trust culture and (well-functioning) institutions are highly interrelated. Literature shows that culture in the form of generalized macro-trust cannot be completely separated from economic and institutional development. Both the literature addressing the trust–growth relationship and that focussing on the antecedents of trust find evidence of a strong relationship between trust and well-functioning institutions and cultural (religious) traditions.

This implies that the relationships between trust, culture, institutions and economic development are complex, and empirical studies suffer from various identification problems. Putnam himself describes the causal arrows among civic involvement, reciprocity, honesty and social trust as being as tangled as well-tossed spaghetti (Putnam 2000: 137). He suggests two social equilibria exist (Putnam *et al.* 1993: 177–181). Virtuous circles result in social equilibria with high levels of cooperation, trust and civic engagement. Conversely, the absence of these traits in the uncivic community is also self-reinforcing. This process of cumulative causation suggests that there may be at least two broad equilibria toward which all societies tend to evolve and which, once attained, tend to be self-reinforcing. The possibility of these two equilibria has also been suggested by others (Rothstein and Uslaner 2005; You and Khagram 2005; Dixit 2009). Empirically, the evidence for the existence of these social equilibria is rather thin and mostly based on correlations over time. Rothstein and Uslaner (2005) report a correlation of .81 for the twenty-two countries included in both the 1981 and the 1990 samples of the WVS, and a correlation of .85 between the twenty-eight countries in the 1990 and 1995 samples. Generalized trust levels are rather sticky or change only in decades, not years. A similar observation holds for levels of inequality. GINI scores of economic inequality are highly correlated over time. Galbraith[15] reports a correlation of .71 between economic inequality measures in 1963 and 1996 for a sample of thirty-seven countries.

Evaluating the trust literature, we can only agree with Putnam that the relationships between trust, culture, institutions and economic development seem like well-tossed spaghetti. However, this would also suggest our understanding of trust has not improved and no clear theoretical ideas exist on how to proceed. We do not think that such a conclusion does justice to the reality. What may have looked like

---

[15] http://utip.gov.utexas.edu/

well-tossed spaghetti a few years ago now starts to be unraveled in different components. Thanks to the trust literature, we have improved our insights and understanding of how trust relates to culture and institutions. However, what this also shows is that scholars need to be very precise in defining their concepts and carefully describe their chain of logic in order to avoid being trapped in an intricate web of causal linkages.

A theory on trust and institutions should at least deal with the multi-level problem of trust and the different types of trust. We know micro-trust is influenced by higher-level factors such as the well-functioning of institutions. In this respect, it is interesting to refer to the work by Bachmann (2001) and Yoo and Lee (2009). They analyze the context-specificity of trust and argue that the process of trust creation and the function of trust should be seen in the broader social setting. More specifically, in relating macro to micro, Bachmann argues that in developed countries such as the United Kingdom and Germany, institutional differences result in differences in the process of trust-building and types of micro-trust. He empirically shows that "while in both countries, trust is highly valued as an efficient means of coping with uncertainty, in the British socio-economic system, which is a prime example of extensive de-regulation, trust is a much more scarce resource than in the German business environment, which is still characterized by tight regulation and a strong institutional order. If/when trust occurs in the British system, it is likely to be *personal trust* constituted on the basis of individual experiences, rather than *system [generalized] trust* produced by reference to the institutional framework" (Bachmann 2001: 353). Yoo and Lee (2009) reach a similar conclusion after comparing trust and social capital in France and Korea. The observation that trust may depend on formal and informal institutions and vary with institutional context is the starting point for Farrell (2005) and Farrell and Knight (2003). According to Farrell and Knight (2003: 539), a theory on trust and institutions would do three things. First, it would establish micro-level explanations that identify the causal relationships among trust [social capital], institutions and social cooperation. Second, it would present a dynamic account of the ways in which trust and social capital can emerge and be maintained over time. Third, it would assess the conditions under which this process is likely to occur.

What does the trust–growth literature imply for the field of culture and economic behavior?
Given the identification and validity problems as discussed in this chapter, we think that the trust literature that emerged in the slipstream of Knack and Keefer's (1997) paper has helped us in many ways, but should not be considered core contributions to the debate on the role of culture in economics. Too many theoretical and empirical problems are associated with this measure and the theoretical construct to claim that the trust literature has showed that culture affects economic growth. As Moore (1999: 75) puts it: "We are trying to do empirical research on a fragile conceptual base. The concept of trust remains elusive, and useful empirical measures still evade us." Manski (2000: 117) has been particularly critical: "The broadening of economic theory has coincided with new empirical research by economists on social interactions. Unfortunately, the empirical literature has not shown much progress." He mentions two problematic aspects. First, the use of ambiguous theoretical concepts such as social capital and trust and poor measurement of these issues result in studies that maintain no or only little connection to economic theory. Second, the type of data used do not allow for a proper study of actual social interactions. "The findings of empirical studies are often open to an uncomfortably wide range of interpretations" (Manski 2000: 117). He suggests two routes out of this problem:

1. Empirical researchers need to be much clearer on the questions they address. Limit the use of jargon with ambiguous meaning.
2. Empirical studies need to be based upon better data. Manski has a clear preference for more experimental-based research.

This does not solve all problems in the field of trust and culture, however. The notorious micro–macro problem as explicitly identified in the trust literature holds more broadly for the entire field of culture and economics. Empirical studies often use survey results based on individual responses. We already discussed the methodological challenges associated with the aggregation of micro to macro and the risk of an ecological fallacy in Chapter 5 (Section 5.2). The leap from micro to macro by simply aggregating these individual scores may not be a legitimate one if – theoretically – the aggregation procedure is affected by interaction effects between individuals. This literature already dates back to Veblen's concept of conspicuous consumption, which basically shows that individual utility functions are affected by social interactions (Veblen 1994 [1899]; Pollak 1976; Bagwell and Bernheim 1996; Glaeser *et al.* 2003; Arrow and Dasgupta 2009). Manski discusses three types of interactions. First, *endogenous interactions*, in which the propensity of an agent to behave in some way varies with the behavior of the group. Second, *contextual interactions*, wherein the propensity of an agent to behave in some way varies with exogenous characteristics of the group members. Third, *correlated effects*, wherein agents in the same group tend to behave similarly because they have similar individual characteristics or face a similar institutional environment (Manski 2000: 127). It is especially the first type, the endogenous interactions, which constitute problems for the translation of micro-insights to macro-outcomes.

Trust relates to all three types of interaction. To start with the correlational effects, as we discussed in this chapter, individual characteristics (age, gender, employed or not, etc.) and, perhaps more importantly, the quality and type of the institutional setting partly determine the reported levels of generalized trust. But exogenous interactions exist as well. Exogenous characteristics of the group, for example the social distance between individuals within a group, the presence of outward threats, all affect the individually reported level of trust. Finally, trust arises endogenously depending on the average trustworthiness of a group. If other people of a group act as trustees, then, all else being equal, oneself is also more willing to act as a trustee.

This context dependency of trust complicates matters considerably. The choice to use trust in regression models explaining economic growth differentials not only poses a micro–macro challenge, it also leaves us with the associated challenge to distinguish between endogenous and contextual interactions (Fehr 2009). The aggregate trust measure does not allow researchers to reveal whether a trusting environment affects individual behavior and trust scores (endogenous interaction), or whether aggregate trust scores are simply the aggregation of independent individuals. Manski (2000) labels this the reflection problem. This is relevant because, as we have shown, if trust is solely based upon well-functioning institutions (contextual interaction), then the only logical policy prescription would be to create good governance systems. Together with the supposed lack of internal validity (does the trust measure really measure trust?), this implies that we cannot unambiguously interpret the results from these trust studies.

Manski's (2000) solution consists of a plea for a more experimental approach in tackling social interaction. Although this may indeed provide us with more insights at the group level, it does not solve the level issue in cross-country studies. We also think there is still room to improve the empirical measure of trust. Miller and Mitamura (2003) make a plea for a multidimensional measure which attenuates measurement and conceptual problems associated with single-item variables. This is actually what scholars concerned with micro-trust do. As we discussed, surveys on inter-firm cooperation and the associated levels of trust between the interacting firms, for example, ask for multiple aspects of trust. Scholars interested in using aggregate-level trust measures could potentially benefit from looking more closely at micro-trust studies.[16] As mentioned previously Owen and Videras (2009) provide a recent study in which such a multidimensional route is taken.

Alternatively, it has been suggested that we change our conceptualization of trust. James Sr. (2002) argues that the word trust may be misplaced as long as it is framed in terms of prisoner dilemma games, because trust as prudence (based on fear of loss of reputation or retaliation) is not true trust, according to him. Following Williamson (1993), James Sr. wonders whether it is really trust when you know your partner has an incentive to be trustworthy. In his view, trust when vulnerability is retained is a much stronger concept than trust derived from incentives. To understand why people trust each other even when the possibility of opportunistic behavior exists is the key question. Many economists have framed the trust concept in a rational setting by building upon game-theoretical or new institutional economic theories. But by doing so, they have not explained why, in the absence of incentives, people trust other people and why some societies may perhaps score higher on this type of trust than others.

In conclusion, the interest in trust as a component of culture has certainly contributed to our understanding of the complex relations between trust, culture, institutions and economic development.

---

[16] The multi-level problem and the problem of preference interaction are also related to the difference between stated and revealed preferences. One of the reasons why revealed preferences may provide us with better insights is the fact that this in a way reflects *ex-post* behavior *after* potential influence of social interaction, whereas stated preferences – as measured in most of the WVS questions – are *ex-ante* preferences.

However, as we have shown in this chapter, many theoretical, methodological and empirical challenges remain. The most pressing is the nature of the relation between trust and culture. There are many aspects of this relationship that we still do not understand and a rich research agenda lies ahead. A social interaction approach, in which interactions between individual actors are modeled and the multi-level problem is explicitly addressed, seems most promising.

8 | *International business*

8.1 Introduction

After looking at entrepreneurial culture and trust, we devote this chapter to the relationship between culture, cultural differences, and the international organization and production of economic activity. As we explain in more detail below, the field of international business (IB) is at least partly defined in terms of its attempt to understand the role of culture.[1] Since the 1970s, IB scholars have expended a great deal of effort to increase our understanding of the role of culture in explaining the organization of international production. This concerns not only patterns of foreign direct investment (FDI) and trade but also the way culture and cultural differences affect the economic organization of these international activities (entry-mode strategies). Given international economists' recent interest in multinational heterogeneity (e.g. Melitz 2003; Bernard *et al.* 2003, 2007; Yeaple 2005, 2008) and in the role of culture in economic behavior (see previous chapters), we take a closer look at the field of IB to see what we can learn from this literature.

This chapter is structured as follows. In order to make clear why studies in international business are relevant and important to discuss in the context of this book, we first define the field of international business. We describe the type of research questions IB scholars typically try to answer and show that Hofstede's culture framework has

---

[1] We focus on national culture here and not organizational or professional culture. Whereas national culture relates primarily to deep-seated values, organizational culture relates primarily to shared beliefs in organizational practices and processes (Hofstede *et al.* 1990). Conceptual and empirical studies on the interplay between these different types of culture and the way they affect managerial decision-making processes are scarce. Simon and Lane (2004) distinguish between types of cultural differences and argue over which type of cultural difference matters most. Another example is the study by Pothukuchi *et al.* (2002).

shaped IB research in many ways. Specifically, using Hofstede's culture dimensions, Kogut and Singh (1988) introduced a measure of cultural distance. This measure is used extensively in IB. We discuss the concept and measure of cultural distance and evaluate how it has served as an input in research focussed on explaining FDI and trade patterns, and the entry-mode strategies of internationalizing firms. IB scholars are also engaged in studies addressing the relationship between culture, managerial values and behavior. Comparative management studies focus on explaining why, and especially, how, differences in managers' cultural backgrounds drive their management styles and decisions. This includes the way employees with different cultural backgrounds interact in the workplace. In the final section, we extrapolate these insights to draw lessons for our more general quest to understand the role of culture in economics. We explicitly discuss (i) the potential for spillovers between IB scholars and international economists and (ii) the methodological lessons that can be learned from the IB literature and how these feed into our overall discussion on culture in economics.

8.2 Defining the field of international business and how culture fits in

IB is a field that does not constitute a separate discipline. Instead it combines and builds upon insights from economics, strategic management and comparative business systems (Negandhi 1983). In defining the field, Caves (1998) clearly sees IB as a field that slices across the grain of areas of study in business administration. According to Caves, "strategy, finance, marketing, organizational behavior, human-resource management each has its domain of decision making within the firm and its stock of models, frameworks, and research problems for addressing them. International business designates not a class of decisions, but a group of firms that face decision-making problems beyond those that confront single-nation business, or they encounter the same problems transformed by their international context" (Caves 1998: 5). Although Caves does not mention economics as a separate discipline and concentrates on business administration, the fact is that much of the current – and even more past – research is based on, derived from or closely related to international economics. For many economics-oriented scholars in IB, the field of IB originated out of the study of FDI, but differentiated from economic approaches by a more empirical approach and one in which the multinational firm was not a black box but was specifically included in the analysis (Shenkar 2004; Buckley 2002). The international or comparative context forms the common denominator in the research agenda of both groups of IB scholars (i.e. the more economics-oriented IB scholars and the more business-oriented IB scholars). In 1970 – which saw the first issue of the *Journal of International Business Studies* – Nehrt *et al.* (1970) defined IB according to the following criteria (*see also* Ricks 1985):

1. It is concerned with firm-level business activity that crosses national boundaries or is conducted in a location other than the firm's home country.
2. It is concerned with the interrelationship between the operations of the business firm and international or foreign environments in which the firm operates.
3. It does not include studies devoted to economic development, development planning, foreign trade and the international monetary system, which belong to development and international economics. Excluded also are studies of foreign legal, political, economic and social environments; these belong to the fields of law, political science, economics and behavioral science unless the study itself relates the environment directly to the organizational, operational or decision-making problems of international business.
4. It does not include studies of business activities in given foreign countries – a study of marketing channels in Turkey is still a study about domestic business in Turkey.
5. As an exception to point 4, however, comparative business studies are included within this definition. For example, a study of pharmaceutical marketing channels in Germany, Italy, Brazil and Japan, which makes comparisons and analyzes the causes and effects of similarities and differences, would be considered IB research.

These five criteria broadly sketch the field of IB (and what is *not* IB). In following the above criteria, Buckley (2002) argues that more than thirty years later, IB scholars have been particularly successful in explaining three key topics.

1. Explaining the patterns of foreign direct investment.
2. Explaining the existence, strategy and organization of multinational enterprises (MNEs).

3. Understanding and predicting the development of the internation-alization of firms and the new developments of globalization.

Each of these three areas represents a specific time period. The explanation of FDI patterns was prominent on the IB agenda in the period after the Second World War until the 1970s. Despite these early studies, explaining the geography of MNE activity remains a popular topic in IB given the ongoing articles on FDI and its location. The interest which IB scholars pay to cross-country patterns of foreign-owned value-adding activity has remained consistently high, as witnessed by the recent debate as to whether MNEs are spreading their activities equally across all parts of the globe or are instead concentrating them in specific regions (Dunning *et al.* 2007; Rugman and Verbeke 2004, 2007).

According to Buckley (2002), the strategy and organization of the MNE dominated the IB agenda between 1970 and 1990. Major theoretical developments in this period concern Dunning's OLI (ownership, location, internalization) theory (*see* Dunning 1980, 1993; Dunning and Lundan 2008) and the application of internalization and transaction costs theories to the MNE (Buckley and Casson 1976; Hennart 1982). Even today, the transaction costs theory is a dominant research tradition in IB and applications go beyond explanations of the mere existence of the MNE, but for example also include the modes of foreign entry (as discussed below). The last key area in which IB scholars have been successful, according to Buckley (2002), has been the improvement of our understanding of the process of globalization. Due to increasing flexibility demands, internationalizing firms were looking for new types of cooperation both within the firm, between headquarter and subsidiary (Bartlett and Ghoshal 1989), and between firms, in terms of international joint ventures and alliances. One important issue in all these sub-fields has been the role of culture and cultural differences.

In his analysis of important future research questions, Buckley (2002) clearly sees a role for culture and IB research, not as a separate sub-field but parallel to and cross-fertilizing "mainstream" IB research. According to Buckley, IB is at least partly defined by its attention to cultural differences and the comparative method. The importance of culture and cultural differences is reflected in recent discussions in the *Journal of International Business Studies* concerning the methodologies required to properly incorporate the role of culture and cultural differences in IB research (*see* special issue in *JIBS*, volume 37 issue 6 and Sivikumar and Nakata 2001; Maseland and Van Hoorn 2009, 2010).

The main database for measuring culture in IB has been Hofstede's (1980, 2001) pioneering work. A number of projects have been initiated since then, such as the World Value Survey, Schwartz's culture framework and the GLOBE project (*see* Chapter 5). Despite the fact that Hofstede's work has been criticized for "reducing culture to an overly simplistic four or five dimension conceptualization; limiting the sample to a single multinational company (IBM); failing to capture the malleability of culture over time; and ignoring within-country heterogeneity" (Kirkman *et al.* 2006: 286), it is generally acknowledged that Hofstede's (1980) work on *Culture's Consequences* has been a major impetus for the field of IB. The impact of Hofstede's seminal work on culture cannot be underestimated and is clearly reflected in Kirkman *et al.*'s review (2006) of empirical research incorporating Hofstede's cultural framework. In this review, Kirkman *et al.* examine 180 articles published in top-tier journals between 1980 and 2002 that empirically assessed the four or five dimensions of Hofstede's framework. Limiting themselves to major management and (cross-cultural) applied psychology journals, they show a broad range of topics exists in which one or multiple Hofstede dimensions have been applied. These are, for example, change management, human resource management, negotiation issues, entrepreneurship, entry modes, innovation and foreign direct investment.

An important assumption that often remains implicit concerns the stability of culture over time (Yaprak 2008). As described in previous chapters, the discussion on cultural convergence vs. that of divergence is still open, and the view of culture as a dynamic process has been gaining ground in social sciences. Despite some limited discussion regarding the stability of cultural values (Leung *et al.* 2005) in IB as well, IB scholars generally assume that cultures, or at least cultural differences, are stable. Doing so helps to reduce ambiguity and makes life easier for scholars. It allows for a discussion of the fit between a certain culture and specific managerial and organizational practices, because it makes behavioral outcomes more predictable (Erez and Earley 1993; Weick and Quinn 1999; Leung *et al.* 2005). This, in turn, allows researchers to include culture in their IB theories without running the risk of including a partly random component, or one that changes over time. In doing so, many scholars refer to Hofstede (1980, 2001), who himself claimed that mental programs of people around the world do not change rapidly but remain relatively constant over time. In line with Inglehart's thesis discussed in Chapter 4, Hofstede asserts that cultural shifts are relative as opposed to absolute. Alternatively, if cultures would be converging as, for example, argued by Heuer *et al.* (1999), this would logically imply that IB-related practices would become increasingly similar and a substantial part of the rationale for the existence of IB as a field of research would vanish.

A second key assumption related to the above discussion concerns the homogeneity of cultures. This homogeneity implies that foreign cultures can be treated as a single unit. The saying "when in Rome, do as the Romans do" is a pillar in the vast majority of IB research and has led to an adaptation paradigm. In other words, when firms cross borders, they have to adapt to local cultures in order to be successful and these local cultures are considered to be homogenous. This explains why a larger cultural distance between two locations (almost always countries) is argued to impede investment flows. This homogeneity and associated adaptation assumption are related to the assumption on stability and the discussion on value convergence or divergence, because globalization might lead not so much to convergence or divergence of values between countries as to increased divergence within countries. That is, the question on convergence or divergence need not be the relevant one if it is the within-country value diversity that increases. This directly impacts IB research as the assumption on homogenous home and host cultures does not hold any longer if that would be the case. And if cultures cannot be "treated" as homogenous any longer, it triggers a question on adaptation, i.e. who to adapt to? In other words, what if the "Romans all do different things and have different values"? As far as we know, there is no study in which this question is explicitly addressed, most probably because of the empirical difficulties associated with measuring value diversity in countries.[2]

---

[2] An interesting first attempt to study value consensus can be found in Schwartz and Sagie (2000), who study value consensus by measuring the standard deviation of ten motivational types of values from Schwartz's framework. As

Irrespective of (or perhaps thanks to) these simplifying assumptions, Shenkar (2001) claims that culture and cultural differences have had three primary thrusts in the field of FDI-related studies (cf. Buckley 2002). The first relates to the explanation of location of FDI, including the sequence of such investments. The second field pertains to the explanation of choice of entry mode into foreign markets. The third is related to the second and considers the success of MNE affiliates in international markets. Hence, following Shenkar (2001), we discuss first the relationship between cultural distance (CD) and FDI, and second that between CD and entry-mode research. But before doing so, we discuss the operationalization of the cultural distance concept in IB. This is important as this specific index was a privileged asset of IB scholars but is now slowly making its way into related fields such as international economics and international finance (De Groot *et al.* 2005; Belot and Ederveen 2006; Siegel *et al.* 2008a, 2008b; Beugelsdijk and Frijns 2010).

8.3 Cultural distance: concept, measurement and critique

8.3.1 Concept

As already explained, IB research has concentrated on the cultural differences between countries engaging in international business activity. Managers pursuing international expansions, exporting or setting up plants abroad are confronted with national cultural settings that differ from their own. The IB literature clearly indicates that both exporters and market- and efficiency-seeking MNEs suffer from a liability of foreignness, meaning that they incur additional costs which indigenous firms do not incur (Hymer 1976; Zaheer 1995; Caves 1996; Miller and Eden 2006). Cultural differences between home and host countries have been put forward as an important source of this liability of foreignness. Culturally more distant countries tend to have norms and values that are more different from those of a firm's home country, resulting in increasingly divergent organizational and managerial

they write themselves, their results should be interpreted with care, because they use a non-representative sample of school teachers. Moreover, they do not take into account the dispersion of values at the individual level – something which is necessary to measure the diversity of values in a country – but use an indirect measure.

practices, communication and negotiation styles, desired behaviors, consumer preferences, and effective marketing tactics (Hofstede 1980; Kogut and Singh 1988; Schneider and De Meyer 1991; Ralston *et al.* 1993; Adler 1986; Campbell *et al.* 1988; Ngo *et al.* 1998; Van Mesdag 2000).

Although most IB scholars have focussed on cultural distance, the concept of CD is strongly related to (and embedded in) a broader and older concept called psychic distance. According to Dow and Karutnaratna (2006: 578), psychic distance is one of the most commonly cited yet vaguely measured constructs within the realm of international business. They trace the origin of psychic distance back to Beckerman (1956). Although it recently made its way into research on trade flows by international economists (more on that later), it has been popularized in IB by the Uppsala school of internationalization. Starting in the mid-1970s, researchers at the Uppsala school included psychic distance in their research in a structured way by looking at (i) the establishment of a formal definition. Johanson and Vahlne (1977: 24) defined psychic distance as "the sum of factors preventing the flow of information to and from the market." The sum of factors includes several elements, ranging from differences in language, political systems, cultural differences and level of economic development; (ii) the measurement of psychic distance, and (iii) its potential applications, focussing on entry modes and location choice. This early work on psychic distance clearly sees cultural distance as an element of the overall psychic distance. More recent contributors, such as Boyacigiller (1990) and Evans *et al.* (2000), follow this line of reasoning. In other words, cultural distance is seen as part of the broader concept of psychic distance.

Ideally, psychic distance is theorized and measured at the individual level, i.e. at the level of the individual manager making a decision (O'Grady and Lane 1996). This is not only theoretically the most correct way to conceptualize psychic distance, it also allows researchers to discriminate between overlapping phenomena. Dow and Karutnaratna (2006: 579) argue in this context that "differences in culture may increase the psychic distance between countries, but it may also be highly correlated with differences in customer preferences." In other words, in their view it may be important to disentangle the different elements that make up the overall concept of psychic distance. They propose thinking of psychic distance as a sequence of related constructs, and distinguish between so-called psychic distance stimuli and what they call the perceived psychic distance (PD_p). The psychic distance stimuli are the macro-level factors such as language, culture and religion. PD_p is the decision-maker's perception of psychic distance and will be a function of the psychic distance stimuli to which they are exposed, but that perception will be moderated by the decision-maker's sensitivity to those stimuli. A manager's sensitivity will depend on his international experience, age and education, amongst other factors. Hence, in Dow and Karutnaratna's vision, CD and psychic distance are different concepts. Despite the conceptual differences between cultural and psychic distance, the dominant logic in IB concerns cultural distance and not psychic distance, and the two concepts are often used interchangeably. Therefore we concentrate on cultural distance as it is used most often in IB research (O'Grady and Lane 1996).

8.3.2 Measurement

In most studies, CD is operationalized by the Kogut and Singh (1988) index, which is based on the differences in the scores on the four (or five) Hofstede dimensions between two countries. These differences are corrected for differences in the variance of each dimension and then arithmetically averaged. Algebraically:

$$CD_j = \sum_{i=1}^{4}\{(I_{ij} - I_{iUS})^2 / V_i\}/4$$

where CD_j is the cultural distance between country j and the home country (e.g. the US), I_{ij} is country j's score on the ith cultural dimension, I_{iUS} is the home-country score on this dimension and V_i is the variance of the score of the dimension. One of the likely reasons why the concept of the CD and the Kogut and Singh index is so popular among IB scholars is the fact that a relatively "soft" theoretical aspect such as cultural differences can be operationalized in such a "hard" way, allowing for its inclusion in large-scale statistical analyses.

Occasionally, CD is calculated as a Euclidean distance version of the Kogut and Singh index, for example in Barkema and Vermeulen (1997) and Brouthers and Brouthers (2001). Unlike the Kogut and Singh index, this measure does not give equal weights to the differences in the scores on each of Hofstede's dimensions and, hence, does not assume that each dimension is equally important in determining the cultural distance between countries. Instead, in line with the concept of Euclidean distance, it computes their distance in a four-dimensional space as the square root of the sum of the squared differences in the scores on each cultural dimension. Formally:

$$CD_j = \sqrt{\sum_{i=1}^{4} \{(I_{ij} - I_{iUS})^2 / V_i\}}$$

where CD_j is the cultural distance between country j and the home country (e.g. the US), I_{ij} is country j's score on the ith cultural dimension, I_{iUS} is the score of the US on this dimension and V_i is the variance of the score of the dimension. Although this Euclidean distance measure is often presented as an alternative of the KS measure, it is highly correlated with the KS measure and very often yields similar results.

8.3.3 Critique

Over time, the concept of CD and its measure have been criticized. The most comprehensive critique comes from Shenkar (2001), who criticizes the CD concept on the grounds of conceptual and methodological properties. The first relates to what he calls the illusion of symmetry, the illusion of stability, the illusion of linearity, the illusion of causality and the illusion of discordance. Regarding methodological properties, Shenkar (2001) mentions the assumption of corporate homogeneity and the assumption of spatial homogeneity.[3] We discuss each of them below.

- *The illusion of symmetry*: the CD measure implicitly assumes that the CD between country A and B is similar to the distance between country B and country A. However, in practice, there need not be such an identical role for home and host countries. It may be much easier for Chinese firms to invest in the US, than vice versa.
- *The illusion of stability*: as CD is measured at a single point in time, the CD is assumed to be constant over time. If cultures change, it may be relevant to point out that the CD between home and host may be different at the time of entry than by the time performance or the

---

[3] Shenkar (2001) also mentions *the assumption of equivalence*, implying that all dimensions are equally important. As this was also part of his comment labeled the illusion of discordance, we do not consider this a separate point of critique.

affiliate's survival is measured. Relatedly, firms may gain experience and the CD for subsequent decisions may be smaller than that for the first acquaintance (e.g. Hennart 1991).

- *The illusion of linearity*: the implication of using one measure of CD for explaining location of MNE activity, the entry mode chosen and the subsequent success of these foreign activities is that CD affects all these different phenomena in a linear way. This can be questioned. The Uppsala school of stepwise internationalization (*see* later) clearly shows that the effect of CD may depend on a firm's learning curve and hence is not linear.

- *The illusion of causality*: a tendency exists to concentrate on the effects of CD, while the impact of CD should be seen as part of a broader picture, including geopolitical distance, market size, political instability, etc. Distance is a multidimensional construct. In this context it is interesting to refer to Huang's 2007 article in which he shows that physical distance is related to underlying cultural characteristics. Using Hofstede's uncertainty avoidance measure, he shows that the impact of geographic distance on trade flows is moderated by the willingness to accept uncertainty; the same absolute number of kilometers is perceived differently.

- *The illusion of discordance*: the assumption in many of the papers using CD is that all aspects of the cultural distance between home and host countries matter equally, whereas it can easily be argued that for some aspects some dimensions of a culture matter more than other dimensions. Implicitly, the argument is that all cultural dimensions can substitute for each other, while some dimensions may be complementary (*see also* Sivakumar and Nakata 2001).

- *The assumption of corporate homogeneity*: by using national cultural measures, the CD concept incorporates variance only at the national cultural level and assumes a lack of variance at the corporate level. This has been argued not to be true (Hofstede *et al.* 1990). The relationship between organizational and corporate culture is a complex one and corporate culture may moderate or mediate the impact of national cultural differences (and vice versa).

- *The assumption of spatial homogeneity*: by calculating CD on the basis of national-level sores, potential intra-country variation is excluded. Also, a firm's exact location in a country is not measured, thus excluding potential border effects reducing the size of the CD and leading to overestimations of the CD.

Despite this criticism, there is some evidence that the KS measure of CD correlates positively with *perceptual* measures of cultural differences. Drogendijk and Slangen (2006) use multiple indicators of cultural distance in their study explaining the choice between greenfield and acquisition. Comparing Hofstede, Schwartz and survey-based perceptual measures, they find that all measures behave in a similar direction and the explanatory power of the cultural distance based on Hofstede and Schwartz is comparable. Magnussen *et al.* (2008: 183) write after an extensive empirical comparison of multiple culture measures that "the CD [cultural distance] construct based on Hofstede is shown to compare favorably with other frameworks."

Given that both market-selection (location-choice) and entry-mode decisions have been argued to be related to cultural or psychic distance (Shenkar 2001; Tihanya *et al.* 2005; Dow and Karutnaratna 2006), we continue our discussion on the role of cultural distance by focussing on these two issues. We first discuss the relationship between CD and the location choice of MNEs by studying FDI patterns. We then turn to the economic organization of international production (i.e. entry-mode strategies) and the role of CD.

8.4 How cultural distance affects type and location of MNE activity

8.4.1 Cultural explanations of the geography of multinational activity

One of the arenas in which the CD index has been applied is in the field explaining aggregate patterns of trade and FDI. Although a long tradition exists in international economics to explain trade flows between countries by so-called gravity equations (Tinbergen 1962), the application of these models to aggregate MNE activity (often FDI flows/stocks) has started only relatively recently. Gravity models postulate that merchandise trade or FDI flows between countries depend on several characteristics of these countries, notably their economic size and level of economic development, and on factors stimulating or discouraging FDI or exports between countries (Bergstrand 1985; Brainard 1997). These factors include transportation costs, typically proxied by the presence or absence of a shared land border and by geographic distance, and formal trade barriers, often proxied by the presence or absence of free trade agreements.

In terms of the role of cultural differences and international economic activity, Beckerman (1956) was the first to suggest that trade flows are hampered not only by geographic but also by cultural distance, as trading partners from culturally more distant countries are generally less familiar with one another. This conjecture has been empirically supported by scholars who have found that countries trade less with one another if they have a different dominant religion or do not share an official language (Geraci and Prewo 1977; Srivastava and Green 1986; Anderson and Marcouiller 2002; Frankel and Rose 2002; Yeyati 2003; De Groot *et al.* 2004; Rose 2004; Subramanian and Wei 2007). Using more sophisticated measures of national cultural differences, Dow and Karutnaratna (2006) found that their new cardinal measure of religious differences between countries had a significantly negative impact on bilateral trade flows, while their new cardinal measure of language differences and the KS index of cultural distance generally had non-significant effects.[4]

Only few studies have directly related cultural distance to FDI flows or other indicators of aggregate MNE activity. Loree and Guisinger (1995) explain the determinants of US outward FDI and focus on the role of policy (e.g. institutional quality or tax rates) and non-policy (e.g. cultural distance) variables. They find a significant negative effect of cultural distance for the 1977 data, but not for the 1982 sample. They ascribe this insignificant result to an acculturation process among multinational managers, which may have reduced the impact of cultural distance (Loree and Guisinger 1995: 294). Grosse and Trevino (1996) report a non-significant effect of cultural distance explaining US FDI inflows, but a significant negative effect when using sales data of foreign affiliates in a more advanced model. Sethi *et al.* (2003) aim to explain changing trends in flows and determinants of FDI and compare the extent to which European and Asian host countries attract US FDI outflow. Their Kogut and Singh index yields a significant negative

---

[4] Note that the new measure by Dow and Karutnaratna (2006) bears no relation to the language variable introduced by Tabellini (2007b), as discussed in Chapter 7. Whereas the first is based on language families and the fraction of people speaking a foreign language in a country, Tabellini's language indicator refers to the structure of nouns.

effect, turning insignificant when including existing FDI stock as a control variable.

Cultural distance indicators have also been included as control variables in gravity equations. For example, in relating levels of corruption to FDI, Cuervo-Cazurra (2006), Kwok and Tadesse (2006a) and Habib and Zurawicki (2002) have included a range of alternative indicators of cultural distance, such as common language (Cuervo-Cazurra 2006), the difference on Hofstede's power distance and individualism dimensions (Kwok and Tadesse 2006a) or the Kogut and Singh index (Habib and Zurawicki 2002). In line with the other studies, these results are mixed as well.

Whereas the majority – if not all – of these studies use Hofstede's dimensions, mostly by calculating the Kogut–Singh cultural distance score, Siegel *et al.* (2008a) use Schwartz's (1994, 1999) model of culture dimensions. They find broad confirmation for a negative effect of cultural distance on bilateral FDI flows, but also show that some of Schwartz's culture dimensions are positively related to bilateral FDI flows. In a follow-up study, Siegel *et al.* (2008b) explore the role of one of the Schwartz culture dimensions – the degree of a country's egalitarianism and the difference on this dimension between two countries – in more detail and relate it to a set of international investment outcomes. They generally find that a larger distance on the egalitarianism dimension reduces cross-border debt and equity flows.

The problem with (almost) all these studies on trade and FDI is twofold. First of all, they have considered overall FDI and trade flows, whereas theory tells us that a distinction should be made between types of FDI and types of trade. The total amount of FDI consists of horizontal FDI and vertical FDI. Horizontal FDI is driven by access to local markets (Root 1998). Although vertical FDI has a broad interpretation in the literature (Braconier *et al.* 2005), FDI can be labeled as vertical if it includes vertically integrated MNEs, where local affiliates trade (in intermediate goods or services) with other parts of the firm (Braconier *et al.* 2005: 447). Root (1998) refers to vertical FDI as factor-seeking investment, which can be either raw material-seeking or low costs production-seeking. This distinction between horizontal and vertical FDI is relevant because the effect of cultural distance is likely to differ not only between these types of FDI (as shown by Slangen and Beugelsdijk 2010) but also between types of trade. Total trade consists of both intra-firm (associated with vertical FDI) and inter-firm or arm's length trade (substituting for horizontal FDI). Although we are not aware of any formal empirical test, we can expect that the impact of cultural distance is likely to be smaller on intra-firm trade than on arm's length trade, because of the former's lower level of interaction with the host-country culture.

Second, the impact of cultural distance on trade and FDI cannot be studied in isolation (as has been done so far) because trade and FDI are interrelated (Lipsey and Weiss 1984; Brainard 1997; Blonigen 2001; Head and Ries 2001; Pantulu and Poon 2003; Girma *et al.* 2005).[5] Horizontal FDI may substitute for arm's length trade and vertical FDI is associated with complementary intra-firm exports. And as the choice between exporting abroad or producing locally has been shown to depend on cultural distance (more on that in the next section), the impact of cultural distance on (horizontal) FDI and (arm's length) exports cannot be studied separately. Firms may choose to substitute one type of serving foreign markets with another type, depending on the cultural distance.

As far as we know, the only study that has looked at the role of cultural distance by explicitly comparing its impact on (arm's length) exports and (horizontal) FDI has been Slangen *et al.* (2007). The authors use the Hofstede-based KS index of cultural distance and clean their data on US exports from intra-firm trade. They use entry-mode theory (*see* next sub-section for details on this literature) to develop hypotheses on the relation between cultural distance and aggregate (arm's length) exports. Because of the substitution between exports and local production, firms may choose exports when cultural distance is large and choose the more risky mode of local production

---

[5] An extensive (mostly theoretical) literature on the substitute-complement debate exists, and the more fine-grained empirical evidence suggests that whether home-country exports and host-country-based affiliates are substitutes or complements depends on the type of foreign affiliate (cf. Clausing 2000: 192). When foreign affiliates represent vertical downstream investments, home-country exports are likely to increase (i.e. complementarity), because such affiliates often procure intermediate inputs from their parents. Vertical investments are thus likely to stimulate intra-firm trade (Andersson and Frederiksson 1996). However, when foreign affiliates represent horizontal market-seeking investments, home-country exports are likely to decrease (i.e. substitution), since the outputs sold by these affiliates to unaffiliated parties will no longer be sold directly from the home country. In such cases foreign affiliates and exports can thus be considered rival ways of serving foreign markets.

when cultural distance is relatively small. Testing their hypotheses, the authors find that increasing cultural distance is associated with lower levels of (horizontal) FDI and higher levels of aggregate (arm's length) exports. This is an important conclusion because it directly feeds into the discussion among international economists on firm heterogeneity. Their study shows that besides heterogeneity in firm characteristics (such as level of productivity), substitute options available to individual firms influence macro-level relationships between patterns of international trade and multinational production on the one hand and cultural distance on the other.

8.4.2 Entry-mode research and cultural differences

A considerable amount of research in IB concerns the firm's foreign-market entry (Slangen and Hennart 2007). This foreign-entry-mode literature aims to identify the determinants of an MNE's choice between different modes of foreign market entry by modeling certain entry modes as substitutes for one another (for a comprehensive review, *see* Datta *et al.* 2002). Many studies have examined the determinants of an MNE's choice between entering foreign markets through high-commitment modes requiring substantial resources, such as wholly owned and majority-owned affiliates, and entering them through lower-commitment modes requiring fewer resources, such as exports, licensing and joint ventures. There is general agreement that this choice depends to a considerable extent on the cultural distance to the target country, with many studies arguing that, as this distance increases, market-seeking MNEs are increasingly likely to enter that country through low-commitment rather than high-commitment entry modes (Anderson and Gatignon 1986; Hill *et al.* 1990; Root 1998; Brouthers and Brouthers 2001).

The theories on entry mode and internationalization are influenced by two major schools of thought. The first is transaction costs theory and the second is the Uppsala school describing a stepwise internationalization process of firms (Anderson 1993). The latter theory basically argues that firms begin their internationalization process in countries that are psychically close before venturing to more distant countries (Johanson and Vahlne 1977; Drogendijk 2001; Clark and Pugh 2001). Although, as Shenkar (2001) correctly points out, it is unclear whether the stepwise internationalization process from exports to local production coincides with an incremental increase in cultural distance, it is generally argued that firms can overcome cultural distance once they have learned to deal with that in a step-wise manner. Firms are predicted to start the process of internationalization by entering into culturally close markets and to enter more distant markets at a later stage. A crucial assumption is obviously that psychically close countries are more similar and that similarity is easier to manage than dissimilarity. However, as O'Grady and Lane (1996) argue, starting the internationalization process by entering countries physically close to the home country may also result in failure because the perceived similarity may lead to an underestimation of the true differences. Although empirical support for the Uppsala thesis is not terribly strong (Benito and Gripsrud 1992), the theory is prominent among IB scholars. Most probably this is because the model has a practical, common-sense appeal to it (O'Grady and Lane 1996: 314).

Interestingly enough, the dynamic Uppsala entry-mode approach is mixed with the static transaction costs theory of the firm (Williamson 1975, 1985, 1998). Basically its application to entry modes can be seen as an extension of the transaction cost theory of the MNE by looking at cultural distance as a source of uncertainty. With CD increasing, firms deal with this uncertainty by internalizing foreign activities. In other words, the theory predicts that if CD is high, firms will choose more control-oriented modes of foreign entry because complete and accurate information on the subsidiaries' activities is difficult to obtain. Mostly, scholars have studied the choice between licensing and FDI, or between wholly owned subsidiaries (WOS) and partially owned international joint ventures (IJV), or greenfield vs. acquisition (for a critical overview *see* Slangen and Hennart 2007).

The rationale for this supposed relationship between CD, control and entry mode is based on the argument that MNE managers expect ventures in culturally more distant countries to encounter greater difficulties because such countries have norms, values, consumer preferences and business practices that differ from those in the MNE's home country (Hofstede 1980; Kogut and Singh 1988; Caves 1996). They are therefore unwilling to commit major resources to ventures in culturally distant countries (Root 1998), as doing so would result in high exit costs should these ventures fail (Hill *et al.* 1990; Kim and Hwang 1992). By entering culturally dissimilar countries through low-commitment entry modes, MNE managers reduce cross-cultural difficulties and exit costs (Hill *et al.* 1990).

The entry-mode literature thus proposes that MNE managers anticipate the greater liability of foreignness associated with operating local affiliates over that associated with exporting, leading their preference for exports over majority-owned local affiliates to increase with the cultural distance to the target country (Dunning 1993; Root 1998). Despite its broad acceptance, the argument can also be reversed (Gatignon and Anderson 1988). "A firm may prefer low control to compensate for its lack of knowledge in high CD situations, relying on a local partner to contribute local knowledge" (Shenkar 2001: 521). Hence, the theoretical argument regarding the relation between CD and entry mode can be both a negative and a positive one (Tihanya *et al.* 2005). In a similar vein, scholars have related CD to MNE performance and have argued for both a positive and a negative relationship. On the one hand, increasing CD is associated with intra-organizational conflicts and managerial problems (Li and Guisinger 1992). On the other hand, it has been argued that MNEs can enter culturally distant countries because of the organizational advantages their foreign activities may provide. MNEs may benefit from the foreign operations because they can integrate newly acquired skills and knowledge into their operations which may positively affect their performance (Morosini *et al.* 1998). In these cases, cultural distance can be argued to have a positive effect, a hypothesis that seems to be gaining ground given some recent publications on the role of cultural distance as a source of attraction (Beugelsdijk and Slangen 2010), or as a double-edged sword affecting acquisition performance in negative and positive ways (Reus and Laffont 2009).

Empirical studies on the entry-mode choice are abundant (Gatignon and Anderson 1988; Kim and Hwang 1992; Shane 1994; Barkema and Vermeulen 1997; Contractor and Kundu 1998; Hennart and Larimo 1998; Arora and Fosfuri 2000; Brouthers and Brouthers 2001), with many of them finding that, as cultural distance increases, MNEs are increasingly likely to choose low-commitment entry modes such as exports, licensing and joint ventures over wholly owned subsidiaries. It is beyond the scope of this chapter to discuss all these in detail. A meta-analysis of the role of CD on entry-mode choice, but also on the relationship between CD and MNE performance, is provided by Tihanya *et al.* (2005). Based on fifty-five articles published in top-tier journals, the results of their meta-analysis suggest that "cultural distance does not appear to be directly related to entry mode choice, international diversification, or MNE performance across prior empirical studies" (Tihanya *et al.* 2005: 278–279). Testing for moderator effects, the authors do find some indications of a role for cultural distance, suggesting that the measurement instrument used, the MNE origin, industry type and host country of investment are all important variables that have not been taken into account sufficiently so far. They suggest improving cultural distance measures (cf. Shenkar's 2001 critique) and theoretical frameworks on the relationship between culture and organizational practices (cf. Slangen 2006). In sum, whereas cultural distance is strongly associated with entry-mode research, both theoretically and empirically, the IB literature is inconclusive about its specific role (*see also* Siegel *et al.* 2008a for a similar conclusion).

So far we have discussed the literature in IB dealing with cultural distance. This cultural distance concept is used to explain how *differences* in values affect choices of actors and not how absolute "levels" of values affect behavior. One area in IB in which the role of cultural content (not cultural distance) and the nature of the relationship between culture and economic decision-making are specifically theorized upon is in the field of comparative management studies.

8.5 Comparative management: managerial values and international cooperation

Without the ambition to provide a full picture of the field of comparative management (for that *see* Koen 2005), some basic insights are relevant in the context of this book. As mentioned in the introduction to this chapter, comparative management is mainly concerned with the way culture and differences in culture affect managerial decision-making. One reason why this is interesting in the context of this book is that IB scholars develop specific theoretical hypotheses on the effect of culture. They do not so much argue that culture matters but much more *how* culture matters. Second and related, because IB has analyzed the role of culture in economic decision-making in such detail, these insights serve as micro-foundations of the role of culture in the aggregate analyses of trade and FDI. For these two reasons, we think a discussion of some of these studies is interesting and relevant in the context of this book. First we discuss the relationship between culture and managerial values in an intracultural setting (unilateral). After that we explore the literature on international management in an intercultural setting (dyadic). This sequence is logical, because "understanding cultural differences in expectation-formation and decision-making can provide significant insights into dynamic cooperation in cross-cultural business relationships" (Scott-Marshall and Boush 2001: 874). Many scholars in IB implicitly start from a unilateral approach before delving into the dyadic aspects.

8.5.1 Managerial values

As with the entrepreneurial trait research discussed in Chapter 6, we may expect that certain cultural traits affect the behavior of managers and the way they communicate, their leadership style, organizational commitment and problem-solving styles. Hence, to understand differences in managerial behavior it is important to relate to differences in culture. In this subsection we provide some examples merely to sketch the general approach of IB scholars in assessing the relationship between culture and managerial values. The interaction between partners from different cultures is discussed in the next subsection. The field of managerial values is obviously extensive and goes far beyond the scope of this book. We will discuss only a representative selection of papers. We do so not because we consider the specific contents of these papers to be directly relevant for many economists, but because the general lessons that can be learned are. As we discuss in detail in the final section, one strong element in many of these studies is the fact that scholars theorize and test *how* culture matters.

The article by Agarwal *et al.* (1999) is a nice illustration of this typical approach. Comparing 184 US sales persons with 181 Indian sales persons, Agarwal *et al.* (1999) focus on the leadership behavior of the managers of these salespersons and the interaction between the manager and the salesperson. Although their empirical findings are mixed, this approach is typical for IB. The authors select a sample of countries – in this case the US and India – based on a fundamental difference in the "cultural endowment" of these countries. Whereas the US scores relatively high on Hofstede's Individualism dimension, India scores relatively low. The reverse holds for Hofstede's dimension of Power Distance. Agarwal *et al.* (1999) specifically argue that subordinates in low-power-distance and high-individualism societies show a tendency to attribute job performance to their personal efforts, whereas subordinates in high-power-distance and low-individualism societies experience greater stress if supervisors have a more controlling leadership style. Hence, these differences have implications for the way people and groups of people are most effectively managed. (*See also* Pillai *et al.* 1999 and Pellegrini and Scandura 2006 on leadership styles, Gibson 1995 on gender differences and culture, Waldman *et al.* 2006 on leadership and corporate social responsibility values and Hofstede *et al.* 2002 on leadership goals.)

Based on a similar set-up comparing managerial behavior in a set of culturally different countries, Morris *et al.* (1998) compare the conflict management style of managers in the US, China, India and the Philippines. In line with their theoretical expectations derived from Hofstede's multidimensional framework, they find that in solving conflicts, US managers tend toward a competing style and the Chinese managers tend toward an avoiding style. Similarly, Tinsley and Pillutla's (1998) experiment with 153 students from Hong Kong and 78 US students indicates that the latter are more likely to subscribe to self-interest and joint problem-solving norms in negotiations. The Hong Kong students, meanwhile, were more likely to subscribe to norms of equality.

The fact that cultural differences lead to differences in management styles is particularly relevant for ex-patriate managers working for multinational companies. These ex-pats are almost always socialized in a home-country context and are expected to manage an affiliate in a host country characterized by a different set of values and norms. For this reason, IB scholars have also engaged in understanding ex-patriate management (e.g. Brewster and Scullion 1997; Leiba-O'Sullivan 1999; Jun *et al.* 2001), even including the role of the ex-patriate's spouse (Stewart-Black and Gregersen 1991). Similar examples can be found in human resource management (Adler and Bartholomew 1992; Brewster 1993; Schuler *et al.* 1993; Harris *et al.* 2003) and international marketing (Peterson and Jolibert 1995; Verlegh and Steenkamp 1999; De Mooij 2010). For example, country-of-origin research in international marketing has found that consumers frequently favor goods manufactured by local firms over otherwise similar goods manufactured by foreign MNEs (Bilkey and Nes 1982 and Samiee 1994), even when the latter products are manufactured locally (Knight 1999).

In most of these studies, scholars typically theorize and relate certain aspects of a culture to a specific phenomenon of interest. For example, building on Hofstede's classification, Schuler and Rogovsky (1998) theorize and find that both seniority-based compensation systems and skill-based compensation systems are more likely to be found in countries with higher levels of uncertainty avoidance. Relating individualism to pay-for-performance systems and bonus or commission practices, their results suggest that culture is an important explanatory variable in understanding the variation in compensation practices between countries. In a similar vein, researchers have related specific cultural dimensions to international differences in accounting and budget practices (Ueno and Sekaran 1992), corporate capital structures (Chui *et al.* 2002), work standardization practices (Harrison *et al.* 2000; Newburry and Yakova 2006), job satisfaction and job exit strategies (Kanungo and Wright 1983; Thomas and Au 2002), opinion seeking and information exchange among consumers (Dawar *et al.* 1996), corporate entrepreneurship (Morris *et al.* 1994) and employee benefit plans and social security programs (Goad Oliver and Cravens 1999).

8.5.2 *International cooperation*

Parallel but not unrelated to the literature on managerial values, a relatively small literature exists on the behavioral aspects of international business relationships. Given the aggregate cultural dimensions of Hofstede and others, it would in principle be fairly easy to provide some national-level scores on how we would expect people to behave in certain circumstances. Linking the aggregate scores to individual behavior – though also criticized as constituting an ecological fallacy (*see* Chapter 7 on trust) – has been a popular way to conceptualize and operationalize cooperation between individuals from different cultures. As discussed before, the aggregate effect of cultural distance between home and host countries on trade or FDI is often studied by including the KS index. Whereas most research using the cultural distance measure (the KS index) implicitly refers to the problems associated with intercultural interaction, the underlying micro-level processes remain a black box. The obvious problem with large-scale analyses of international business negotiations at the *individual* level is the logistical difficulties of bringing together a large number of participants from different countries (Lee *et al.* 2006). At the same time, it is generally accepted that international negotiations in an intercultural setting create additional sources of tension compared with negotiations in an intracultural setting (Adler and Graham 1989; Kumar 1997; Barry *et al.* 2004). Cultural differences create or enhance potential communication problems and reduce the general level of empathy felt in the negotiation process (Triandis 1995). These additional complexities in international negotiations are caused by language differences and differences in nonverbal behaviors, values and patterns of thought (Lee *et al.* 2006).

A comprehensive overview of the literature on negotiations and the role of affect is provided by Kumar (1997). Depending on the nature of the negotiation process being either embedded in a situation of so-called contrient interdependence (individuals have opposing goals) or of promotive interdependence (individuals have goals that are positively linked with each other), Kumar lists three variables that form the origins of affective responses in negotiations. These are the image of one's counterpart, the distributive and procedural justice associated with the negotiation process and differences in the culture of actors. Regarding image, Kumar notes that when the image is negative, ambiguous stimuli may trigger an affective response and the nature of the affective response will implicate the other actor. Images may be self-reinforcing. With respect to justice, Kumar follows the traditional distinction between distributive and procedural justice. The former deals with the fairness of allocated outcomes, while the latter concerns the way these outcomes have been realized. Interestingly enough, Kumar (1997) provides a number of references claiming that certain behavioral aspects of the procedural justice in negotiations are equally important across cultures. According to Kumar, emotions caused by procedural (in)justice have a longer duration compared with emotions caused by distributive (in)justice.

The third aspect – and in the context of this chapter the most relevant one – that is related to both image and justice is culture and differences in culture (*see also* Li and Cropanzano 2009; Ren and Gray 2009). Following Boyacigiller *et al.* (1996), Kumar presents emotions due to perceived cultural differences as a group-level phenomenon and conceptualizes culture as group identity. "Actions posing a threat to a group's identity are culturally variable, and this variability problematizes interaction across different cultural groups. What may be trivial or a non-offense in one cultural group may be viewed with much alarm by members of another cultural group (Li and Cropanzano 2009).

Compounding the problem is the fact that cultural groups also differ in the intensity of the sanctions they apply when cultural norms are violated" (Kumar 1997: 89). In sum, cultural norm violations are related to the strength of the affective response and cultural differences may slow down the process of negotiation because the different parties with their different operational norms need time to get acquainted. Against this theoretical background of the role of affect in negotiations and the moderating role of cultural differences, we discuss some empirical findings that have been obtained so far.

In an experimental analysis of negotiations between Chinese and Americans, Lee *et al.* (2006) find that tension is present for both groups, but in a different way. In line with their expectations, tension with the Chinese managers was emotional and influenced by the atmosphere of the cooperation during the negotiations. For the Chinese, a cooperative atmosphere reduced the perceived tension and increased empathy toward the Americans. The investigators also showed that higher levels of tension had a negative effect on empathy levels and trustworthiness and resulted in negative expectations about cooperation with Americans in the future. Both the Americans and the Chinese rated the levels of cooperation in their own teams (intracultural) as higher than that of their foreign partners. This finding has been established by other people as well. Brett and Okumura (1998) and Adair *et al.* (2001) investigated both intra- and intercultural negotiations between Japanese and American managers and found that (a) there are main effects of culture on the behavior of these managers and also that (b) intercultural negotiations are more difficult than intracultural negotiations. Based on a negotiation simulation game in a group of 462 American, Canadian and Japanese business people, Adler and Graham (1989) explicitly test the assumption that managers behave similarly in both intra- and inter-cultural settings. They find that behaviors in cross-cultural negotiations differ in important ways. A similar observation has been made by Rao and Hashimoto (1996), who compared the behavior of Japanese managers dealing with Japanese subordinates and Canadian subordinates. They found that significant differences in strategies existed that were associated with the national culture of the subordinates. In other words, "the face-to-face conduct of negotiations may be influenced by behavioral discrepancies when persons of different cultural backgrounds are brought together" (Sawyer and Guetzkow 1965, in Adler and Graham 1989: 517). This clearly shows the complexity of the role of culture in understanding negotiation processes.

The attitude toward cooperative strategies has been the focus in a study by Steensma *et al.* (2000). Based on survey research among 484 entrepreneurs from Australia, Finland, Greece, Indonesia, Mexico, Norway and Sweden, they relate Hofstede's dimensions to the individual attitude of these entrepreneurs toward cooperative strategies. They find that entrepreneurs from societies that are masculine and individualistic have a lower appreciation for cooperative strategies compared with entrepreneurs from societies that are feminine and collectivist. According to Dyer and Chu (2000: 603–604), masculine cultures view cooperation in general as a sign of weakness and individualistic societies place a high value on independence and control. Entrepreneurs from individualist cultures place greater emphasis on contractual safeguards. The essence of Steensma *et al.* (2000) is that *all cultures have their own specific cooperative strategies*, providing further evidence that in case of intercultural cooperation, negotiation clashes, frustrations and (negative) emotions are most likely to occur; or are at least more likely than in intracultural settings in which every actor involved is familiar with the negotiation routines and underlying values.

Scott-Marshall and Boush (2001) have investigated the decision-making process of export managers in Peru and the US. What is interesting about their paper is that they also track the dynamic role of cultural differences in import–export relationships. Using a scenario-based questionnaire, they find that the influence of cultural differences gradually fades away in favor of personal characteristics and the relationship-specific history. This suggests that if the process of interaction unfolds in a positive way, the moderating role of cultural differences is reduced. These differences may be especially relevant in understanding initial stages of intercultural interaction. But once a certain level of trust has been achieved, cultural differences matter no more (or less).

8.6 Discussion: *how* culture matters

As we described in our definition of IB, its origin can partly be traced back to international economics. However, since the 1970s the two subdisciplines of international economics and international business have diverged substantially. Both international economics and IB share an interest in the MNE and the international organization of production, but the two fields co-exist in relative isolation, with limited interaction. In line with our earlier discussion of a culture of economics in Chapter 4, we could argue that economics and IB have come to constitute different cultures, with different stocks of common knowledge, shared meanings and heroes. Each field has its own top journal (the *Journal of International Economics* and the *Journal of International Business Studies*, respectively) and main conferences, which severely limits the amount of spillovers between the two related fields. This separation is even more striking when taking into account the shared historical importance attached to works by, for example, Vernon's Harvard Multinational Enterprise Project at Harvard Business School in 1965 and Kindleberger's work entitled *American Business Abroad, six lectures on direct investment*, published in 1969. The divergence since the 1970s holds for the methodological frameworks applied (formal vs. descriptive), the role of the multinational firm (black-box or main variable of interest) and the type of data used (secondary vs. survey-based), but not for some of the core questions in both fields. Given the recent development in international economics to incorporate firm-level characteristics in (formal) models of international economic activity, the potential for spillovers has increased recently.[6]

[6] One of the recent articles in the *Journal of International Economics* (*JIE*), entitled "Cross-border mergers and acquisitions *vs*. greenfield foreign direct investment: The role of firm heterogeneity" by Nocke and Yeaple (2007), is a nice example. The authors develop a general equilibrium model that includes heterogeneous firms and complement previous research published in *JIE* that has tried to tackle the issue of firm-level heterogeneity in explaining the international organization of production by multinational enterprises (Grossman *et al.* 2006; Grossman and Helpman, 2004; Ruckman, 2004). The Nocke and Yeaple article is especially interesting as it briefly refers to the management strategy literature. As discussed in this chapter, one of the entry-mode choices that has been studied extensively in IB is that between greenfield and acquisition entry, exactly the one studied by Nocke and Yeaple. Unfortunately, these authors do not refer to this literature at all in their otherwise insightful paper. The IB literature on this topic has offered abundant empirical evidence that an MNE's choice between greenfield and acquisition entry indeed depends on firm-level factors. As touched upon in this chapter, these firm-level factors include an MNE's technological know-how, its international and host-country experience, its level of diversification and its experience with greenfields and acquisitions, among others. We feel that the Nocke and Yeaple (2007) paper could have benefited tremendously from these studies, had they been aware of their existence.

So given this process of convergence, what can economists learn from IB and the way IB scholars deal with culture?

The fact that IB scholars have gone beyond the argument that culture matters and aim to show how culture matters is an important lesson for economists interested in dealing with culture as an object of study. IB shows us the need not just to look at the economic effects of different cultures doing comparative analysis but also to study the effects of cultural distances and relations between cultures. Approaching culture in such a more interactive, dynamic way offers a richer perspective to deal with cultural heterogeneity than that often employed by economists. What we can also learn from IB is the need to move beyond the simple inclusion of a culture variable in our models and empirically estimate whether this variable is significant. We need to theorize on how, under what circumstances and according to what time frame (dynamic) which aspects of culture matter for the phenomenon of interest (cf. Shenkar 2004 and Earley 2006). If anything, IB scholars have shown that not all cultural predispositions matter in all aspects of IB. For economists, this means that instead of simply including a culture dimension such as Hofstede's uncertainty avoidance, they need to theorize on why uncertainty avoidance would matter in this case. Claiming that culture is related to a country's financial system is not an interesting hypothesis. What is required in this case is a careful theory prescribing how culture, for example its level of uncertainty avoidance, may be correlated with tolerated levels of price uncertainty (inflation) and how this may affect the way in which people have "organized" their monetary policy and the associated level of central bank independence (*see* Chapter 9 for a more elaborate discussion on this topic). More generally, the literature discussed in this chapter shows that economists can learn from IB that:

(a) economists need to theorize more how certain culture dimensions or cultural differences affect the phenomenon of interest;

(b) an extensive literature exists relating firm behavior to cultural characteristics of home and host countries (and the differences between home and host), yielding important micro-level insights;

(c) aggregate analyses of culture and patterns of trade and FDI require a detailed understanding of the way culture affects micro-level firm behavior.

The intrinsic interest of IB scholars in culture has resulted in a relatively fine-grained understanding of culture, both theoretically and empirically. At the same time, IB scholars and economists have shared historical roots and a shared interest in improving our understanding of the global distribution of MNE activity and the determinants of this distribution. Although we have witnessed an increased divergence between international economics and IB in the last few decades, the recent trend in international economics in which firm-level heterogeneity is taken into account may positively affect the spillover potential. Given its preoccupation with culture and cultural differences, IB is a rich and powerful source of knowledge for (international) economists who wish to include culture in their analysis.

9 | Comparative corporate governance

9.1 Introduction

Two related developments explain the interest of corporate governance scholars in the role of culture. First, practitioners in the field of corporate governance have discovered the relevance of cultural differences, which has subsequently led to a revised perspective of pension funds, international securities agencies, the OECD, the World Bank and the IMF on corporate governance, one in which national cultural differences play an important role (Licht 2001). Second, and parallel to this inductive – practice-oriented – route toward the recognition of culture, a more deductive, theory-driven route has pushed the interest in culture as well. Economic growth theorists have pointed toward the importance of a well-functioning corporate governance system, which raised the subsequent question as to why quality differences in corporate governance regimes exist. This triggered an intense debate on the origin of such differences. Recent research suggests that historical differences in legal origin and culture help explain such differences.

In comparing corporate governance regimes scholars have turned toward legal origin of societies (countries) and developed a range of measures to proxy for a nation's legal origin. Like the Hofstede dimensions in the field of international business (as discussed in the previous chapter), these measures of legal origin have become a cornerstone of empirical studies in financial economics and comparative corporate governance. When discussing legal origin, scholars frequently refer to the role of culture and a society's cultural background. The causal chain of logic often includes explicit references to a role of culture. Despite the intuitive attractiveness of relating legal origin directly or indirectly to culture, many scholars struggle with the concept of culture. It is unclear whether legal origin is seen *as* culture (it is, just like culture, an exogenous factor) or whether there is a relationship between legal origin *and* culture. Given the way many scholars have operationalized legal origin, it actually shares almost all of the characteristic elements of our definition of culture as discussed in Chapter 1. Both legal origin and culture are inherited, specific, exogenous, man-made, systems of thought and concern values and norms.

In this literature, culture is often interpreted as an exogenous driver of a process of infinite regress (from growth to financial systems to corporate governance to legal origin to culture), but should somehow also fit the neoclassical optimality framework commonly used in financial economics. Stulz and Williamson write that 'we would expect individuals to trade off the costs and benefits of specific cultural values' (Stulz and Williamson 2003: 338). This inclusion of culture in an otherwise standard economic framework creates a methodological challenge and raises questions that help us in our understanding of culture in economics in general. In other words, we include this chapter because it forces us to reflect on culture as an optimal outcome of deliberate choices, discusses the notion of optimality of values, introduces the phenomenon of an infinite regress explicitly and triggers a range of questions related to measurement and operationalization.

In the following section we first define corporate governance. Many definitions exist and we explain how we interpret corporate governance in the context of this book. We subsequently discuss the traditional distinction that is often made in financial economics, i.e. bank-based vs. market-based systems. Then, we introduce the contemporary distinction between common law and civil law regimes. In Section 9.3 we describe how legal origin has been related to differences in corporate governance regimes. We assess the way culture has been included in this field of research in Section 9.4 and in Section 9.5 we provide a critical evaluation of this comparative corporate governance approach. Section 9.6 concludes.

9.2 Corporate governance systems and legal origin

9.2.1 Corporate governance

Corporate governance consists of the 'whole set of legal, cultural, and institutional arrangements that determine what publicly traded corporations can do, who controls them, how that control is exercised, and how the risks and returns from the activities they undertake are allocated' (Blair 1995: 3). In financial economics, corporate governance deals primarily with the agency problem, i.e. the separation between manager and owner. Starting with Berle and Means (1932), financial economists have been concerned with the risk of insiders expropriating the investments made by outsiders because of a lack of control.[1] Instead of investing the capital in the most effective and efficient way, managers would pursue "prestige, power, or the gratification of personal zeal" (Berle and Means 1932: 122). This conflict of interest between principal and agent forms the core of the field of corporate governance. "At the extreme of no investor protection, the insiders can steal a firm's profits perfectly efficiently. Without a strong reputation, no rational outsider would finance such a firm" (LaPorta *et al.* 2000: 6). Because of this preoccupation with the risks investors run, corporate governance concentrates on the protection of these investors and the set of legal mechanisms through which outside investors are protected against the risk of expropriation by insiders.[2] More extensive discussions of corporate governance can be found in Blair (1995), Shleifer and Vishny (1997) and Becht *et al.* (2005).

The central thesis in *comparative* corporate governance is the acknowledgment that to properly understand the patterns of corporate finance in different countries – i.e. the protection of shareholders and creditors – we need to understand the characteristics of the legal system. One of the reasons why research along these lines has become so popular is the (perhaps obvious) finding in the early and mid-1990s that well-developed financial systems directly affect economic growth rates in a positive way. As a logical next step, questions were raised trying to explain why some countries have well-developed financial

---

[1] An interesting historical account of how Berle developed his thesis on expropriation risk and the context in which this took place can be found in Licht (2003). A more general discussion of the evolutionary development of securities regulation and the historical role of norms in contemporary securities law in the UK and the US can be found in Banner (1998).

[2] This contractarian approach to the relationship between investor and manager is not without criticism (Davis 2005). For example, complementary to Berle and Means' (1932) explanation of the rise of the modern corporation, Roy (1997) takes a non-functionalist perspective and traces the legal, political and class roots of this rise. Fligstein (1990) has focussed on the role of the state in explaining the development of these corporations in the twentieth century (*see also* Campbell *et al.* 1991). Despite these critical accounts on the "efficient history" (Davis 2005), the dominant paradigm in financial economics is agency theory and the focus on the risk of expropriation by insiders and the control by investing outsiders.

systems while in other countries it seems to be extremely difficult to develop laws and contract enforcement mechanisms that support the operation of financial markets (Beck *et al.* 2001). In explaining these differences, research has concentrated on the legal origin of corporate governance systems (LaPorta *et al.* 2008).

Culture in this field is often proxied by legal origin, more specifically the distinction between common and civil law countries. Following Merryman (1985: 2), "the legal tradition relates the legal system to the culture of which it is a partial expression." Of course, a cheap (though partly justified) comment on such an approach would be to criticize this field for an incomplete conceptualization and operationalization of culture. As we have seen in previous chapters, culture as a system of values is a complex phenomenon and to limit the concept and measurement of culture to differences in legal families seems rather simplistic. We will return to this criticism in the concluding section of this chapter. For now, it is impossible to deny the importance and prominence of this institutional explanation of differences in corporate governance. It is a vibrant field of research and many scholars working in this field present their studies as contributions to the broader field of culture (and institutions, however defined) and economics. Hence, we feel that a closer discussion is warranted.

Traditionally, financial systems are described according to the distinction between bank-based and market-based systems. Since the early 1990s, an increasing number of financial economists, personified by LaPorta, Lopez-de-Silanes, Shleifer, Vishny (LLSV) and Zingales have studied the antecedents or origins of the differences in corporate governance by looking at differences in legal traditions (Zetzsche 2007).

9.2.2 Bank-based vs. market-based typology

Regarding types of financial system, the most basic distinction made is the one between bank-based and market-based systems. Countries such as Germany and Japan are traditionally associated with bank-based systems, whereas the United States and the United Kingdom are associated with market-based systems. A bank-based system can be described as a relationship-based type of corporate governance in which a main bank provides finance *and* governance to a firm. In market-based types of corporate governance, finance is provided by a large number of (anonymous) investors via equity markets. The bank-based view emphasizes the role of banks as "financial intermediators in ameliorating information asymmetries and intertemporal transaction costs." The market-based view, meanwhile, stresses the importance of well-functioning "securities markets in providing incentives for investors to acquire information, impose corporate control, and custom design financial arrangements" (Levine 2002: 3). Hence, bank-based systems are more relational, while market-based systems are more arm's length (Kwok and Tadesse 2006b). Traditionally, both development economists and corporate finance theorists viewed debt and equity financing as substitutes. Over time, many economists have argued that bank-based systems are better at mobilizing savings, identifying good investments and exerting corporate control, particularly during take-off stages of economic development with relatively weak institutional environments, whereas market-based view proponents have emphasized the advantage of (relatively anonymous) markets in allocating capital (Levine 2002; Carlin and Mayer 2003).

The disadvantage of a bank-based system compared with a market-based system is that the former is based on rather close ties between firms and banks and the funding possibilities for outsiders (e.g. multinationals) may be relatively limited (Levine 2002). In a bank-based system, powerful banks can stymie innovation by extracting informational rents, protecting established firms with close bank–firm ties from competition and colluding with firm managers impeding efficient corporate governance (Levine 2002). At the same time, such relational ties can affect credit ratings of firms in a bank-based system in a positive way, because it leads to lower monitoring costs or lower credit risks (Purda 2008). In the end, as argued by LaPorta *et al.* (1998, 1999) and empirically confirmed by Levine (2002), it may not so much be the distinction between bank-based or market-based but the quality of these two systems that matters. The more recent financial services view has gone beyond the simple discussion on markets vs. banks and places the analytical spotlight on creating better functioning banks and markets. At least for economic growth it has been shown that the type of system does not matter, but the extent to which investor rights are protected in both systems does. LaPorta *et al.* (1997) have shown that, on average, countries with higher ratios of debt to GDP also have bigger stock markets. Thus, the issue may not be banks *or* markets but the quality of the financial services offered. In general, well-functioning financial markets (of either type) reduce the costs of external finance for firms (Rajan and Zingales 1998).

Although other classifications do exist – for example a classification based on the Glass-Steagall Act, in which a distinction is made between countries formally restricting ownership of corporate equity by banks (US) and countries that do not have such regulations (Germany) – contemporary literature in financial economics concentrates on the extent of investor protection.[3] In this focus on investor protection, attention has shifted toward the legal position of investors, be it shareholders or creditors.

9.2.3 Legal traditions

The legal approach to corporate governance is based on the view that protection of outsiders, be it shareholders or creditors, originates in the legal system. This implies both the *type* of laws and the *enforcement* of these laws. According to LaPorta *et al.* (2000, 2008), the legal approach is a logical step in the evolutionary development of the field of financial economics. They argue that it extends seminal contributions by Modigliani and Miller (1958), Jensen and Meckling (1976) and Hart (1995). Although Modigliani and Miller (1958) focussed on the firm as a collection of investment projects and associated cash flows, they did not explain why the cash flow would return to the original investors. Jensen and Meckling (1976) introduced the notion of financial claims of investors and the risk of insider expropriation by focussing on (financial) contracts. Hart (1995) extended this by framing the financial contract as one element of a broader residual control rights that investors may have (power to change directors, to force dividend payment, etc.). However, both Jensen and Meckling and the residual control rights framework are based on the well-functioning of the legal system. And this logically leads to the conceptual idea that types of law, and the quality of their enforcement, are a fundamental part of the system of corporate governance.

Researchers in this field typically argue that there are historical reasons for differences in corporate governance regimes. Because legal

---

[3] *See* Zetzsche (2007) for an elaborate distinction between i) bank based versus market based, ii) common law versus civil law, iii) shareholder versus stakeholder, and iv) explicit versus implicit systems of corporate control. In the context of this book, we concentrate on legal origin.

families originated before financial markets had developed, there is no problem of endogeneity and legal origin is seen as a valid exogenous (instrumental) variable in explaining differences in corporate governance systems. "Legal families appear to shape the legal rules, which in turn shape financial markets" (LaPorta *et al.* 2000: 9). In classifying legal families, a key distinction is made between common law systems and civil law systems. Common law originates in England and civil law has Roman roots. Both common law and civil law tradition (especially France and Spain) have spread throughout the world by means of conquest, borrowing or imitation and imperialism. LaPorta *et al.* (1998, footnote 1) do not take into account religious law, e.g. Islamic law (Sharia), because they consider these to be less relevant and they focus on secular legal traditions.[4]

Both the civil and the common law traditions have historical roots (LaPorta *et al.* 1998; Beck *et al.* 2001; Glaeser and Shleifer 2002; Stulz and Williamson 2003; Zetzsche 2007; LaPorta *et al.* 2008). The civil law tradition is based on Roman law and uses statutes and codes as major means of ordering legal material. As a consequence it is practiced by legal scholars who formulate the rules. Not taking into account village-level tribunals, civil law is oldest and most widely distributed around the world. However, it is not uniform and three subtraditions are distinguished: the French, German and Scandinavian civil law, each with their own specific historical trajectory. The French civil law tradition was shaped by Napoleon in the early nineteenth century and has been exported to Belgium, the Netherlands, Italy and a number of former colonies in the Near East and Southern Africa and through Spain and Portugal, as well as in southern and Central America. The German civil law code was developed at the end of the nineteenth century (Bismarck's unification of the German states) and has influenced and shaped law systems in Austria, Japan and Korea, amongst others. The Scandinavian law family is seen as a separate tradition because it was less derivative of Roman law than the French and German law

---

[4] The exclusive focus on civil and common law is understandable from a Western point of view, but triggers fundamental questions. For example, to label civil law – with its roots in Rome where authority was derived from the divine emperor – as secular is an anachronism (*see also* Zetzsche 2007). Similarly, to label religious law as irrelevant can be disputed because the question is, irrelevant to whom? To put it bluntly, the focus on common and civil law runs the risk of being an ethnocentric classification. We discuss this in detail in Section 6 of this chapter.

systems. In contrast with the civil law system, common law is formed by judges who have the specific task of solving disputes and these judges do not base themselves on general scholarly contributions but use precedents from judicial decisions made in the past. Common law has its roots in England and was exported to the United States, Canada, Australia and many other countries, often former colonies of England.

Generally speaking, research along the legal origin "paradigm" seems to suggest that it is not true that some countries protect shareholders and others protect creditors, as the distinction between bank-based and market-based systems would suggest, but some countries protect all outside investors better than others (LaPorta *et al.* 2000, 2008). The typical hypothesis regarding the extent to which investors are protected and the legal origin of countries is that countries with a common law tradition perform better. To test this thesis, scholars have measured aspects of corporate governance and linked these aspects to a country's legal origin. These empirical approaches have focussed on the protection of shareholder rights, creditor rights and the enforcement of both. We discuss the theoretical reasoning and the empirical arguments in the next section.

9.3 Differences in investor protection regimes

9.3.1 Explanations

In understanding the logic of how differences in legal origins shape financial systems, more specifically why common law systems are assumed to be better at protecting investors than civil law systems are, four basic explanations are put forward. Parallel to the judicial explanation and the political explanation (LaPorta *et al.* 2000, 2008), there are the legal adaptability approach and the endowment view. The essence of the judicial explanation is best summarized by LaPorta *et al.* themselves (2000: 9): "Legal rules in the common law system are usually made by judges, based on precedents and inspired by general principles such as fiduciary duty of fairness. Judges are expected to rule on new situations by applying these general principles even when specific conduct has not yet been described or prohibited in the statutes. (. . .) The expansion of legal precedents to additional violations of fiduciary duty, and the fear of such expansion, limit the expropriation by the insiders in common law countries."

LaPorta *et al.* (2000) continue discussing the civil law system. "Laws in civil law systems are made by legislatures, and judges are not supposed to go beyond the statutes and apply 'smell tests' of fairness opinions. As a consequence, a corporate insider who finds a way not explicitly forbidden by the statutes to expropriate outside investors can proceed without fear of an adverse judicial ruling. Moreover in civil law countries, courts do not intervene in self-dealing transactions as long as these have a plausible business purpose. The vague fiduciary duty principles of the common law are more protective of investors than the bright line rules of the civil law, which can often be circumvented by sufficiently imaginative insiders." Obviously this reasoning is based on the assumption that judges are inclined to protect outside investors instead of the insiders. This is where the additional political explanation comes in.

The political explanation of the superior investor protection in common law vs. civil law countries is based on the observation that the state has historically had a greater role in regulating business in civil law countries than in common law countries. This explanation is grounded in the differences between the relative power of a king and property owners across European states. In England, common law was influenced by the fact that property law was developed to protect private property against the crown and over time this protection was extended to investors. In contrast with England, parliament in civil law countries such as France and Germany was weaker and the state did not surrender its power over economic decisions to independent courts (LaPorta *et al.* 2000, 2008; Glaeser and Shleifer 2002). The key explaining variable in this political–historical approach is the power of the government vs. that of the judiciary, and civil law is in fact a proxy for a strong state. That is not to say that values do not play a role in such an explanation. In fact, Zetzsche (2007) documents extensively how religious values are intertwined with views on the role of the state and that of commercial corporations. Empirical evidence for the thesis of higher levels of government intervention in civil law countries is provided by LaPorta *et al.* (1999). The authors claim to have found that the amount and quality of regulation, prevalence of red tape and bureaucratic delays are higher in civil law countries, particularly in French civil law countries.

Parallel to these "static" legal origin and political historical explanations, scholars have tried to explain differences in the quality of financial systems in terms of geographical endowments and the extent to which legal systems are flexible. This latter approach does not assume a fixed relation between legal origin several hundred years ago and a country's current corporate governance system, but refers to what degree both law systems allow for changes in laws. This legal adaptability approach holds that common law is inherently dynamic because of the case-by-case approach.[5] French civil law is relatively more fixed because it was conceived as a complete, unambiguous, internally consistent system resulting in more rigid laws concerning financial transactions (Beck *et al.* 2001). And because financial systems have developed, it is argued that the common law approach has been better able to stay "in touch" with the commercial and financial needs of an economy. Hence, "differences in legal tradition influence legal system adaptability, which in turn shapes financial development" (Beck *et al.* 2001: 489).

The endowment view holds that geography, topology and the associated climatic characteristics of a country (including diseases) shape the development of institutions, including the financial institutions (Diamond 1997; Acemoglu *et al.* 2001; Easterly and Levine 2003). As institutions have spread partly through conquest by European colonizers, this endowment approach has been used to explain the nature of the institutions (exploitive or long-lasting settlements) in former colonies. Hospitable endowments favored the construction of settler colonies, where Europeans established secure property rights (Beck *et al.* 2003). A general problem with this endowment-based explanation is that explanations can be orthogonal. For example, it has been argued that lands with high rates of disease and poor large-scale agricultural farming possibilities do not develop economically and financially because of their small scale and the associated lack of specialization (*see* Beck *et al.* 2001). However, in explaining the difference between North and South American economic development, it has been argued that the large-scale farming possibilities in South America have resulted in institutions aimed at protecting the vested interests of a few landholders. Meanwhile, North American small-scale farming has resulted in more egalitarian institutions (Engerman

---

[5] Beck *et al.* (2001) also refer to the German civil law system as a more dynamic system than the French civil law system. For details we refer to Beck *et al.* (2001: 489).

and Sokoloff 1997, 2002). These differences have resulted in different systems of property rights, including some basic characteristics of the financial system. For an empirical test of the legal-adaptability and endowment view we refer to Beck *et al.* (2001, 2003). They find that both legal origin and a country's geographical endowments are important determinants of stock market development and private property rights protection.

Notwithstanding the difficulty in distinguishing between these explanations, a whole range of initiatives has been undertaken since the mid-1990s to explore empirical characteristics of financial systems, most notably LaPorta *et al.* (1998) and subsequent studies by LLSV. In doing so, scholars have typically concentrated on investor rights (both shareholder and creditor) and the enforcement of these rights.

9.3.2 Differences in shareholder and creditor rights

Shareholder rights encourage the development of equity markets, as measured by the valuation of firms, the number of listed firms and the rate at which firms go public (LaPorta *et al.* 1997, 2000, 2008). LaPorta *et al.* (1998) operationalize shareholder rights along two key dimensions, i.e. anti-director rights and mandatory dividend, of which the first seems to be most important and is a composite measure consisting of five underlying items. The anti-director rights index captures the extent to which the legal system favors minority shareholders against managers or dominant shareholders in the corporate decision-making process, including the voting process itself. The underlying items relate to the presence or absence of practices such as (i) if shareholders are required to show up in person or send an authorized representative if they wish to vote, (ii) cumulative voting for directors or proportional representation on the board and minority shareholders being allowed to name a proportional number of directors, (iii) the percentage of share capital needed to call an extraordinary shareholders' meeting, (iv) an oppressed minority mechanism is in place, (v) the minimum percentage of share capital that entitles a shareholder to call for an extraordinary shareholder meeting is less than the sample median (10 percent). (*See* LaPorta *et al.* 1998: 1127–1128 for further details.) The total score of the anti-director rights index ranges from 0 to 5, where a country such as Belgium scores 0 and Canada and the United States score 5. The mandatory dividend index reflects the extent to which firms are allowed to pay out a certain fraction of their declared earnings as dividends. According to LaPorta *et al.* (1998), this index may be seen as a legal substitute for the weakness of other protections of minority shareholders.

Ten years after the 1998 seminal contribution by LLSV, Djankov *et al.* (2008) published a revised anti-director index and a new measure for shareholder protection called the self-dealing index. Since 1998, the anti-director index developed by LLSV had been criticized on numerous grounds (some of which will be discussed next). The revised index relies on similar basic dimensions of corporate law, but defines them with greater precision and for a larger number of countries (seventy-two vs. forty-four). In addition, Djankov *et al.* (2008) developed a new so-called anti-self-dealing index, which according to them is developed not so much on an ad hoc basis but based on theoretical grounds. Assembled with the help of Lex Mundi law firms across the world, the index is derived on the basis of an example of self-dealing and lawyers from seventy-two countries are asked how investors are protected (both *ex ante* and *ex post*) against this agency problem. Based on a range of items relating to disclosure, approval and litigation, Djankov *et al.* (2008) develop their self dealing index.

In Table 9.1 we show the scores on this composite shareholder rights indices for the different law groups. For the scores of the individual countries we refer to Table 2 in LaPorta (1998) and the various tables in Djankov *et al.* (2008). Djankov *et al.* (2008) feel that the anti-self-dealing index is the most complete index proxying investor protection.

As becomes clear from the scores on the different indices depicted in Table 9.1, the common law countries score highest on shareholder rights and the French and German civil law countries score lowest. Note that this index reflects a composite measure and LaPorta *et al.* (1998) and Djankov *et al.* (2008) also show the results for the individual dimensions. In both cases, a similar picture emerges: "Relative to the rest of the world, common-law countries have a package of laws most protective of shareholders" (LaPorta 1998: 1129). The reverse holds for French civil law countries. The difference in the shareholder rights score between French civil law and common law countries is also statistically significant (at 1 percent). Although the German civil law countries score equally low on the 1998 composite indicator of the shareholder rights protection index, this seems to be particularly

Table 9.1. *Shareholder and creditor protection*

	Shareholder rights index (anti-director index, LaPorta *et al.* 1998)	Revised anti-director index (Djankov *et al.* 2008)	Anti-self-dealing index (Djankov *et al.* 2008)	Creditor rights index (LaPorta *et al.* 1998)
English common law heritage	4	4.19	.66	3.11
French civil law heritage	2.33	2.91	.33	1.58
German civil law heritage	2.33	3.04	.38	2.33
Scandinavian civil law heritage	3	3.80	.39	2
World average	3	3.37	.44	2.3

Source: LaPorta *et al.* (1998) and Djankov *et al.* (2008)

caused by two sub-items (the relatively high frequency of the one share – one vote system and the question as to whether minority shareholders have legal mechanisms against oppression by directors).

Creditor rights encourage the development of lending (LaPorta *et al.* 1997). Laws protecting creditors are primarily concerned with bankruptcy and reorganization procedures. These include measures enabling creditors to repossess collateral, to protect their seniority and to make it harder for firms to seek court protection in reorganization (LaPorta *et al.* 2000). Similar to the operationalization of shareholder rights, creditor rights are also proxied by a composite measure consisting of five underlying items. These items all refer to the position of creditors in case of reorganizations (*see* LaPorta *et al.* 1998: 1135 for details). As shown in Table 9.1, the common law countries score highest (3.11) on creditor rights and the French civil law countries score lowest (1.58). This difference is also statistically significant. The German civil law countries score in between and do not differ significantly from the English common law countries. Interestingly, the United States scores lowest within the group of the common law countries (1 vs. the group average of 3.11). Updated scores for creditor rights provided by Djankov *et al.* (2007) do not change this overall picture.

In sum, though minor differences exist between common law and civil law countries on some individual items, the picture that emerges from the scores developed by LaPorta *et al.* (1998) and Djankov *et al.* (2008) and shown in Table 9.1 is that the group of common law countries have the highest shareholder and investor protection and that especially French civil law countries provide the lowest protection of both shareholders and creditors. The German and Scandinavian civil law countries are in between. A full explanation as to why common law systems are better at protecting investors than civil law systems remains absent, but Glaeser and Shleifer (2002: 1222) point to the fact that expropriation by insiders is difficult to control by a single rule. This is difficult because a "broad range of creative behavior designed to expropriate investors 'falls between the cracks' in the rules." And because the common law system is not based on a system of bright line rules, it may be better equipped to deal with agency problems.

9.3.3 Differences in enforcement

LaPorta *et al.* (2000) and especially LaPorta *et al.* (1998) and Djankov *et al.* (2008) provide extensive evidence on enforcement and legal origin. Their argument to take enforcement into account is based on the premise that a strong system of legal enforcement could potentially substitute for weak rules. Using a variety of databases, LaPorta *et al.* (1998) use five measures of law enforcement: (i) efficiency of the judicial system, (ii) rule of law, (iii) corruption, (iv) risk of expropriation by the government and (v) likelihood of contract repudiation by the government. In addition to these five measures they use a measure for the quality of the accounting standards. Djankov *et al.* (2008) develop a public enforcement measure based on the extent to which fines and criminal sanctions apply to behavior ranging from criminal intent to obtain unlawful profits to breaches of duties and care and loyalty. Table 9.2 summarizes the scores on the different indicators for the different country clusters.

Taking into account that the quality of enforcement is positively correlated with level of economic development, law enforcement in terms of efficiency of the judiciary and lack of corruption is highest in Scandinavia and Germany (both civil law countries). Except for Djankov

Table 9.2. *Enforcement*

	Efficiency of judicial system	Rule of law	Corruption	Risk of expropriation	Risk of contract repudiation	Accounting standards	Public enforcement (Djankov *et al.* 2008)
English common law heritage	8.15	6.46	7.06	7.91	7.41	69.62	.32
French civil law heritage	6.56	6.05	5.84	7.46	6.84	51.17	.42
German civil law heritage	8.54	8.68	8.03	9.45	9.47	62.67	.48
Scandinavian civil law heritage	10	10	10	9.66	9.44	74	.55
World average	7.67	6.85	6.9	8.05	7.58	60.93	.41

Source: LaPorta *et al.* (1998) and Djankov *et al.* (2008)

et al.'s 2008 index, the French civil law countries score lowest on all aspects of the quality of law enforcement. Common law countries are generally in between. Instead of substituting for the lower levels of shareholder and investor protection, the enforcement indices suggest that low investor protection, be it shareholders or creditors, coincides with low levels of enforcement. Djankov *et al.*'s 2008 measure of public enforcement provides a slightly different picture, in the sense that differences between common law and civil law are not significant. It is, however, still the case that French civil law countries score relatively low on this new index.

In sum, the mainstream literature in this field typically argues that laws vary significantly across countries because of differences in legal origin. It is found that "civil laws give investors weaker legal rights than common laws do, independent of level of per capita income. Common law countries give both shareholders and creditors – relatively speaking – the strongest, and French civil law countries the weakest, protection. German civil law and Scandinavian countries generally fall in between the other two. The quality of law enforcement is the highest in Scandinavia, and German civil law countries, next highest in common law countries, and again the lowest in French civil law countries" (LaPorta *et al.* 1998: 1116). The reason why the results on enforcement measures are mixed and not as clear as the scores on investor protection could be linked with the fact that enforcement involves the likelihood that criminal sanctions are actually imposed (rather than their mere existence). Unfortunately, so far no data exist on actual enforcement practices, although it can be expected that the literature will move in this direction in the near future.

9.3.4 Consequences

The fact that legal origin is such an important determinant of the type and especially the quality of financial systems in terms of the protection of investors has additional consequences (*see* Fergusson 2006 for an overview). First of all, the extent to which investors – both shareholders and creditors – are protected determines the quality of the overall financial system. This is important because it has been shown that high-quality financial systems are an important determinant of economic growth. By enhancing savings, turning these savings into capital and investments, and the fact that investors exercise some control

over their capital, well-developed financial systems improve the alloca-
tive efficiencies of capital (Wurgler 2000) and affect economic growth
in a positive way (King and Levine 1993; Levine and Zervos 1998;
Beck *et al*. 2000). Moreover, investor protection and overall financial
development are associated with the extent to which markets decline
during financial crises; financial crises, measured in terms of exchange
rate depreciation and stock market decline, are deeper in low investor
protection countries (Johnson *et al*. 2000)[6] and with the greater ability to fund faster growing firms (Demirgüç-Kunt and Maksimovic
1998).

Second, differences in investor protection affect the ownership structure of firms. Poor investor protection will lead to concentrated control
for a number of reasons (LaPorta *et al*. 1998, 2000). Given that legal
origin affects the extent to which investors are protected, and the extent
to which investors are protected affects ownership structures because
poor investor protection is associated with concentrated ownership
(LaPorta *et al*. 1998), legal origin indirectly also determines the structure of ownership in firms. Shleifer and Vishny (1997) mention two
types of costs associated with large investors. First, in contrast with
dispersed ownership, the risk is larger because large investors are not
diversified. Second, large investors represent their own interests and
these need not coincide with the other (smaller) investors in the firm
(or with the employees and managers).

These are just two main consequences that have been derived from
this law and finance literature. Obviously there are more. However,
in the context of this book, three questions need to be asked at this
point. First, how does legal origin relate to culture? Second, can legal
origin proxy for culture? Third, what can we learn from the legal origin
literature? We discuss the second question in the concluding section;
first we discuss the link between legal origin and culture.

9.4 From legal origin to culture

Driven by the argument and findings that legal origin has shaped
differences in corporate governance regimes, as a next step a limited number of studies concentrate on the differences in legal origin.

---

[6] Note that this study does not include the 2009 financial crisis.

As will be discussed below, some of them have provided explanations of the differences in legal origin by using the standard efficiency
framework commonly used in economics (Glaeser and Shleifer 2002),
whereas others struggle to fit an exogenous factor called culture into an
otherwise standard efficiency framework (Stulz and Williamson 2003).
Yet another group of scholars has included culture without an explicit
attempt to embed the explanation in a standard economic framework
(Licht *et al.* 2007). These multiple approaches toward culture as a
driver of differences in legal origin and corporate governance regimes
are a broader reflection of the struggle on how to include culture in
economics.

9.4.1 Optimality and 0–1 interpretations of culture and legal origin

The mainstream legal origin literature clearly suggests that common
law regimes are optimal from an economic point of view. A different question is why some countries developed a common law and
others developed a civil law regime. Guided by the economic efficiency
framework, Glaeser and Shleifer (2002) present an historical overview
and develop a formal model based on a simple yet effective trade-off.
They start from the premise that the historical evolution of legal systems in England (common law) and France (civil law) started in the
twelfth and thirteenth centuries and that the political system in this
period has left some permanent marks on the way the legal system
developed and has shaped the choice of royal judges vs. independent
juries (cf. Zetzsche 2007). The trade-off they present is "between a
judge incentivized by the king and therefore less vulnerable to local
magnate pressure, and a jury, whose preferences are closer to those of
the community but which faces no incentives and can be more easily
coerced" (Glaeser and Shleifer 2002: 1202). Based on a social welfare point of view, they argue that given the political constellation
in that period, the choice made for the legal system in both France
and England was efficient and optimal. Based on the key parameters
in their model, Glaeser and Shleifer (2002) explain both the emergence of the two different systems and their respective convergence in
the twentieth century. Their approach raises the question of how this
efficient history fits the optimality argument made in the legal origin

literature (with common law regimes performing better). How can the historical development of both systems be driven by optimality and efficiency, but the subsequent economic performance of one of the two systems be sub-optimal? A similar "struggle" can be found in more contributions, for example the one by Stulz and Williamson (2003), who explore whether differences in culture, operationalized as religious heritage, explain differences in investor protection. The rationale for them to look specifically at religious heritage is that religion is argued to shape the system of beliefs and the attitude toward market institutions.

Starting from the popular premise that Protestantism is more favorable toward market institutions,[7] Stulz and Williamson (2003: 322) wish to test whether "simple culture proxies can help explain the diversity in the protection of investor rights consistently across countries" (Stulz and Williamson 2003: 322). Their starting point is that "we would expect individuals to trade off the costs and benefits of specific cultural values" (Stulz and Williamson 2003: 338) and they interpret culture as religious heritage (Catholicism vs. Protestantism and Christian vs. non-Christian) and language (English as a main language or not). Their methodical approach has a data-mining character in the sense that they explore almost all possible correlations between religious heritage, language, legal origin and investor protection. Their findings are mixed and interpretation of their statistical results is not easy. For example, with respect to shareholder rights, they find that legal origin is more important than religious heritage, supporting the law and finance literature. However, they also find that culture, measured as religious heritage, is more important than legal origin when explaining creditor rights; within the group of civil law countries, Catholic countries score lower on creditor rights. Finally, enforcement

---

[7] As we have already described in the chapter on trust, non-hierarchical religions are argued to create more favorable conditions for horizontal ties enabling trust. In financial economics, it is typically argued that the economic organization of a religion also affects the financial market contracting; Catholic nations are associated with smaller financial markets. The reason for arguing so is that the Calvinist reformation is associated with a decentralization effort and an abolition of the hierarchical structure of the Catholic Church. And decentralization limits rent seeking and corruption. The fact that Lutheran and Calvinist reformers emphasize that individuals need to read the Bible themselves, and can reach correct decisions based on their own reading, empowers individuals (Stulz and Williamson 2003; Zetzsche 2007).

is explained by both legal origin and culture, with Spanish-speaking Catholic countries showing lower levels of law enforcement. Their results also indicate that Protestant countries have better enforcement of rights than do Catholic countries, but this result is not robust for inclusion of language.

In addition to their blurred findings, another problem of their approach (or reason for their mixed findings) is the interpretation of their results for "culture," which are based on dummies for religion and language. Such a fixed-effects approach is not uncommon (*see* e.g. Licht *et al.* 2007) but may lead to substantial validity problems; given that they are group-based country dummies, the question rises as to what these dummies really measure. A dummy for classifying a country as Protestant or Catholic is very simplistic even if the classification is carefully done, as in the study by Stulz and Williamson (2003). Given that religious heritage is highly correlated with legal origin (French legal origin with Catholicism and common law with Protestant heritage), the interpretation of the statistical results when using both variables simultaneously is complex. For example, Stulz and Williamson (2003) make a distinction between Germany and France as civil law countries by pointing to their Protestant, respectively Catholic heritage. However, as La Porta *et al.* (1998) have shown, the civil code between Germany and France is not the same, and instead of measuring religious heritage, the 0–1 Protestant–Catholic dummy may in fact reflect this difference in civil law regime. In other words, interpretation problems arise because of validity issues moderated by an omitted variable bias. At a more substantive level, if we interpret culture as a system of values, what does the 0–1 distinction between Catholics and Protestant have to do with culture? As we described in Part I of this book, values are not an either-or category but are continuous and multidimensional. And even accepting this 0–1 framework, interpretation problems arise, because we cannot distinguish between the causal mechanism driving the statistical effect of the religion dummy; is it the economic organization of a specific religion (decentralized Protestant and hierarchical Catholic) or the theologically value-based differences between religious traditions? In sum, studies such as those by Glaeser and Shleifer (2002) and Stulz and Williamson (2003) exemplify the problems of disentangling legal origin and culture and illustrate the difficulty of including culture in an otherwise standard efficiency optimality framework.

9.4.2 Systems of values, local optimality and corporate governance regimes

Studies that go beyond the 0–1 classification of culture and include value frameworks such as Hofstede's or Schwartz's multidimensional operationalization of culture do exist. A useful starting point in this context is the contributions by Banner (1998), Coffee (2001) and Licht and his co-authors (Licht 2001, 2003, 2008; Licht *et al.* 2005). In his article entitled "The mother of all path dependencies: toward a cross-cultural theory of corporate governance systems," Licht uses the cultural values frameworks developed by Schwartz and Hofstede to argue that national cultures "play a role in both the origin and future development of corporate governance systems" (Licht 2001: 147). He describes a broad range of potential relationships between aspects of corporate governance (for example, shareholding structures, executive compensation, and self-dealing regulation) and one or more of the culture dimensions as developed by Hofstede or Schwartz. Banner (1998) and Coffee (2001) do the same but at a more general level linking values and the development of (securities) law systems.

In a follow-up article, Licht *et al.* (2005) explicitly seek to go beyond the legal origin approach and establish a set of empirical relations between shareholder and creditor rights and specific values. More specifically, they test all possible correlations between LLSV's 1998 anti-director rights index, the creditor rights index and key cultural dimensions of both Hofstede and Schwartz. They hypothesize that greater reliance on concrete legal rules enforceable in the courts (higher creditor and shareholder rights) is positively associated with Schwartz's cultural dimension of mastery and negatively related to the harmony dimension. Along similar lines, Licht *et al.* (2005) hypothesize on the relation between the Hofstede dimensions of individualism (high) and uncertainty avoidance (low) and the degree of investor protection. Based on extensive correlation and regression analyses (but occasionally using relatively small samples), they find some support for their hypotheses and show that "combining classifications based on cultural dimensions and legal families can yield insights obscured by using one approach only" (Licht *et al.* 2005: 251). Their result stands orthogonal to the results obtained by LaPorta *et al.* (2008), who include Hofstede's dimensions as additional controls next to legal origin dummies in explaining investor protection (the creditor rights index) and find that legal origin is significant and the culture variables are not. This fairly simplistic regression on just one dimension of investor protection leads LaPorta *et al.* (2008) to conclude that legal origin dummies are not just a proxy for culture. Despite Licht *et al.*'s (2005) additional step in analyzing investor protection regimes, and the operationalization of culture as a system of values, the contribution by Licht *et al.* (2005) lacks some focus. This is probably caused by the broad nature of the research question. More focussed value-based approaches addressing just one aspect of the corporate governance regime are, for example, Chui *et al.* (2002), De Jong (2002) and Kwok and Tadesse (2006b).

Following the "tradition" of the law and finance literature, Kwok and Tadesse (2006b) try to explain the size and quality of the stock market and relate cross-country differences to value differences. Countries with higher levels of uncertainty avoidance (Hofstede's measure) are associated with larger, bank-based financial systems, because compared with stock market-based financial systems, bank-based systems are associated with superior risk-reducing capabilities. More important, perhaps, in the legal origin context is that the regression results obtained by Kwok and Tadesse also seem to suggest that this uncertainty avoidant effect exists next to the effect of legal origin. Hence, both common law countries and countries that score low on uncertainty avoidance have larger and better developed stock markets. These results are robust for a two-stage least squares approach in which geographical endowments (continent dummies) and religious heritage (percentage of Catholics, Protestants or Muslims) are included as instruments for uncertainty avoidance, suggesting the causal link runs from culture to type of financial systems instead of vice versa.

Another example of a value-based approach toward cultural explanations in finance can be found in Chui *et al.* (2002), who wish to explain the cross-national differences in debt ratios (financial leverage). Based on extensive theoretical argumentation, they hypothesize how and which cultural values might influence firms' capital structures. They build on Schwartz's framework and find that conservatism (associated with moderation, social order, security and status-quo maintenance) and mastery (associated with being ambitious, successful, being independent) are both negatively related to the use of debt finance. Firms from countries in which people stress these values are characterized by a lower debt ratio. Conservatism and mastery jointly explain 44 percent of the cross-national variance in debt ratios. Interestingly, when Chui *et al.* (2002) control for legal origin using LLSV's classification of legal families, they still find confirmation for their hypotheses. Moreover, they test their thesis at both the country and the firm level. Their results are also robust for inclusion of variables measuring financial institutional development and other well-known determinants of debt ratio at the firm level, such as firm size and profitability.

To explicitly counter the "data-mining-lack-of-theory-criticism," De Jong (2002) has theorized on the relationship between a key construct in financial economics, i.e. central bank independence, and a country's value system. Focussing on Hofstede's uncertainty avoidance, he has tested the hypothesis that countries that are relatively uncertainty avoidant have higher levels of central bank independence. His causal logic is based on the idea that uncertainty avoidance is associated with lower levels of inflation (price uncertainty) and central bank independence is one of the key mechanisms for relatively low levels of inflation. Logically this would imply a causal link between uncertainty avoidance and central bank independence, a claim for which he indeed finds empirical support.

All the above approaches aim to establish a link between culture and governance systems. One key difference between the first group focussing on legal origin and culture as 0–1 variables and the second group of studies using a system of values approach (based on, for example, Hofstede or Schwartz) is that the latter group explicitly or implicitly starts from the notion that different combinations of culture and governance exist and these need not suffer from relative differences in optimality. In other words, studies in comparative corporate governance have a perspective on culture which is either in line with the neoclassical optimality (efficiency) framework or a perspective in which multiple (equally optimal) combinations are allowed for.[8] It is

---

[8] This latter approach based on the fit between culture and institutions is clearly reflected in the argument by Licht (2001) when he writes: "Suppose that Germans, in general, are (statistically) significantly more sensitive than Americans to issues like equality, social justice, and mutual help; Americans in contrast put more emphasis on ambition, success, wealth and social power. If Greece, for example, decided to reform its corporate governance system, Greek experts might consider adopting the German model of corporate governance, with its paradigmatic corporate governance structure of large blockholdings, mandatory employee representation on the supervisory board, relatively opaque disclosure, et cetera. Alternatively, Greece might consider imitating the American model, with dispersed ownership of shares, ample discretion to the

especially in the first group of studies that economists struggle to fit culture in.

9.5 Critique of the law and finance literature

Although the argument that historically determined differences in legal traditions explain international differences in financial systems is a powerful one, it is not without criticism. LaPorta *et al.* (1998) themselves acknowledge that their indices do not cover merger and takeover rules, they cover disclosure only partially and they do not cover stock exchange rules of financial institutions. As already explained, Djankov *et al.* (2008) develop a new measure of anti-self-dealing explicitly to take into account some of these criticisms. More fundamental critique that goes beyond these straightforward measurement issues can be organized along several dimensions. One can criticize the internal logic of the legal origin approach and one can criticize the legal approach as such, including the claim that it is perhaps rather simplistic to operationalize legal origin and culture as a 0–1 distinction.

9.5.1 Convergence between legal families

The classification of countries by different law systems is based upon historically shaped patterns. It can, however, be questioned whether these 0–1 classifications still represent the differences in law systems because of convergence since their origins in the twelfth and thirteenth centuries. Coffee (2000) argues that there has been considerable convergence between common and civil law systems. The impact of globalization and internationalization affects securities laws so that national law systems do not exist side by side any more (Roe 1998). This is illustrated by a historical study of EU business regulation, in which Wigger and Nölke (2007) show that European regulation has become distinctly more Anglo-Saxon in recent years. Glaeser and Shleifer (2002) provide an economic explanation for the convergence

board of directors (with no employee representation) and an aggressive disclosure regime. *Adopting features of the German corporate governance system would be much smoother than adopting the American system if Greeks shared more cultural values with Germans*" (Licht 2001: 150–151, emphasis added).

of these systems in the twentieth century. Politically-oriented analyses of convergence effects have been put forward as well. (*See* Haber *et al.* (2007) for a broad overview of political theories and financial development and Acemoglu *et al.* (2004) for an overview of political explanations of economic development.) Roe (2003) has argued that politics and not legal systems shape corporate governance systems. And going beyond the 0–1 classification, Berkowitz *et al.* (2003) show that the way the law was initially transplanted and received is a more important determinant than the supply of law from a particular legal family.

Rajan and Zingales (2003) do not so much focus on the question of whether convergence has taken place or not but argue that no large differences existed at all between continental Europe and the United States in terms of the size of their equity markets (in fact, the European equity market was relatively more developed) before the First World War. Instead, the political environment (isolation and nationalism) in the early twentieth century negatively affected the subsequent financial development, leading to differences between these groups of countries. This leads Rajan and Zingales (2003) to conclude that "structural theories" stressing the role of time-invariant factors such as legal origin and culture are at minimum incomplete. This critique by Rajan and Zingales (2003) triggered LaPorta *et al.* (2008) to develop a counter-argument. Using Rajan and Zingales' (2003) own data sources, LaPorta *et al.* (2008) claim to have shown that a careful reinterpretation of these data actually supports their legal origin view. Their critical remarks that there were no differences in equity markets between common and civil law countries at the start of the twentieth century is, according to LaPorta *et al.* (2008), based on a misinterpretation of the data.

Taking specific issue with the convergence question, Balas *et al.* (2008) follow up on Djankov *et al.* (2003a) and develop historical scores for the latter's measure of procedural formalism, a measure of how heavily the law regulates the procedure. Balas *et al.* (2008) claim to show that if anything, there has been a process of divergence in the design of the legal process for civil litigation between civil and common law countries since the starting date of their analysis (since 1950). Using different data for a twenty-five-year period, Djankov *et al.* (2007) report lack of convergence as well. With more and more data becoming available, we can expect that more of these studies will be undertaken, testing the legal origin argument by tracing convergence vs. divergence of regimes or outcomes of these regimes in terms of investor protection. So far the evidence seems mixed.

9.5.2 Functional equivalence

A second point of critique is related to the above convergence argument and concerns the question of what the functional difference between these legal families is. Even if these differences in legal origins still exist, the question arises as to whether different legal systems really lead to functional differences. This question points to the potentially important difference between the process of lawmaking vs. the contents of the law (Berkowitz *et al.* 2003). In other words, instead of making a relatively superficial distinction between legal families, we should look at the true functional differences (cf. Coffee 2001).

In a general discussion of numerical comparative law, Siems (2005) argues that the numerical method of natural sciences cannot simply be copied by the social sciences because of the context specificity. Law is complex, prescriptive and cannot be reduced to numbers because one compares apples and oranges. According to Siems (2005), it will only lead to "pseudo-science." He does not suggest dropping all initiatives to quantify law and legal effectiveness, but he proposes to classify law systems on functional grounds. So instead of ranking the presence of rules in countries as a 1, or as a 0 in another country, we need to take notice of the micro-structure of these laws and the way they function.

Against this background, Lele and Siems (2007a, 2007b) scrutinize laws protecting shareholders in India, the UK and the US (2007a) and add Germany and France in another study (2007b). Based on an analysis of sixty items related to shareholder protection over a thirty-five-year period, they find that (i) within common law countries there exists a great diversity in shareholder protection, leading them to conclude that a classification "into one single group according to their legal origins seems almost naïve" (Lele and Siems 2007b: 8); (ii) there are no deep differences between shareholder protection in civil law and common law countries; and (iii) despite some convergence in shareholder protection since the 1990s, there is no indication of a general Americanization of the law on shareholder protection, and instead they show evidence indicating the presence of a European legal culture, with the US taking a separate position compared with these other four countries. (In fact, they show that it is the UK which can be considered most mainstream by being the least different from all the other countries.)

In an even more detailed account of shareholder rights in the US, Belgium and France, Cools (2004) convincingly shows that the selection of items included in LaPorta *et al.*'s (1998) anti-director index is ad hoc and contains some coding errors. Djankov *et al.* (2008) have taken into account some of these critical notions in the revised anti-director's index and the anti-self-dealing index developed in 2008, but part of Cools' critique still holds. For example, she finds that similar institutions can have a different effect as a consequence of other rules, thereby pointing to the presence of institutional complementarities. After an extensive and detailed account of the individual practices included in the anti-director's index developed by LaPorta *et al.* (1998), Cools (2004: 40) concludes that the "difference between common and civil law with regard to shareholder protection is not as straightforward as the numbers in *Law and Finance* suggests." The difference between the coding strategies by LaPorta *et al.* (1998) and Cools (2004) is related to the fact that Cools looks at the actual power distribution between managers and owners, instead of the mere presence of rights. Her study of effective control in American, Belgian and French corporations also indicates that it is very difficult, if not impossible, to rank shareholder rights regimes in terms of relative efficiency. Within the broader institutional framework, she seems to suggest that each system may have its own way of achieving efficiency. In a related article, Armour *et al.* (2008) not only develop new longitudinal data but also show that although common law countries may have exhibited a greater over-all level of shareholder protection than civil law countries, the latter group experienced a greater increase in shareholder protection over the period 1995–2005, suggesting convergence in *actual* levels of investor protection.

9.5.3 Ethnocentrism

Apart from the question on the relevance of the common and civil law distinction, more meta-sociological critique on the culturally bound perceptions of corporate governance exists as well. Davis (2005) writes in this context that "behind much of the recent work in law and economics is a rather stylized depiction of the American (or Anglo–American) system of corporate governance that is often at odds with how that system operates on the ground." Pointing to the corporate scandals at the turn of the twenty-first century, he argues that "the American system is hardly an arm's-length meritocracy organized around impersonal institutions, as portrayed in the theories" (Davis 2005: 156). In a similar vein, it can be questioned to what extent the finding that the English language dummy is associated with better accounting practices (remember the study by Stulz and Williamson 2003) might be based on the fact that it is exactly these English-speaking countries that define what good accounting standards are. Lele and Siems (2007b) describe how this US bias may have driven the scores developed in the law and finance literature. They point to the selection of variables to be included and those to be excluded. For example, cumulative voting is one of the items included in the LaPorta *et al.* (1998) index and is a big issue in the US, but cumulative voting does not play a major role in Germany and France. (Note, however, that Djankov *et al.* (2008) do try to solve this specific issue in their revised anti-director's index.) Alternatively, the minority protection index used in LaPorta *et al.* (1998) does not take into account the risk of expropriation of minority shareholders by majority blockholders. In some non-US countries, however, it may be important to take this into account. Berndt (2002, in Lele and Siems 2007b) has shown that when taking into account these alternative mechanisms and developing a revised index, Germany performs better than the US (in contrast with the LLSV 1998 index). The essence of comparative law is that it should not contain a country bias and some authors claim that the law and finance literature does not cover this sufficiently.[9] Finally, in addition to the stylized way of presenting corporate governance systems, the taxonomy of major legal systems itself has been criticized as

---

[9] One of the leading text books on comparative law writes in this context: "Europeans and Americans must be constantly aware, when studying non-Western legal systems and culture, that they must not approach or appraise these systems from their Western viewpoints or judge them by European or American standards. For example, some Western lawyers concluded in the 1970s that China has no legal system because she has no attorneys in the American or European sense, no independent judiciary, no Codes, and since the Cultural Revolution, no system of legal education. Yet, this is surely to judge a non-Western system by Western standards, rather like the Western visitor who assumed there was no 'proper' music played in China because he did not see any Western instruments in the Chinese court hall he visited" (De Cruz 1999: 223).

being "Euro–American-centric" (Licht *et al.* 2005: footnote 40) and has been described as an evolutionary tree, with the American system at the top (Licht 2001: 157). Taking a radical perspective, one might even suspect that to an Anglo-Saxon economist, any scale is valid only when it puts France against the Anglo-Saxon world. In this sense, it may pay to consider this literature itself as a product of a specific culture: "French-bashing" is a deep-rooted trait of British and US culture (and vice versa). As a consequence, any typology that puts France and the US on the same end of a scale, opposed to Britain, will not be considered convincing.

9.6 Discussion

9.6.1 Optimality of values

As described in Section 9.4, scholars in comparative corporate governance struggle with the conceptualization of legal origin and culture. The (often implicit) assumption still is that an "optimal" culture exists and that we can empirically trace this best combination of culture, institutions and economic performance by regressing a set of proxies on whatever measure of economic success by using a proper set of exogenous instruments to deal with the chain of the causality between culture, governance and outcomes. As an illustration, we refer to Stulz and Williamson, who have talked about path dependencies and the link between legal origin and religious heritage, but also write that "we would expect individuals to trade off the costs and benefits of specific cultural values" (Stulz and Williamson 2003: 338). This explicitly assumes (i) one unique best set of values, with "best" defined along the economic efficiency dimension, and (ii) that people will search for these and accept them in some rational search process.

There are two objections to such a perspective. First, even if we can establish one unique best set of values and institutions through extensive empirical analysis, the question is to what extent this set's optimality is dependent on the current political and economic context. In the contemporary world order, it makes economic sense to have corporate governance structures, accounting standards and values that are reasonably compatible with those of the United States. Such a low cultural and institutional distance would facilitate economic relations with the world's biggest economy and is therefore economically beneficial to any country. However, to derive from this that US standards are universally optimal is in danger of mistaking might for right.

Second, the assumption that people search for and accept a unique best set of values by trading of costs and benefits goes against our intuitive ideas about what culture is. In fact, isn't a key characteristic of a culture – often defined as a shared system of values and norms of behavior – that one does *not* question the usefulness of its behavioral guidelines? While much of the literature seems to start from the premise that values matter and that different values are associated with different institutions (including corporate governance), there is at the same time this underlying quest among economists to find the best, i.e. most efficient, performing model.

Once one takes a perspective of culture which is more in line with the description of culture as provided in Chapter 1, and accepting Stulz and Williamson's (2003) argument that a crucial difference exists between formal regulations and what managers actually do, the entire idea of studying the origin of corporate governance regimes by looking at a 0–1 distinction between common and civil law systems becomes rather peculiar. As the very existence of corporate governance research concerns the incompleteness of contracts and the risk of expropriation by insiders because of the impossibility of controlling everything, a manager's room to maneuver implies a role for their underlying value system to affect the decisions made. Moreover, this especially holds for common law countries because "in common law countries, managers and boards have more flexibility than they do in civil law countries" (Stulz and Williamson 2003: 347). Exactly because of the room for discretionary effort in corporate governance, we need to know the actual drivers of managers' behavior if we want to study how culture matters. And when taking this perspective, the study of culture in terms of a 0–1 religion, legal origin or language dummy does not cover the true scope of managerial behavior. We believe that it may at maximum capture only some of the very broad norms related to these 0–1 categories, but fail to measure actual value dispositions. And it certainly does not measure culture as a system. In other words, one potentially interesting way out of the awkward discussion on optimality of values is to make a conceptual turn and study how values affect decision-making in the context of incomplete contracts and risk of expropriation. Such a value-based approach could be applied to test the key assumption in corporate governance that every manager would behave according to the standard predictions of the principal agent model. The extent to which managers behave according to this model could differ depending on a society's culture. The risk of expropriation by insiders may be partly culturally determined and this may affect the type of formal institutions required to cope with this. "The upshot of this reasoning is that accountability mechanisms may look and function in fundamentally different ways according to (. . .) the social environment in which [these managers] interact" (Licht 2003: 36), leading to the hypothesis that the "one size fits all optimum cannot apply to all countries" (Zetzsche 2007). A study that takes such a perspective of culture as a system of values substituting for legal institutions is the one by Coffee (2001). Starting from the premise that "corporate behavior may be shaped and determined by social norms rather than by legal rules," he hypothesizes that other factors such as social cohesion play a role in determining the extent to which corporate governance systems function properly (and may explain why common law regimes do not necessarily outperform civil law regimes). Along similar lines, it has been argued that shared cultural values lead to shared accounting values which lead to a nation's accounting system (Han *et al.* 2010). Culture and legal systems co-develop in such a view.

9.6.2 Exogeneity vs. endogeneity

So far, the way culture is included in finance is based on the premise that cultural differences lead to different governance systems, which lead to different economic outcomes. As with the nature of the empirical studies on the economic importance of trust as described in Chapter 7, this reflects a traditional two-stage model from culture to institutions to performance. According to Licht *et al.* (2007), feedback mechanisms exist between culture, governance and economic outcomes, and this creates an endogeneity problem. In the context of corporate governance, evidence exists linking cultural origin proxied by differences in legal tradition and the type of financial or corporate governance system. There is, however, no robust link established between type of financial system and economic performance of these systems. Surveying the literature on corporate governance, Shleifer and Vishny (1997: 773) conclude that "despite a great deal of controversy, we do not believe that either the theory or the evidence tells us which of the [three] principal corporate governance systems is the best." Levine (2002) reached a similar conclusion when comparing bank-based and market-based systems and their effect on economic growth. Together with some of the earlier evidence on shareholder rights, this seems to suggest that it is not so much the type of corporate governance that matters for economic success but the quality.

In a way this is a comforting thought, because legal origin is not a "Tinbergen" variable that can be changed at will. Legal origin, a country's economic development path, political history and its financial systems are highly endogenous, and interrelated. One cannot push a legal origin button and expect fundamental changes, but this is perhaps not necessary either if each system is optimal in its own way. Legal origin and culture are both inherited, specific, exogenous, man-made, systems of thought, and concern values and norms. The discussion, then, is perhaps not so much about legal origin or culture but about whether the view of culture as exogenous is correct, whether we should not see culture, including legal origin, as something dynamic, evolving under influence of political considerations and other developments. Such a perspective on the fundamental relationship (or fit) between culture and formal institutions and the type of economic organization also affects the nature of the econometrics that can be applied to test hypotheses in this area. "Many of the variables commonly treated as exogenous are inadequate for controlling reverse causality in relations between cultural and legal variables. They may have had reciprocal causal relations with law and/or culture either directly or through economic factors. The menu of truly exogenous variables is thus largely limited to bio-geographical factors and to major historical events" (Licht *et al.* 2005: 245). In other words, to tackle the chain of causality associated with the link between culture, institutions or governance and economic outcomes, the traditional tool of economists to use two Stage-Least-Squares techniques becomes limited because of a lack of exogenous instruments in such a perspective on culture and legal origin.

In conclusion, in this chapter we have studied the legal origin thesis, i.e. performance differences in corporate governance regimes can be traced back to differences in legal families. Legal origin is subsequently related to country-specific political and historical developments and culture broadly defined. This infinite regress from economic growth to financial systems to corporate governance regimes to legal families to culture and/or historical developments is not only typical for this literature but also nicely illustrates how culture is often included in economics more broadly. We described how scholars struggle with the position of culture in this debate: is culture a truly exogenous variable, or a variable that is (or can be made) subject to the neoclassical optimality framework? Moreover, we showed how culture and legal origin are interrelated and that existing measures very often yield an uncomfortably wide range of possible interpretations of empirical analyses. Just like the analysis of trust as discussed in a previous chapter, empirical studies on comparative corporate governance run into identification problems. In the next chapter and the final part of the book, we integrate these insights with those generated in the previous chapters.

PART III

Evaluation

10 | *Discussion*

10.1 Introduction

In the first part of this book, we discussed the historical origins of the debate about culture in economics. We have shown how culture and economics over the course of centuries evolved into opposite concepts, the one being about collective, inherited and particular structures and perspectives, the other embracing individual, rational choice as a universal behavioral principle. This deep-rooted opposition sets the stage for any attempts to reintegrate culture and economics, be it from the side of cultural theory or economics. The fundamental nature of this opposition makes attempts to address culture in economics challenging, more so than is often realized. We discussed several of the theoretical and methodological challenges and the ways economists have confronted them in Chapters 4 and 5 respectively. The second part of this book dealt with research into culture in economics in practice. We critically discussed the treatment of culture in the literature about entrepreneurship, trust, international business and corporate governance. In all of this literature, we observed a number of difficulties in aligning economics and culture.

Now it is time to make up the balance and take these two discussions together. The aim of this concluding chapter is to show that the theoretical and methodological oppositions discussed in the first part of the book are not just abstract, conceptual tensions of concern only to those working on abstract theoretical levels, but that they translate into practical difficulties for economists studying culture in practice. It also presents new ideas on how to deal with these tensions and provides directions for future research. This is important, because we believe economists should not let the difficulties involved in studying culture in economics lead them to abandon the subject. The odd position of the culture concept in economics is precisely what makes it such a potential source of enrichment for economic thought. Not only does

addressing culture open up new perspectives for an improved understanding of the world, it also forces us to critically reflect upon our
own discipline and its methodological and theoretical premises, which
can only lead to a better economic science.

We structure this chapter along the lines of the main conflicts
between economics and culture. Section 10.2 discusses the tension
between economics' methodological individualism and the collective
nature of culture. Section 10.3 addresses that tension between culture
as inherited structure and economics as a science dealing with rational choice. Section 10.4 deals with the opposition between economics'
ambition to identify universal principles and insights and culture's
focus on the particular. Subsequently, we place these discussions in
their political–economic context. We conclude with a summary of our
main insights and ideas.

10.2 Economic individualism vs. cultural collectivism

It has been stressed repeatedly throughout the various chapters of this
book that the relationship between the individual and the collective, or
alternatively the multi-level aspects of preference formation, are implicitly in the background when attempting to include culture in economics
(Licht 2008). As we have shown in Chapter 2, culture has, over time,
evolved into a concept that explicitly deals with structures and identity
on a collective level. Preferences, ideas and behavior that are specific to
the individual are not generally deemed to be culture. At the same time,
economics has developed into a discipline focussing explicitly on individual, micro-level decision-making. This contrast makes it inherently
difficult to integrate culture into the economic framework.

10.2.1 Theoretical juxtaposition

Looking back upon the literature discussed throughout this book, we
conclude that the collective tends to enter economic analysis in two
ways. The first is the way in which the macro-level has traditionally
been addressed in economics: as a derivative of micro-outcomes. Most
economists claim to adhere to such a kind of "methodological individualism." Although the precise meaning of this term is rather unclear
(Hodgson 2007a, 2007b), it generally involves the view that any economic relationships or outcomes observed at the macro-level should be

retraceable to individual decision-making. In practice, linking micro-
to macro-level is seen as a primarily mathematical challenge, which
generally involves the assumption of universal representative actors.

The second way in which the collective enters economics can be
found in approaches such as new institutionalism which take factors
such as embeddedness more seriously. In this view, there are collective
sources of preferences and constraints on individual rational decision-
making. These might be labeled institutions, mental maps or culture.
Here, the collective enters not so much as a result of individual choices
but as one of many external factors informing them.

These two ways of approaching the relationship between the micro-
and macro-level generate a tension in economic thought. In the first
approach, the collective does not exist as something in itself. Macro-
level outcomes are merely the total of a number of independent individual decisions. They are informative, but they do not matter for behavior. Social phenomena can be explained by individual actions alone.
In the second approach, however, the collective level is something that
affects and informs individual decisions. In this view, social reality cannot be explained by individual behavior alone, but we need to include
social structures in our explanations as well (Hodgson 2007a; Licht
2008). The collective has, in some senses, a life of its own.

From micro to macro and back

Trying to get the two approaches together, as the culture in economics
debate does, brings about both practical problems and more fundamental, methodological issues. Practically speaking, the idea that
the macro-level affects micro decision-making complicates aggregation exercises significantly. Rather than individual outcomes adding
up to a macro-outcome, there are feedback loops as well. The limitations of the "traditional" way of dealing with micro- and macro-
issues by simple aggregation of the behavior of representative agents
have been put on the agenda, most notably by Blundell and Stoker
in their 2005 *Journal of Economic Literature* article. A first obvious
limitation is the fact that in real life, universal representative actors do
not exist. Insights in behavioral economics have stressed the necessity
to deal with heterogeneity among agents. Adding up heterogeneous
agents rather than universal representative actors adds considerable
complexity to any micro–macro aggregation. It is not an impassable
hurdle, however. Blundell and Stoker (2005) describe ways to deal with

the complexities associated with aggregating heterogeneous individual consumption patterns, labor participation and income.

Second, beyond heterogeneity, a small but rapidly expanding literature discusses the endogeneity of preferences. Behavior of individual agents has an influence not just on general outcomes but also on the conduct of other agents. Taking both heterogeneity and endogeneity seriously is crucial, not just for the study of culture in economics but for economics in general. It implies at the minimum a mathematically far more sophisticated way of moving from the individual to the macro-level than by simply adding up micro-level insights. Whether this is enough is the question; sceptical scholars will argue that in the end any formal procedure linking micro to macro will have to build on some aggregation mechanism and such a mechanism will never be able to take all interactions into account.

From individualism to culture and back

The challenge posed by the introduction of culture into the economic framework goes beyond the mathematical complexities of aggregation, however. The problems discussed by Blundell and Stoker (2005) and the literature on endogenous preferences deal with only a part of the problem, though admittedly an important part. The more fundamental issue is that incorporating culture as something that exists at the collective level implies acknowledging that social phenomena cannot be explained entirely in terms of individuals *alone*. Social phenomena should be explained in terms of individuals plus social structures at the collective level, such as culture. This view is a crucial step away from the methodological individualism that appears an essential element of the economic approach (Hodgson 2007a).

A famous quote by Friedrich Hayek clearly points out the difference. According to Hayek (1967: 70–71, emphasis added): "The overall order of actions in a group is in two respects more than the totality of regularities observable in the actions of individuals and cannot be wholly reduced to them. It is not only in the trivial sense in which the whole is more than the mere sum of its parts but presupposes also that these elements are related to each other in a particular manner. *It is more also because the existence of those relations which are essential for the existence of the whole cannot be accounted for wholly by the interaction of the parts but only by their interaction with an outside world both of the individual parts and the whole.*"

In other words, the idea that all economic explanations must be retraceable to micro-level decisions is problematic. Were it only for the first, "trivial" reason, mathematically more complex aggregation procedures in the directions discussed above might hypothetically still do the trick. Harder to overcome is the second reason put forth by Hayek, why "wholes," such as culture, are ultimately irreducible to individual actions and choices. Even if we were to retrace the emergence of culture to individual decisions, this does not take away the fact that culture enters our thinking and our actions as a collective entity. Individual Americans, for example, do not confront "American culture" as merely their actions and interrelations. As Anderson (1991) points out, communities like "America" are imagined in the sense that no actual relations exist between the members. Rather, it is the idea of a collective whole called American culture that unites individual Americans and opposes it to individuals and imagined communities in the outside world. American culture, even while it may be the product of individual actions and relations, enters individual decision-making as a whole with an existence of its own. That is what the idea of culture implies: culture has meaning as something that binds the collective and distinguishes it from the outside world. As such, it enters individual decision-making, which is very hard to reconcile with strict methodological individualism.

10.2.2 *Methodical challenges: cross-level interaction*

The challenge to link collective culture to individual behavior also enters as a key methodical issue in empirical research. Research on culture in economics has primarily taken the form of cross-cultural regressions in which comparisons are made at the country level. To tackle the challenge of bridging the gap between economic individualism and collective culture, we believe that a combination with other methods is warranted. There are two methods that are hardly used by economists but which we think can help push the research frontier in this field. First, especially management scholars have used fine-grained methods to properly undertake case studies (Yin 1993, 1994; Eisenhard 1989, 1991). More generally, so-called grounded theory approaches provide rich empirical material, and robust methods exist to extrapolate the insights generated in these cases and produce theoretical material that is built upon causal logical arguments. Although many economists are reluctant to do this themselves (and often also lack the training to do so properly), we would like to draw attention to cases performed in related disciplines. An example of such a case is D'Iribarne's (1989) study on aluminum plants in France, the US and the Netherlands and the cultural differences in management and organization on the work floor. Combining case material with more traditional economic modeling and econometric large-scale tests offers great opportunities for triangulation. Both emic and etic approaches suffer from shortcomings and combining these approaches will generate a new wave of enthusiasm and research opportunities.

A second relatively new method originating in sociology concerns multi-level techniques (Snijders and Bosker 1999). Multi-level techniques are suitable to study nested data structures, for example when individual-level dependent variables are explained by independent variables at the individual level and at higher levels. Individual-level scores are nested in these higher-level scores and the most interesting part of multi-level techniques is the ability to distinguish random slopes coefficients. Or alternatively, to empirically establish to what extent individual-level drivers differ depending on different contexts. The idea to distinguish between levels of analysis is not new for many econometricians, but the focus on cross-level interaction may be new for many of us. So far this multi-level technique is mainly applied in sociology and social-psychology, which is not surprising given sociologists' orientation toward understanding group effects, especially social stratification theorists. Moreover, many sociologists are familiar with structural equation modeling and it is a logical next step in the tradition of this methodical family to take issue with nested structures (Cheung and Au 2005).

Multi-level applications in the field of culture and economics are so far scarce and to our knowledge only some working papers exist in which, for example, individual levels of trust are explained by looking at cross-level interactions between individual characteristics (e.g. employed or not) and societal-level characteristics (e.g. high levels of income inequality as reflected in high GINI scores) (e.g. Wang and Gordon 2007). These types of approaches are important because they shed light on the individual and the contextual effects, and their interrelationship, and thereby contribute explicitly to the relationship between trust and institutions in specific, and the structure–agency debate more generally. Given the recent surge in multi-level cross-cultural psychology (*see*, for example, the recent book by Van de Vijver *et al.* 2008 and the fifth volume in the *Research in Multi Level Issues* series by Yammarino and Dansereau 2006), we may expect these multi-level techniques to be gaining prominence in the field of culture and economics (Cheung *et al.* 2006). However, we should be clear: multi-level techniques will not completely solve the micro–macro problem, nor the endogenous preference-formation issue. It is technically more precise, and closer to the theoretical arguments many of us aim to test, but it is not a panacea for all the methodological problems discussed in this book. Having said this, however, we cannot suppress our excitement in this area; the future will show whether economists indeed take up this multi-level challenge.

10.3 Exogenous structures vs. rational agents

In the previous section, we discussed the tension between economists' adherence to a form of methodological individualism and their increasing interest in culture, which resides at the collective level. We argued that the desire to include culture in economic analysis not only highlights problems of aggregation but also puts more fundamental methodological issues on the table. More specifically, we claimed that taking culture seriously implies that one has to let go of (strict) methodological individualism and include collective factors as explanatory variables in the analysis. What is more, we showed that although collective norms, values and identities are ultimately constituted by actions of individuals, the resulting culture enters our minds and our decisions as a collective whole rather than as a collection of individual decisions and their relations.

10.3.1 Theoretical juxtaposition

Taking this one step further, we argue that this difference is not just about levels but also about the distinction between structure and agency. In the economic perspective, social structures are seen as retraceable to choices by agents. The concept of culture, by contrast, implies something more than that; it is something with a life of its own. Where economics focusses on individual choices, culture enters the economic model as a given to the individual. People do not make rational choices about the content or form of their culture – they perceive it as a given, exogenous structure (Licht 2008). If individuals were to "trade off the costs and benefits of specific cultural values," as Stulz and Williamson (2003: 338) want it, they would not be bound by these cultural values. For culture to be culture, and to influence our behavior rather than being an outcome, it has to be an exogenous input to the individual's choices. This puts culture in direct opposition to rational choice. That, on the one hand, is what makes it difficult to reconcile with economic theory. On the other hand, it is also what makes culture so interesting to the economist. Reducing culture to a (by)product of individual actions is perhaps a way of bringing culture and economics together. However, it does so by dissolving the meaning and added value of the concept "culture." If introducing culture is to add something to economic theory, it must be conceived as having a life of its own and not be reducible to individual actions.

Discussions such as the one about trust in Chapter 7 illustrate this. Ex ante it may be questionable whether a book on culture should discuss trust as extensively as we have done in our book. Is trust culture? True, many economists talk about culture and use trust measures to operationalize culture. Trust is about human-made, ideational factors influencing behavior and outcomes, and may be specific to a certain community. However, the attractiveness of trust as a proxy for culture in economics is that trust, in contrast to other possible proxies, has a calculative component which can meaningfully be studied by means of rational choice theory. This makes trust a relatively easy-to-fit concept in generally accepted economic models. As we have discussed in Chapter 7, the calculative component of trust at the same time creates doubts about its cultural character; if it is simply a matter of rational choice, is trust really culture? When discussing differences in trust levels, are we not talking about rational responses to differences in institutions rather than culture? The question emerging in Chapter 7 is what component and type of trust belongs to culture and what is determined by calculative types of processes. But this question is informed by a specific conception of culture as opposed to rational, calculative choices and actions of individuals. Behavior that can be analyzed on the basis of rational choice models is not considered cultural. Culture is about inherited customs and beliefs that are determined on a collective level and may be irrational from the individual point of view. Behind this discussion again lies a conception of culture as an exogenous factor.

Only things that cannot be reduced to material circumstances, rational choice, political or legal factors are deemed culture.

Hence, we observe a difficulty in integrating cultural structures into the rational choice framework of economic thinking. Since the non-calculative and collective character of culture is ingrained in the concept itself, any study analyzing social structures from an individual rational choice framework cannot be about culture. This simplistic dichotomy between rational and irrational (cultural) behavior does no justice to many of the recent developments in our knowledge about human decision-making. Many studies have shown that full rationality is in fact not normal behavior (*see* Conlisk 1996 for an overview) and that it has to be abandoned in favor of bounded rationality. The concept of rationality has been opened up to include more of our empirical insights about how people actually make decisions – the turn to cognitive sciences and neuro-economics is illustrative. As North (2005: 64) argues, "what we mean by rationality requires explicit specification for social scientists in general, but especially for those who employ rational choice models. If we are going to employ the choice theoretic approach we must be explicit about just how people arrive at choices they make. Being explicit entails specification of the subjective models people possess to interpret information and of the information they receive." In turning toward mental models and cognitive processes, authors like North seek to trace culture down to cognitive processes (Denzau and North 1994; North 1990, 2005). In a similar way, Williamson (2000) argues that beliefs, norms and values are rooted in people's cognitive characteristics. These contributions dissolve much of the discrepancy between the rational choice model and culture. If (bounded) rationality comes to be defined as how we make decisions in practice, deviations from the rational model are no longer possible. What previously was deemed culture thus becomes an element of bounded rationality. Culture is then rooted in the natural constraints on our rationality.

Alternative approaches to the problem

An alternative route to address the structure–agency problem is provided by the structuration theory of Anthony Giddens (1984, 1991) (*see also* Hodgson 2007b). Giddens argues that, rather than being two different, difficult-to-reconcile concepts, structure and agency are constituted by each other. Structures exist only within the actions of agents; but agents can act meaningfully only because in their minds, the world is structured. The structural relation between handing over money and getting goods in return, for example, exists only as long as people keep reproducing it. Yet, people continue handing over money and expecting goods in return only because they believe this structural relation to exist. Once we forget about the meaning of money and stop giving goods in exchange for it, the structure disappears and all we are left with are useless pieces of paper. This also shows that if there were no structural relations between cause and effect in our perceived social environment, it would be impossible to do anything. The structural relation of exchanging money for goods gives meaning to individual actions of buying and enables individuals to obtain goods. It is because we act in such structural ways that our agency comes about. Without doing so, we would be severely limited in our agency, as there would not be any (predictable) social consequences to our actions. This perspective opens the door for a third possible way of adding culture to the economic rational choice model: culture might be seen neither as preferences nor as constraints but as constituting agency by framing choices. Rational choice is possible only if there are consequences to our choices. Such consequences require that people structure their society in such a way that certain acts have certain effects; the choice between buying apples and pears exists only because the grocer and I agree upon the structure of me handing money to her resulting in my ownership of either an apple or a pear. Without shared, acted-upon ideas about actions and consequences in a society, rational choice cannot exist. Such shared, acted-upon ideas may very well be called culture.

We do not believe structuration theory is the definitive answer to the challenge of reconciling culture with the rational choice approach of economics. For one thing, it is rather vague about how it can be made relevant to empirical research, something which will definitely put off many economists. What structuration theory does show, however, is that a more creative, reflective way of thinking about methodological issues such as structure–agency can offer promising new directions. The desire to integrate culture in economics requires us to do so.

10.3.2 Methodical challenges: infinite regress

The problem of structure vs. agency enters empirical research most visibly in the debate about so-called "deep determinants" of economic growth. Searching for explanations for structural differences in economic performance between societies, researchers have come across the problem that the economic model in principle does not allow for structural differences in behavior between groups. Facing similar conditions, the neoclassical choice model predicts that groups of rational actors will not make structurally different choices. Hence, if structural differences in performance exist, these must be ultimately reducible to differences in structural conditions. Institutional and cultural explanations for growth divergence are not satisfactory from this perspective. Both institutions and culture are human-made; in the economic framework, they are the result of choices by individuals. If differences in human-made culture and institutions are responsible for differences in performance, this begs the question why societies adopt different cultures and institutions.

One solution is that cultural differences between groups exist due to differences in material conditions. Cultural patterns can be explained by tracing them back to environmental constraints. Culture, in this view, is a rational response to material circumstances (*see* Chapter 9). Habits have grown out of this rational response (e.g. Harris 1979; Hofstede 2001; North 2005). This new institutional view on habits and culture as a rational response to environmental circumstances is at odds with old institutional economics in which these are not perceived as rational answers to environmental conditions, but are seen as autonomous structures. Moreover, it conflicts with the intuitive understanding of culture as something that cannot be rationally negotiated by individuals. As we argued in Chapter 1, one of the essential aspects of culture is that one does not question the validity of its behavioral guidelines.

Ultimately, the problem lies in the limitations of the rational choice framework of economic analysis when dealing with issues such as culture. On the one hand, culture is invoked as a structural constraint in much institutional theory (Greif 1994; North 1990; Williamson 2000) and empirical research (*see* Chapter 9 for example). On the other hand, the adherence to rational choice implies that culture cannot be such a constraint, since it itself is seen as a product of individual choices. Of course, there is an important time dimension to this discussion. Values may indeed be the result of a rational historical process in which geography is one of the drivers, but those historically grown value systems cannot be argued to be a rational response to circumstances arising today. In other words, culture may indeed be a rational response to environmental conditions, but only to the extent that these are historically grown.[1] That does not take away the question of why different cultures have been adopted by different societies, leading to differences in performance. In order to explain differences between societies, in the end we need exogenous factors. The literature about the deep determinants of growth can be seen as a quest for such truly exogenous factors, underlying all observed differences. Unfortunately, there is a problem in finding exogenous variables (Fehr 2009), because the menu of truly exogenous variables is short (Licht *et al.* 2007).

To illustrate these issues, recall the discussion in the previous chapter of the process with which financial economists have gradually become interested in legal origin. After establishing that economic growth was in important ways related to the quality of financial markets and, more specifically, the degree of investor protection, it was subsequently argued and found that differences in investor protection are again related to differences in law regimes. But going one step further (or in fact back), differences in law regimes have to do with the distinction between common and civil law, which has historical and political roots again. And these are embedded in geographical endowments according to some, which in turn could be argued to be the product of factors such as migration patterns. The point is that this process of backtracking causality in the end boils down to an infinite regress.

We think that the current trend in financial economics to perform such an infinite regress is representative for much of the ongoing work in the field of culture and economics. A prime example of the infinite regress is the recent work by Spolaore and Wacziarg (2006), who study the role of *genetic* distance in explaining income differences. They find that the amount of time elapsed since two populations' last common

---

[1] This of course triggers the question as to why cultural behavior has evolved as a rational response to material circumstances, but then stops responding rationally to changes in circumstances. This is especially a pressing problem in a world of increased migration flows, since these would entail moving people to environments to which their culture is not tailored, according to the theory. A striking example of how problematic such notions can be is the philosophy of Lee Kuan Yew, former leader of Singapore. Lee has argued that the Chinese, socialized in a harsh climate which necessitated hard labor and endurance, naturally acquired the upper hand when moving to the Malay Peninsula, where the population's culture had evolved in a benign climate which fostered laziness and indulgence (Barr 1999).

ancestors (interpreted as genetic distance) is significantly related to pairwise income differentials. A more general discussion on the role of genetic architecture vs. environmental conditions (nature/nurture) can be found in North (2005 Chapter 3) and Williamson (2000).

Infinite regress often results in a tendency to fine slice the theoretical route linking culture and economics into its constituent parts and test the parts of this culture–performance chain. As long as the goal of such a "fine-slicing" method is to understand the process itself, and not to find the ultimate factor driving the causal chain of logic linking culture to economic outcomes, the problem of infinite regress will be relatively limited. What does it help us if we can establish that in the end everything is determined by geographic endowments? Isn't it much more relevant and interesting to know how the process itself unfolds? What does it help a policy maker if we can tell him or her that it is the geography that causes the poor economic performance of their country? Similar to Hodgson's (1998) critique on the wish to start from a so-called institution-free state of nature to understand the origin of institutions, we think the most interesting research questions do *not* emerge out of the quest for a culture-free state of nature by means of infinite regress. To study the process of how cultures develop, and how culture and differences in culture affect economic behavior, is not only theoretically more rewarding but also more useful from a practical point of view. Assuming economists aim to understand the drivers (and consequences) of economic behavior, we think the study of a "zero-equilibrium" is not that interesting, but the process toward and from such an equilibrium is.

This does not mean that we find the current studies along this line useless. The fact that these studies have been performed has contributed tremendously to our understanding of culture and it has also resulted in our discussion of the problem of infinite regress. What it also implies is that our thoughts regarding fruitful routes for future research are shaped by this observation. If the multi-peak model holds (*see* below for details), it may be much more interesting to understand how culture shapes the equilibrium forces in the different societal systems and drives economic outcomes in these different systems. Hence, not the "universal" model of economic growth and the "optimal" cultural values are relevant any more, but how culture and preference structures lead to different types of economic behavior and aggregate outcomes (*à la* Greif 2006). These different types of economic organization may have different ways to achieve economic growth and need not lead to differences in economic efficiency by definition. Such a comparative economic organization approach is a fruitful angle to include culture in economics.

10.4 Economic universalism and cultural contingency

In Chapter 2, we have seen how economics evolved into a discipline studying universal principles of behavior. Culture, by contrast, refers to structures and ideas that are inherent to a certain group's identity. This opposition between culture's particularity and economics' universalism creates another source of tension for scholars studying culture in economics.

10.4.1 Theoretical juxtaposition

The conceptualization of culture as being about collective differences leads to the question of how different cultures are. The discussion of entrepreneurial culture in Chapter 6 illustrates this. In this literature, some authors develop measures of culture specifically geared to capture the extent to which a society has entrepreneurial values, while others focus on general measures of cultural dimensions which can be related to rates of entrepreneurship. Such a choice reflects a conceptual difference between a position of culture as a concept for which you have to develop unique dimensions reflecting a society's unique aspects (and societies differ in the relevant dimensions) or as a universal concept having similar dimensions all over the world (and societies differ only in their score on these dimensions). This opposition can be reduced to a fundamental choice all researchers in this field have to make: the choice between an emic perspective, focussing on distinctions that are meaningful to the members of a given culture, and an etic perspective, relying on categories and analyses provided by outsiders. This choice emerges from an underlying conception of culture as referring to specific structures and behavior. Those parts of behavior that are shared by all humankind, we do not consider cultural; culture is only about those parts that are unique to certain groups. This conception of culture as difference triggers the question of how unique culture has to be. Is the specificity a matter of differences in degree on universally meaningful dimensions? Or are cultures so fundamentally different that no meaningful comparisons are possible at all? Those who are arguing the first cling to an etic perspective; those holding the second position argue only emic analysis is possible.

If the relationship between culture and economic outcomes is culture specific, this triggers a discussion on the proper choice of outcome variables. If each society with its distinct set of preferences behaves according to these preferences, we may expect that different outcomes will be achieved; one society stressing work and competition will achieve higher levels of material well-being than other societies stressing leisure and harmony, which will achieve lower levels of material well-being but higher levels of equality. This does not, however, automatically mean that levels of total perceived well-being differ between these societies. For example, the relation between income and happiness is culture specific, because the importance of material income is not equal in all societies. Alternatively, in a standard utility function the importance of friends and family translates into a reduction of working time (Beugelsdijk and Smulders 2003), resulting in lower income levels but not necessarily in lower levels of subjective well-being. Although this book has mostly been on economic (in)efficiency, it may be equally interesting to study how culture affects other outcome parameters such as happiness and other measures of subjective well-being. If the utility derived from certain choices is not defined solely in terms of financial gains and losses but for example in terms of perceived happiness, the link between rationality and utility does hold and still fits the standard economic framework.

Hence, the nature of the economic outcome may differ because of different cultural endowments. Rationality is universal, values differ and hence each society stresses its own aspects of economic performance. In practical terms, such reasoning would imply that it is still possible to apply Hofstede's or Schwartz's multidimensional culture framework and rank societies on, for example, uncertainty avoidance. And given that countries score high or low on this dimension, it is rational for people in these societies to develop an institutional system that fits their underlying set of preferences. Though theoretically neat, this approach yields empirical problems. A regression on happiness levels using uncertainty avoidance as a cultural characteristic to establish a link between culture and happiness will probably be flawed, because if people do not like uncertainty avoidance, you may expect them to develop an institutional system in such a way that uncertainties are limited (e.g. by social safety nets). A significant negative effect between happiness and uncertainty avoidance may in this case not imply that uncertainty-avoiding societies are less happy, but that the way the institutional system minimizes uncertainty does not function properly. Again, this solution to the contingency problem is theoretically attractive but empirically complex.

With this line of reasoning, rational behavior also implies that different economic outcomes are stressed in these societies, e.g. work vs. leisure. A regression relating the scores on a specific value system to one aspect of economic performance, e.g. economic growth, will yield significant relationships, but the underlying question is what such a finding really means. Does it imply that economic growth can be achieved only in societies with these specific cultural characteristics? Is there a single culture that is economically optimal?

Toward a multi-peak landscape?

The above discussion on cultural contingency leads us to present the relationship between culture and economic behavior as a two-step procedure including economic organization aspects (Licht *et al.* 2007). The link between culture and economic outcomes runs through institutions shaping the organization of economic activities (Djankov *et al.* 2003). Although we have focussed explicitly on culture and do not intend to extensively discuss the role of formal institutions in this book, some remarks are nevertheless warranted for the sake of our argument.

To make our point regarding the existence of multiple equilibrium combinations of culture and economics, let us first consider the alternative, a one-peak system. This is graphically presented in Figure 10.1. It shows a three-dimensional picture in which the z-axis reflects economic efficiency and the x- and y-axes represent dimensions of a country's institutional system. These dimensions of a country's institutional system are embedded in a society's value system and reflect the aggregate outcome regarding the choices of individuals triggered by their underlying preferences. The picture shows that despite the existence of multiple combinations of institutional dimensions, only one optimal combination exists. Every deviation from this single-peak equilibrium yields lower levels of efficiency, reflected in the lower z-scores of the alternative combinations of institutions. This single-peak model is dominant in much theoretical and empirical work in economics. In the culture and economics discussion, the single-peak model implies that

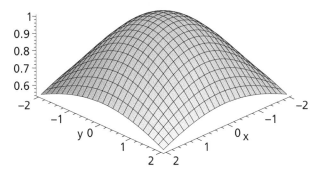

Figure 10.1. Single-peak model

an optimal culture exists and deviations from this optimal culture lead to lower levels of economic performance. In this case, culture matters by leading to deviations from the one optimal model. But as we have argued above, including culture in economics may require some revisions of this single-peak model.

Following the argument made earlier, the culture–economics framework changes in a multi-peak landscape in which each society's value system is associated with different institutional systems and different scores on different aspects of economic outcomes (Djankov *et al.* 2003; Pryor 2008). As North (2005: 49–50) puts it: "Belief systems embody the internal representation of the human landscape. Institutions are the structure that humans impose on that landscape in order to produce the desired outcome. Belief systems therefore are the internal representation and institutions the external manifestation of that representation." In other words, underneath these peak models lies the assumption that culture, or belief systems, affect the way institutions are developed (and vice versa) and certain institutional combinations are associated with certain economic outcomes (Greif 2006). This implies that "we must have not only a clear understanding of the belief structure underlying the existing institutions but also margins at which the belief system may be amenable to changes that will make possible the implementation of more productive institutions" (North 2005: 163).

There are two ways to present the above idea conceptually and graphically. Version 1 implies that different cultures stress different outcomes. In this case it would perhaps be better to speak of multiple one-peak systems, in which each culture is associated with an

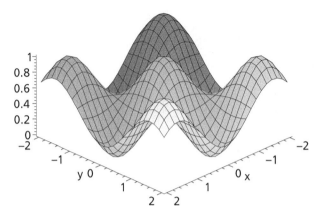

Figure 10.2. A multi-peak landscape

outcome that is optimal according to its own criteria. Culture matters in this model, not because of the existence of one unique optimal model but because of multiple peaks scoring optimally on different economic outcome dimensions. Each peak reflects a combination of institutions embedded in underlying value systems and one aspect of economic performance. Because objectives and criteria differ between cultures, meaningful comparison on a single standard of economic performance is problematic. Changing the figure accordingly results in Figure 10.2. In this multiple one-peak model version, the representation in Figure 10.2 implies that on each specific outcome measure, societies with the associated value system score highest. The z-axis in this case reflects a vector of economic outcomes, and each peak has its own 'z.'

Version 2 of the multi-peak model is less radical, as it still leaves room for meaningful intercultural comparison. It assumes that different cultures lead to different institutional systems, but this does not necessarily translate into differences in certain economic outcomes. Each peak in Figure 10.2 represents a society's score on some measure of economic performance that is equally meaningful to all societies. This measure might be economic efficiency; the underlying idea then is that economic efficiency is not so much a culture-specific objective but a measure of the degree to which a society has been capable of achieving its own objectives. In other words, it is a way of comparing scores on different 'z's. An alternative interpretation of such a multi-peak model is that peaks represent subjective well-being. Subjective well-being is often presented as a measure of the degree to which people in different societies are accomplishing the values they hold dear. "If societies have different sets of values, people in them are likely to consider different criteria relevant when judging the success of their society" (Diener and Suh 2000: 3). The recent surge in studies on well-being and happiness is a logical outcome of the perhaps broader ambition to include cultural diversity in economics. Starting with Easterlin (1974, 1975) in the 1970s, the study of happiness and well-being has more recently attracted the attention of economists such as Blanchflower and Oswald (2004), Di Tella *et al.* (2001), Fleurbaey (2009), Frey and Stutzer (2002), Helliwell (2006) and Layard (2005).[2]

From cultural content to consistence and coherence

This interpretation of the multi-peak model is basically about coherence. Economic efficiency and subjective well-being are both measures of the extent to which institutions and culturally contingent objectives are consistent with each other. If they are, economic efficiency and well-being are high, regardless of the nature of these objectives and institutions. Veenhoven (2000), for example, shows that variations in institutional structures, such as the extent of the welfare state, have no effect on well-being. This makes sense from the perspective of the multi-peak model; societies attaching importance to a welfare state will be happy creating one, while societies not wanting a welfare state will be equally happy not developing one. A similar argument has been made by Hall and Soskice (2001), who argue that different institutional systems do not necessarily perform differently in terms of economic growth rates. In Hall and Soskice's argument, which is based on developed, mostly democratic nations, the focus lies on the compatibility of institutions with each other. They delineate two models, the liberal market economy and the coordinated market economy, which are seen as internally coherent systems. Countries with corporate governance

---

[2] This is not to deny that sociologists have been involved in happiness research for a much longer time (e.g. Ruut Veenhoven's work on happiness starting in the early 1980s and his world database on happiness) and that the basic idea of a broader utility function can already be found in the works of "pre-modern" economists and philosophers such as Mill, Bentham and Smith. The point is, however, that the acceptance of such (empirical) work among economists is from more recent times.

systems, industrial relations systems and other institutions that are congruent either with those of a liberal market economy or with those of a coordinated market economy are expected to perform well. Nations with less coherent institutional frameworks, mixing industrial relations of a liberal market economy with the corporate governance systems of a coordinated market economy, for example, are expected to perform less well.

In a setting of developing societies, we might interpret this coherence thesis differently, however. Developing societies often suffer from an unfinished process of state formation and are often fragmented along regional, ethnic or class lines. Where in developed nations it perhaps makes sense to assume 'z' to be the same for the whole society, in many developing countries this assumption is almost certainly inappropriate. As a result, coherence is not so much about the compatibility of institutions with each other but more about the extent to which institutions designed and developed by one group fit the objectives and ideas of society as a whole. An institutional system might be very coherent in itself, but if it is geared only toward the objectives of a tiny minority of the population, it does not contribute to the general economic well-being of society. In other words, economic efficiency might be seen as a reflection of the degree to which a country's economic institutions are representative of its total variety of culturally contingent objectives.

This interpretation perhaps allows us a way out of the difficult debate about the role of culture in development. As we have seen, modernization theory already saw lack of development at least in part as a cultural problem. More recently, Harrison (1985; Harrison and Huntington 2000) has reissued the claim that underdevelopment is a state of mind.[3] In light of the discussion in this book, we can say that such claims are problematic, as they clearly subscribe to a single-peak view, measuring the world by only one – likely to be ethnocentric – standard. However, succumbing to the position in which everything is culturally contingent is hardly more attractive. It is, after all, fairly obvious that cultures of tribalism, nepotism or corruption negatively

---

[3] Such thinking is deeply engrained in American society and has historical roots. Abraham Lincoln framed it in the following way: "The man who labored for another last year, this year labors for himself, and next year he will hire others to labor for him" and that the only reason for a worker's failure to rise out of wage labor would be "his dependent nature" or perhaps "improvidence, folly, or singular misfortune" (*see* Friedman 2005: 57).

affect economic well-being and growth. The argument put forward here makes it possible to not so much see issues such as tribalism or nepotism as aspects of "the" culture of a country but to see them as lack of coherence between various cultures and identities within a society, each struggling for dominance.[4] This makes sense: where a tiny elite of one ethnic group rules a country in a predatory way at the expense of other ethnic groups, one can hardly blame the culture of the country as a whole for this. The fact that there is not one, single culture is precisely the problem. Interestingly, Greif's (2006) discussion on the formation of the city state of Genoa resembles aspects of this reasoning; unification (in Greif's analysis caused by external threats) has been put forward as a source of economic success. Platteau (2009) argues that the existence of various strong ethno-regional identities in a country is likely to prevent the emergence of a single, effective institutional framework, which negatively affects growth. This builds on a wider interesting literature about the relationship between ethnic homogeneity and economic performance, showing that ethnic fractionalization is bad for economic welfare (Alesina *et al.* 1999; Alesina *et al.* 2003; Easterly and Levine 1997; Mauro 1995).

Addressing diversity

In conclusion, there have been various ways in which the literature has dealt with cultural diversity in modeling economic behavior and performance. The single-peak model and the two versions of the multi-peak model are attempts to capture complex relationships between culture and economics. We do not wish to present any of these models as the ultimate solution to the questions raised here because none of them is. Even in the second version of the multi-peak model, for example, the question remains as to what operationalization of economic efficiency is genuinely not culture specific. The tension between universality and particular context thus remains. However, we do think that conceptualizing the very general position of culture in economics in terms of single- and multi-peak landscapes helps us push the debate. The peak models are in line with North's recent ideas on the existence of multiple equilibria: "While the sources of productivity growth are well

---

[4] As we have seen in Chapters 2 and 3, such a view of culture as contested and dynamic is also more in line with more current approaches in anthropology and sociology (e.g. Appadurai 1996; Bourdieu 2005a; Wolf 1999).

known, the process of economic growth is going to vary with every society, reflecting the diverse cultural heritages and the equally diverse geographic, physical and economic settings" (North 2005: 165).

Note that these multi-peak models do not imply that the concept of equilibrium is being dropped, "only" that the idea of one unique best equilibrium may require some revision. This universal model is deeply engrained in economics, but triggered by the culture research, and the associated discussion on rationality, the logical next step seems to be to reconceptualize our single-peak model and start exploring the implications of such a multi-peak model or the existence of multiple single-peak models.

10.4.2 Methodical challenges: how cultural differences matter

The challenge for empirical researchers interested in culture is to find ways to do justice to cultural contingency, while at the same time deriving general insights about economic processes. Measurement is a main problem here. In order to measure cultural differences, we need criteria and research methods that are equivalent over different cultural settings. Cultural contingency, however, implies that the meaning and relevance of such methods may be culture specific. This problem is most obvious in survey-based methods such as Hofstede's (1980, 2001),[5] which can be criticized for asking questions that may be understood differently across cultures and which refer to concepts that may not be equally central to various cultural identities.

A field explicitly dealing with this tension between universality and cultural contingency is (cross-cultural) experimental economics (e.g. Greif 2006; Henrich *et al.* 2004; Ostrom 2005; Camerer 2003, 2005). Economic experiments so far have focussed on showing that people do not always behave according to the (rational) economic (efficiency) framework. Cross-cultural experiments have additionally revealed that part of the economic behavior of individuals is specific to societies (Henrich *et al.* 2006; Herrmann *et al.* 2008; Gächter and Herrmann

---

[5] The problem is explicitly addressed in other surveys such as Schwartz (1994, 2006). Schwartz's approach includes a theoretical grounding and a survey of respondents to validate the equivalent meaning of the survey items across cultures.

2009). In our view, the key challenge for experimental economists will be to go beyond the by now well-established insight that culture matters and move on to the question of how culture matters precisely (as we have argued in Chapter 8 in the context of international business) and how it evolves. Experiments in different cultural and institutional settings can, for example, yield additional insights regarding the role of culture in economic decision-making. Remember the discussion in Chapter 7 on trust and the different results between survey-based trust measures and experimental-based trust measures in Tanzania and Sweden (Danielson and Holm 2005).

However, as discussed in Chapter 5, such cross-cultural experiments are not without problems (Samuelson 2005). First of all, the fact that experimental behavior varies in different societies may come as a shock for many economists assuming universal behavior. But for those social scientists who start from the premise that cross-cultural variance is associated with differences in behavior, including economic choices, these findings may not be that breathtaking. As such, the plea in Henrich *et al.*'s (2004) book for further investigation of the cultural foundations of social preferences seems rather tautological. Second, preferences as shown in experiments depend on the game *and* the context in which it is played, where the experiment can [only] control the former (Samuelson 2005: 495). This critique on experimental economics is typically found among cultural anthropologists. Any experiment suffers to some degree from such environmental indeterminacies and this is especially relevant when the explicit goal of the experiments is to show the context-specific variance. Again, the problem is that if culture is about differences, cultural contingency might affect the comparability of the cultures under study. Just as survey-based cultural dimensions can be criticized for applying alien categories to cultures, cross-cultural experiments can be charged with setting up games that have altogether different meanings and relevance in various contexts. Variance in outcomes of an ultimatum game may not so much reflect differences in the degree of cooperative attitudes as differences in the understanding of the game itself. The fundamental question is *how* different cultures are. Experiments can help us in this respect, but are not *the* answer to our problems.

One possible way forward for cross-cultural economic research is shown by the international business literature discussed in Chapter 8.

In this literature, culture is perceived as collective difference: the shared pattern of values that distinguishes one group of people from another group of people. However, rather than taking a comparative angle and asking which culture or institutions are best to achieve a certain outcome, IB scholars are often more interested in the question of how cultural differences matter if one is to cooperate with people from another cultural context. The focus lies on the impact of cultural differences rather than on the different impacts of cultures; or, from a more normative angle, on the question of what is the best way to deal with other cultures rather than what is the best culture. The strong point of IB in this matter is its clear theoretical route linking (differences in) values to managerial behavior and choices of multinational firms. Instead of arguing that culture is related to a certain phenomenon and testing this by regressing a broad range of proxies for culture on this phenomenon of interest, many IB scholars explicitly theorize on how certain dimensions of culture affect certain aspects of economic behavior in certain ways. Their subsequent test is often much more specific and detailed. However, in doing so, some of these studies suffer from the ecological fallacy, because micro-level causal reasoning is derived from aggregate cultural characteristics. The paradox of this route is the fact that its strength is also its weakness, and there is no easy way out of this.

10.5 The political–economic dimension

We have shown in the first part of the book that contemporary efforts to include culture in economics have been shaped by the way in which culture and economics drifted apart historically. The opposition between economic behavior and culture as a collective structure that is irrational and exogenous to the individual is no exception to this. It is rooted in the opposition of Romanticism to the idea of progress, in which a focus on particular customs and traditions of a society stood as defence against the universalizing onslaught of artificial civilization. Later on, under the influence of imperialism, this opposition became associated with the dichotomy of the West vs. the rest of the world. The West consisted of civilized, rational agents, whereas the rest of the world was governed by irrational collective traditions.

This goes to show that power structures affect our thinking about culture and economics. As we have seen in the historical chapters, the politically-economic dominant position of Northwest Europe has affected much of what has been written about 'the East' over the years. Said (1995) has shown that the representation of the non-Western world by Western authors has been severely distorted for a long time. This is not just a matter of mistakes we made in the past. Even today, ideas such as Asian Values, which have more than a smack of such Orientalism about them, can readily find acceptance. One's position in the world's power structures thus continues to affect our ideas and thoughts, and authors would do well to reflect on their potential biases and preconceptions, especially when it comes to sensitive issues such as culture.

This is not always an easy thing to do, for the impact of power structures on our thinking often runs deep. As we argued in the first chapters of this book, for example, issues as fundamental as the division of the social sciences and the associated adherence of economics to methodological individualism itself reflect the distribution of power. Throughout the literature, authors have repeatedly pointed out that methodological individualism is logically separate from political individualism (Schumpeter 1908; Hodgson 2007a). Strictly speaking, this is obviously true: methodological individualism prescribes only how social phenomena should be explained; it does not say how they are, let alone how they should be. That does not mean that the choice for and application of a methodological approach are not informed by the political–economic context. Nor does it mean that such choices have no political–economic effects.

If we look at the history of the debate about culture in economics, for example, we observe that "cultural" explanations in terms of collective structures governing behavior have been particularly enthusiastically employed when studying "The Other." The division of labor in social sciences that assigned individual rationality to economics and irrational culture to disciplines such as sociology and anthropology also had a geographical component to it. Economics dealt with the behavior of "normal," enlightened individuals in one's own society. Sociology dealt with deviant groups, anthropology with "other" societies. This selective choice for methodological, individualistic explanations was informed by the deep-rooted idea that "other" societies were governed by static, irrational, collective traditions in contrast to the educated, purposive and self-thinking Western individual. It represents an "Us" vs. "Them" thinking in which the "Them" has a subordinate position.[6] Moreover, it reproduced such ideas in social science; it was not until the late 1970s that the authors in the so-called neoclassical counterrevolution began applying economic insights that had been derived from the 'own' societies to developing economies (e.g. Lal 1983).

Should we care about the political–economic dimension of economic thinking about culture? Throughout this book, we have argued that we should. Ideas and conceptions may support and reproduce structures of power that, upon reflection, we might not really like to support. An important example of the way in which research is both informed by and informing the political–economic context is the common focus on nations as units of analysis. As we have seen in Chapter 2, part of the legacy of the historical school is the common focus on nations in culture studies. The emergence of the idea of national culture was linked to the trend of Romantic nationalism that facilitated the emergence of nation-states in the nineteenth century. Nowadays, the nation usually enters as the level at which culture is thought to reside in economic publications. Although this may be appropriate in some cases, one should be aware of the fact that research using the nation as unit of culture is informed by and reproduces the idea of one state, one nation, one culture. This focus obscures internal struggles between groups with different ideas and beliefs within countries. This is important because culture is an idea acted upon by individuals. Culture matters for behavior. It channels actions, fosters cooperation, forges unity and mobilizes support. Therefore it matters along which boundaries the cultural community is imagined; it matters who is defining the community and how. If researchers unquestioningly take over imagined communities along national lines, they can (marginally) contribute to the idea of national unity, which has political repercussions.

Another illustration of the political–economic dimension to research emerges from our discussion of comparative corporate governance. We have clearly described the potential US bias that may exist in the current measures of level of investor protection (Chapter 9). We have also referred to literature arguing that the debate in financial economics over the superiority of the common law regimes is not so much a

---

[6] On a different level, the subordinate position of cultural anthropology relative to economics in terms of academic status and funding can be seen as a derivative of this.

"real" issue but a reflection of power structures in the world centered around US domination (including in academia). The point is, of course, that whatever the truth may be, the end result may be the same, i.e. common law countries being (perceived as) superior investor protection regimes. Such a self-fulfilling prophecy illustrates the potential risk of including culture in economics without properly correcting for ethnocentric biases in this type of research. More generally, the idea that there is one optimal way of behavior, so that poorer, less successful societies really have no choice but to become more like the rich and powerful, tends to reproduce poor societies' subordinate position. When it comes to the role of culture in the economy, we would therefore do well to remember the warning words of Keynes (1936: 383): "The ideas of economists and political philosophers, both when they are right and when they are wrong, are more powerful than is commonly understood."

10.6 Conclusion

In this book, we have discussed the past and present of the debate about culture in economics. We have seen how culture was an inherent part of economic thought up until the nineteenth century. The combined arrival of marginalism in economics and the interpretation of culture as irrational, collective differences set culture and economics apart.

We observe that culture is making a remarkable comeback in economic thought. The renewed inclusion of culture in economics is a vibrant and promising "new" development, which we fully endorse. Developments in experimental economics and cross-cultural surveys bode well for the future. The increasing theoretical sophistication of institutional and behavioral economics is also promising. More so than new insights coming from these new developments so far, we are encouraged by the questions economists today are asking (again). The formation of preferences, the process of decision-making, the institutions characterizing a market economy and the role of history in economic change are all firmly on the research agenda. We see a move away from overtly narrow interpretations of methodological individualism toward an increased interest in social interactions and intersubjective meanings and beliefs. We believe these developments have the potential to reinvigorate economics and make the overarching field of culture in economics a crucial one in the coming decades.

Table 10.1. *Overview of conceptions of culture*

	Economic	Culture
Methodological	Individual	Collective
	Agents	Exogenous structures
	Universal	Particular
Theoretical	Rational choice	Cultural systems
	Single-peak	Multi-peak
Political	Us	Them
	Modern/Western	Traditional/Eastern

At the same time we hope to have made clear that the focus on culture in economics yields a methodological minefield. The concepts of culture and economics have evolved in opposite directions, making it more problematic to reconcile the two than is often acknowledged. The opposition between culture and economics consists of several dimensions and is closely related to how economics has defined itself. On each dimension, the idea of culture can be seen as taking in the one extreme, while economics takes the other. Table 10.1 gives an overview of the oppositions underlying the conceptions of culture and the economic, on a methodological, theoretical and political level.

Economics is concerned with a universally applicable model of choices and actions made by individuals; culture is conceptualized as very much the negative of this – it refers to particular deviations from the universal model, consisting of collective structures, which to the individual are given facts.

The methodological dichotomies within our conception of culture and the economic become visible when they are translated into theoretical positions. They lie at the root, for example, of the difficulties in aligning the concepts of personalized trust and generalized trust discussed in Chapter 7. Personalized trust is an interpretation of trust fitting a world made up by autonomous, individual actors. Behind the concept of generalized trust, by contrast, lies a vision of a world governed by collective structures, not directly retraceable to individual agency but setting the stage for individual behavior. The rational choice approach also fits a conception of the world in terms of individual agency, whereas the view of the world in terms of cultural systems is rooted in a structuralist worldview. The etic approach of economics springs from the idea that economics is studying universal types of behavior. The emic approach of ethnography coincides with a world-view in which cultures are unique, closed systems that are mutually incomparable.

If one insight arises from our overview of the recent literature, there-fore, it is that the methodological fault lines along which economics and culture got separated in the early twentieth century continue to have an impact on current attempts at reintegration. Many of the cur-rent attempts at including culture in economics start out from the basic opposition between the two and then seek to bring them together. As a result, contributions often take an uneasy middle ground between two perhaps incompatible extremes:

- Balancing between universalism and cultural relativism, contribu-tions tend to adopt single-peak cultural contingency.
- Balancing between rationality and the idea of non-rational, cul-tural structures affecting choices and behavior, contributions adopt bounded rationality.
- Balancing between structure and agency, contributions retrace struc-tures to natural constraints (infinite regress), redefining nurture as nature.
- And most importantly, balancing between culture and economics, contributions adopt a culture *and* economics perspective.

We believe that in order to successfully include culture in economics, we ought to redefine culture and economy in such a way that they are no longer opposites in the first place. However, that requires a more dynamic view of culture and cultural differences, in which individual action stands more central. A successful inclusion of culture may also imply that economics might need to rethink its single-peak orienta-tion and the associated penchant for universal theory. Fortunately, such new developments are on their way. We expect that the nature of the questions asked will change further in the near future. From the latest wave of mainly cross-country regressions trying to estab-lish causal links between parts of the culture–economic performance chain, we expect a move toward comparative economic organization approaches. In our view, the question of how preferences, embedded in underlying value systems, shape economic behavior and result in choices between competing alternatives is the core of the economic discipline. Method-wise, there are also some interesting and promising developments. Cross-cultural experiments, multi-level methods and triangulation by using emic and etic methods will improve our understanding of the economic role of culture. We are confident that culture will continue to be a promising field of research in economics.

References

Acemoglu, D., Johnson, S. and Robinson, J. 2001. "The colonial origins of comparative development: an empirical investigation," *American Economic Review* 117: 1231–1294.

2005. "Institutions as the fundamental cause of long run growth," in P. Aghion and S. Durlauf (eds.) *Handbook of Economic Growth*. North Holland: Elsevier, pp. 385–472.

Achrol, R.S. 1997. "Changes in the theory of interorganizational relations in marketing: toward a network paradigm," *Journal of the Academy of Marketing Science* 25: 56–71.

Acs, Z. and Audretsch D. 2003. *Handbook of Entrepreneurship Research: an interdisciplinary survey and introduction*. Boston, MA: Kluwer Academic Publishers.

Adair, W.L., Okumura, T. and Brett, J.M. 2001. "Negotiation behavior when cultures collide: the United States and Japan," *Journal of Applied Psychology* 86.3: 371–383.

Adler, N.J. 1983. "A typology of management studies involving culture," *Journal of International Business Studies*, 14.2: 29–47.

1986. "Communicating across cultural barriers," in N. Adler (ed.) *International Dimensions of Organizational Behaviour*. Boston, MA: Kent Publishing, pp. 50–75.

Adler, N.J. and Bartholomew, S. 1992. "Academic and professional communities of discourse: generating knowledge on transnational human resource management," *Journal of International Business Studies* 23: 551–569.

Adler, N.J. and Graham, J.L. 1989. "Cross-cultural interaction: the international comparison fallacy?" *Journal of International Business Studies* 20: 515–537.

Agarwal, S., Decarlo, T.E. and Vyas, S.B. 1999. "Leadership behavior and organizational commitment: a comparative study of American and Indian salespersons," *Journal of International Business Studies* 30.4: 727–743.

Ahlerup, P., Olsson, O. and Yanagizawa, D. 2009. "Social capital vs institutions in the growth process," *European Journal of Political Economy* 25: 1–14.

Akçomak, S. and Ter Weel, B. 2009. "Social capital, innovation and growth: evidence from Europe," *European Economic Review* 53: 544–567.

Akerlow, G. and Kranton, R. 2000. "Economics and identity," *Quarterly Journal of Economics* 115.3: 715–753.

Albert, M. 1991. *Capitalisme Contre Capitalisme*. Paris: Seuil.

Alesina, A., Baqir, R. and Easterly, W. 1999. "Public goods and ethnic divisions," *Quarterly Journal of Economics* 114(4): 1243–1284.

Alesina, A., Devleeschauwer, A., Easterly, W., Kurlat, S. and Wacziarg, R. 2003. "Fractionalization," *Journal of Economic Growth* 8: 155–194.

Alesina, A. and La Ferrara, E. 2000. "Participation in heterogeneous communities," *The Quarterly Journal of Economics* 115.3: 847–904.

Alesina, A. and La Ferrara, E. 2002. "Who trusts others?" *Journal of Public Economics* 85.2: 207–234.

Algan, Y. and Cahuc, P. 2010. "Inherited trust and growth," *American Economic Review* (in press).

Almond, G. and Verba, S. 1963. *The Civic Culture: Political Attitudes and Democracy in Five Nations*. Princeton, NJ: Princeton University Press.

American Economic Association. 1899. "Discussion – the President's Address," *Economic Studies: publication of the American Economic Association* 4(1): 108–111.

Amit, R.K., MacCrimmon, R., Zietsma, C. and Oesch, J.M. 2001. "Does money matter? Wealth attainment as the motive for initiating growth oriented ventures," *Journal of Business Venturing* 16: 119–143.

Anderson, B. 1991 [1983]. *Imagined Communities*. London, New York: Verso.

1998. *The Spectre of Comparisons: Nationalism, Southeast Asia, and the World*. London: Verso.

2005. *Under Three Flags*. London and New York: Verso.

Anderson, E. and Gatignon, H. 1986. "Modes of foreign entry: a transaction cost analysis and propositions," *Journal of International Business Studies* 17(3): 1–26.

Anderson, J.E. and Marcouiller, D. 2002 "Insecurity and the pattern of trade: an empirical investigation," *Review of Economics and Statistics* 84(2): 342–352.

Anderson, O. 1993. "On the internationalization process of firms: a critical analysis," *Journal of International Business Studies* 24.2: 209–231.

Andersson, T. and Frederiksson, T. 1996. "International organization of production and variation in exports from affiliates," *Journal of International Business Studies* 27(2): 249–263.

Aoki, M. 2001. *Toward a Comparative Institutional Analysis*. Stanford, CA: MIT Press.

Appadurai, A. 1996. *Modernity at Large: cultural dimensions of globalization*. Minneapolis, MN: University of Minnesota Press.

Armour, J., Deakin, S., Sarkar, P., Siems, M. and Singh, A. 2008. "Shareholder protection and stock market development: an empirical test of the legal origins hypothesis," University of Cambridge, CBR working paper.

Arora, A. and Fosfuri, A. 2000. "Wholly-owned subsidiary versus technology licensing in the worldwide chemical industry," *Journal of International Business Studies* 31(4): 555–572.

Arrow, K. 1971. "Political and economic evaluation of social effects and externalities," in M. Intriligator (ed.) *Frontiers of Qualitative Economics*. Amsterdam: North-Holland, pp. 3–25.

Arrow, K. and Dashgupta, P.S. 2009. "Conspicuous consumption, inconspicuous leisure," *The Economic Journal* 119: F497–F516.

Arts, W., Halman, L. and Hagenaars, J. (eds.) 2003. *The Cultural Diversity of European Unity*. Leiden/Boston, MA/New York: Brill Academic Publishers.

Ashraf, N., Camerer, C.F. and Loewenstein, G. 2005. "Adam Smith, behavioral economist," *Journal of Economic Perspectives* 19.3: 131–145.

Audretsch, D. and Keilbach, M. 2004. "Entrepreneurship and regional growth: an evolutionary interpretation," *Journal of Evolutionary Economics* 14: 605–616.

Axelrod, R. 1984. *The Evolution of Cooperation*. New York: Basic Books.
1986. "An evolutionary approach to norms," *American Political Science Review* 80: 1095–1111.

Azzi, C. and Ehrenberg, R. 1975. "Household allocation of time and church attendance," *Journal of Political Economy* 83: 27–56.

Baars, P. 1988. *Anachronisme en Historisch Besef*. Den Haag: Nijgh en van Ditmar University.

Bachmann, R. 2001. "Trust, power and control in trans-organizational relations," *Organization Studies* 22: 337–365.

Bae, S. 2008. "Is the death penalty an Asian value?" *Asian Affairs* 39(1): 47–56.

Bagwell, L.S. and Bernheim, B.D. 1996. "Veblen effects in a theory of conspicuous consumption," *The American Economic Review* 86.3: 349–373.

Bahry, D., Kosolapov, M., Kozyreva, P. and Wilson, R.K. 2005. "Ethnicity and trust: evidence from Russia," *American Political Science Review* 99.4: 521–532.

Balas, A., La Porta, R., Lopez-de-Silanes, F. and Shleifer, A. 2008. "The divergence of legal procedures," NBER working paper 13809, Cambridge, MA: NBER.

Banfield, E.C. 1958. *The Moral Basis of a Backward Society.* New York: Free Press.

Banner, S. 1998. *Anglo-American Securities Regulation: cultural and political roots, 1690–1860.* New York: Cambridge University Press.

Barkema, H.G. and Vermeulen, F. 1997. "What differences in the cultural backgrounds of partners are detrimental for international joint ventures?" *Journal of International Business Studies* 28.4: 845–864.

Barney, J.B. and Hansen, M.H. 1995. "Trustworthiness as a source of competitive advantage," *Strategic Management Journal* 15: 175–90.

Barr, M.D. 1999. "Lee Kuan Yew: race, culture and genes," *Journal of Contemporary Asia* 29.2: 145–166.

Barro, R.J. 1991. "Economic growth in a cross section of countries," *Quarterly Journal of Economics* 106: 407–443.

Barro, R.J. and McCleary, R.M. 2003. "Religion and economic growth across countries," *American Sociological Review* 68(5): 760–781.

Barro, R.J. and Sala-I-Martin, X. 1995. *Economic Growth.* New York: McGraw-Hill.

Barry, B., Fulmer, I.S. and Van Kleef, G.A. 2004. "I laughed, I cried, I settled: the role of emotion in negotiation," in M.J. Geldland and J.M. Brett (eds.) *The Handbook of Negotiation and Culture.* Stanford, CA: Stanford Business Books, pp. 71–91.

Bartlett, C. and Ghoshal, S. 1989. *Management across Borders: the transnational solution.* Boston, MA: Hutchinson Business Books.

Bartley, R. and Bartley, S. 2000. "Stigmatizing Thorstein Veblen: a study in the confection of academic reputations," *International Journal of Politics, Culture and Society* 14.2: 363–399.

Baumol, W. 1968. "Entrepreneurship in economic theory," *The American Economic Review* 58: 64–71.

  1993. *Entrepreneurship, Management, and the Structure of Payoffs.* Cambridge: MIT Press.

Becht, M., Bolton, P. and Röell, A. 2005. "Corporate governance and control," European Corporate Governance Institute working paper, available at www.ssrn.com/abstract_id=343461.

Beck, T., Demirgüç-Kunt, A. and Levine, R. 2001. "Legal theories of financial development," *Oxford Review of Economic Policy* 17.4: 483–501.

  2003. "Law, endowments and finance," *Journal of Financial Economics* 70: 137–181.

Beck, T., Levine, R. and Loayza, N. 2000. "Finance and the source of growth," *Journal of Financial Economics* 58: 261–300.

Becker, G. 1965. "A theory of allocation of time," *Economic Journal* 75: 493–517.

1973. "A theory of marriage: part I," *Journal of Political Economy* **81**.4: 813–847.

1976. "Altruism, egoism, and genetic fitness: economics and sociobiology," *Journal of Economic Literature* **14**.3: 817–826.

Becker, G. and Murphy, K. 2000. *Social Markets: The Marriage of "Economic" and "Social" Forces*. Cambridge, MA: Harvard University Press.

Beckerman, W. 1956. "Distance and the pattern of intra-European trade," *The Review of Economics and Statistics* **38**: 31–40.

Beidelman, T.O. 1993. "Review of Mary Douglas' risk and blame: essays in cultural theory," *American Anthropologist* **95**.4: 1065–1066.

Bell, D. 1973. *The Coming of Post-industrial Society*. New York: Basic Books.

Bellemare, C. and Kroger, S. 2007. "On representative social capital," *European Economic Review* **51**: 183–202.

Belot, M. and Ederveen, S. 2006. "Cultural and institutional barriers in migration between OECD countries," CPB Netherlands Bureau for Economic Policy Analysis, working paper.

Ben-Ner, A. and Putterman, L. 2009. "Trust, communication and contracts: an experiment," *Journal of Economic Behavior and Organization* **70**: 106–121.

Benedict, R. 2005 [1934]. *Patterns of Culture*. New York: Mariner Books.

Benito, G. and Gripsrud, G. 1992. "The expansion of foreign direct investments: discrete rational location choices or cultural learning process?," *Journal of International Business Studies* **3**: 461–476.

Bentley, G. 1987. "Ethnicity and practice," *Comparative Studies in Society and History* **29**.1: 24–55.

Berger, P. and Pullberg, S. 1965. "Reification and the sociological critique of consciousness," *History and Theory* **4**.2: 196–211.

Berggren, N. and Jordahl, H. 2006. "Free to trust: economic freedom and social capital," *Kyklos* **59**.2: 141–169.

Bergstrand, J.H. 1985. "The gravity equation in international trade: some micro economic foundations and empirical evidence," *Review of Economics and Statistics* **67**(3): 474–481.

Berkowitz, D., Pistor, K. and Richard, J. 2003. "Economic development, legality, and the transplant effect," *European Economic Review* **47**: 165–195.

Berle, A.A. and Means, J.G. 1932. *The Modern Corporation and Private Property*. New York: Macmillan.

Bernard, A. 2006. "Firms in international trade," *NBER Reporter research summary* Fall.

Bernard, A., Eaton, J., Bradford Jensen, J. and Kortum, S. 2003. "Plants and productivity in international trade," *American Economic Review* 93.4: 1268–1290.

Bernard, A., Redding, S. and Schott, P. 2007. "Comparative advantage and heterogeneous firms," *Review of Economic Studies* 74: 31–66.

Betz, H.K. 1997. "The role of ethics as part of the historical methods of Schmoller and the older historical school," in P. Koslowski (ed.) *The Theory of Ethical Economics in the Historical School*. Berlin, Heidelberg, New York, Tokyo: Springer, pp. 81–104.

Beugelsdijk, S. 2006. "A note to the theory and measurement of trust in explaining differences in economic growth," *Cambridge Journal of Economics* 30: 371–387.

2007. "Entrepreneurial culture, regional innovativeness and economic growth," *Journal of Evolutionary Economics* 17.2: 187–210.

2008. "Trust, institutions and the generally speaking question: a reply to Uslaner," *Cambridge Journal of Economics* 32.4: 633–638.

Beugelsdijk, S. and Frijns, B. 2010. "A cultural explanation of the foreign bias in international asset allocation," *Journal of Banking and Finance* 34: 2121–2131.

Beugelsdijk, S., de Groot, H. and Van Schaik, A.B.T.M. 2004. "Trust and economic growth; a robustness analysis," *Oxford Economic Papers* 56.1: 118–134.

Beugelsdijk, S., Koen, C.I. and Noorderhaven, N.G. 2006. "Organizational culture and relationship skills," *Organization Studies* 27: 833–854.

Beugelsdijk, S. and Slangen, A.H.L. 2010. "The impact of national cultural distance on the number of foreign website visits by U.S. households," *CyberPsychology & Behavior* 13.2: 201–205.

Beugelsdijk, S. and Smulders, S. 2003. "Bonding and bridging social capital: which type is good for economic growth?" in W. Arts, L. Halman and J. Hagenaars (eds.) pp. 147–184.

Beugelsdijk, S. and Smeets, R. 2008. "Entrepreneurial culture and economic growth; revisiting McClelland's thesis," *American Journal of Economics and Sociology* 67.5: 915–939.

Beugelsdijk, S. and Van Schaik, A.B.T.M. 2005a. "Differences in social capital between 54 Western European regions," *Regional Studies* 39.8: 1053–1064.

2005b. "Social capital and growth in European regions: an empirical test," *European Journal of Political Economy* 21.2: 301–324.

Bilkey, W.J. and Nes, E. 1982. "Country-of-origin effects on product evaluations," *Journal of International Business Studies* 13(1): 89–99.

Bjørnskov, C. 2007. "Determinants of generalized trust. A cross country comparison," *Public Choice* 130: 1–21.

2009. "Social trust and the growth of schooling," *Economics of Education Review* 28: 249–257.

Blair, M. 1995. *Ownership and Control: re-thinking corporate governance for the 21st century*. Washington, DC: Brookings Institution Press.

Blanchflower, D. and Oswald, A.J. 1998. "What makes an entrepreneur," *Journal of Labor Economics* 16: 26–60.

2004. "Well being over time in Britain and the USA," *Journal of Public Economics* 88: 1359–1387.

Blanchflower, D., Oswald, A.J. and Stutzer, A. 2001. "Latent entrepreneurship across nations," *European Economic Review* 45: 680–691.

Blaug, M. 1992. *Economic History and the History of Economics*, New York: Harvester Wheatsheaf.

Blonigen, B.A. 2001. "In search of substitution between foreign production and exports," *Journal of International Economics* 53: 81–104.

Blundell, R. and Stoker, T. 2005. "Heterogeneity and aggregation," *Journal of Economic Literature* 43.2: 347–391.

Boas, F. 1930. "Anthropology," in E. Seligman and A. Johnson (eds.) *Encyclopedia of the Social Sciences, Vol. 2*, New York: Macmillan: 73–110.

Boggs, C. 2001. "Social capital and political fantasy: Robert Putnam's bowling alone," *Theory and Society* 30: 281–297.

Boix, C. and Posner, D.N. 1998. "Social capital: explaining its origins and effects on government performance," *British Journal of Political Science* 28: 686–693.

Bond, M.H. and Chi, V.M-Y. 1997. "Values and moral behaviour in mainland China," *Psychologia* 40(4): 251–264.

Bond, N. 2006. "Eliminating the 'social' from 'Sozialökonomik'," *Economic Sociology* 7.2: 7–15.

Bourdieu, P. 1998a. "L'essence de néolibéralisme," *Le Monde Diplomatique*, March: 3.

1998b. "A reasoned utopia and economic fatalism," *New Left Review*, I, 227: 125–130.

2005a. "Principles of an economic anthropology" in N. Smelser and R. Swedberg (eds.) *Handbook of Economic Sociology* (2nd edn.). Princeton, NJ: Princeton University Press, pp. 75–89.

2005b. *The Social Structures of the Economy*. Cambridge, MA: Polity Press.

Bowles, S. 1998. "Endogenous preferences: the cultural consequences of markets and other economic institutions," *Journal of Economic Literature* 36: 75–11.

2004. *Micro Economics: behaviour, institutions and evolution*. Princeton, NJ: Russell Sage Foundation, Princeton University Press.

Boyacigiller, N. 1990. "The role of expatriates in the management of interdependence, complexity and risk in multinational corporations," _Journal of International Business Studies_ 21.3: 357–381.

Boyacigiller, N.A., Kleinberg, M.J., Philips, M.E. and Sackmann, S.E. 1996. "Conceptualizing culture," in B.J. Punnett and O. Shenkar (eds.) _Handbook of International Management Research_. Cambridge, MA: Blackwell, pp. 157–191.

Boyd, R. and Richerson, P.J. 1985. _Culture and the Evolutionary Process_. Chicago, IL: University of Chicago Press.

Braconier, H., Norback, P.J. and Urba, D. 2005. "Multinational enterprises and wage costs: vertical FDI revisited," _Journal of International Economics_ 67: 446–470.

Brainard, S.L. 1997. "An empirical assessment of the proximity-concentration trade-off between multinational sales and trade," _American Economic Review_ 87(4): 520–544.

Brandstätter, H. 1997. "Becoming an entrepreneur – a question of personality structure?" _Journal of Economic Psychology_ 18: 157–177.

Braunerhjelm, P., Acs, Z.J., Audretsch, D.A. and Carlsson, B. 2010. "The missing link: knowledge diffusion and entrepreneurship in endogenous growth," _Small Business Economics_ 34(2): 105–125.

Brehm, J. and Rahn, W. 1997. "Individual level evidence for the causes and consequences of social capital," _American Journal of Political Science_ 41: 999–1023.

Brett, J.M. and Okumura, T. 1998. "Inter- and intracultural negotiations: U.S. and Japanese negotiations," _Academy of Management Journal_ 41.5: 495–510.

Brewer, A. 1990. _Marxist Theories of Imperialism_. London: Routledge.

Brewster, C. 1993. "Developing a 'European' model of human resource management," _International Journal of Human Resource Management_ 4.4: 765–785.

Brewster, C. and Scullion, H. 1997. "A review and agenda for expatriate HRM," _Human Resource Management Journal_ 7.3: 32–42.

Brewster-Smith, M. 1964. "The Achieving Society, a review essay," _History and Theory_ 3: 371–381.

Brock Smith, J. and Barclay, D.W. 1997. "The effects of organizational differences and trust on the effectiveness of selling partner relationships," _Journal of Marketing_ 61: 3–21.

Brockhaus, R.H. 1982. "The psychology of an entrepreneur," in C. Kent, D.L. Sexton and K.H. Vesper (eds.) _Encyclopedia of Entrepreneurship_. Englewood Cliffs, NJ: Prentice Hall, pp. 39–56.

Brockhaus, R.H. and Horovitz, P.S. 1986. "The psychology of the entrepreneur," in D.L. Sexton (ed.) _The Art and Science of Entrepreneurship_. Cambridge, MA: Ballinger Publishing.

Brons, L. 2005. *Rethinking the Culture–economy Dialectic*. Dissertation, University of Groningen.

Brouthers, K.D. and Brouthers, L.E. 2001. "Explaining the national cultural distance paradox," *Journal of International Business Studies* 32(1): 177–189.

Brumann, C. 1999. "Writing for culture: why a successful concept should not be discarded," *Current Anthropology*, 40 Supplement, special issue: *Culture: a second chance?*, S1–S27.

Buchan, J. 2006. *The Authentic Adam Smith: His life and ideas*. New York: Atlas Books/Norton.

Buchan, N., Croson, R. and Dawes, R. 2002. "Swift neighbors and persistent strangers: a cross-cultural investigation of trust and reciprocity in social exchange," *American Journal of Sociology* 108.1: 168–206.

Büchner, S., Gonzalez, L.G., Guth, W. and Levati, M.V. 2004. "Incentive contracts versus trust in three person ultimatum games: an experimental study," *European Journal of Political Economy* 20: 673–694.

Buckley, P. 2002. "Is the international business agenda running out of steam?" *Journal of International Business Studies* 33.2: 365–373.

Buckley, P. and Casson, M. 1976. *The Future of the Multinational Enterprise*. London: Macmillan.

Busenitz, L. and Lau, C. 1996. "A cross cultural cognitive model of new venture creation," *Entrepreneurship Theory and Practice* 20.4: 25–39.

Butler, J., Giuliano, P. and Guiso, L. 2009. "The right amount of trust," NBER working paper 15344, Cambridge, MA: NBER.

Camerer, C. 2003. *Behavioral Game Theory–Experiments in Strategic Interaction*. Princeton, NJ: Princeton University Press.

Camerer, C. and Fehr, E. 2006. "When does 'economic man' dominate social behaviour?" *Science* 311: 47–52.

Camerer, C. and Loewenstein, G. 2003. "Behavioral economics: past, present and future," in C. Camerer, G. Loewenstein and M. Rabin (eds.) *Advances in Behavioral Economics*. Princeton, NJ: Princeton University Press.

Camerer, C., Loewenstein, G. and Prelec, D. 2005. "Neuroeconomics: how neuroscience can inform economics," *Journal of Economic Literature* 53: 9–64.

Camerer, C., Loewenstein, G. and Rabin, M. (eds.) 2003. *Advances in Behavioral Economics*. Princeton, NJ: Princeton University Press.

Campbell, J., Rogers Hollingsworth, J. and Lindberg, L.N. 1991. *Governance of the American Economy*. Cambridge, MA: Cambridge University Press.

Campbell, N.C.G., Graham, J.L., Jolibert, A. and Meissner, H.C. 1988. "Marketing negotiations in France, Germany, the United Kingdom, and the United States," *Journal of Marketing* 52(2): 49–62.

Carlin, B.I., Dorobantu, F. and Viswathan, S. 2009. "Public trust, the law, and financial investment," *Journal of Financial Economics* 92: 321–341.

Carlin, W. and Mayer, C. 2003. "Finance, investment, and growth," *Journal of Financial Economics* 69: 191–226.

Carree, M. and Thurik, R. 2003. "The impact of entrepreneurship on economic growth," in Z. Acs and D. Audretsch (eds.) *Handbook of Entrepreneurship Research*. Boston, MA: Kluwer Academic Publishers, pp. 437–471.

Carrol, C., Byung-Kun, R. and Changyong, R. 1994. "Are there cultural effects on saving? Some cross-sectional evidence," *The Quarterly Journal of Economics* 109(3): 685–699.

Casey, T. 2004. "Social capital and regional economies in Britain," *Political Studies* 52: 96–117.

Casson, M. 1993. "Cultural determinants of economic performance," *Journal of Comparative Economics* 17: 418–442.
  2003 [1982]. *The Entrepreneur, an Economic Theory* (2nd edn.). Aldershot: Edward Elgar.

Casson, M. and Godley, A. 2000. *Cultural Factors in Economic Growth*. Berlin, Heidelberg, New York: Springer.

Caulkins, D. and Peters, C. 2002. "Grid group analysis, social capital, and entrepreneurship in North American immigrant groups," *Cross-cultural Research* 36.1: 48–72.

Caves, R. 1996. *Multinational Enterprise and Economic Analysis* (2nd edn.). Cambridge, UK: Cambridge University Press.
  1998. "Research on international business: problems and prospects," *Journal of International Business Studies* 29.1: 5–19.

Centraal Bureau voor de Statistiek. 2004. *Bevolking: Kerncijfers 2004*. Voorburg/Heerlen: CBS.

Chai, S.-K. 1997. "Rational choice and culture: clashing perspectives or complementary modes of analysis?" in R. Ellis and M. Thompson (eds.) *Culture Matters*. Boulder, CO: Westview Press, pp. 45–56.

Chell, E., Haworth, J. and Brearley, S. 1991. *The Entrepreneurial Personality: concepts, cases and categories*. London: Routledge.

Chen, C.C., Greene, P.G. and Crick, A. 1998. "Does entrepreneurial self-efficacy distinguish entrepreneurs from managers?" *Journal of Business Venturing* 13: 295–316.

Cheung, M. and Au, K. 2005. "Applications of multilevel structural equation modeling to cross cultural research," *Structural Equation Modeling* 12.4: 598–619.

Cheung, M., Leung, K. and Au, K. 2006. "Evaluating multi level models in cross cultural research," *Journal of Cross Cultural Psychology* 37.5: 522–541.

Chinese Culture Connection. 1987. "Chinese values and the search for culture-free dimensions of culture," *Journal of Cross-Cultural Psychology* 18(2): 143–164.

Chui, A.C.W., Lloyd, A.E. and Kwok, C.C.Y. 2002. "The determination of capital structure: is national culture a missing piece to the puzzle?" *Journal of International Business Studies* 33.1: 99–127.

Clark, G. 1988. "Economists in search of culture: the unspeakable in pursuit of the inedible?" *Historical Methods* 21: 161–164.

Clark, T. and Pugh, D.S. 2001. "Foreign country priorities in the internationalization process: a measure and an exploratory test on British firms," *International Business Review* 10: 285–303.

Clarke, H., Kornberg, A., McIntyre, C., Bauer-Kaase, P. and Kaase, M. 1999. "The effect of economic priorities on the measurement of value change," *American Political Science Review* 93: 637–647.

Clausing, K.A. 2000. "Does multinational activity displace trade?" *Economic Inquiry* 38.2: 190–205.

Clifford, J. 1989. "Comments on Paul A. Roth 'Ethnography without tears'," *Current Anthropology* 30.5: 561–563.

Clifford, J. and Marcus, G. 1986. *Writing Culture: the poetics and politics of ethnography*. Berkeley, CA: University of California Press.

Coase, R. 1984. "The new institutional economics," *Journal of Institutional and Theoretical Economics* 140: 229–231.

1990. *The Firm, the Market and the Law*. Chicago, IL: University of Chicago Press.

Cochran, T.C. 1960. "Cultural factors in economic growth," *Journal of Economic History* 20: 515–530.

Cochrane, S.H. 1975. "Children as by-products, investment goods and consumer goods: a review of some micro-economic models of fertility," *Population Studies* 29(3): 373–390.

Coffee, J. 2000. "Convergence and its critics: what are the preconditions to the separation of ownership and control?" Columbia Law School working paper 179.

2001. "Do norms matter? A cross country examination of private benefits of control," Columbia Law and Economics working paper 183, available at http://ssrn.com/abstract=257613.

Colander, D. and Klamer, A. 1987. "The making of an economist," *The Journal of Economic Perspectives (1986–1998)* 18;1(2): 95–111.

Coleman, J.S. 1990. *Foundations of Social Theory*. Cambridge, MA: Harvard University Press.

Collier, M.J. 1989. "Cultural and intercultural communication competence: Current approaches and directions for future research," in M.K. Asante and W.B. Gudykunst (eds.) *Handbook of International and Intercultural Communication*. London: Sage Publications, pp. 287–301.

Conlisk, J. 1996. "Why bounded rationality?" *Journal of Economic Literature* 34.2: 669–700.

Contractor, F.J. and Kundu, S.K. 1998. "Mode choice in a world of alliances: analyzing organizational forms in the international hotel sector," *Journal of International Business Studies* 29(2): 325–358.

Cools, S. 2004. "The real difference in corporate law between the United States and continental Europe: distribution of powers," Harvard John M. Olin discussion papers no. 490, Harvard University.

Costa, D. and Kahn, M. 2003. "Civic engagement and community heterogeneity: an economist's perspective," *Perspectives on Politics* 1: 103–111.

Crockett, H.J. 1962. "Review of the Achieving Society," *Social Forces* 2: 208–209.

Cromie, S. 2000. "Assessing entrepreneurial inclinations: some approaches and empirical evidence," *European Journal of Work and Organizational Psychology* 9.1: 7–30.

Croson, R. and Konow, J. 2009. "Social preferences and moral biases," *Journal of Economic Behavior & Organization* 69: 201–212.

Cuervo-Cazurra, A. 2006. "Who cares about corruption?" *Journal of International Business Studies* 37: 807–822.

Daly, G.G. 1998. "Entrepreneurship and business culture in Japan and the U.S.," *Japan and the World Economy* 10: 487–494.

Danielson, A. and Holm, H.J. 2005. "Tropic trust versus Nordic trust: experimental evidence from Tanzania and Sweden," *The Economic Journal* 115: 505–532.

Das, T.K. and Teng, B.S. 2001. "Trust, control and risk in strategic alliances: an integrated framework," *Organization Studies* 22: 251–283.

Dasgupta, D. 1988. "Trust as a commodity," in D. Gambetta (ed.) *Trust. The Making and Breaking of Cooperative Relations*. Oxford: Blackwell, pp. 49–72.

Datta, D.K., Herrmann, P. and Rasheed, A.A. 2002. "Choice of foreign market entry mode: critical review and future directions," in M.A. Hitt and J.L.C. Cheng (eds.) *Managing Transnational Firms: resources, market entry and strategic alliances. Advances in International Management* 14. Amsterdam: JAI Press, pp. 85–153.

Davidsson, P. 1995. "Culture, structure and regional levels of entrepreneurship," *Entrepreneurship and Regional Development* 7: 41–62.

2004. *Researching Entrepreneurship*. New York: Springer.

Dávila, A. 2001. *Latinos, Inc.: the marketing and making of a people*. Berkeley, CA: University of California Press.

Davis, D. and Davenport, C. 1999. "Assessing the validity of the postmaterialism index," *American Political Science Review* 93: 649–664.

Davis, G.F. 2005. "New directions in corporate governance," *Annual Review of Sociology* 31: 143–162.

Davis, J. and Klaes, M. 2003. "Reflexivity: curse or cure?" *Journal of Economic Methodology* 10.3: 329–352.

Dawar, N., Parker, P.M. and Price, L.J. 1996. "A cross-cultural study of interpersonal information exchange," *Journal of International Business Studies* 27.3: 497–516.

De Cruz, P. 1999. *Comparative Law in a Changing World* (2nd edn.). London: Cavendish.

De Groot, H., Linders, G., Rietveld, P. and Subramanian, U. 2004. "The institutional determinants of bilateral trade patterns," *Kyklos* 57(1): 103–123.

De Groot, H., Linders, G., Slangen, A. and Beugelsdijk, S. 2005. "Cultural and institutional determinants of bilateral trade patterns," Tinbergen discussion paper 05–074/3.

De Jong, E. 2002. "Why are price stability and statutory independence of central banks negatively correlated? The role of culture," *European Journal of Political Economy* 18: 675–694.

De Mooij, M. 2010. *Global Marketing and Advertising: Understanding Cultural Paradoxes*. Thousand Oaks, CA: Sage Publications.

De Mooij, M. and Hofstede, G. 2002. "Convergence and divergence in consumer behavior: implications for international retailing," *Journal of Retailing* 78: 61–69.

Dekker, P., Koopmans, R. and Van Den Broek, A. 1997. "Voluntary associations, social movements and individual political behaviour in Western Europe: a micro-macro puzzle," in J. Van Deth (ed.) *Private Groups and Public Life: social participation, voluntary associations and political involvement in representative democracies*. London: Routledge.

Delhey, J. and Newton, K. 2005. "Predicting cross-national levels of social trust: global pattern of Nordic exceptionalism?" *European Sociological Review* 21.4: 311–327.

DellaVigna, S. 2009. "Psychology and economics: evidence from the field," *Journal of Economic Literature* 47.2: 315–372.

Demirgüç-Kunt, A. and Maksimovic, V. 1998. "Law, finance and firm growth," *Journal of Finance* 53.5: 2107–2137.

Denzau, A. and North, D. 1994. "Shared mental models: ideologies and institutions," *Kyklos* 47(1): 3–32.

D'Iribarne, P. 1989. *La Logique de l'honneur – Gestion des entreprises et traditions nationales*. Paris: Editions de Seuil.

Di Tella, R., MacCulloch, R. and Oswald, A.J. 2001. "Preferences over inflation and unemployment, evidence from surveys of happiness," *The American Economic Review* 91: 335–341.

Diamond, J. 1997. *Guns, Germs and Steel, the Fates of Human Societies*. New York: W.W. Norton.

Dieckmann, O. 1996. "Cultural determinants of economic growth: theory and evidence," *Journal of Cultural Economics* 20: 297–320.

Diener, E. and Suh, E.M. 2000. "Measuring subjective well being to compare the quality of life of cultures," in E. Diener and E.M. Suh (eds.) *Culture and Subjective Well Being*. Cambridge, MA: MIT Press, pp. 3–12.

DiMaggio, P. 1994. "Culture and economy," in N. Smelser and R. Swedberg (eds.) *Handbook of Economic Sociology*. Princeton, NJ: Princeton University Press, pp. 27–57.

DiPasquale, D. and Glaeser, E. 1996. "The LA riot and the economics of urban unrest," NBER working paper no. 5456, Cambridge, MA: NBER.

Dixit, A. 2009. "Governance institutions and economic activity," *American Economic Review* 99.1: 5–24.

2009. "Governance institutions and economic activity" (AEA Presidental Address), *American Economic Review* 99.1: 5–24.

Djankov, S., Glaeser, E., LaPorta, R., Lopez-de-Silanes, F. and Shleifer, A. 2003. "The new comparative economics," *Journal of Comparative Economics* 31.3: 595–619.

Djankov, S., La Porta, R., Lopez-de-Silanes, F. and Shleifer, A. 2003a. "Courts," *Quarterly Journal of Economics* 118.2: 453–517.

2008. "The law and economics of self-dealing," *Journal of Financial Economics* 88: 430–465.

Djankov, S., McLiesh, C. and Shleifer, A. 2007. "Private credit in 129 countries," *Journal of Financial Economics* 84: 299–329.

Dollar, D. and Kraay, A. 2003. "Institutions, trade, and growth," *Journal of Monetary Economics* 50(1): 133–162.

Dore, R. 1967. *Aspects of Social Change in Modern Japan*. Princeton, NJ: Princeton University Press.

1990. "Reflections on culture and social change," in G. Gereffi and D.L. Wyman (eds.) *Manufacturing Miracles*, Princeton, NJ: Princeton University Press, pp. 353–367.

Dore, R., Lazonick, W. and O'Sullivan, M. 1999. "Varieties of capitalism in the twentieth century," *Oxford Review of Economic Policy* 15.4: 102–20.

Dore, R. and Whittaker, D.H. 2001. *Social Evolution, Economic Development, and Culture: what it means to take Japan seriously*. Cheltenham: Edward Elgar.

Douglas, M. 1973. *Natural Symbols*, 2nd edn. London: Barrie & Jenkins.

1986. *How Institutions Think*, Syracuse, NY: Syracuse University Press.

1999. "Four cultures: the evolution of a parsimonious model," *Geojournal* **47**: 411–415.

Douglas, M. and Isherwood, B.C. 1979. *The World of Goods*. Boston, MA: Basic Books.

Douglas, M. and Wildavsky, A. 1982. *Risk and Culture: an essay on the selection of technical and environmental dangers*. Berkeley, CA: University of California Press.

Dow, D. and Karutnaratna, A. 2006. "Developing a multidimensional instrument to measure psychic distance stimuli," *Journal of International Business Studies* **37**: 578–602.

Drogendijk, R. 2001. *Expansion Patterns of Dutch Firms in Central and Eastern Europe, Learning to Internationalize*, CentER dissertation series, Tilburg University, The Netherlands.

Drogendijk, R. and Slangen, A. 2006. "Hofstede, Schwartz, or managerial perceptions? The effects of different cultural distance measures on establishment mode choices by multinational enterprises," *International Business Review* **15**.4: 361–380.

Drucker, P. 1985. *Innovation and Entrepreneurship*. New York: Harper & Row.

Dunning, J. 1980. "Toward an eclectic theory of international production: some empirical tests," *Journal of International Business Studies* **11**: 9–31.

1993. *Multinational Enterprises and the Global Economy*. Wokingham: Addison-Wesley Publishing Company.

Dunning, J., Fujita, M. and Yakova, N. 2007. "Some macro data on the regionalization–globalization debate: a comment on the Rugman–Verbeke thesis," *Journal of International Business Studies* **38**: 177–199.

Dunning, J. and Lundan, S. 2008. *Multinational Enterprises and the Global Economy* (2nd edn.). Wokingham: Addison-Wesley Publishing Company.

Durkheim, E. and Fauconnet, P. 1903. "Sociologie et sciences sociales," *Revue philosophique* **55**: 465–497.

Durlauf, S.N. 2002a. "On the empirics of social capital," *Economic Journal*, **112**: F459–479.

2002b. "Bowling alone: a review essay," *Journal of Economic Behaviour and Organisation* **47**: 259–273.

Durlauf, S.N. and Fafchamps, M. 2004. "Social capital," NBER working paper series no. 10485. Cambridge, MA: NBER.

Dyer, J. and Chu, W. 2000. "The determinants of trust in supplier–automaker relationships in the U.S., Japan, and Korea," *Journal of International Business Studies* **31**.2: 259–285.

Earl, P.E. 2005. "Economics and psychology in the twenty-first century," *Cambridge Journal of Economics* **29**: 909–926.

Earley, C.P. 2006. "Leading cultural research in the future: a matter of paradigms and taste," *Journal of International Business Studies* **37**: 922–931.

Easterlin, R. 1974. "Does economic growth improve the human lot? Some empirical evidence," in P. David and M. Reder (eds.) *Nations and Households in Economic Growth*. New York: Academic Press.

1975. "Will raising the incomes of all increase the happiness of all?" *Journal of Economic Behavior and Organization* **27**: 35–48.

Easterly, W. and Levine, R. 1997. "Africa's growth tragedy: policies and ethnic divisions," *Quarterly Journal of Economics* **112**.4: 1203–1250.

2003. "Tropics, germs and crops: how endowments influence economic development," *Journal of Monetary Economics* **50**: 3–39.

Edgeworth, Francis. 1879. "The hedonical calculus," *Mind* 4(15): 394–408.

Eisenhardt, K.M. 1989. "Building theories from case study research," *Academy of Management Review* **14**:4: 532–550.

1991. "Better stories and better constructs: the case for rigor and comparative logic," *Academy of Management Review* **16**:3: 620–627.

Eisenstadt, S.N. 1968. "Review article: some new looks at the problem of relations between traditional societies and modernization," *Economic Development and Cultural Change* 16.3: 436–450.

Engels, F. 1888. "An F.A. Sorge in Hoboken, 10.sept. 1888," in: Marx, K. & F. Engels (1962–68), *Werke*, Berlin: Dietz, vol. 37, 93.

Engerman, S. and Sokoloff, K. 1997. "Factor endowments, institutions, and differential paths of growth among new world economies," in S. Haber (ed.) *How Latin America Fell Behind*. Stanford, CA: Stanford University Press, pp. 260–304.

2002. "Factor endowments, inequality, and the paths of development among New World economies," NBER working paper 9259, Cambridge, MA: NBER.

Erasmus, C.J. 1962. "Review of the Achieving Society," *American Anthropologist* **64**: 622–625.

Erez, M. and Earley, P.C. 1993. *Culture, Self-identity, and Work*. Oxford: Oxford University Press.

Eriksen, T. 1993. *Ethnicity & Nationalism*. London: Pluto Press.

Etounga-Manguelle, D. 2000. "Does Africa need a cultural adjustment programme?" in S.P. Huntington and L.E. Harrison (eds.) *Culture Matters: how values shape human progress*. New York: Basic Books.

Evans, J., Treadgold, A. and Mavondo, F. 2000. "Explaining export development through psychic distance," *International Marketing Review* 17.2: 164–168.

Fagenson, E.A. 1993. "Personal value systems of men and women entrepreneurs versus managers," *Journal of Business Venturing* 8: 409–430.

Fallows, J. 1994. *Looking at the Sun: the rise of the new East Asian economic and political system*. New York: Pantheon.

Farrell, H. 2005. "Trust and political economy. Institutions and the sources of inter-firm cooperation," *Comparative Political Studies* 38.5: 459–483.

Farrell, H. and Knight, J. 2003. "Trust, institutions, and institutional change: industrial districts and the social capital hypothesis," *Politics & Society* 31.4: 537–566.

Fehr, E. 2008. "On the economics and biology of trust." Presidential Address, 2008 Annual Meeting of the European Economic Association, August 2008, Milan.

2009. "Economics and biology of trust," *Journal of the European Economic Association* 7.2–3: 235–266.

Fergusson, L. 2006. "Institutions for financial development: what are they and where do they come from?" *Journal of Economic Surveys* 20.1: 27–69.

Fernandez, J. 1986. *Persuasions and Performances: The Play of Tropes in Culture*. Bloomington, IN: Indiana University Press.

Fernandez, R. 2007. "Women, work, and culture," NBER working paper 12888. Cambridge, MA: NBER.

2008. "Culture and economics," in S. Durlauf and L. Blume (eds.) *New Palgrave Dictionary of Economics* (2nd edn.). London and New York: Macmillan.

Fernandez, R. and Fogli, A. 2005. "Culture: an empirical investigation of beliefs, work, and fertility," NBER working paper 11268. Cambridge, MA: NBER.

2006. "Fertility: the role of culture and family experience," *Journal of the European Economic Association* 4.2: 552–561.

Fershtman, C. and Gneezy, U. 2001. "Discrimination in a segmented society: an experimental approach," *Quarterly Journal of Economics* 116.1: 351–377.

Fetchenhauer, D. and Dunning, D. 2009. "Do people trust too much or too little?" *Journal of Economic Psychology* 30: 263–276.

Fine, B. 2001. *Social Capital Versus Social Theory: political economy and social science at the turn of the millennium*. New York: Routledge.

2002. "Economic imperialism: a view from the periphery," *Review of Radical Political Economics* 34(2): 187–201.

Finison, L.J. 1976. "The application of McClelland's national development model to recent data," *The Journal of Social Psychology* 98: 55–59.

Flanagan, S. 1982a. "Changing values in advanced industrial societies: Inglehart's silent revolution from the perspective of Japanese findings," *Comparative Political Studies* **14**.4: 403–444.

1982b. "Measuring value change in advanced industrial societies: a rejoinder to Inglehart," *Comparative Political Studies* **15**: 403–444.

Fleurbaey, M. 2009. "Beyond GDP: the quest for a measure of social welfare," *Journal of Economic Literature* **47**(4): 1029–1075.

Fligstein, N. 1990. *The Transformation of Corporate Control*. Cambridge, MA: Harvard University Press.

Florida, R. 2002. *The Rise of the Creative Class: and how it's transforming work, leisure, community and everyday life*. New York: Basic Books.

Fölster, S. 2000. "Do entrepreneurs create jobs?" *Small Business Economics* **14**: 137–148.

Fox, R. 1985. *Lions of the Punjab: culture in the making*. Berkeley, CA: University of California Press.

François, P. 2002. *Social Capital and Economic Development*. London: Routledge.

Franke, R.H., Hofstede, G. and Bond, M.H. 1991. "Cultural roots of economic performance: a research note," *Strategic Management Journal* **12**: 165–173.

Frankel, J. and Rose, A. 2002. "An estimate of the effect of common currencies on trade and income," *Quarterly Journal of Economics* **117**(2): 437–466.

Freedman, D.A. 2001. "Ecological inference and the ecological fallacy," *International Encyclopedia for the Social and Behavioral Sciences* **6**: 4027–4030.

Freeman, K.B. 1976. "The significance of McClelland's achievement variable in the aggregate production function," *Economic Development and Cultural Change* **24**: 815–824.

Freire, P. 1972. *Pedagogy of the Oppressed* (trans. M. Bergman Ramos). New York: Herder and Herder.

Frey, B. and Stutzer, A. 2002. *Happiness and Economics*. Princeton, NJ: Princeton University Press.

Frey, S.R. 1984. "Does N-achievement cause economic development? A cross lagged panel analysis of the McClelland thesis," *The Journal of Social Psychology* **122**: 67–70.

Freytag, A. and Thurik, R. 2007. "Entrepreneurship and its determinants in a cross country setting," *Journal of Evolutionary Economics* **17**: 117–131.

Friedman, B. 2005. *The Moral Consequences of Economic Growth*. New York: Vintage Books.

Fritsch, M. 2004. "Entrepreneurship, entry and performance of new business compared in two growth regimes: East and West Germany," *Journal of Evolutionary Economics* 14: 525–542.

Fukuyama, F. 1992. *The End of History and the Last Man.* New York: Free Press.

Fukuyama, F. 1995. *Trust: the social virtues and the creation of prosperity.* New York: Free Press.

Gächter, S. and Herrmann, B. 2009. "Reciprocity, culture, and human cooperation: Previous insights and a new cross-cultural experiment," *Philosophical Transactions of the Royal Society B – Biological Sciences* 364: 791–806.

Gächter, S., Herrmann, B. and Thöni, C. 2005. "Cross-cultural differences in norm enforcement," *Behavioral and Brain Sciences* 28(6): 822–823.

Gambetta, D. 1988. *Trust: making and breaking cooperative relations.* Oxford: Blackwell Publishers.

Ganesan, S. 1994. "Determinants of long term orientation in buyer–seller relationships," *Journal of Marketing* 58: 1–19.

Gatignon, H. and Anderson, E. 1988. "The multinational corporation's degree of control over foreign subsidiaries: an empirical test of a transaction cost explanation," *Journal of Law, Economics, and Organization* 4.2: 305–336.

Geertz, C. 1973. "Thick description: toward an interpretive theory of culture," in *The Interpretation of Cultures,* New York: Basic Books, pp. 3–30.

1983. *Local Knowledge: further essays in interpretive anthropology.* New York: Basic Books.

Gellner, E. 1992. *Reason and Culture: the historic role of rationality and rationalism.* Oxford: Blackwell.

Georgellis, Y. and Wall, H. 2000. "What makes a region entrepreneurial? Evidence from Britain," *The Annals of Regional Science* 34: 385–403.

Geraci, V.C. and Prewo, W. 1977. "Bilateral trade flows and transport costs," *The Review of Economics and Statistics* 59(1): 67–74.

Ghandi, L. 1998. *Postcolonial Theory: a critical introduction.* New York: Columbia University Press.

Gibson, C. 1995. "An investigation of gender differences in leadership across four countries," *Journal of International Business Studies* 26: 255–279.

Giddens, A. 1974. *Max Weber over politiek en sociologie* (trans. H.O. van den Berg). Meppel, The Netherlands: Boom.

1984. *The Constitution of Society.* Cambridge, UK: Polity Press.

1991. *Modernity and Self-Identity*. Stanford, CA: Stanford University Press.

1992. "Introduction," in M. Weber 1992. *The Protestant Ethic and the Spirit of Capitalism* (trans. Talcott Parsons, 1930). London, New York: Routledge, pp. vii–xxvi.

Gilleard, C.J. 1989. "The Achieving Society revisited: a further analysis of the relation between national economic growth and need achievement," *Journal of Economic Psychology* 10: 21–34.

Gillespie, N. and Dietz, G. 2009. "Trust repair after an organizational level failure," *Academy of Management Review* 34.1: 127–145.

Gintis, H. 2008. "Punishment and Cooperation," *Science* 319: 1345–1346.

Girma, S., Kneller, R. and Pisu, M. 2005. "Exports versus FDI: an empirical test," *Review of World Economics: Weltwirtschaftliches Archiv* 141(2): 193–218.

Glaeser, E., Laibson, D., Scheinkman, J. and Souter, C. 2000. "Measuring trust," *Quarterly Journal of Economics* 115: 811–846.

Glaeser, E., LaPorta, R., Lopez-de-Silanes, F. and Shleifer, A. 2004. "Do institutions cause growth?" *Journal of Economic Growth* 9(3): 271–303.

Glaeser, E., Scheinkman, J. and Sacerdote, B. 2003. "The social multiplier," *Journal of the European Economic Association* 1.2: 345–353.

Glaeser, E. and Shleifer, A. 2002. "Legal origins," *Quarterly Journal of Economics* 117.4: 1193–1229.

Goad Oliver, E. and Cravens, K. 1999. "Cultural influences on managerial choice: an empirical study of employee benefit plans in the United States," *Journal of International Business Studies* 30.4: 745–762.

Goldin, C. and Katz, L. 1999. "Human capital and social capital: the rise of secondary schooling in America: 1910–1940," *Journal of Interdisciplinary History* 29.4: 683–723.

Gradstein, M. and Justman, M. 2002. "Education, social cohesion, and economic growth," *The American Economic Review* 92.4: 1192–1204.

Gramsci, A. 1980 [1977]. *Grondbegrippen van de Politiek: Hegemonie, Staat, Partij* (trans. by M. Horn). Nijmegen, The Netherlands: Socialistische Uitgeverij Nijmegen.

Granato, J., Inglehart, R. and Leblang, D. 1996. "The effect of cultural values on economic development: theory, hypotheses, and some empirical tests," *American Journal of Political Science* 40: 607–631.

Greif, A. 1994. "Cultural beliefs and the organization of society: a historical and theoretical reflection on collectivist and individualist societies," *Journal of Political Economy* 102.5: 912–950.

2006. *Institutions and the Path to the Modern Economy; lessons from medieval trade*. Cambridge, UK: Cambridge University Press.

Greif, A., Milgrom, P. and Weingast, B. 1994. "Coordination, commitment and enforcement: the case of merchant guilds," *Journal of Political Economy* 102(4): 745–776.

Grilo, I. and Thurik, R. 2006. "Entrepreneurship in the old and new Europe," in E. Santarelli (ed.) *Entrepreneurship, Growth and Innovation*. Berlin, Heidelberg, New York: Springer, pp. 75–103.

Grosse, R. and Trevino, L.J. 1996. "Foreign direct investment in the United States, an analysis by country of origin," *Journal of International Business Studies* 27.1: 139–155.

Grossman, G.M. and Helpman, E. 2004. "Managerial incentives and the international organization of production," *Journal of International Economics* 63: 237–262.

Grossman, G.M., Helpman, E. and Szeidl, A. 2006. "Optimal strategies for the multinational firm," *Journal of International Economics* 70: 216–238.

Guerrero, D.C. and Serro, M.A. 1997. "Spatial distribution of patents in Spain: determining factors and consequences on regional development," *Regional Studies* 31: 381–390.

Guiso, L. 2008. "A test of narrow framing and its origin," CEPR discussion paper 7112 (version October 1, 2008).

Guiso, L., Sapienza, P. and Zingales, L. 2003. "People's opium? Religion and economic attitudes," *Journal of Monetary Economics* 50: 225–282.

2006. "Does culture affect economic outcomes?" *Journal of Economic Perspectives* 20.2: 23–48.

2009. "Cultural biases in economic exchange," *Quarterly Journal of Economics* 124.3: 1095–1131.

Gulati, R. 1995. "Does familiarity breed trust? The implications of repeated ties for contractual choice in alliances," *Academy of Management Journal* 38: 85–112.

1998. "Alliances and networks," *Strategic Management Journal* 19: 293–317.

Haber, S., North, D.C. and Weingast, B. (eds.). 2007. *Political Institutions and Financial Development*. Stanford, CA: Stanford University Press.

Habib, M. and Zurawicki, L. 2002. "Corruption and foreign direct investment," *Journal of International Business Studies* 33(2): 291–307.

Hall, P. and Soskice, D. 2001. *Varieties of Capitalism: the institutional foundations of comparative advantage*. New York: Oxford University Press.

Hall, R. and Jones, C.I. 1999. "Why do some countries produce so much more output per worker than others?" *Quarterly Journal of Economics* 114: 83–116.

Hall, S. 1995. "New cultures for old," in D. Massey and P. Jess (eds.) *A Place in the World? Places, cultures and globalization.* Oxford: Oxford University Press, pp. 175–214.

Haller, M. 2002. "Theory and method in the comparative study of values: critique and alternative to Inglehart," *European Sociological Review* 18: 139–158.

Hampden-Turner, C. and Trompenaars, A. 1993. *The Seven Cultures of Capitalism.* London: Doubleday.

Han, S., Kang, T., Salter, S. and Yoo, Y.K. 2010. "A cross country study on the effects of national culture on earnings management," *Journal of International Business Studies* 41: 123–141.

Hardin, R. 2002. *Trust and Trustworthiness.* New York: Russell Sage Foundation.

Hargreaves Heap, S. and Zizzo, D.J. 2009. "The value of groups," *American Economic Review* 99.1: 295–323.

Harris, H., Brewster, C. and Sparrow, P. 2003. *International Human Resource Management.* London: Chartered Institute for Personnel and Development.

Harris, J. and De Renzio, P. 1997. "'Missing link' or analytically missing?: the concept of social capital," *Journal of International Development* 9: 919–937.

Harris, M. 1979. *Cultural Materialism: the struggle for a science of culture.* New York: Random House.

  1985. *Good to Eat: riddles of food and culture.* New York: Simon & Schuster.

Harris Bond, M. 1988. "Invitation to a wedding: Chinese values and economic growth," in D. Sinha and H. Kao (eds.) *Social Values and Development: Asian perspectives.* New Delhi: Sage Publications, pp. 197–209.

Harrison, G.L., McKinnon, J.L., Wu, A. and Chwo, C.W. 2000. "Cultural influences on adaptation to fluid workgroups and teams," *Journal of International Business Studies* 31.3: 489–505.

Harrison, L.E. 1985. *Underdevelopment is Just a State of Mind: the Latin American case.* Lanham, MD: University Press of America.

  1992. *Who Prospers? How Cultural Values Shape Economic and Political Success.* New York: HarperCollins, Basic Books.

Harrison, L.E. and Huntington, S. 2000. *Culture Matters: how values shape human progress.* New York: Basic Books.

Hart, O. 1995. *Firms, Contracts and Financial Structure.* London: Oxford University Press.

Hau, C. 2000. *Necessary Fictions: Philippine literature and the nation 1946–1980.* Manila: Ateneo de Manila University Press.

Hayek, F. 1967. *Studies in Philosophy, Politics, and Economics.* London: Routledge.

Head, K. and Ries, J. 2001. "Overseas investment and firm exports," *Review of International Economics* 9(1): 108–122.

Heide, J.B. and John, G. 1992. "Do norms matter in marketing relationships?" *Journal of Marketing* 56: 32–44.

Heilbroner, R. 1999. *The Worldly Philosophers: the lives, times, and ideas of the great economic thinkers.* New York: Simon & Schuster.

Heilbroner, R. and Milberg, W. 2002. *The Making of Economic Society.* Upper Saddle River, NJ: Prentice Hall.

Helliwell, J.F. 2006. "Well-being, social capital and public policy: what's new?" *Economic Journal* 116: C34–C45.

Helliwell, J.F. and Putnam, R. 1995. "Economic growth and social capital in Italy," *Eastern Economic Journal* 21.3: 295–307.

Hennart, J.F. 1982. *A Theory of the Multinational Enterprise.* Ann Arbor, MI: University of Michigan Press.

1991. "The transaction costs theory of joint ventures: an empirical study of Japanese subsidiaries in the United States," *Management Science* 37.4: 483–497.

Hennart, J.F. and Larimo, J. 1998. "The impact of culture on the strategy of multinational enterprises, does national origin affect ownership decisions?" *Journal of International Business Studies* 29.3: 515–537.

Henrich, J. 2000. "Does culture matter in economic behavior? Ultimatum game bargaining among the Machiguenga of the Peruvian Amazon," *American Economic Review* 90.4: 973–979.

Henrich, J., Boyd, R., Bowles, S., Camerer, C., Fehr, E. and Gintis, H. (eds.). 2004. *Foundations of Human Sociality: economic experiments and ethnographic evidence from fifteen small-scale societies.* Oxford: Oxford University Press.

Henrich, J., Boyd, R., Bowles, S., Camerer, C., Fehr, E., Gintis, H. and McElreath, R. 2001. "In search of homo economicus: behavioural experiments in 15 small-scale societies," *The American Economic Review* (papers and proceedings) 91.2: 73–78.

Henrich, J., McElreath, R., Barr, A., Ensminger, J., Barret, C., Bolyantz, A., Camilo Cardenas, J., Gurven, M., Gwako, E., Henrich, N., Lesorogol, C., Marlowe, F., Tracer, D. and Ziker, J. 2006. "Costly punishment across human societies," *Science* 312: 1767–1770.

Herrmann, B., Thöni, C. and Gächter, S. 2008. "Antisocial punishment across societies," *Science* 319: 1362–1367.

Herrmann-Pillath, C. 2006. "Cultural species and institutional change," *Journal of Economic Issues* 40.3: 539–575.

Herskovits, M.J. 1948. *Man and his Works.* New York: Knopf.

Heuer, M., Cummings, J.L. and Hutabarat, W. 1999. "Cultural stability or change among managers in Indonesia," *Journal of International Business Studies* 30.3: 599–610.

Heukelom, F. and Maseland, R. 2010. "The economics of paradigm change." Paper presented at ESHET Conference 2010, Amsterdam.

Heydemann, S. 2008. "Institutions and economic performance: the use and abuse of culture in new institutional economics," *Studies in Comparative and International Development* 43: 27–52.

Hill, C.W.L., Hwang, P. and Kim, W.C. 1990. "An eclectic theory of the choice of international entry mode," *Strategic Management Journal* 11: 117–128.

Hill, M. 2000. "'Asian values' as reverse Orientalism: Singapore," *Asian Pacific Viewpoint* 41.2: 177–190.

Hill, M. and Lian, K.F. 1995. *The Politics of Nation Building and Citizenship in Singapore*. London: Routledge.

Hirschman, A.O. 1965. "Obstacles to development: a classification and a quasi-vanishing act," *Economic Development and Cultural Change* 13.4: 385–393.

Hitchcock, D. 1994. *Asian Values and the United States: How much conflict?* Washington, DC: The Center for Strategic and International Studies.

Hodgson, G. 1995. "Varieties of capitalism from the perspectives of Veblen and Marx," *Journal of Economic Issues* 29.2: 575–585.

1998. "The approach of institutional economics," *Journal of Economic Literature* 36: 166–192.

2004. *The Evolution of Institutional Economics*. London: Routledge.

2006. "Institutions, recessions, and recovery in transitional economies," *Journal of Economic Issues* 40.4: 875–894.

2007a. "Meaning of methodological individualism," *Journal of Economic Methodology* 14.2: 211–226.

2007b. "Institutions and individuals: interaction and evolution," *Organization Studies* 28: 95–116.

2009. "The great crash of 2008 and the reform of economics," *Cambridge Journal of Economics* 33.6: 1205–1221.

Hofstede, G. 1980. *Culture's Consequences: International differences in work-related values*. Beverly Hills, CA, London: Sage Publications.

1983. "The cultural relativity of organizational practices and theories," *Journal of International Business Studies* 14: 75–89.

1991. *Cultures and Organizations: Software of the mind*. London: McGraw-Hill.

2001. *Culture's Consequences: Comparing values, behaviors, institutions and organizations across nations* (2nd edn.). Beverly Hills, CA: Sage Publications.

2006. "What did GLOBE really measure? Researchers' minds versus respondents' minds," *Journal of International Business Studies* 37: 882–896.

Hofstede, G. and Bond, M.H. 1988. "The Confucius connection: from cultural roots to economic growth," *Organizational Dynamics* 16: 4–21.

Hofstede, G., Neuijen, B., Ohavy, D. and Sanders, C. 1990. "Measuring organizational cultures: a qualitative and quantitative study across twenty cases," *Administrative Science Quarterly* 35: 386–416.

Hofstede, G., Van Deusen, C.A., Mueller, C.B. and Charles, T.A. 2002. "What goals do business leaders pursue? A study in fifteen countries," *Journal of International Business Studies* 33.4: 785–803.

Hooghe, M., Reeskens, T., Stolle, D. and Trappers, A. 2006. "Ethnic diversity, trust and ethnocentrism and Europe; a multi level analysis of 21 European countries," Paper presented at the 102nd Annual Meeting of the American Political Science Association, Philadelphia, 31 August–3 September.

Hoselitz, B. 1954. "Problems of adapting and communicating modern techniques to less developed areas," *Economic Development and Cultural Change* 2.4: 249–268.

1957. "Non-economic factors in economic development," *The American Economic Review* (papers and proceedings) 47: 28–41.

1962. "Review of the Achieving Society," *The American Journal of Sociology* 68: 129–130.

House, R.J., Hanges, P.J., Javidan, M., Dorfman, P.W. and Gupta, V. 2004. *Culture, Leadership and Organizations: The Globe study of 62 societies.* Thousand Oaks, CA: Sage Publications.

House, R.J., Javidan, M. and Dorfman, P. 2001. "Project GLOBE: an introduction," *Applied Psychology: an international review* 50.4: 489–505.

Huang, R.R. 2007. "Distance and trade: disentangling unfamiliarity effects and transport cost effects," *European Economic Review* 51(1): 161–181.

Hult, G.T.M., Ketchen, D.J., Griffith, D.A., Finnegan, C.A., Gonzalez-Padron, T., Harmancioglu, N., Huang, Y., Berk Talay, M. and Tamer Cavusgil, S. 2008. "Data equivalence in cross cultural international business research: assessment and guidelines," *Journal of International Business Studies* 39: 1027–1044.

Hume, D. 1976 [1757]. *The Natural History of Religion.* Edited by J.V. Price. Oxford: Clarendon.

Huntington, S. 1993. "The clash of civilizations," *Foreign Affairs* 72.3: 22–50.

1996. *The Clash of Civilizations and the Remaking of the World Order.* New York: Simon & Schuster.

Hymer, S.H. 1976. *The International Operations of National Firms: A study of foreign direct investment.* Cambridge, MA: MIT Press.

Iannaccone, L. 1992a. "Heirs to the Protestant ethic? The economics of American Fundamentalists," in M.E. Marty and R. Scott Appleby (eds.) *Fundamentalisms and the State: Remaking politics, economics, and militance.* Chicago, IL: The University of Chicago Press, pp. 342–366.

1992b. "Sacrifice and stigma: reducing free-riding in cults, communes, and other collectives," *Journal of Political Economy* 100.2: 271–291.

Iannaccone, L. and Berman, E. 2006. "Religious extremism: the good, the bad, and the deadly," *Public Choice* 128(1): 109–129.

Inglehart, R. 1977. *The Silent Revolution: Changing values and political styles in advanced industrial societies.* Princeton, NJ: Princeton University Press.

1981. "Post-materialism in an environment of insecurity," *The American Political Science Review* 75.4: 880–900.

1990. *Culture Shift in Advanced Industrial Society.* Princeton, NJ: Princeton University Press.

1997. *Modernization and Postmodernization: Cultural, economic and political change in 43 societies.* Princeton, NJ: Princeton University Press.

2006. "Mapping global values," *Comparative Sociology* 5.2–3: 115–136.

Inglehart, R. and Baker, W.E. 2000. "Modernization, cultural change, and the persistence of traditional values," *American Sociological Review* 65: 19–51.

Inglehart, R. and Carballo, M. 1997. "Does Latin America exist? (And is there a Confucian culture?): a global analysis of cross-cultural differences," *PS: Political Science and Politics* 30.1: 34–46.

Jackman, R.W. and Miller, R.A. 1996. "A renaissance of political culture?" *American Journal of Political Science* 40.3: 632–659.

James, Sr. H. 2002. "The trust paradox: a survey of economic inquiries into the nature of trust and trustworthiness," *Journal of Economic Behavior and Organization* 47: 291–307.

Javidan, M., House, R.J., Dorfman, P.W, Hanges, P.J. and Sully de Luque, M. 2006. "Conceptualizing and measuring cultures and their consequences: a comparative review of GLOBE's and Hofstede's approaches," *Journal of International Business Studies* 37: 897–914.

Jennings, A. 1998. "Veblen, Thorstein," in J. Davis, D.W. Hands and U. Mäki (eds.) *Handbook of Economic Methodology.* Cheltenham and Northampton: Edward Elgar, pp. 528–531.

Jensen, M. and Meckling, W. 1976. "Theory of the firm: managerial behavior, agency costs and ownership structure," *Journal of Financial Economics* 3: 305–360.

Johanson, J. and Vahlne, E.J. 1977. "The internationalization process of the firm – a model of knowledge development and increasing foreign market participation," *Journal of International Business Studies* 8: 22–32.

Johnson, S., Boone, P., Breach, A. and Friedman, E. 2000. "Corporate governance in the Asian financial crisis," *Journal of Financial Economics* 58: 141–186.

Johnson, S.L., Cullen, J.B., Sakano, T. and Takenouchi, H. 1996. "Setting the stage for trust and strategic integration in Japanese–US cooperative alliances," *Journal of International Business Studies* 27: 981–1004.

Jovanovic, B. 1994. "Firm formation with heterogeneous management and labor skills," *Small Business Economics* 6: 185–191.

Jun, S., Gentry, J.W. and Hyun, Y.J. 2001. "Cultural adaptation of business expatriates in the host marketplace," *Journal of International Business Studies* 32.2: 369–377.

Kahani-Hopkins, V. and Hopkins, N. 2002. "'Representing' British Muslims: the strategic dimension to identity construction," *Ethnic and Racial Studies* 25.2: 288–309.

Kahn, H. 1979. *World Economic Development: 1979 and beyond.* Boulder, CO: Westview Press.

Kahneman, D. 2003. "Maps of bounded rationality: psychology for behavioral economics," *The American Economic Review* 93(5): 1449–1475.

Kahneman, D. and Tversky, A. 1979. "Prospect theory, an analysis of decision under risk," *Econometrica* 47: 263–291.

Kanbur, R. 2002. "Economics, social science, and development," *World Development* 30.3: 477–486.

Kangasharju, A. 2000. "Regional variation in firm formation: panel and cross-section data evidence from Finland," *Papers in Regional Science* 79: 355–373.

Kanungo, R. and Wright, R. 1983. "A cross-cultural comparative study of managerial job attitudes," *Journal of International Business Studies* 14: 115–129.

Karlan, D., Mobius, M., Rosenblat, T. and Szeidl, A. 2009. "Trust and social collateral," *Quarterly Journal of Economics* 124.3: 1307–1361.

Katona, G. 1962. "Review of the Achieving Society," *The American Economic Review* 52: 580–583.

Katzner, D. 2008. *Culture and Economic Explanation: Economics in the US and Japan.* Abingdon: Routledge.

Keynes, J.M. 1936. *The General Theory of Employment, Interest, and Money.* London: Macmillan.

Khoo, B.T. 2002. "Nationalism, capitalism, and 'Asian values'," in F. Loh Kok Wah and B.T. Khoo (eds.) *Democracy in Malaysia: Discourses and practices.* Richmond, Surrey: Curzon, pp. 51–73.

Kihlstrom, R. and Laffont, J.J. 1979. "A general equilibrium entrepreneurial theory of firm formation based on risk aversion," *Journal of Political Economy* 87: 719–748.

Kim, D.J. 1994. "Is culture destiny? The myth of Asia's anti-democratic values," *Foreign Affairs* 73(6): 189–194.

Kim, P.H., Dirks, K.T. and Cooper, C.D. 2009. "The repair of trust: a dynamic bilateral perspective and multilevel conceptualization," *Academy of Management Review* 34.3: 401–422.

Kim, W.C. and Hwang, P. 1992. "Global strategy and multinationals' entry mode choice," *Journal of International Business Studies* 23.1: 29–53.

Kindleberger, C. 1969. *American Business Abroad*, six lectures on direct investment. New Haven, CT, London: Yale University Press.

King, R. and Levine, R. 1993. "Finance and growth: Schumpeter might be right," *Quarterly Journal of Economics* 108.3: 717–737.

Kirkman, B.L., Lowe, K.B. and Gibson, C. 2006. "A quarter century of Culture's consequences: a review of empirical research incorporating Hofstede's cultural values framework," *Journal of International Business Studies* 37.3: 285–320.

Kirzner, I. 1997. "Entrepreneurial discovery and the competitive market process: an Austrian approach," *Journal of Economic Literature* 35: 60–85.

Klein, K., Dansereau, F. and Hall, R. 1994. "Levels issues in theory development, data collection, and analysis," *Academy of Management Review* 19.2: 195–229.

Kluckhohn, C. and Leighton, D. 1946. *The Navaho*. Cambridge, MA: Harvard University Press.

Knack, S. 2000. "Social capital and the quality of government: evidence from the US states," World Bank Policy research working paper no. WPS 2504.

2003. "Groups, growth and trust: cross country evidence on the Olson and Putnam hypotheses," *Public Choice* 117: 341–355.

Knack, S. and Keefer, P. 1997. "Does social capital have an economic payoff? A cross country investigation," *Quarterly Journal of Economics* 112.4: 1251–1288.

Knight, F. 1921. *Risk, Uncertainty and Profit*. Chicago, IL: The University of Chicago Press.

Knight, G.A. 1999. "Consumer preferences for foreign and domestic products," *Journal of Consumer Marketing* 16.2: 151–162.

Koen, C. 2005. *Comparative International Management*. London: McGraw-Hill.

Kogut, B. and Singh, H. 1988. "The effect of national culture on the choice of entry mode," *Journal of International Business Studies* 19.3: 411–432.

Kopytoff, I. 1986. "The cultural biography of things: commoditization as process," in A. Appadurai (ed.) *The Social Life of Things: Commodities in cultural perspective*. New York: Cambridge University Press, pp. 64–91.

Koslowski, P. 1997. "Economics as ethical economy in the tradition of the historical school," in P. Koslowski (ed.) *The Theory of Ethical Economics in the Historical School*. Berlin, Heidelberg, New York, Tokyo: Springer, pp. 1–14.

Kostova, T. 1997. "Country institutional profiles: concept and measurement," *Academy of Management Best Paper Proceedings*: 180–189.

Kreps, D. 1990. "Corporate culture and economic theory," in J.E. Alt and K.A. Shepsle (eds.) *Perspectives on Positive Political Economics*. Cambridge University Press, UK, pp. 90–143.

Kroeber, A.L. and Kluckhohn, C. 1963. *Culture: A critical review of concepts and definitions*. New York: Vintage Books.

Kumar, R. 1997. "The role of affect in negotiations: an integrative overview," *Journal of Applied Behavioral Science* 33.1: 84–100.

Kumlin, S. and Rothstein, B. 2005. "Making and breaking social capital: the impact of welfare state institutions," *Comparative Political Studies* 38.4: 339–365.

Kuran, T. 2003. "The Islamic commercial crisis: institutional roots of economic underdevelopment in the Middle East," *The Journal of Economic History* 63(2): 414–447.

2009. "Explaining the economic trajectories of civilizations: the systemic approach," *Journal of Economic Behavior and Organization* 71(3): 593–605.

Kwok, C.C.Y. and Tadesse, S. 2006a. "The MNC as an agent of change for host-country institutions: FDI and corruption," *Journal of International Business Studies* 37: 767–785.

Kwok, C. and Tadesse, S. 2006b. "National culture and financial systems," *Journal of International Business Studies* 37: 227–247.

La Ferrara, E. 2002. "Inequality and group participation: theory and evidence from rural Tanzania," *Journal of Public Economics* 85.2: 235–273.

Lal, D. 1983. *The Poverty of Development Economics*. London: The Institute of Economic Affairs.

1985. "The misconceptions of 'development economics'," *Finance and Development* 22: 10–13.

1998. *Unintended Consequences: The impact of factor endowments, culture, and politics on long run economic performance*. Cambridge, MA: MIT Press.

Landes, D. 1998. *The Wealth and Poverty of Nations*. London: Abacus.

Lane, C. and Bachmann, R. 1998. *Trust within and between Organizations*. Oxford: Oxford University Press.

Lane, J.-E. and Ersson, S. 2005. *Culture and Politics: A comparative approach*. Aldershot: Ashgate.

LaPorta, R., Lopez-de-Silanes, F. and Shleifer, A. 1999. "Corporate control around the world," *Journal of Finance* 54: 471–517.

   2008. "The economic consequences of legal origin," *Journal of Economic Literature* 46.2: 285–332.

LaPorta, R., Lopez-de-Silanes, F., Shleifer, A. and Vishny, R. 1997. "Legal determinants of external finance," *Journal of Finance* 106: 1131–1150.

   1998. "Law and finance," *Journal of Political Economy* 106: 1113–1155.

   1999. "The quality of government," *Journal of Law, Economics and Organization* 15: 222–279.

   2000. "Investor protection and corporate governance," *Journal of Financial Economics* 58: 3–27.

Layard, R. 2005. *Happiness: Lessons from a new science*. New York: Penguin Press.

Lazear, E. 1999. "Culture and Language," *Journal of Political Economy* 107: S95–126.

   2000. "Economic imperialism," *Quarterly Journal of Economics* 115(1): 99–146.

Lee, K., Yang, G. and Graham, J.L. 2006. "Tension and trust in international business negotiations: American executives negotiating with Chinese executives," *Journal of International Business Studies* 37: 623–641.

Lee, S.Y., Florida, R. and Acs, Z.J. 2004. "Creativity and entrepreneurship: a regional analysis of new firm formation," *Regional Studies* 38.8: 879–891.

Leff, N.H. 1979. "Entrepreneurship and economic development: the problem revisited," *Journal of Economic Literature* 17: 46–64.

Leiba-O'Sullivan, S. 1999. "The distinction between stable and dynamic cross-cultural competencies: implications for expatriate trainability," *Journal of International Business Studies* 30.4: 709–725.

Leibenstein, H. 1968. "Entrepreneurship and development," *The American Economic Review* (papers and proceedings) 58: 72–83.

Lele, P. and Siems, M. 2007a. "Shareholder protection," CESifo DICE Report 1: 3–9.

   2007b. "Shareholder protection: a leximetric approach," *Journal of Corporate Law Studies* 7.1: 17–50.

Leung, K. 2006. "Editor's introduction to the exchange between Hofstede and GLOBE," *Journal of International Business Studies* 37(6): 881.

Leung, K., Bhagat, R.S., Buchan, N.R., Erez, M. and Gibson, C.B. 2005. "Culture and international business: recent advances and their implications for future research," *Journal of International Business Studies* 36: 357–378.

Levi-Strauss, C. 1966. *The Savage Mind*. Chicago, IL: University of Chicago Press.

1980 [1950]. *Tristes Tropiques*. Paris: Plon.

Levine, R. 2002. "Bank-based or market-based financial systems: which is better?" *Journal of Financial Intermediation* 11: 1–30.

Levine, R. and Zervos, S. 1998. "Stock markets, banks and economic growth," *American Economic Review* 88.3: 537–558.

Levitt, S.D. and Dubner, S.J. 2005. *Freakonomics: A rogue economist explores the hidden side of everything*. London: Allen Lane.

Levy, Jr., M. 1962. "Some aspects of 'individualism' and the problem of modernization in China and Japan," *Economic Development and Cultural Change* 10.3: 225–240.

1992. "Confucianism and modernization," *Society* 29.4: 15–20.

Lewicki, R.J. and Bunker, B.B. 1996. "Developing and maintaining trust in work relationships," in R.M. Kramer and T.R. Tyler (eds.) *Trust in Organizations: Frontiers of theory and research*. Thousand Oaks, CA: Sage, pp. 114–139.

Lewin, S.B. 1996. "Economics and psychology: lessons for our own day from the early twentieth century," *Journal of Economic Literature* 34.2: 1293–1323.

Lewis, D. 1969. *Convention, A Philosophical Study*. Cambridge, MA: Harvard University Press.

Li, A. and Cropanzano, R. 2009. "Do East Asians respond more/less strongly to organizational justice than North Americans? A meta analysis," *Journal of Management Studies* 46.5: 787–805.

Li, C. 1997. "Confucian value and democratic value," *Journal of Value Inquiry* 31(2): 183–194.

Li, J. and Guisinger, S. 1992. "The globalization of service multinationals in the triad regions: Japan, Western Europe and North America," *Journal of International Business Studies* 23: 675–696.

Licht, A. 2001. "The mother of all path dependencies: toward a cross-cultural theory of corporate governance systems," *Delaware Journal of Corporate Law* 26: 147–205.

2003. "The maximands of corporate governance: a theory of values and cognitive style," *European Corporate Governance Institute (ECGI) law working paper 16/2003*: http://ssrn.com/abstract=469801.

2008. "Social norms and the law: why peoples obey the law," *Review of Law & Economics* 4.3: 715–750.

2010. "Entrepreneurial motivations, culture and the law," in A. Freytag and R. Thurik (eds.) *Entrepreneurship and Culture*. Heidelberg: Springer, pp. 11–40.

Licht, A., Goldschmidt, C. and Schwartz, S. 2005. "Culture, law, and corporate governance," *International Review of Law and Economics* 25: 229–255.

2007. "Culture rules: the foundations of the rule of law and other norms of governance," *Journal of Comparative Economics* 35: 659–688.

Licht, A. and Siegel, J.I. 2006. "The social dimensions of entrepreneurship," in M. Casson and B. Yeung (eds.) *Oxford Handbook of Entrepreneurship*. Oxford: Oxford University Press, pp. 511–539.

Lincoln, J., Olson, J. and Hanada, M. 1978. "Cultural effects on organizational structure: the case of Japanese firms in the United States," *American Sociological Review* 43.6: 829–847.

Lindert, P. 1996. "What limits social spending?" *Explorations in Economic History* 33.1: 1–34.

Linsley, P. and Shrives, P. 2009. "Mary Douglas, risk and accounting failures," *Critical Perspectives on Accounting* 20: 492–508.

Lipsey, R.E. and Weiss, M.Y. 1981. "Foreign production and exports in manufacturing industries," *Review of Economics and Statistics* 63: 488–494.

Lodge, G. and Vogel, E. 1987. *Ideology and National Competitiveness: An analysis of nine countries*. Boston, MA: Harvard University Press.

Loree, D.W. and Guisinger, S. 1995. "Policy and non-policy determinants of US equity foreign direct investment," *Journal of International Business Studies* 26(2): 281–299.

Lucas, R.E. 1978. "On the size distribution of business firms," *Bell Journal of Economics* 9: 508–523.

Luhmann, N. 1979. *Trust and Power*. Chichester: John Wiley and Sons.

1988. "Familiarity, confidence, trust," in D. Gambetta (ed.) *Trust. Making and breaking of cooperative relations*. Oxford: Blackwell, pp. 94–107.

Lumpkin, G.T. and Dess, G.G. 1996. "Clarifying the entrepreneurial orientation construct and linking it to performance," *Academy of Management Review* 21.1: 135–172.

Luttmer, E. 2001. "Group loyalty and the taste for redistribution," *Journal of Political Economy* 109.3: 500–528.

Luttmer, E. and Singhal, M. 2008. "Culture, context, and the taste for redistribution," *NBER working papers 14268*.

Lyman, S. and Douglass, W. 1973. "Ethnicity: strategies of collective and individual impression management," *Social Research* 40: 344–365.

Lynn, R. 1991. *The Secret of the Miracle Economy. Different national attitudes to competitiveness and money.* London: The Social Affairs Unit.

MacIntosh, R. 1998. "Global attitude measurement: an assessment of the World Values Survey postmaterialism scale," *American Sociological Review* 63: 452–464.

Magnussen, P., Wilson, R.T., Zdravokovic, R., Zhou, J.X. and Westjohn, S. 2008. "Breaking the cultural clutter; a comparative assessment of multiple cultural and institutional frameworks," *International Marketing Review* 25.2: 183–201.

Malinowski, B. 1969 [1944]. *A Scientific Theory of Culture and Other Essays.* Oxford: Oxford University Press.

Mangeloja, E. 2005. "Economic growth and religious production efficiency," *Applied Economics* 37.20: 2349–2359.

Mankiw, N.G., Romer, D. and Weil, D. 1992. "A contribution to the empirics of economic growth," *Quarterly Journal of Economics* 107: 407–431.

Manski, C.F. 2000. "Economic analysis of social interactions," *Journal of Economic Perspectives* 14.3: 115–136.

Markus, G. 1993. "Culture: the making and the make-up of a concept (an essay in historical semantics)," *Dialectical Anthropology* 18: 3–29.

Marwell, G. and Ames, R. 1981. "Economists free ride, does anyone else? Experiments on the provision of public goods IV," *Journal of Public Economics* 15.3: 295–310.

Marx, K. 1859. "Zur Kritik der Politischen Ökonomie," in Marx and Engels Marx (1962–68), *Werke*, Berlin: Dietz, 13: 1–160.
    1978 [1867]. *Het Kapitaal, Vol. 1.* Translated by I. Lipschitz. Haarlem: De Haan.

Marx, K. and Engels, F. 1848. *Manifest der Kommunistischen Partei*, in Marx and Engels (1962–68), *Werke*, Berlin: Dietz, 4, 459–493.

Maseland, R. 2006. *Embedding Economics: the constitution of development and reform in Malaysia and the Philippines.* Dissertation, Radboud University Nijmegen.

Maseland, R. and Van Hoorn, A. 2009. "Explaining the negative correlation between values and practices: a note on the Hofstede–GLOBE debate," *Journal of International Business Studies* 40.3: 527–532.
    2010. "Values and marginal preferences in international business," *Journal of International Business Studies* 41.8 (in press).

Maseland, R. and Peil, J. 2008. "Assessing the new Washington pluralism from the perspective of the Malaysian model," *Third World Quarterly* 29.6: 1175–1188.

Mauro, P. 1995. "Corruption and growth," *Quarterly Journal of Economics* 110.3: 681–712.

Mauss, M. 1970 [1925]. *The Gift: Forms and functions of exchange in archaic societies*. Translated by Ian Cunnison. London: Routledge and Kegan Paul.

Mayer, R.C., Davis, J.H. and Schoorman, F.D. 1995. "An integrative model of organizational trust," *Academy of Management Review* 20: 709–734.

Mazur, A. and Rosa, E. 1977. "An empirical test of McClelland's 'Achieving Society' Theory," *Social Forces* 55: 769–774.

McAllister, D.J. 1995. "Affect- and cognition-based trust as foundations for interpersonal cooperation in organizations," *Academy of Management Review* 38: 24–59.

McCleary, R. and Barro, R. 2006. "Religion and economy," *Journal of Economic Perspectives* 20.2: 49–72.

McClelland, D. 1961. *The Achieving Society*. Princeton, NJ, Toronto, New York: Van Nostrand.

1965. "A reply to Schatz's critique," *Quarterly Journal of Economics* 79: 242–245.

McClelland, D., Atkinson, J., Clark, R. and Lowell, E. 1953. *The Achievement Motive*. New York: Appleton-Century-Crofts Inc.

McCloskey, D.N. 1983. "The rhetoric of economics," *Journal of Economic Literature* 21: 481–571.

1998. *The Rhetoric of Economics*. Madison, WI: University of Wisconsin Press.

McGowan, P. and Purkitt, H.E. 1979. *Demystifying "National Character" in Black Africa: A comparative study of culture and foreign policy*. Denver, CO: Graduate School of International Studies, University of Denver.

McGrath, R.G. and MacMillan, I. 1992. "More like each other than anyone else? A cross cultural study of entrepreneurial perceptions," *Journal of Business Venturing* 7: 419–429.

McGrath, R.G., MacMillan, I. and Scheinberg, S. 1992. "Elitists, risk-takers, and rugged individualists? An exploratory analysis of cultural differences between entrepreneurs and non-entrepreneurs," *Journal of Business Venturing* 7: 115–135.

McKnight, D.H., Cummings, L.L. and Chervany, N.L. 1998. "Initial trust formation in new organizational relationships," *Academy of Management Review* 23: 473–490.

McSweeney, B. 2002a. "Hofstede's model of national cultural differences and their consequences: a triumph of faith – a failure of analysis," *Human Relations* 55: 89–118.

2002b. "The essentials of scholarship: a reply to Hofstede," *Human Relations* 55: 1363–1372.

Melitz, M. 2003. "The impact of trade on intra-industry realloca-
tion and aggregate industry productivity," *Econometrica* 71: 1695–
1725.

Menger, C. 1969 [1883]. *Untersuchungen über die Methode der Sozialwis-
senschaften und der politischen Okonomie insbesondere, Ges. Werke.
Vol. 2.* Tubingen: Mohr.

Merritt, A. 2000. "Culture in the cockpit: do Hofstede's dimensions replicate?" *Journal of Cross Cultural Psychology* 31: 283–301.

Merryman, J.H. 1985. *The Civil Law Tradition.* Stanford, CA: Stanford
University Press.

Miller, A.S. and Mitamura, T. 2003. "Are surveys on trust trustworthy?"
Social Psychology Quarterly 66.1: 62–70.

Miller, S.R. and Eden, L. 2006. "Local density and foreign subsidiary performance," *Academy of Management Journal* 49.2: 341–356.

Mishler, W. and Rose, R. 2001. "What are the origins of political trust?
Testing institutional and cultural theories in post communist societies,"
Comparative Political Studies 34.1: 30–62.

Misztal, B.A. 1996. *Trust in Modern Societies.* Oxford: Blackwell.

Mitchell, R., Seawright, K. and Morse, E. 2000. "Cross cultural cognitions
and the venture creation decision," *Academy of Management Journal*
43.5: 974–993.

Mitchell, W. 1929. "Obituary," *The Economic Journal* 39.156: 646–650.

Modigliani, F. and Miller, M. 1958. "The cost of capital, corporation
finance, and the theory of investment," *American Economic Review*
48: 261–297.

Moore, M. 1999. "Truth, trust and market transactions: what do we know?"
Journal of Development Studies 36.1: 74–88.

Moorman, C., Zaltman, G. and Deshpandé, R. 1992. "Relationships
between providers and users of market research: the dynamics of trust
within and between organizations," *Journal of Marketing Research* 29:
314–328.

Morgan, M.S. and Rutherford, M. 1998. *From Interwar Pluralism to Post-
war Neoclassicism.* Durham: Duke University Press.

Morgeson, F.P. and Hofmann, D.A. 1999. "The structure and function of
collective constructs: implications for multi-level research and theory
development," *Academy of Management Review* 24: 249–265.

Morishima, M. 1982. *Why Has Japan Succeeded? – Western technology and the Japanese ethos.* Cambridge, UK: Cambridge University
Press.

Morosini, P., Shane, S. and Singh, H. 1998. "National cultural distance
and cross border acquisition performance," *Journal of International
Business Studies* 29: 137–158.

Morris, C.T. and Adelman, I. 1988. *Comparative Patterns of Economic Development 1850–1914*. Baltimore, MD: John Hopkins University Press.

Morris, M.H., Davis, D.L. and Allen, J.W. 1994. "Fostering corporate entrepreneurship: cross-cultural comparisons of the importance of individualism versus collectivism," *Journal of International Business Studies* 25: 65–89.

Morris, M.W., Williams, K.Y., Leung, K., Larrick, R., Teresa-Mendoza, M., Bhatnager, D., Li, J., Kondo, M., Luo, J.L. and Hu, J.C. 1998. "Conflict management style: accounting for cross national differences," *Journal of International Business Studies* 29.4: 729–748.

Murray, H.A. 1938. *Explorations in Personality*. New York: Oxford University Press.

Nash, M. 1964. "Social prerequisites to economic growth in Latin America and Southeast Asia," *Economic Development and Cultural Change* 12.3: 225–242.

Nee, V. and Swedberg, R. (eds.) 2005. *The Economic Sociology of Capitalism*. Princeton, NJ and Oxford: Princeton University Press.

Negandhi, A.R. 1983. "Cross cultural management research: trend and future directions," *Journal of International Business Studies* 14: 17–28.

Nehrt, L., Truitt, F. and Wright, R. 1970. *International Business Research: Past, present and future*. Indiana University Graduate School of Business.

Newburry, W. and Yakova, N. 2006. "Standardization preferences: a function of national culture, work interdependence and local embeddedness," *Journal of International Business Studies* 37: 44–60.

Ngo, H., Turban, D., Lau, C. and Lui, S. 1998. "Human resource practices and firm performance of multinational corporations: influences of country of origin," *International Journal of Human Resource Management* 9: 632–652.

Nocke, V. and Yeaple, S. 2007. "Cross-border mergers and acquisitions vs. greenfield foreign direct investment: the role of firm heterogeneity," *Journal of International Economics* 72.2: 336–365.

Noland, M. 2005. "Religion and economic performance," *World Development* 33(8): 1215–1232.

Noorderhaven, N., Thurik, R., Wennekers, A. and Van Stel, A. 2004. "The role of dissatisfaction and per capita income in explaining self-employment across 15 European countries," *Entrepreneurship Theory and Practice* 28.5: 447–466.

Nooteboom, B. 2002. *Trust*. Cheltenham: Edward Elgar.

North, D. 1973. *The Rise of the Western World: A new economic history*. Cambridge, UK: Cambridge University Press.

1981. *Structure and Change in Economic History*. New York: Norton.

1990. *Institutions, Institutional Change and Economic Performance*. Cambridge, UK: Cambridge University Press.

1992. "Institutions, ideology and economic performance," *CATO Journal* 11: 477–499.

2005. *Understanding the Process of Economic Change*. Princeton, NJ: Princeton University Press.

Nuyen, A.T. 1999. "Chinese philosophy and western capitalism," *Asian Philosophy* 9.1: 71–80.

O'Grady, S. and Lane, H.W. 1996. "The psychic distance paradox," *Journal of International Business Studies* 27.2: 309–333.

OECD. 1998. *Fostering Entrepreneurship*. Paris: OECD.

2000. *OECD Employment Outlook*. Paris: OECD.

Olson, M. 1982. *The Rise and Decline of Nations*. New Haven, CT: Yale University Press.

Ostrom, E. 2005. *Understanding Institutional Diversity*. Princeton, NJ: Princeton University Press.

Ostrom, E. and Walker, J. 2003. *Trust and Reciprocity: Interdisciplinary lessons from experimental research*. New York: Russell Sage Foundation.

Ostwald, W. 1907. "The modern theory of energetics," *The Monist* 17: 481–515.

Owen, A. and Videras, J. 2009. "Reconsidering social capital: a latent class approach," *Empirical Economics* 37: 555–582.

Pantulu, J. and Poon, J. 2003. "Foreign direct investment and international trade: evidence from the US and Japan," *Journal of Economic Geography* 3: 241–259.

Pareto, V. 1972 [1906]. *Manual of Political Economy*. London: Macmillan.

Patten, C. 1996. "Asian values and Asian success," *Survival* 38(2): 5–12.

Paxton, P. 1999. "Is social capital declining in the United States? A multiple indicator assessment," *American Journal of Sociology* 105: 88–127.

2002. "Social capital and democracy: an interdependent relationship," *American Sociological Review* 67: 254–277.

Peil, J. 1999. *Adam Smith and Economic Science: A methodological reinterpretation*. Cheltenham and Northampton: Edward Elgar.

Pellegrini, E.K. and Scandura, T.A. 2006. "Lead member exchange (LMX), paternalism, and delegation in the Turkish business culture: an empirical investigation," *Journal of International Business Studies* 37: 264–279.

Penrose, E. 1959. *The Theory of the Growth of the Firm*. Oxford: Blackwell.

Peterson, R. and Jolibert, A. 1995. "A meta-analysis of country-of-origin effects," *Journal of International Business Studies* 26.4: 883–900.

Petterson, T. 2006. "Religion in contemporary society: eroded by human well-being, supported by cultural diversity," *Comparative Sociology* 5.2–3: 231–257.

Peukert, H. 2001. "On the origins of modern evolutionary economics: the Veblen legend after 100 years," *Journal of Economic Issues* 35.3: 543–555.

Pillai, R., Scandura, T.A. and Williams, E.A. 1999. "Leadership and organizational justice: similarities and differences across cultures," *Journal of International Business Studies* 30.4: 763–779.

Platteau, J.P. 1994. "Behind the market stage, where real societies exist, Part I: the role of public and private order institutions," *Journal of Development Studies* 30.3: 533–577.

2000. *Institutions, Social Norms and Economic Development*. Amsterdam: Harwood Academic Publishers and Routledge.

2009. "Institutional obstacles to African economic development: state, ethnicity, and custom," *Journal of Economic Behavior and Organization* 71(1): 669–689.

Polanyi, K. 1957. *Trade and Market in the Early Empires*. Glencoe, IL: Free Press.

1975 [1944]. *The Great Transformation*. New York: Octagon Books.

1977. *The Livelihood of Man*. New York, London: Academic Press.

Pollak, R.A. 1976. "Interdependent preferences," *The American Economic Review* 66.3: 309–320.

Popkin, S.L. 1979. *The Rational Peasant: The political economy of rural society Vietnam*. Berkeley, CA: University of California Press.

Poterba, J. 1997. "Demographic structure and the political economy of public education," *Journal of Policy Analysis and Management* 16.1: 48–66.

Pothukuchi, V., Damanpour, F., Choi, J., Chen, C.C. and Park, S.H. 2002. "National and organizational culture differences and international joint venture performance," *Journal of International Business Studies* 33: 243–265.

Potter, D.M. 1962. "Review of the Achieving Society," *Business History Review* 36: 470–473.

Priddat, B.P. 1997. "Intention and failure of W. Roscher's Historical Method of national economics," in P. Koslowski (ed.) *The Theory of Ethical Economics in the Historical School*, Berlin, Heidelberg, New York, Tokyo: Springer, pp. 15–35.

Pryor, F.L. 2005. "National values and economic growth." *American Journal of Economics and Sociology* 64.2: 451–483.

2008. "Culture rules: a note on economic systems and values," *Journal of Comparative Economics* 36: 510–515.

Puranem, P. and Vanneste, B. 2009. "Trust and governance: untangling a tangled web," *Academy of Management Review* 34.1: 11–31.

Purda, L. 2008. "Risk perception and the financial system," *Journal of International Business Studies* 39: 1178–1196.

Putnam, R. 2000. *Bowling Alone: The collapse and revival of American community.* New York: Simon and Schuster.

Putnam, R., Leonardi, R. and Nanetti, R.Y. 1993. *Making Democracy Work.* Princeton, NJ: Princeton University Press.

Rainer, H. and Siedler, T. 2009. "Does democracy foster trust?" *Journal of Comparative Economics* 37: 251–269.

Rajan, R. and Zingales, L. 1998. "Financial dependence and growth," *American Economic Review* 88.3: 559–586.

2003. "The great reversals: the politics of financial development in the twentieth century," *Journal of Financial Economics* 69(1): 5–50.

Ralston, D.A., Gustafson, D.J., Mainiero, L. and Umstot, D. 1993. "Strategies of upward influence: a cross-national comparison of Hong Kong and American managers," *Asia Pacific Journal of Management* 10.2: 157–175.

Rao, A. and Hashimoto, K. 1996. "Intercultural influence: a study of Japanese expatriate managers in Canada," *Journal of International Business Studies* 27: 443–466.

Rauch, A. and Frese, M. 2000. "Psychological approaches to entrepreneurial success. A general model and an overview of findings," in C.L. Cooper and I.T. Robertson (eds.) *International Review of Industrial and Organizational Psychology.* Chichester: Wiley, pp. 101–142.

Ren, H. and Gray, B. 2009. "Repairing relationship conflict: how violation types and culture influence the effectiveness of restoration rituals," *Academy of Management Review* 34.1: 105–126.

Reus, T. and Laffont, B. 2009. "The double edged sword of cultural distance in international acquisitions," *Journal of International Business Studies* 40.8: 1298–1316.

Reynolds, P., Bygrave, W., Autio, E. and Hay, M. 2002. *Global Entrepreneurship Monitor; executive report.* Wellesley, MA: Babson College, Kauffman Foundation and London Business School.

Ricks, D.A. 1985. "International business research: past, present and future," *Journal of International Business Studies* 16.2: 1–4.

Ring, P.S. and Van de Ven, A. 1992. "Structuring cooperative relationships between organizations," *Strategic Management Journal* 13: 483–498.

Robbins, D.K., Pantuosco, L.J., Parker, D.F. and Fuller, B.K. 2000. "An empirical assessment of the contribution of small business employment to US state economic performance," *Small Business Economics* 15: 293–302.

Robbins, L. 1932. *An Essay on the Nature and Significance of Economic Science*. London: Macmillan.

Robinson, W.S. 1950. "Ecological correlations and the behavior of individuals," *American Sociological Review* 15: 351–357.

Rodrik, D., Subramanian, A. and Trebbi, F. 2004. "Institutions rule: the primacy of institutions over geography and integration in economic development," *Journal of Economic Growth* 9.2: 131–165.

Roe, M. 1998. "Comparative corporate governance," in P. Newman (ed.) *Palgrave Dictionary on Law and Economics*. London: Palgrave, pp. 339–346.

  2003. *Political Determinants of Corporate Governance: Political context, corporate impact*. New York: Oxford University Press.

Roland, G. 2004. "Understanding institutional change: fast-moving and slow-moving institutions," *Studies in Comparative Institutional Development* 38: 109–131.

Root, F.R. 1998. *Entry Strategies for International Markets* (2nd edn.). San Francisco, CA: Jossey-Bass Publishers.

Roscher, W. 1918 [1854]. *Grundlagen der Nationalökonomie*. Stuttgart and Berlin: Gotta'sche Buchhandlung Nachfolger.

Rose, A.K. 2004. "Do we really know that the WTO increases trade?" *American Economic Review* 94.1: 98–114.

Rosen, S. 1997. "Austrian and neoclassical economics: any gains from trade?" *Journal of Economic Perspectives* 11: 139–152.

Rosenberg, M. 1956. "Misanthropy and political ideology," *American Sociological Review* 21: 690–695.

Ross, D. 1991. *The Origins of American Social Science*. Cambridge, UK: Cambridge University Press.

Rostow, W. 1960. *The Stages of Economic Growth*. Cambridge, UK: Cambridge University Press.

Roth, A., Prasnikar, V., Okuno-Fujiwara, M. and Zamir, S. 1991. "Bargaining and market behavior in Jerusalem, Ljubljana, Pittsburgh, and Tokyo: an experimental study," *American Economic Review* 81:1068–1095.

Roth, F. 2009. "Does too much trust hamper economic growth?" *Kyklos* 62.1: 103–128.

Roth, P. 1989. "Ethnography without tears," *Current Anthropology* 30.5: 555–569.

Rosenstein-Rodan, P. 1943. "Problems of industrialisation of Eastern and South-Eastern Europe," *The Economic Journal* 53: 202–211.

Rothstein, B. 2003. "Social capital, economic growth and quality of government: the causal mechanism," *New Political Economy* 8.1: 49–73.

Rothstein, B. and Uslaner, E. 2005. "All for all; equality, corruption and social trust," *World Politics* 58: 41–72.

Rotter, J.B. 1966. "Generalised expectancies for internal versus external control of reinforcement," *Psychological monographs: general and applied* 80: 609.

Rousseau, D., Sitkin, S.B., Burt, R.S. and Camerer, C. 1998. "Introduction to special topic forum: not so different after all: a cross discipline view of trust," *Academy of Management Review* 23: 393–404.

Roy, W.G. 1997. *Socializing Capital: The rise of the large industrial corporation in America*. Princeton, NJ: Princeton University Press.

Rubin, J. 1963. "Review of The Achieving Society," *The Journal of Economic History* 23: 118–121.

Rubinstein, A. 2006. "Discussion of behavioral economics at the World Congress of the Econometric Society 2005," downloaded and accessed on March 3, 2008 at www.arielrubinstein.tau.ac.il/papers/behavioral-economics.pdf

Ruckman, K. 2004. "Mode of entry into a foreign market: the case of U.S. mutual funds in Canada," *Journal of International Economics* 62: 417–432.

Rugman, A.M. and Verbeke, A. 2004. "A perspective on regional and global strategies of multinational enterprises," *Journal of International Business Studies* 35(1): 3–19.

2007. "Liabilities of regional foreignness and the use of firm-level versus country-level data, a response to Dunning *et al.* (2007)," *Journal of International Business Studies* 38: 200–205.

Rutherford, M. 2001. "Institutional economics: then and now," *Journal of Economic Perspectives* 15(3): 173–194.

Sahlins, M. 1976. *Culture and Practical Reason*. Chicago, IL: Chicago University Press.

Said, E. 1995 [1978]. *Orientalism*. London: Penguin.

Sako, M. 1992. *Prices, Quality and Trust: Interfirm relations in Britain and Japan*. Cambridge, UK: Cambridge University Press.

Sala-i-Martin, X. 1997. "I just ran two million regressions," *The American Economic Review* 87(2): 178–183.

Samiee, S. 1994. "Customer evaluation of products in a global market," *Journal of International Business Studies* 25.3: 579–604.

Samuelson, L. 2005. "Foundations of human sociality: a review essay," *Journal of Economic Literature* 43: 488–497.

Saxenian, A.L. 1994. *Regional Advantage: Culture and competition in Silicon Valley and Route 128*. Cambridge, MA: Harvard University Press.

Schatz, S.P. 1965. "Achievement and economic growth: a critique," *Quarterly Journal of Economics* 79: 234–241.

1971. "*N* achievement and economic growth: a critical appraisal," in P. Kilby (ed.) *Entrepreneurship and Economic Development.* New York: Free Press.

Scheré, J. 1982. "Tolerance for ambiguity as a discriminating variable between entrepreneurs and managers," *Proceedings of the Academy of Management* **42**: 404–408.

Schmitz, J.A. 1989. "Imitation, entrepreneurship, and long-run growth," *Journal of Political Economy* **97**: 721–739.

Schneider, G., Plümper, T. and Baumann, S. 2000. "Bringing Putnam to the European regions, on the relevance of social capital for economic growth," *European Urban and Regional Studies* **7**.4: 307–317.

Schneider, S.C. and De Meyer, A. 1991. "Interpreting and responding to strategic issues: the impact of national culture," *Strategic Management Journal* **12**: 307–320.

Schuler, R., Dowling, P. and De Cieri, H. 1993. "An integrative framework of strategic international human resource management," *The International Journal of Human Resource Management* **5**.3: 717–764.

Schuler, R.S. and Rogovsky, N. 1998. "Understanding compensation practice variations across firms: the impact of national culture," *Journal of International Business Studies* **29**.1: 159–177.

Schultz, T. 1975. *Economics of the Family: Marriage, children, and human capital.* Chicago, IL: University of Chicago Press.

Schumpeter, J.A. 1908. *Das Wesen und der Hauptinhalt der theoretischen Nationalökonomie.* Munich and Leipzig: Duncker und Humblot.

1909. "On the concept of social value," *Quarterly Journal of Economics* **23**(2): 213–232.

1934. *The Theory of Economic Development.* Cambridge, MA: Harvard University Press.

1951. "Change and the entrepreneur," in R.V. Clemence (ed.) *Essays of J.A. Schumpeter.* Reading, MA: Addison-Wesley.

1954 [1920]. "Max Webers Werk," in *Dogmenhistorische und biographische Aufsätze.* Tübingen: J.C.B. Mohr: pp. 108–117.

1955. *History of Economic Analysis.* London: George Allen & Unwin Ltd.

Schwartz, S.H. 1994. "Beyond individualism/collectivism: new cultural dimensions of values," in U. Kim, H.C. Triandis, C. Kagitçibasi, S.C. Choi and G. Yoon (eds.) *Individualism and Collectivism: Theory, method, and applications.* Thousand Oaks, CA: Sage, pp. 85–119.

1999. "A theory of cultural values and some implications for work," *Applied Psychology, an International Review* **48**.1: 12–47.

2004. "Mapping and interpreting cultural differences around the world," in H. Vinken, J. Soeters and P. Ester (eds.) *Comparing Cultures.* Leiden: Brill Academic Publishers, pp. 43–73.

2006. "A theory of cultural value orientations: explication and applications," *Comparative Sociology* 5.2–3: 137–182.

Schwartz, S.H. and Sagie, G. 2000. "Value consensus and importance: a cross national study," *Journal of Cross Cultural Psychology* 31: 465–497.

Schwarz, M. and Thompson, M. 1990. *Divided We Stand: Redefining politics, technology and social choice.* Hemel Hempstead: Harvester Wheatsheaf.

Schweder, R.A. 2001. "Culture: contemporary views," in N.J. Smelser and P.B. Baltes (eds.) *International Encyclopedia of the Social and Behavioral Sciences.* Amsterdam: Elsevier.

Scott-Marshall, R. and Boush, D.M. 2001. "Dynamic decision making: a cross cultural comparison of U.S. and Peruvian export managers," *Journal of International Business Studies* 32.4: 873–893.

Sekaran, U. 1983. "Methodological and theoretical issues and advancements in cross-cultural research," *Journal of International Business Studies* 14.2: 61–73.

Seligman, A. 1997. *The Problem of Trust.* Princeton, NJ: Princeton University Press.

Sennett, R. 2006. *The Culture of the New Capitalism.* New Haven, CT and London: Yale University Press.

Sen, A. 2006. *Identity and Violence: The illusion of destiny.* New York and London: W.W. Norton & Company.

Sent, E.-M. 2005. *The Science of Economics, The Economics of Science.* Inaugural Lecture, Radboud University Nijmegen, The Netherlands.

Sethi, D., Guisinger, S.E., Phelan, S.E. and Berg, D.M. 2003. "Trends in foreign direct investment flows: a theoretical and empirical analysis," *Journal of International Business Studies* 34.4: 315–326.

Sexton, D.L. and Bowman, N. 1985. "The entrepreneur: a capable executive and more," *Journal of Business Venturing* 1.1: 129–140.

Shane, S. 1992. "Why do some societies invent more than others?" *Journal of Business Venturing* 7: 29–46.

1993. "Cultural influences on national rates of innovation," *Journal of Business Venturing* 8: 59–73.

1994. "The effect of national culture on the choice between licensing and direct foreign investment," *Strategic Management Journal* 15.8: 627–642.

2003. *A General Theory of Entrepreneurship.* Aldershot: Edward Elgar.

Shenkar, O. 2001. "Cultural distance revisited: towards a more rigorous conceptualization and measurement of cultural differences," *Journal of International Business Studies* 32.3: 519–535.

2004. "One more time: international business in a global economy," *Journal of International Business Studies* 35: 161–171.

Shleifer, A. and Vishny, R.W. 1997. "A survey of corporate governance," *Journal of Finance* 52.2: 737–783.

Siegel, J.I., Licht, A. and Schwartz, S.H. 2008a. "Egalitarianism, cultural distance and FDI: a new approach." Working paper SSRN.com/abstract=957306 (version January 2, 2008).

2008b. "Egalitarianism, and international investment." Working paper SSRN.com/abstract=899082 (version September 19, 2008).

Siems, M. 2005. "Numerical comparative law: do we need statistical evidence in law in order to reduce complexity?" *Cardozo Journal of International and Comparative Law* 13: 521–540.

Silver, B. and Dowley, K. 2000. "Measuring political culture in multiethnic societies: reaggregating the World Values Survey," *Comparative Political Studies* 33: 517–550.

Simmel, G. 1950. *The Sociology of Georg Simmel*. Translated and edited by K. Wolff. Glencoe, IL: The Free Press.

Simon, D.G. and Lane, P.J. 2004. "A model of cultural differences and international alliance performance," *Journal of International Business Studies* 35: 306–319.

Sivakumar, K. and Nakata, C. 2001. "The stampede toward Hofstede's framework: avoiding the sample design pit in cross-cultural research," *Journal of International Business Studies* 32.3: 555–574.

Slangen, A.H.L. 2006. "National cultural distance and initial foreign acquisition performance: the moderating effect of integration," *Journal of World Business* 41.2: 161–170.

Slangen, A.H.L. and Beugelsdijk, S. 2010. "The impact of institutional hazards on foreign multinational activity: a contingency perspective," *Journal of International Business Studies* 41: 980–995.

Slangen, A.H.L., Beugelsdijk, S. and Hennart, J.F. 2007. "Does national cultural distance really reduce trade flows? An examination of arm's length US exports and foreign affiliate sales." Paper presented at the Academy of International Business (AIB) Conference 2006, Atlanta.

Slangen, A.H.L. and Hennart, J.F. 2007. "Greenfield versus acquisition: a review of the empirical foreign establishment mode literature," *Journal of International Management* 13.4: 403–429.

Smelser, N. and Swedberg, R. (eds.) 1994. *Handbook of Economic Sociology*. Princeton, NJ: Princeton University Press.

Smith, A. 1976 [1759]. *The Theory of Moral Sentiments*. Edited by D. Raphael and A. Macfie. Oxford: Oxford University Press.

1999 [1776]. *The Wealth of Nations* (ed. by A. Skinner) London: Penguin.

Smith, P. 2006. "When elephants fight, the grass gets trampled: the GLOBE and Hofstede projects," *Journal of International Business Studies* 37: 915–921.

Smith, P. and Bond, M. 1998. *Social Psychology across Cultures*. London: Prentice Hall Europe.

Smith, P., Bond, M. and Kagitcibasi, C. 2006. *Understanding Social Psychology across Cultures: Living and working in a changing world*. London: Sage.

Smith, T.W. 1997. "Factors relating to misanthropy in contemporary American society," *Social Science Research* 26: 170–196.

Snijders, T. and Bosker, R. 1999. *Multi Level Analysis*. Thousand Oaks, CA: Sage.

Sobel, J. 2002. "Can we trust social capital?" *Journal of Economic Literature* 40: 139–154.

Soltow, J.H. 1968. "The entrepreneur in economic history," *The American Economic Review* (papers and proceedings) 58: 84–92.

Søndergaard, M. 1994. "Hofstede's consequences: a study of reviews, citations and replications," *Organization Studies* 15.3: 447–456.

Spence, J.T. 1985. "Achievement American style: the rewards and costs of individualism," *American Psychologist* 40: 1285–1295.

Spickard, J.V. 1989. "A guide to Mary Douglas's three versions of Grid/Group Theory," *Sociological Analysis* 50.2: 151–170.

Spolaore, E. and Wacziarg, R. 2006. "The diffusion of development." NBER working paper 12153, Cambridge, MA: NBER.

Srivastava, R.K. and Green, R.T. 1986. "Determinants of bilateral trade flows," *Journal of Business* 59.4: 623–640.

Stanczak, G. 2006. "Strategic ethnicity: the construction of multi-racial/multi-ethnic religious community," *Ethnic and Racial Studies* 29.5: 856–881.

Stanfield, J. 1998. "Polanyi, Karl," in J. Davis, D.W. Hands and U. Mäki (eds.) *Handbook of Economic Methodology*. Cheltenham and Northampton: Edward Elgar, pp. 366–368.

Steensma, K., Marino, L. and Weaver, M. 2000. "Attitudes towards cooperative strategies: a cross cultural analysis of entrepreneurs," *Journal of International Business Studies* 31.4: 591–609.

Stevenson, H.H. and Jarillo, J.C. 1990. "A paradigm of entrepreneurship: entrepreneurial management," *Strategic Management Journal* 11: 17–27.

Stewart-Black, J. and Gregersen, H.B. 1991. "The other half of the picture: antecedents of spouse cross-cultural adjustment," *Journal of International Business Studies* 22.3: 461–477.

Stigler, G.J. and Becker, G. 1977. "De Gustibus non est Disputandum," *American Economic Review* **67**.2: 76–90.

Stolle, D. and Rochon, T. 1998. "Are all associations alike? Member diversity, associational type and the creation of social capital," *American Behavioral Scientist* **42**: 47–65.

Stulz, R.M. and Williamson, R. 2003. "Culture, openness, and finance," *Journal of Financial Economics* **70**: 313–349.

Suarez-Villa, L. 1989. *The Evolution of Regional Economies: Entrepreneurship and regional change*. London: Praeger.

Subramanian, A. and Wei, S.J. 2007. "The WTO promotes trade, strongly but unevenly," *Journal of International Economics* **72**.1: 151–175.

Suddle, K., Beugelsdijk, S. and Wennekers, S. 2006. "Entrepreneurial culture as determinant of nascent entrepreneurship," SCALES paper EIM Zoetermeer, available at www.eim.net/pdf-ez/N200519.pdf.

2010. "Entrepreneurial culture as a determinant of nascent entrepreneurship," in R. Thurik and A. Freytag (eds.) *Entrepreneurship and Culture*. Heidelberg, Dordrecht, London and New York: Springer, pp. 227–244.

Summers, R. and Heston, A. 1991. "The Penn World Table (Mark 5): an expanded set of international comparisons, 1950–1988," *Quarterly Journal of Economics* **106**(2): 327–368.

Sunderland, P., Taylor, E. and Denny, R. 2004. "Being Mexican and American: negotiating ethnicity in the practice of market research," *Human Organization* **63**.3: 373–380.

Swank, D. 1996. "Culture, institutions, and economic growth: theory, recent evidence, and the role of communitarian polities," *American Journal of Political Science* **40**.3: 660–679.

Tabellini, G. 2007a. "Institutions and culture," Presidential lecture European Economic Association (EEA), Budapest meeting, August 30.

2007b. "Culture and institutions: economic development in the regions of Europe," Working paper IGIER Bocconi University (version April 2007, first version 2005).

2008a. "The scope of cooperation: values and incentives," *Quarterly Journal of Economics* **123**.3: 905–950.

2008b. "Institutions and culture," *Journal of the European Economic Association* **6**.2/3: 255–294.

Tang, L. and Koveos, P.E. 2008. "A framework to update Hofstede's cultural value indices: economic dynamics and institutional stability," *Journal of International Business Studies* **39**: 1045–1063.

Tarrow, S. 1996. "Making social science work across space and time: a critical reflection on Robert Putnam's Making Democracy Work," *The American Political Science Review* **90**: 389–398.

Temple, J. 1999. "The new growth evidence," *Journal of Economic Literature* 37: 112–156.

Thaler, R. 1991. *Quasi Rational Economics*. New York: Russell Sage Foundation.

1992. *The Winner's Curse: Paradoxes and anomalies of economic life*. New York: Free Press.

(ed.). 1993. *Advances in Behavioral Finance*. New York: Russell Sage Foundation.

2000. "From homo economicus to homo sapiens," *Journal of Economic Perspectives* 14(1): 133–141.

(ed.). 2005. *Advances in Behavioral Finance*. Princeton, Princeton University Press.

The Economist. 1992. "The resumption of history," *The Economist* 325.7791: 67–69.

2009. "What went wrong with economics?" *The Economist* 392.8640: 11–12.

Thomas, A.S. and Mueller, S.L. 2000. "A case for comparative entrepreneurship: assessing the relevance of culture," *Journal of International Business Studies* 31(2): 287–301.

Thomas, D.C. and Au, K. 2002. "The effect of cultural differences on behavioral responses to low job satisfaction," *Journal of International Business Studies* 33(2): 309–326.

Thompson, M., Ellis, R. and Wildavsky, A. 1990. *Cultural Theory*. Boulder, CO, San Francisco, CA and Oxford: Westview Press.

Thurik, R. and Grilo, I. 2007. "Determinants of entrepreneurial engagement levels in Europe and the US." Jena: Max Planck Institute of Economics working paper 0207.

Tihanya, L., Griffith, D.A. and Russell, C.J. 2005. "The effect of cultural distance on entry mode choice, international diversification and MNE performance," *Journal of International Business Studies* 36.3: 270–283.

Tilman, R. 2004. "Karl Mannheim, Max Weber, and the problem of social rationality in Thorstein Veblen," *Journal of Economic Issues* 38.1: 155–172.

Timmons, J.A. 1978. "Characteristics and role demands of entrepreneurship," *American Journal of Small Business* 3: 5–17.

Tinbergen, J. 1962. *Shaping the World Economy*. New York: Twentieth Century Fund.

Tinsley, C.H. and Pillutla, M.M. 1998. "Negotiating in the United States and Hong Kong," *Journal of International Business Studies* 29.4: 711–728.

Todd, E. 1985. *The Explanation of Ideology: Family structures and social systems*. Oxford, New York: Blackwell.

Tomlinson, E.C. and Mayer, R.C. 2009. "The role of causal attribution dimensions in trust repair," *Academy of Management Review* **34**.1: 85–104.

Tönnies, F. 2001 [1887]. *Community and Civil Society* [Gemeinschaft und Gesellschaft], translated by Hollis and edited by Harris, Cambridge.

Torsvik, G. 2000. "Social capital and economic development: a plea for the mechanisms," *Rationality and Society* **12**.4: 451–476.

Triandis, H. 1972. *The Analysis of Subjective Culture*. New York: Wiley-Interscience.

1995. *Culture and Social Behavior*. New York: McGraw-Hill.

Trompenaars, F. 1994. *Riding the Waves of Culture: Understanding diversity in global business*. Burr Ridge, IL: Irwin.

Tylor, E. 1924 [1871]. *Primitive Culture; 2 Vols (7th edn.)*. New York: Brentano's.

Ueno, S. and Sekaran, U. 1992. "The influence of culture on budget control practices in the USA and Japan: an empirical study," *Journal of International Business Studies* **23**.4: 659–694.

Uhlaner, L. and Thurik, R. 2007. "Postmaterialism influencing total entrepreneurial activity across countries," *Journal of Evolutionary Economics* **17**: 161–185.

Uslaner, E.M. 2002. *The Moral Foundations of Trust*. Cambridge, UK: Cambridge University Press.

2008. "The foundations of trust: macro and micro," *Cambridge Journal of Economics* **32**: 289–294.

Uzzi, B. 1996. "The sources and consequences of embeddedness for the economic performance of organizations: the network effect," *American Sociological Review* **61**: 674–698.

Van de Vijver, F., Van Hemert, D. and Poortinga, Y. (eds.) 2008. *Multilevel Analysis of Individuals and Cultures*. New York: Psychology Press.

Van Mesdag, M. 2000. "Culture-sensitive adaptation or global standardization – the duration-of-usage hypothesis," *International Marketing Review* **17**.1: 74–84.

Van Oorschot, W., Arts, W. and Gelissen, J. 2006. "Social capital in Europe: measurement and social and regional distribution of a multifaceted phenomenon," *Acta Sociologica* **49**.2: 149–165.

Van Oudenhoven, J.P. 2001. "Do organizations reflect national cultures? A 10-nation study," *International Journal of Intercultural Relations* **25**: 89–107.

Van Stel, A., Carree, M. and Thurik, R. 2005. "The effect of entrepreneurial activity on national economic growth," *Small Business Economics* **24**: 311–321.

Veblen, T. 1909. "The limitations of marginal utility," *Journal of Political Economy* 17.9: 620–636.

1994 [1899]. *Theory of the Leisure Class: An economic study in the evolution of institutions*. London: Penguin Classics UK.

1998 [1898]. "Why is economics not an evolutionary science?" *Cambridge Journal of Economics* 22: 403–414.

Veenhoven, R. 2000. "Wellbeing in the welfare state: level not higher, distribution not more equitable," *Journal of Comparative Policy Analysis* 2.1: 91–125.

Verlegh, P. and Steenkamp, J.B. 1999. "A review and meta analysis of country-of-origin research," *Journal of Economic Psychology* 20.5: 521–546.

Voltaire. 1963 [1756]. *Essai sur les mœurs et l'esprit des nations et sur les principaux faits de l'histoire depuis Charlemagne jusqu'à Louis XIII.* Paris: Classiques Garnier.

Wagner, J. and Sternberg, R. 2002. "Personal and regional determinants of entrepreneurial activities: empirical evidence from the REM Germany." IZA Discussion paper 624, Bonn, Germany.

Waldman, D.A. and 35 co-authors. 2006. "Cultural and leadership predictors of corporate social responsibility values of top management: a GLOBE study of 15 countries," *Journal of International Business Studies* 37: 823–837.

Wallerstein, I. 1960 "Ethnicity and national integration," *Cahiers d'etudes africaines* 1.3: 129–139.

Wallis, W. 1930. *Culture and Progress.* New York: Whittlesey House.

Wang, L. and Gordon, P. 2007. "Trust and institutions: a multi level analysis," working paper, mimeo.

Weber, M. 1908. "Die Grenznutzlehre und das psychophysische Grundgesetz," *Archiv für Sozialwissenschaft und Sozialpolitik* 27.2: 546–558.

1921. *Economy and Society.* New York: Bedminster Press.

1989. *Die Wirtschaftsethik der Weltreligionen Konfuzianismus und Taoismus; Schriften 1915–1920*, Tübingen: Mohr.

1992 [1930]. *The Protestant Ethic and the Spirit of Capitalism.* Translated by T. Parsons. London, New York: Routledge.

2005. *Die Wirstschaftsethik der Weltreligionen: Das Antike Judentum: Schriften und Reden 1911–1920* (hrsg. von Eckart Otto), Tübingen: Mohr.

Weick, K.E. and Quinn, R.E. 1999. "Organizational change and development," *Annuals Review of Psychology* 50: 361–386.

Weil, D. 2009. *Economic Growth* (2nd edn.). Boston, MA: Pearson, Addison Wesley.

Weisskopf, W.A. 1962. "Review of The Achieving Society," *Journal of Political Economy* 70: 311–313.

Wennekers, S. 2006. *Entrepreneurship at country level: economic and noneconomic determinants*. Erasmus Research Institute for Management (ERIM), Dissertation Rotterdam University.

Wennekers, S., van Stel, A., Thurik, R. and Reynolds, P. 2005. "Nascent entrepreneurship and the level of economic development," *Small Business Economics* 24: 293–309.

Wennekers, S. and Thurik, R. 1999. "Linking entrepreneurship and economic growth," *Small Business Economics* 13: 27–55.

Whiteley, P. 2000. "Economic growth and social capital," *Political Studies* 48: 443–466.

Whitrow, G. 1988. *Time in History: The evolution of our general awareness of time and temporal perspective*. Oxford: Oxford University Press.

Wiener, M.J. 1981. *English Culture and the Decline of the Industrial Spirit, 1850–1980*. Cambridge, UK: Cambridge University Press.

Wigger, A. and Nölke, A. 2007. "Enhanced roles of private actors in EU business regulation and the erosion of Rhenish capitalism: the case of antitrust enforcement," *Journal of Common Market Studies* 45.2: 487–513.

Wildavsky, A. 1987. "Choosing preferences by constructing institutions: a cultural theory of preference formation," *The American Political Science Review* 81.1: 4–21.

Williamson, O.E. 1975. *Markets and Hierarchies, Analysis and Antitrust Implications*. New York: Free Press.

1985. *The Economic Institutions of Capitalism*. New York: Free Press.

1993. "Calculativeness, trust and economic organization," *Journal of Law and Economics* 36: 453–486.

1998. "Transaction cost economics: how it works; where it is headed," *De Economist – Quarterly Review of the Royal Netherlands Economic Association* 146: 23–58.

2000. "The new institutional economics: taking stock, looking ahead," *Journal of Economic Literature* 38: 595–613.

Winterbottom, M.R. 1953. *The relation of childhood training in independence to achievement motivation*. Dissertation, University of Michigan.

Wolf, E.R. 1999. *Envisioning Power: Ideologies of Dominance in Crisis*. Berkeley, Los Angeles, CA, London: University of California Press.

Wong, P.K., Yuen, P.H. and Erkko, A. 2005. "Entrepreneurship, innovation and economic growth," *Small Business Economics* 24: 335–350.

Wood, R. and Bandura, A. 1989. "Social cognitive theory of organizational management," *Academy of Management Review* 14: 361–384.

World Bank. 1993. *The East Asian Miracle: Economic growth and public policy.* New York: Oxford University Press.

Wundt, W. 1911–1920. *Völkerpsychologie: eine Untersuchung der Entwicklungsgesetze von Sprache, Mythus und Sitte.* I–X. Leipzig: Kröner.

Wurgler, J. 2000. "Financial markets and the allocation of capital," *Journal of Financial Economics* 58: 187–214.

Wuthnow, R., Hunter, J.D., Bergesen, A. and Kurzweil, E. 1984. *Cultural Analysis.* Boston, MA, London: Routledge and Kegan Paul.

Yammarino, F. and Dansereau, F. 2006. *Multi Level Issues in Social Systems. Research in Multi Level Issues* series volume 5. Oxford: JAI Press.

Yaprak, A. 2008. "Culture study in international marketing: a critical review and suggestions for future research," *International Marketing Review* 25.2: 215–229.

Yeager, L.B. 1997. "Austrian economics, neoclassicism and the market test," *Journal of Economic Perspectives* 11: 153–165.

Yeaple, S. 2005. "A simple model of firm heterogeneity, international trade, and wages," *Journal of International Economics* 65: 1–20.

2008. "Firm heterogeneity and the structure of US multinational activity: an empirical analysis," NBER working paper 14072. Cambridge: NBER.

Yelvington, K. 1991. "Ethnicity as practice? A comment on Bentley," *Comparative Studies in Society and History* 33.1: 158–168.

Yeyati, E.L. 2003. "On the impact of a common currency on bilateral trade," *Economic Letters* 79: 125–129.

Yin, R. 1993. *Applications of Case Study Research.* Beverly Hills, CA: Sage Publishing.

2002. *Case Study Research: Design and methods* (3rd edn.). Beverly Hills, CA: Sage Publishing.

Yonay, Y. and Breslau, D. 2006. "Marketing models: the culture of mathematical economics," *Sociological Forum* 21(3): 345–386.

Yoo, T. and Lee, S.H. 2009. "In search of social capital in state-activist capitalism: elite networks in France and Korea," *Organization Studies* 30: 529–547.

You, J.S. 2005. "Inequality and corruption as correlates of social trust: fairness matters more than similarity." Kennedy School of Government Working Paper Series No. 29, Harvard University.

You, J.S. and Khagram, S. 2005. "A comparative study of inequality and corruption," *American Sociological Review* 70.1: 136–157.

Young, C. 1983. "The temple of ethnicity," *World Politics* 35(4): 652–662.

Zaheer, A., McEvily, B. and Perrone, V. 1998. "Does trust matter? Exploring the effects of interorganisational and interpersonal trust on performance," *Organisation Science* 9: 141–159.

Zaheer, S. 1995. "Overcoming the liability of foreignness," *Academy of Management Journal* **38**.2: 341–363.

Zak, P.J. and Knack, S. 2001. "Trust and growth," *The Economic Journal* **111**: 295–321.

Zerfu, D., Zikhali, P. and Kabenga, I. 2009. "Does ethnicity matter for trust? Evidence from Africa," *Journal of African Economies* **18**.1: 153–175.

Zetzsche, D. 2007. "An ethical theory of corporate governance history." Center for Business and Corporate Law Research Paper Series 0006 (02/2007): downloaded from http://ssrn.com/abstract=970909.

Ziegler, C. 2007. *Favored Flowers: Culture and economy in a global system.* Durham: Duke University Press.

Zucker, L.G. 1986. "Production of trust: institutional sources of economic structure, 1840–1920," *Research in Organizational Behaviour* **8**: 53–111.

Index